A Curse upon the Nation

A Curse upon the Nation

RACE, FREEDOM, AND EXTERMINATION
IN AMERICA AND THE ATLANTIC WORLD

Kay Wright Lewis

The University of Georgia Press
Athens

Paperback edition, 2019
© 2017 by the University of Georgia Press
Athens, Georgia 30602
www.ugapress.org
All rights reserved
Set in 10.5/13.5 Adobe Garamond Pro by Graphic Composition, Inc.

Most University of Georgia Press titles are
available from popular e-book vendors.

Printed digitally

The Library of Congress has cataloged the
hardcover edition of this book as follows:
Names: Lewis, Kay Wright, 1958– author.
Title: A curse upon the nation : race, freedom, and extermination
    in America and the Atlantic world / Kay Wright Lewis.
Description: Athens : The University of Georgia Press, 2017. | Includes
    bibliographical references and index.
Identifiers: LCCN 2017003724 | ISBN 9780820351278 (hardcover : alk. paper) |
    ISBN 9780820351261 (e-book)
Subjects: LCSH: Slavery—United States—Influence. | Violence—
    United States—History. | Slave insurrections—Historiography. |
    African Americans—Crimes against. | Racism—United States—History. |
    Fear—Political aspects—United States. | Genocide—Public opinion. |
    United States—Race relations—History.
Classification: LCC E184.A1 L477 2017 | DDC 305.800973—dc23
LC record available at http://lccn.loc.gov/2017003724

Paperback ISBN 978-0-8203-5547-4

In memory of my muse,
Sylvia Lorraine Wright,
a beautiful and brilliant woman

CONTENTS

A Curse upon the Nation

INTRODUCTION

The Legacy and Human Cost of Slavery

In the spring of 1918, when Mary Turner made what a mob considered "unwise remarks" about the lynching of her husband, who she claimed was innocent of any wrongdoing, "the people took exceptions to her remarks as well as her attitude."[1] Members of the mob, out for vengeance for what they called the "personal outrages and violence, especially against helpless women and children," were not to be deterred from sending the message that no one in the black community could seek legal or extralegal justice and live. They took Mary from her house on a Sunday afternoon and strung her up by her ankles a few yards from Folsom's Bridge in Lowndes County, Georgia. They poured gasoline on her clothes and set her on fire. After the clothes were burned off her body, Mary, who was eight months pregnant at the time, was cut with "a sharp instrument . . . her stomach being entirely opened." Miraculously, her eight-month-old infant was still alive, and it fell out of Mary's womb onto the ground. The baby made "two cries" but then was "crushed by the heel of a member of the mob." The formerly pregnant woman was "riddled with bullets from high-powered rifles until it was no longer possible to recognize it as the body of a human being." Mary was not even allowed the dignity of being buried by her own kinfolk; instead, she and her infant were buried by the mob "ten feet from the tree," with a whiskey bottle and a cigar stub marking the location of this particularly brutal execution.[2]

At least eleven other African Americans in this part of South Georgia were lynched, and more than five hundred fled the region, fearing for their lives. Most African Americans living in the South during the Jim Crow era did not receive equal treatment by the criminal justice system. This did not deter Mary from speaking out, but clearly hundreds of other African Americans were so terrorized that, rather than confront the lawless mobs, they left Lowndes County. Horrific violence against black men, women, and children in the postemancipation South had a long and complicated history in America, and white southerners knew that they had the upper hand politically, socially, and economically. Without law enforcement on their side, African Americans "knew that they could not fight back effectively, they could not protect themselves, and . . . they could not expect protection from their persecutors." "Any slight conflict . . . would bring down upon the head of the defenseless the full weight of naked physical violence," something that Mary deliberately chose to take on when she called for justice in the murder of her husband.[3] Racialized violence was a salient part of everyday life in the African American community in the Jim Crow South, but it also had roots in the historical legacy of slavery.

The silence surrounding the history of how and why racialized violence toward African Americans became inscribed in race relations in America, continuing throughout the civil rights era, is entangled with how certain narratives are privileged over others in the production and creation of what is considered fact or truth. This erasure is made manifest by the countless testimonies of African Americans about the violence they experienced and the trauma that such violent events caused in their lives, events that have not been acknowledged. Although the majority of African Americans lynched during and after the Civil War were men, many women and children were also murdered during the centuries when slavery reigned. The notion of the inevitability of America's "Manifest Destiny," which is entangled with ideas of white supremacy, obfuscates the fact that extermination was part of a racialized ideology used to sustain the institution of enslavement and the slave trade. For African Americans enslaved and free in America, however, their memories of the conflict and trauma remained significant well into the civil rights era. For those enslaved and free, racial extermination was not "unthinkable."[4] And here lies the chasm that this work attempts to fill, between historical production and memory, between authentic experience and the meaning of those experiences. Indeed, African Americans remembered the fear and trauma that this discourse generated among enslaved and free people with an exactitude that requires full acknowledgment.

Intuitively, we know that this sort of violence did not begin as a postemancipation South phenomenon, the South that saw the rise of the Ku Klux Klan, where white Americans set upon black Americans and where occasionally African Americans armed themselves in self-defense. It had a prehistory that extends back to the initial decades of English colonization and the development of slavery in America. Historian Claude Clegg argues that white Americans saw "blackness as a troubling counternarrative" that disrupted their vision of America as a "neo-European preserve" and precluded their ideas of ending slavery and implementing immediate emancipation.[5] White ideas about what would happen if black Americans were given freedom and equality led to assertions of war and of black and white extermination during the eighteenth and nineteenth centuries, ideas that shaped and nurtured racial violence well into the twentieth century. Tracing the origins of exterminatory warfare in the United States reveals why this particular strategy of violence emerged and how it became raced, because European ideas linking race to savagery and barbarianism were evident in the Atlantic World. People defined as savages and barbarians were subjected to extermination, which was justified by theories of who was more civilized.[6] The history of these ideas, in part, helps explain the ferocity of the violence that black women like Mary Turner experienced during Reconstruction and the Jim Crow era. It exposes the probability that white southerners did not develop a new emotional state after the Civil War but were rather perpetuating an inherited set of ideas about black bodies and, indeed, black humanity.

The foundation for race-based violence in America emanated from a type of warfare used for centuries by Europeans and some Africans. What we today call "total warfare," which military historian John Grenier calls "unlimited war" or "*petite guerre*," is a strategy where one side attempts to destroy its enemy's will to fight by "killing and intimidating" the enemy's noncombatant populations, namely, women, children, and the elderly.[7] But for Europeans, extermination referenced the killing of women and children generally. In Europeans' view, West African nations practiced extermination in war as well. Thus, historically, the term "extermination" was used to describe the envisioned slaughter of large populations of white and black people in the Atlantic World.[8] The institution of African enslavement, as it was practiced, was always poised to disintegrate into an exterminatory war, a war that white Americans were determined black Americans would lose. Yet over time, most African Americans deliberately sought strategies of nonviolence to win their freedom from enslavement and oppression. Anglo-Americans, however, continued to believe in the potential necessity of black extermination if a race war should ensue, making the threat of extermination an essential tool for maintaining the institution of enslavement and white supremacy.

The psychological cost of slavery is unveiled in the way that Africans and Europeans dealt with racialized codes of war.[9] Racial extermination was, for the most part, used by masters to make the enslaved "stand in fear."[10] But Europeans also had a deeply rooted anxiety about the cataclysmic nature of slavery because they understood that those they enslaved were human beings who valued their freedom. This created "a condition of tension" between black and white Americans, between master and slave, which perpetuated the idea that exterminatory violence was necessary for black liberation and for white self-defense and racial control.[11] The phenomenological experience for those threatened by a race war and extermination, however, differed for the perpetrators and victims. For African Americans, enslaved and free, the potential for one-sided violence—white on black—was always present and traumatic, especially, as theologian Howard Thurman has argued, when experience and the law taught that "you do not count."[12] The type of trauma that enslaved people experienced, the type that shatters a person's sense of self and creates fear for one's well-being, was handed down from adult to child, from one generation to the next, through oral and "written acts of remembering."[13] This was certainly the case with the advent of racial violence after Nat Turner's rebellion in Southampton, Virginia, John Brown's insurrection at Harpers Ferry, and during and after the Civil War. Indeed, the significance of challenges to white supremacy was remembered well into the twentieth century by the black community. Even if we have sufficiently examined the "origins of [African American] trauma narratives," we have not looked closely enough at the experiences themselves. The "history of trauma," especially this type of trauma—internecine violence, fears of racial extermination, and the demise of the black family, of black women and children—needs to be explored for what it tells us about everyday life for those enslaved and free. Trauma can also function, anthropologist Aaron Denham argues, "as a carrier of cultural and family identity . . . strategies of resilience, for holding on, for surviving. [It is a] non-pathological adaptive response and ability to maintain or 'spring back' . . . after experiencing adversity."[14] This ability to "spring back" is evidenced by the black community's determination to create a "collective memory" or social memory of its experiences as an enslaved and free people, an essential part of African American history for what it tells us about how African Americans endured hardship, how they continued to achieve and prosper despite the challenges they faced, how concerns about racial extermination did not deter their determination to achieve social justice and equality. Thus the social and psychological costs of a war between the races were not the same for those in the oppressed group as for those in the dominant group; therefore, the teleological underpinnings of this rhetoric are paramount to this study.

Extermination as a category of analysis forces us to reevaluate the conditions in which slaves and free blacks exerted power. An examination of black thought and culture reveals these ideas in the "common wind," the tradition of carrying information through oral communication that Africans retained in America.[15] Black people enslaved and free were well aware of what they were up against, as they were shaping their own communities within the African diaspora while Native Americans were being exterminated in their efforts to resist the colonization of their land. Those who were enslaved valued life and consciously saw it as their communal obligation to help keep the black race

alive. And although some slaves transgressed the boundaries of white supremacy by attempting to foment insurrections, for most Africans in the Americas, survival was their form of resistance. At the same time, the difficulty of
coping with a traumatic form of violence that went beyond the whippings,
rape, and separation of families is also apparent, revealing a psychological
cost of slavery not accounted for in economic terms.

While there are a number of published works (primarily generated by
an earlier generation of scholars) that look at racial violence in the post-
Reconstruction era, only a few secondary works allude to the rhetoric of a war
between the races. But they do not analyze it from the African American perspective nor trace its origins back to Africa or Europe, where practices of *petite
guerre* were organized out of already established cultural traditions. Ideas of
a race war were linked to extermination and the deliberate killing of women,
children, and old people, a lineage linking past to future that stands power-
fully for that horrific objective. George Frederickson, in *The Black Image in the
White Mind*, refers to what he calls the "racial prognostication" that early colonists like Thomas Jefferson espoused about the dangers of black freedom.[16]
Jefferson and other slave owners believed that there was always the possibility
of a war between the races, because slave owners understood that slaves, just
like white men, would always try to free themselves by killing off their cap-
tors. Historian Robert Abzug wrote on this subject as well, only he views the
subject through the lens of William Lloyd Garrison's fears about slave rebellions resulting in the extermination of either race.[17] Garrison, an abolitionist
and editor of the antislavery newspaper the *Liberator*, did not advocate that
the enslaved use violence, but he did use the threat of violence to encourage
the abolition of slavery. Like Frederickson, Abzug does not historicize the idea
of extermination from the African American perspective, nor does he suggest
how it shaped African Americans' understanding of the political and social
world in which they lived or how it influenced the institution of slavery and
the business of the Atlantic slave trade. It is as if the rhetoric of a race war
emerged in the public sphere with Garrison and the abolitionists' calls for immediate emancipation instead of being an essential part of the institution of
enslavement from the very beginning.

In his *Crucible of Race*, Joel Williamson discusses these ideas in an attempt
to explain white violence in the post-Reconstruction South. However, Williamson's central argument is that the threat of a violent black revolt, which
first crystallized with Nat Turner's rebellion, triggered deep psychological
trauma for the first three generations of white Americans born after the Civil
War. This thesis is deeply flawed in light of the centrality of exterminatory
violence used against blacks to historically sustain white power from the very

beginning. Williamson also creates the illusion that *white southerners* were the victims in the Jim Crow era.[18] Leon Litwack also explains these ideas with some detail in his *Trouble in Mind*, but he focuses on the post–Civil War and Reconstruction era. Litwack states that blacks organized throughout the South to protect each other in their communities from white violence and abuse, increasingly using a show of arms in either self-defense or retaliation. Race relations became so explosive that concerns about a race war centered white energy on suppressing black aggression. These young blacks, Litwack argues, created a crisis within the white community in the South. Their behavior was grounded in the rejection of the accommodation of their slave fathers.[19] The suggestion that it was black agency that created white aggression in the Jim Crow era does not stand up in light of the endless cycles of internecine violence, the massacres of black men, women, and children that occurred before, during, and after the Civil War. The young African Americans who were born out of slavery were not substantively different from their ancestors who were enslaved, they just took advantage of prevailing opportunities given to them by law. Both arguments have created a mythology about the origins of racial violence in America that needs correction.

Historian Gregory J. W. Urwin, in his examination of Civil War atrocities, *Black Flag over Dixie*, does connect the extermination of African American soldiers with the inherited ideas of racial prejudice generated during slavery, but he does not discuss the longer history of racial conquest through war.[20] Historian Chandra Manning, in *What This Cruel War Was Over*, also discusses how ideas of a race war fueled southern white men's participation in the Confederate army during the Civil War. Recruitment and the fervor to fight for the Confederacy were predicated on a fear of what would happen if slavery were abolished. Certainly, ideas of white extermination were used to stoke white fear of black emancipation and racial equality, and newspapers and politicians across the country imagined black freedom to be a problem because it would mean that black people would be equal to whites.[21] But they also imagined that racial amalgamation would occur. In order to circumvent blacks acquiring social and civic equality and practicing miscegenation, a nineteenth-century term for interracial sex, whites would have to either migrate out of the South, force blacks to live in separate states, colonize blacks in some other country, or reenslave the entire black population. If one of these scenarios did not happen, a race war and black extermination would occur. There has been no examination of the considerable threats of extermination that were made against African Americans during and after the Civil War, and it is essential to examine what *they* thought about these ideas and how they coped with the deadly violence against them in the South and the North. Indeed, concerns about and prophecies of a race war continued into the twentieth century and were even expressed during the civil rights era in the writings and speeches of Marcus Garvey, W. E. B. Du Bois, Martin Luther King Jr., Robert F. Williams, and Malcolm X.

In the early years of the Republic and throughout the nineteenth century, concerns about the possibility of a race war were part of everyday life, and who would win was always contested terrain and uncertain. Guided by the framework of intellectual and social history, historical trauma, and memory, this study of slavery and race uses a breadth of primary sources from the seventeenth to the nineteenth century that reveal a previously ignored perspective of the African diasporic experience. Africans in America viewed the possibility of racial extermination as a serious threat throughout the nineteenth century, a threat that was still very much present in the civil rights era and continues to resonate with some African Americans even today.

If slaves from Africa were successful in killing any of their white oppressors, they were viewed as criminals and were sentenced to death for their crimes. Liberal-republican ideas of freedom, defined as personal "autonomy, or the capacity for human agency," an individual's ability to act and shape his or her own circumstances, ideas that historian François Furstenberg argues emerged during and after the Revolutionary War, never applied to people of African descent. The Republican concept of virtue, inscribed in an individual's willingness to fight for his or her freedom, even if it meant death, was denied to those who did fight against their oppression, and their actions were instead defined as evil acts of savagery and barbarism.[22] And the consequences for resisting enslavement went far beyond the individuals involved. In reality, those who were enslaved were attempting to free themselves from a system of oppression that denied their right to be free, their "personhood" and "humanity." That system was "maintained by a constant climate of coercive violence."[23] Indeed, some whites argued that slavery was an inhumane institution, even calling it a crime against humanity. Slave masters successfully controlled laws and customs that supported enslavement in the African diaspora, but they did not control the minds or the spirits of those Africans who believed that those who oppressed them did so unlawfully and were rightfully their enemies. This was as true for those African warriors on board slave ships during the Middle Passage, for Tacky in Jamaica, Court in Antigua, Jemmy in South Carolina, as it was for Toussaint L'Ouverture in Saint-Domingue, Denmark Vesey in South Carolina, Nat Turner in Virginia, and the thousands of men and women who believed in and supported what these courageous men attempted to do, despite the risk of unchecked retaliation and possible extermination. Black soldiers who fought in the Civil War held beliefs similar to those of African

Americans who did their best to defend themselves and their families from white violence in the post–Civil War and Jim Crow eras.

Yet most people today, white or black, do not know that the history of racialized exterminatory warfare is an essential part of the American story. If "the memory of a people," as scholar Catherine Reinhardt, argues, "is the key to controlling their dynamism, their experience, and their knowledge of their struggles," then the "systematic silencing" of this history has been effective.[24] The reason that extermination as a central tenet of racial control has been obscured is that one side—white people—stood to gain from its usage in particular, yet ever-changing, ways over time. Ideas about race and freedom allowed for unobstructed violence to ensue against those who resisted slavery during the Civil War and Reconstruction and throughout the Jim Crow era. The language of extermination found in the personal letters, newspapers, pamphlets, travel narratives, and creative expressions of slave-owning men and women, as well as in slave narratives, congressional records, and abolitionist tracts, offers fresh insight into the everyday lives of those enslaved and free. It makes what we know about slavery and the nation appear incomplete. Something much bigger was at stake for African Americans. Indeed, the threat of racial extermination was a palpable reason why slaves did not rebel more frequently than they did, especially in the latter part of the antebellum era.

Is this "a history of the impossible," an attempt to uncover what never happened—what never could have happened—a memory, which has been locked away and buried so long ago?[25] For Africans across the diaspora, deadly racial violence was not impossible, because extermination was a real threat, and the killing of black women, children, and the elderly remained part of the black lived experience. From the perspective of Enlightenment philosophers like Guillaume-Thomas, abbé de Raynal, and Marie-Jean-Antoine-Nicolas de Caritat, marquis de Condorcet, exterminatory warfare was not impossible. Although these Enlightenment thinkers were not free from racial assumptions about African people being inferior to whites, men like French historian Raynal argued that those who were enslaved had a right to their freedom, a right inscribed in "natural law."[26] He and others reasoned that "brutes are chained up, and kept in subjection, because they have no notion of what is just or unjust." Africans, however, were well aware of the injustice of being enslaved, whether by other Africans on the continent or by Europeans in the "New World," and therefore, Raynal argued, they had a right to fight against their enslavement. Moreover, Raynal warned in 1770: "Ye nations of Europe . . . Your slaves stand in no need either of your generosity or your counsels, in order to break the sacrilegious yoke of their oppression. . . . There are so many indications of the impending storm, and the Negroes only want a chief, sufficiently courageous, to lead them on to vengeance and slaughter. . . . In all parts the name of the hero, who shall have restored the rights of the human species will be blest. . . . [T]rophies will be erected to his glory."[27] French reformer Condorcet went even further, calling the institution of enslavement a crime. Condorcet stated in 1781 that "reducing a man to slavery, buying him, selling him in servitude: these are truly crimes, and crimes worse than theft. . . . [I]n freeing the slave the law does not attack property but rather ceases to tolerate an action which it should have punished with the death penalty." Government "therefore owes no compensation to the masters of slaves just as [it] owes none to a thief."[28]

The history of these ideas has also been memorialized by important nineteenth-century ethnologists like John Phillip, Sir Charles Lyell, James Prichard, and Robert Knox, who predicted the extermination of darker people of color around the world as early as 1828.[29] In his visit to America in 1845, Lyell noted that whereas a white Georgian aristocrat claimed to understand the "cruelty of slavery," he harbored a strong "anti-negro feeling" that led him to "hope" and was "ready to precipitate measures which would cause the Africans [in America] to suffer that fate which the aboriginal Indians have experienced throughout the Union."[30]

Because the language of extermination was part of the cultural and political currency that European and American slaveholders used to sustain slavery and uphold white supremacy, the notion of paternalism, which is often used to dismiss black extermination as a possibility, becomes a false framework for interpreting what life was like for those enslaved and free.[31] The idea that slavery was a paternalistic institution was first proclaimed in 1918 by historian Ulrich Bonnell Phillips, who described it as an institution "shaped by mutual requirements, concessions, and understandings, producing reciprocal" labor relations on the plantation. Even Phillips, however, understood that whites were aware of the danger in having an enslaved population living in their midst, of the "possibility of [their] social death from negro upheaval." A central problem for slave owners was "their unending task of race discipline," considered necessary to keep blacks from overthrowing white authority and white control.[32] The modern take on paternalism in the works of historian Eugene Genovese, for example, did not stray far from Phillips's theories of reciprocity.[33] Although for many scholars the issue of paternalism as a real construct is a nonstarter, there remains a cadre of scholars who still believe in the notion of southern paternalism.[34] Some historians, for example, Lacy Ford, continue to argue that the idea of paternalism evolved because southerners were plagued with guilt over their involvement in the institution of enslavement.[35] But what value does guilt really have as a human experience if it does not change behavior? If guilt shaped the thinking of white southerners regarding slavery, why did violence against black people escalate instead of decline during the nineteenth century? In seeking an answer to that question, this research reveals that enslaved people were not viewed by whites as helpless victims in the long history of slavery in the Americas and that the enslaved were far from apolitical, as some historians have suggested.[36] We must also consider, in light of the mass violence that enslaved people experienced and their spoken and unspoken anxiety about racial extermination, how a transformational relationship like paternalism could have occurred. The rationale and theories surrounding paternalism, enslavement, race, and freedom that emerged in the seventeenth and eighteenth centuries were fashioned for the sake of empire. These ideas, for the most part, were never real but were myths that have become history. Because the enslaved desired freedom, the anticipation of and potential for war between the races was a central tension within the institution. That fear of race war eliminated any real sense of reciprocity or familial sentimentality between whites and blacks and influenced the formation and evolution of the first racially based and most perniciously violent form of slavery in the history of the world. Nevertheless, through it all, and despite fears of mass violence and racial extermination, African Americans continued to fight for justice and freedom from oppression—to improve their lives and to preserve African American culture and communities in the United States.

The development of the United States into a powerful nation occurred not only because of the courage of the early pioneers and the political brilliance of the Founding Fathers but also through acts of incredible violence toward those enslaved. The manifestation of exterminatory warfare and violent conquest depicted throughout this book had roots in Europe and Africa that spread across the Atlantic World. As slavery became intrinsic to the American way of life, so too did ideas that blacks and whites could never live peaceably together as equals. Southerners remained determined that those enslaved could never be free without that freedom ending in a massacre of the black race, and they intentionally followed through on their convictions during the Civil War and post–Civil War era. Thus, this book looks at how the potential for a race war between blacks and whites shaped the human cost of slavery—and freedom—in ways that have been previously unexamined.

CHAPTER ONE

"Nits Make Lice"

Genocidal Violence in Colonial America

When Europeans first settled in the New World in the seventeenth century, they came with an inherited set of ideas about how to subdue those whom they would soon declare to be savages. In ancient times, it was not uncommon for enemy combatants to either exterminate their foes or enslave them.[1] First encounters in the New World included deep-seated fears that the Native population would plot revenge or attack a European colony that was already on the threshold of calamity. Those fears drove a mentality based on an "us versus them" dichotomy that demanded action. Such fears led to the death of thousands of Native people—men, women, and children—who were seen as collateral damage in what English colonialists viewed as "just wars."[2] Colonists also believed in a divine right to exterminate those whom they deemed uncivilized, and they compared their struggle with that of the Israelites. Increase Mather, preaching to his Puritan congregation in Boston in 1710, argued that "there are Just Wars which the Lord Himself calls men to engage in. . . . God has put a principle of self preservation into his Creatures." Mather also used the example of the Israelites' war against the Ammonites to show how "battles fought with the Enemies of God" should be waged: "Therefore the Children of Israel fought against them and slew them with a great Slaughter: This was just."[3] The colonists, determined to secure lanes of commerce, control, and jurisdiction, enacted the royal command to keep any group that might oppose British imperialism in check and to make those perceived to be in the way of progress "stand in fear."[4]

Uniquely fashioned ideas about just warfare and its necessary tactics and casualties were fundamentally sustained by greed. The more the fledgling colonies prospered and cities grew, the more a culture of violence came to undergird the economies of the new settlements. What began with the enslavement of Native Americans in the early decades of English colonization quickly expanded into a system of institutionalized slavery that imported labor from Africa. The natural resources, climate, and landscape of the American South allowed the development of a networked agricultural economy producing primarily rice and tobacco and eventually cotton, which depended on an enslaved workforce. Such a system, sustained by exhibitions of violence, brute force, and dehumanization, became normalized for its executioners, even as it became symbolic of their own underlying fear of annihilation.

Early European Warfare

Wars of extermination were not born on American soil but were practiced in Western Europe before colonists crossed the Atlantic.[5] The English waged wars of this type against the Irish over land, religious and cultural factionalism in the aftermath of the Christian Reformation, and mercantile interests in the new economy of the mid-sixteenth century. The slaughtering of hundreds of "manne, woman and childe" during the first Desmond Rebellion in Munster, Ireland, in 1569 was rationalized by Thomas Churchyard, an English author and soldier of fortune in the sixteenth century, as the most expedient way to end conflict, since "terrour . . . made short warres." For after "thei sawe the heddes of their dedde fathers, brothers, children, kinsfolke, and freendes, lye on the ground before their faces," the people would be reformed, and "universall peace, and subjection" would prevail. Churchyard further explained that killing the women of Irish soldiers was particularly effective because it ultimately led to the starvation of the "menne of warre," who were incapable of taking care of "their Creates . . . their victualles, and other necessaries."[6] Churchyard was no doubt referencing the brutal policies of Sir Humphrey Gilbert, the appointed governor of Munster, a pioneer of proprietor colonization and an English soldier who was known for piling the slaughtered heads of men, women, and children along the pathway to his tent after battle. In 1566 Gilbert placed the entire village of Munster under martial law. Indifferent to the townspeople's surrender, he ordered their decapitation to set an example of what other Irish people might expect if they resisted English rule.[7]

Despite English tactics of slaughter, which they believed had "subdued the country," many Irish did not concede defeat, and this led to even greater atrocities.[8] For the English, the brutality of the wars in Ireland in the 1560s and 1570s was justified by claims that those fighting against colonization were barbarians and savages and therefore culturally inferior. Ideas of Irish barbarity and paganism were used to rationalize the imposition of martial law.[9] To the English Privy Council, the Irish remained outside the realm of European standards of civilization. It was, they claimed, the duty of England to civilize barbarian people, as Rome had the ancient Brits. Ireland was a nation of "rebellious people" to whom "nothing but feare and force can teach dutie and obedience."[10] But even when they did comply, the Irish were ruthlessly murdered. Despite making unconditional submission to the Earl of Essex, and after three days and nights of "peace, sociality, and friendship" between Brian, the son of Felim Bacagh O'Neill, and the earl in 1574, "Brian . . . and all his people [were] put unsparingly to the sword, men, women, youths, and maidens. . . . This unexpected massacre . . . was sufficient cause of hatred and disgust *of the English* to the Irish."[11]

This type of warfare was not reserved for those who were enemies of the English. As another incident in 1577 attests, "a horrible act of treachery was committed by the English of Leinster and Meath . . . upon that part of the people of Offally and Leix [Ireland] that remained in confederacy with them, and under their protection . . . they were all summoned to shew themselves . . . and on their arrival at that place they were surrounded on every side by four lines of soldiers and cavalry, who proceeded to shoot and slaughter them without mercy, so that not a single individual escaped, by flight or force."[12] And when the Irish remained loyal to Catholicism, despite the establishment of the Protestant Church of England, their loyalty fueled further ideas that they could not or would not assimilate. In the sixteenth and seventeenth centuries, this meant that the Irish faced either banishment from their lands or extermination until they respected the political will and cultural authority of England's Queen Elizabeth I.

Genocidal warfare reached new heights as the English sought intentionally to achieve high casualties through military strategy in the seventeenth century. Historical accounts of the Irish rebellion against colonization and religious oppression in 1641 assert that from the beginning, the English Parliament, under the leadership of King Charles I, pressed for a war of extermination. By 1644 the Parliaments of both England and Scotland, which were engaged in civil war, passed ordinances that "no quarter be given to any Irish who came to England to the King's aid."[13] There was brutality on both sides, and noncombatant populations were in constant jeopardy of becoming casualties of war.[14] Nevertheless, the unprecedented and intentional slaughter of Irish people is well documented: "In one day eighty women and children in Scotland were flung over a high bridge into the water, solely because they were the wives and children of Irish soldiers" who were held there as prisoners of war. People from several villages in Ireland were deliberately trapped by fire in an enclave and "all burnt or killed—men, women, and children."[15] British ferocity was particularly memorable in the massacres of Drogheda and Wexford. Under the severe discipline and leadership of Oliver Cromwell, the lieutenant general of the English army in Ireland, at least three thousand people, "some women and children . . . were put to the sword on September 11 and 12,

1649." Cromwell would later claim, "I wish that all honest hearts may give the glory of this to God alone to whom indeed the praise of this mercy belongs."[16] John Nalson, an English clergyman and historian, was told by a captain in the English army that "no manner of Compassion or Discrimination was shewed either to Age or Sex, but that the little Children were promiscuously sufferers with the Gulley [large knife], and that if any who had some grains of Compassion reprehended the Soldiers for this unchristian inhumanity, they would scoffingly reply, Why? Nits will be Lice, and so would dispatch them."[17] It is at this point that "the saying 'Nits will make lice,' which was constantly employed to justify the murder of Irish children," became part of English vernacular.[18] The extermination of children was the ultimate solution in war, for it thwarted the possibility of revenge and made space for the settlement of a superior English race. It helped fulfill "the grand object of the Revolutionary Party . . . to carry out the wild scheme of unpeopling Ireland of the Irish, and planting it anew with English."[19] The antecedent of these war tactics began nearly a century earlier, but the English policies that sanctioned the final conquest of Ireland, that legitimized possession by force and colonization as God's will, would continue to be employed in the subsequent conquest of America.[20]

American Conceptions of War and Conquest

When the first settlers came to America, they anticipated that there would be trouble in the region. Historian Patrick M. Malone states that "the transmission of concepts of total warfare from Europe to America" was evident as early as 1637, but it began much earlier.[21] Continuity is evident in 1578, when Queen Elizabeth gave Sir Humphrey Gilbert a six-year patent to "discover, finde, search out, and view such remote, heathen and barbarous lands, countreys and territories not actually possessed of any Christian prince or people . . . to have, hold, occupie . . . forever."[22]

Theories about natural "rights and liberties" that prevailed during the English Reformation were conspicuously absent from the rhetoric concerning colonization of the New World.[23] What emerges instead is what historian Francis Jennings called the "conquest myth." Europeans claimed that the New World was "virgin land" settled by savages who were not Christians. Native people were "demons" and "beasts in the shape of men," and Europeans often refused to recognize them as fully human.[24] The designation of indigenous and eventually African people as savages by clergy and government authorities alike profoundly loosened the boundaries of just warfare. Because "savages" were viewed as "irrational" and uncivilized people, they were seen as committing senseless acts of "perpetual violence" rather than being capable of practicing the "rational," organized form of violence that the English claimed defined European warfare.[25] These differences—much like race—were used to justify not only conquest but also enslavement and extermination, and many English settlers who gained their military experience in Ireland had the confidence and formula for how they would induce the "lesser breeds" to cooperate.[26]

The clergy in the seventeenth century reinforced ideas that connected savagery to violence and heathens to damnation. From William Symmonds in England to Increase Mather in what is now Massachusetts, religious leaders were central to shaping and affirming conceptions of war in the American colonies. In 1609 King James I ordered church ministers to use their pulpit to encourage the English to Christianize North America by settling in the colony of Jamestown, Virginia. Rev. Symmonds was one of the first ministers to do so in England. He preached that a missionary impulse should guide colonization and that, like "Worthy Joshuah and most worthy David," England, the country of God's chosen people, had a moral mandate to expand so that its "dominion should be from sea to sea."[27] In another sermon, the English reverend Robert Johnson argued that the intent was not to remove the "savages. . . . Our intrusion into their possessions shall tend to their great good and in no way to their hurt, unless"—and here is the conundrum that indigenous people faced—"as unbridled beastes, they procure it to themselves."[28] Rev. Robert Gray, however, rather bluntly outlined the theocratic justifications and militant intentions for English settlement. Gray claimed that the English had always been "more warlike" than other nations and that "we may justly say, as the children of Israel say here to Joshua, we are a great people." Joshua, "a faithfull and godly Prince," responsible for Israel's holy conquest and the annihilation of the idolaters settled in the land of Canaan, seemed to Gray emblematic of the mission that English adventurers faced in Virginia. Their task was to "bring the barbarous and savage people to the civill and Christian kinde of government, under which they may learne how to live holily, justly, and soberly in this world . . . rather then to destroy them, or utterly to roote them out." If that did not work, however, Gray, who had never been to America, made clear that "we are warranted by this direction of Ioshua, to destroy wilfull and convicted Idolaters, rather then to let them live, if by no other meanes they can be reclaimed."[29]

The mission to encourage settlement in Virginia was effective, and the English arrived in the Americas with a "crusading mentality."[30] God had given them, as superior people, the right to conquer those without religion and without civilization. Through these culturally driven beliefs and religious interpretations, the English believed themselves to be like the Israelites, and they believed that God, as described in the Old Testament, was a "man of warre." If indigenous Americans caused trouble and resisted European settlement through violent means, God directed them, as he had the Hebrews, to "save alive nothing that breatheth."[31]

The fact that there was no central authority governing and shaping policy in the early colonies enabled the colonists to determine the ways in which warfare was waged and how English expansion was rationalized. As such, wars fought in colonial America were distinctive for their brutality. They were more violent and terroristic in nature than wars in Europe and "were waged with a macabre intensity not seen in Europe for generations after the seventeenth century."[32] The English saw Native Americans as dangerous foes "who seemed to possess some strange form of animal cunning, who treated prisoners cruelly, and who would not fight in expected ways."[33] These differences in military culture had a profound impact in shaping future English attempts to decimate and remove entire indigenous populations and ultimately led to Europeans giving up their organized crusade to Christianize Native Americans. As early as 1697, Virginia governor Edmund Andros remarked that "no endeavors to convert the Indians to Christianity have ever been heard of."[34]

War and Subjugation in Virginia

Jamestown, Virginia, was developed in 1607 through a charter granted by King James I to a joint stock company, the Virginia Company of London. These early colonists intended to settle on the land, trade with indigenous peoples, and search for commodities and raw materials to export.[35] The subsequent European invasion of the region created a hostile environment that resulted in a rise in Native American military organization.[36] Ultimately, Native Americans in Virginia were almost entirely extinguished from the region through either disease, wars of extermination, or enslavement. The few who survived and remained in the region became marginalized and subsumed by legislation that lumped Native peoples and Africans together as savages and racial others.

A portrait of European conquest and warfare with the Powhatan Confederacy in Virginia can be found in the narrative of George Percy, a wealthy nobleman from England. In *A Trewe Relacyon*, Percy stated that he and his men followed the orders of Thomas West, 12th Baron de La Warr and the first governor of Virginia, to attack the Paspahegh and Chickahominy people in 1610. Driven by revenge, they killed men, women, and children and captured the "Quene and her Children" in a brutal campaign. Although Percy expressed reluctance to killing the captives, he acquiesced under great pressure from his fellow officers and allowed them to kill the children by throwing them "overboard and shoteinge owtt their Braynes in the water. Yett for all this Crewellty the Sowldiers weare nott well pleased and I had mutche to doe To save the queens lyfe for thatt Tyme." Upon reaching shore, de La Warr, who had served as a soldier in Ireland, seemed displeased that the queen had been left alive and thought it best to "Burne her." Percy, who claimed to be sickened already by the amount of "Blood shedd that day," then agreed to "geve her a quicker dispatche" either by shooting her or by the sword.[37]

The manner in which the English settlers treated the Native people was not without its consequences. In the context of broad-scale European pressures for land and the development of tobacco as an export crop, the murder of a revered and important leader named Nemattanow, or Jack the Feather, of the Powhatan Confederacy fueled an already tense situation that erupted in 1622 with a counterattack by the Pamunkey against the English. Approximately one-third of the Virginia settlers were killed in what was called a massacre. The English were infuriated that "under the bloudy and barbarous hands of the perfidious and inhumane people, contrary to all lawes of God and men, of Nature and Nations, three hundred forty seven men, women, and children [were killed], most by their owne weapons; and not being content with taking away life alone, they fell after againe upon the dead, making as well as they could, a fresh murder, defacing, dragging, and mangling the dead carkasses into many pieces, and carrying some parts away in derision, with base and brutish triumph."[38] The 1622 massacre shocked the Jamestown colony and eventually contributed to the collapse of the Virginia Company of London. Public confidence also waned in England in response to rumors of continued conditions of near starvation and devastating diseases in the colony.[39]

The subsequent retaliation for the attack, however, was considered not only justified but also a blessing for the English, as Native Americans, "these beasts," were viewed as an obstruction and nuisance to white settlement and expansion.[40] As Edward Waterhouse, the Virginia Company secretary, put it in his report: "Our hands which before were tied wit gentlenesse and faire usage, are now set at liberty by the treacherous violence of the Sauvages, not untying the Knot, but cutting it: So that we . . . may now by right of Warre, and law of Nations, invade the Country, and destroy them who sought to destroy us."[41] Capt. John Smith, however, a soldier of fortune in Europe and former president of the council in Jamestown, disagreed. He believed that although the settlers did "have just cause to destroy them by all meanes possible," for the good of the settlement it would be better to avoid having to subjugate the Native Americans. Yet Smith admitted that it would be easier to "civilize them by conquest then faire meanes; for the [first] one may be made at once, but their civilizing will require a long time and much industry."[42] In retaliation, armed forces were sent out to destroy all Indians residing in the areas of the James and York Rivers. Two years later it was customary for colonists to attack Indian settlements every November, March, and July with the hope of "rooting them out for being longer a people upon the face of the Earth."[43]

Through oral tradition, a man known as Uncle Moble Hobson's father, who admitted he had not been a witness, nonetheless transmitted the story of how Native American people along the York and Poquoson Rivers were eliminated after "de white man come." Hobson, a former slave of mixed descent, relayed that his father told him, "Dis whut de white man do. . . . Well, dey cross de Potomac an' dey has to fight de injuns an' dey cross de York an' fit some more tell de kilt all de Injuns or run em' way. When de cross de Poquoson dey fine de Injuns ain't aimin' tuh fight but dey kilt de men an' tek de injun women fo' de wives. Coursen dey warn't no marryin' dem at dat time."[44] The exact time frame of Hobson's story has not been verified, but the Poquoson River was named after an Algonquin group affiliated with the Powhatan Confederacy that had inhabited the area before its colonization by the English. The Algonquins, who were supposedly hostile to the English, would certainly have had good reason to be antagonistic, as the colonists apparently opened Algonquin land for English settlement in 1628. Poquoson became part of York County in 1642–43; this is when the name of the Charles River was changed to the York River. It is conceivable that what Hobson relays is the removal of the Poquoson inhabitants through the retaliatory campaigns in the aftermath of the 1622 massacre, ending with what appears to be unrelenting English aggression.

At face value, the assertion that the atrocity committed by the Pamunkey tribe forced the English to retaliate appears justified, except that many historians concur that at that time, Native peoples did not generally practice exterminatory warfare. After contact with Europeans, however, Native Americans learned quickly that it was in their best interest to operate in what would become the "American way": applying English techniques of massive slaughter that indigenous people themselves frequently experienced during English attacks.[45] Although chronicler and writer William Strachey asserts that Powhatan exterminated the Chesapeakes and many of the Piankatanks due to a divine prophecy, the fact that Powhatan did so does not negate the fact that it was culturally viewed as wrong and against their currently practiced traditions, in which women were valued for their agricultural skills and as mothers.[46] Strachey supports this analysis by further noting that "they seldom make warrs for lands or goods, but for women and children, and principally for revenge. . . . [T]he weroances [officers or commanders], women or children, they put not to death, but keep them captives. They have a method in warre."[47] Although archaeological evidence suggests that Native Americans did practice indiscriminate violence against women and children in the past, it is not clear that the reasons for the carnage were generated by ideas of extermination. What is clear, as Christina Snyder argues, is that when the English colonists arrived in North America, these practices had changed as a result of heightened intertribal warfare and plunging Native populations due to European diseases. Thus, by the end of the seventeenth century, most women and children were either captured for sale or held as captives by other tribes to ensure the survival of various Mississippian clans.[48] By the seventeenth century, the tribes had evolved, and the Native American approach to warfare common to the Eastern Woodland nations became known as the "Law of Innocence." It did not allow for the killing of noncombatants—women, children, and elderly people. Europeans were not responding to savagery; they were creating an environment in which it thrived. And Native American people living in the eastern part of North America, from the Great Lakes region to the Gulf of Mexico, from the Atlantic Ocean to the eastern Great Plains, learned to come to terms with an enduring environment of hostility.

Despite the fact that, collectively, Native Americans in Virginia were substantially weakened by the persistent aggression of Europeans and the threat of Native tribes from bordering regions, the English continued to rationalize exterminatory warfare against the indigenous people in the region and foment fear in cultural and racial terms. In 1666 the English government ordered the militia to exterminate the Doeg, Nanzemond, Portobacco, and Patawomeck tribes residing in Rappachannock County because of their apparent harassment of a few settlers in the upper portions of that region. According to Governor Sir William Berkeley, this was "for revenge," and he ordered that "for the prevention of future mischeifs that the towns of Monzation, Nanzimond and Port Tobacco with the whole nation of the Doegs and Potamacks [Patawomecks] be forthwith prsecuted with war to their utter destruction if possible and that their women and children and their goods . . . be disposed of."[49] This action followed a 1655 law that made it legal to kill Native Americans if it was perceived that they were up to "mischief."[50] It is impossible to know the full outcome of British efforts, but there is evidence that whoever was left of the Patawomeck tribe abandoned their homeland, and there is no further mention of the Patawomecks in the extant historical documents of English colonial history.[51] Some Nanzemond, however, appear to still have been in Virginia in the late 1670s.[52] And enough of the Doeg Indians apparently survived to continue their aggressive resistance against white settlement on their lands in July 1675.[53]

The rebellion led by Nathaniel Bacon, an English colonist, in 1676 was, at its core, a call for racial extermination as a tool to resolve the problems of continued contestations between Native Americans and Europeans over land. In this first of civil actions against English imperial power, Bacon led a coalition of disgruntled white yeoman farmers against the colonial royal governor of Virginia, William Berkeley. Bacon and fur trader William Byrd I, who had lands along the James River, charged that Berkeley was not sufficiently concerned with protecting the Virginia frontier homelands from Doeg and Susquehanna attacks because of his trade monopoly with Native Americans in the region. Berkeley's purported neglect of the colonists' needs heightened the pressure on an already diminished indigenous population.[54]

At the center of this conflict, though, was whether it was appropriate for the colonists to be at "war with all Indians which come not in with their armies, and give Hostages for their fidelity and to ayd against all others."[55] If those who were left of a once-sizeable and influential confederation of peoples, 2,900 members of the Powhatan tribe, did not comply with British demands, then the burgeoning English population of over 30,000 threatened, "We will spare none."[56] Native Americans would have to completely surrender themselves to British rule or else face certain destruction. The killing of Bacon's overseer during one of the Doeg and the Susquehanna raids perhaps made the issue a personal one for Bacon. But most of the English citizens siding with Bacon believed in the "law of nature," which required that "wee defend ourselves before they oppose us . . . take their usual advantage . . . and soe destroy us."[57] Perhaps promises of freedom encouraged the involvement of the eighty slaves and twenty servants who also participated.[58] Nevertheless, the "common cry" that there was no distinction between "Friend or Foe Soe they be Indians" fostered what historian Kathleen Brown calls an "ethic of racist violence" that pushed all Native Americans outside of the protection of English law.[59]

Bacon and his army of three hundred were able to only moderately make good on their promise to kill "those that will destroy us," but what the records do reveal is that his army killed men, women, and possibly children.[60] In one altercation, Bacon and his rebels were successful after stumbling upon Pamunkey Indians who "did not at all oppose, but fled, being followed by Bacon and his Forces killing and taking them Prisoners." The queen of Pamunkey, Cockacoeske, fled with a ten-year-old boy, fearful of returning to her village because "shee happened to meet with a deade Indian woman lying in the way being one of her own nation; which struck such terror in the Queene that fearing their cruelty by that gastly example shee went on her first intended way into wild woodes where shee was lost amd missing from her people for ffourteen dayes." An unidentified elderly Indian woman who was the queen's nurse had been killed earlier after Bacon ordered "his soldiers to knock her in the head, which they did, and they left her dead on the way." Perhaps this was the woman left in "the way" that the queen encountered while making her escape. This woman had remained loyal to her queen by not guiding Bacon and his rebels to the queen's encampment; instead, she led them around for more than a day until at last they discovered her attempt to impede their efforts. In another incident, a "half starved" Native American woman apparently met a similar fate, as did a handful of men and an equal number of women who were attempting to flee from their encampment. Bacon managed to come away with forty-five captives, which he proudly held as plunder.[61] Despite the rebels' limited success in locating the Native American camps, the Pamunkey population was seriously decimated after Bacon's Rebellion.[62] Ironically, Bacon believed that it was the Pamunkeys' committed friendship with the English that made them the greatest threat, "being acquainted and knowing both the manners, customs, and nature of our People, and the Strength, Situation and advantages of the country and so capable of doing hurt and damage to the English."[63]

Bacon was the standard-bearer for all the English hopes "of destroying the Heathen," which continued even after the rebellion was put down. One petition from Isle of Wight County requested that the subsequent commissioners sent by the king continue Bacon's efforts of "war with the Indians that we may have done with them." In Nansemond County, the petitioners also advocated that "all Indians ought to be killed." In their view, this was not only a border issue but also a problem that everyone within the province of Virginia wanted addressed: the removal of Native Americans who were "all of a colour."[64]

After 1676, and because of Nathaniel Bacon's perseverance, the way of life for Native American communities in Virginia fundamentally changed. A series of laws were passed that curtailed the liberties of Native Americans. Deprived of protected status as indigenous people, terrorized Native Americans faced the options of death or enslavement. Voluntary exile was their only alternative. Now Native communities became racialized, as communities of color, and indigenous people engaged in war were to be made slaves if captured. Enslavement made war profitable for Jamestown and incentivized those soldier-citizens who might have previously been reluctant to join in initiatives like Bacon's Rebellion.[65] By 1682 any Native person traveling or living in Virginia could be legally enslaved.[66]

Anglo constructions of racial difference that did not distinguish between Native American slaves and African slaves functioned to diminish the Native American community and delegitimize their claims to their ancestral homelands. Just as they were being extirpated from the regions or enslaved, Africans were being imported as a new source of labor. Although the first "20 and odd Negroes" bought "at the best and easiest rate" were able to integrate into Virginia colonial society as enslaved and eventually free people, fourteen of these first Africans were distinguished by race in the 1623 census.[67] The forced arrival of Africans in Virginia increased rapidly in the 1680s and 1690s, and this expanding population led to the creation of racial distinctions between unfree and free laborers. The potential growth in the number of racially ambiguous colonists threatened social stability, despite the 1662 legislation that made it unlawful for any Christian to have sexual relations with a "negro." Statutes already in place established that the children born from these unions would follow the "condition of the mother," but these laws were hard to enforce. When Virginia lawmakers revisited this issue in 1691, they made the punishment for interracial marriage banishment. This was the first time that Virginia legislators used the word "white," and they specifically identified that the undesirable partners were "Negroes, mulattoes, and Indians." These statutes were created to put "all non-whites in 'their place'" and to prevent mixed-race populations from continuing to grow, which they did anyway, in exponential fashion, from 1690 to the 1720s.[68] After 1785 all mulattoes, as they were called, were considered to be mixed with African blood. Any Native Americans who were found to have "become one fourth mixed with the negro race" were by law "treated as free negroes or mulattoes."[69] Moreover, slave owners and traders made no distinctions between African slaves and Native American slaves. Both groups were sent out into the fields, lived in the same quarters, and were employed in trades or as domestics. They were renamed by their masters, wore the same type of coarse clothing and sometimes were without shoes, and generally suffered similar legal and extralegal debasement.[70] Both African and Native American males were forced to do work considered women's work in their cultures, and they hid in the swamps to evade white violence. Both groups were traumatized due to a general disregard for their traditional burial practices, as in their view, the lack of proper burial rituals prohibited the spirit from reaching the afterlife.[71] Much like African demographics for the slave trade, three Native people would die for every one Native person that was enslaved. By making all Native Americans who did not voluntarily remove themselves or did not become "pseudowhite" indistinguishable within the categories of "Negro" and "slave," white Virginians used race and bondage to further usurp indigenous possession of the land.[72] Those Native Americans who were considered uncivilizable and African by law were stripped of their title to any land in the American South. They were and in many cases still are no longer regarded as indigenous people.[73]

Indeed, a 1705 statute sought to close any legal distinction between Africans and Native Americans in Virginia. It specifically allowed that "all servants imported and brought into this country, by sea or land, who were not Christians in their native country . . . shall be slaves." It further dictated that "all Negroes, mulatto, and Indian slaves within this dominion shall be held to be real estate." The statute was later clarified by the court so that executors of an estate could treat "Negroes . . . as no otherwise than Horses or Cattle." The statute also allowed that the killing of a slave who resisted enslavement was no longer a felony. It became illegal, however, for any Negro, mulatto, or Indian, whether enslaved or free, to fight or strike "any Christian, not being negro, mulatto or Indian." The enslaved could no longer carry arms, or own cattle, or leave home without permission. Slaves also faced the possibility of "dismembering" as a means of controlling those who would run away by "terrifying others from the like practices."[74] Because the English engaged in and subsequently defeated Native Americans in wars and because of the legal definition of many Native Americans as nonwhites, they as a people were never beyond the reach of enslavement or white fears of a war between the races.

In *Notes from Virginia*, Thomas Jefferson canonized the idea in 1789 that a state of war always existed between master and slave. Echoing the fears of other colonists, like Col. William Byrd II and the future president, James Madison, Jefferson expressed his belief in the possible "extermination of the one race or the other," reflecting the view that large numbers of enslaved people were a dangerous threat to those who were their masters and to whites generally.[75] Jefferson, however, did not make the distinction between those slaves who were of indigenous descent, those who were of African descent, and those who were of a racially mixed heritage. By 1789 Native Americans who were racially mixed or enslaved had certainly become part of that group that Jefferson and other white colonists found to be an incompatible element of the Republic. And for Jefferson, chattel slavery and racialized ideas of who could be civilized required that certain people "be removed beyond the reach of mixture."[76]

The clarion call for the destruction of all Native Americans, defined by colonists as uncivilized heathens who were an obstruction to white settlement in the region, did not go unheeded. English concerns about living amongst slaves did not exclude Native Americans, who, as racial outcasts, found themselves outside the boundaries of colonial law by 1705. By the 1820s Native Americans in Virginia had been completely pushed off most of their tribal lands and into the black community because of white anxiety, which saw black and Native Americans as fundamentally the same, legally and racially.[77] That is, both groups were considered antagonistic and resistant to white supremacy. This was true in Virginia and true for the Native Americans in New England as well.

New England Ideas of Just Warfare

The Puritans arrived in the Northeast with ideas that supported the use of exterminatory warfare against Native Americans, whom the Puritans believed were God's enemies. The chronicled animosity between Europeans and Native Americans in the South, well established by 1620, influenced the Puritan settlers' views of indigenous people. Eventually, the Puritans turned a few aggressive actions into a mandate to fulfill God's glory by waging wars of extermination. Thereafter, a substantial number of the already decimated Native American populations in New England suffered enslavement and removal to other British colonies in the South and the West Indies.

Although the Puritans in America believed themselves to be like the Hebrews, who fought wars for self-preservation, their wars often turned into wars of conquest.[78] When Puritan Separatists left England in the pursuit of religious freedom, they dreamed of reestablishing pure Protestantism in the virgin land of North America. They wanted to create a theologically driven civil society based upon the Old Testament, a society they believed existed in "sacred time," that time before people began to live structured lives (known as "profane time"). As God's new chosen people, Puritans believed themselves justified in their decisions about what constituted legitimate land tenure and their divine right to Indian lands in Massachusetts.[79] The pandemics that decimated the once-populous regions of Massachusetts and Connecticut made, according to the Puritans, large swaths of land available for settlement. And, as had occurred in Virginia, Anglo appropriations of Native land created the environment in which Native peoples sporadically attacked white settlers. Eventually, the increased pressure over land tenure became the catalyst for the first war between Anglos and Indians in Connecticut.

Most of the historical accounts of the Pequot War reveal that it did not differ from other wars between Anglos and Indians in terms of what precipitated the conflict.[80] The struggle to mitigate English encroachment, as the English pushed forward to colonize the lands of indigenous people, was the reason wars generally began. What occurred in 1637 was no exception. What is unique, however, is the fact that the leaders of this effort, Maj. John Mason, Capt. John Underhill, and Lt. Philip Vincent, wrote detailed eyewitness accounts about the incident, albeit from the European perspective.

According to John Mason, the Pequots were a "warlike people" who were angry that the English had built Fort Saybrook in the Indian territory of what is now known as Connecticut. They attempted to agitate the English by constantly attacking individual settlers and killing their livestock in the hopes that they would be forced to leave the region. Having already signed away their rights to the Connecticut River valley, the Pequots were determined that English settlement would not permanently expand to the mouth of the Connecticut River.[81] From 1634 to 1637 the three tribes living in the area, the Narragansetts, the Mohegans, and the Pequots, managed to kill thirty-two colonists and to frustrate the militiamen residing at Fort Saybrook, "keeping almost a constant siege." This led Mason to conclude that a just war could be waged and that "it pleased God so to stir up the Hearts of all Men in general." The consensus was that the Pequots had brought the "necessity . . . to engage in an offensive and defensive War" on themselves.[82] Mason took ninety militiamen and recruited five hundred Narragansett Indians, who, according to Mason, were enemies of the Pequots, and traveled across Rhode Island in order to surprise them at their "two Forts," or villages. By the time the English-led forces arrived in Connecticut, it was too late to attack both "Forts" that day, so they made the decision to attack the closest one first. With Captain Underhill leading half of the men, they entered the "Fort" from both sides with the intention "to destroy them by the Sword." They did not see many warriors, and the ones they did see fled from them and hid. Captain Mason then decided, "We must Burn them," and the men immediately set the entire village ablaze. Mason set fire to the west entrance, while Underhill set fire to the south. Everything was consumed by the flames. The men blocked the two exits from the village so that no one could escape the fire, and those who did "perished by the Sword."[83] Underhill noted that other Europeans questioned "why you should be so furious? Should not Christians have more mercy and compassion? But [Underhill said] I would refer you to David's war. . . . [S]ometimes the scripture declareth women and children must perish with the parents. . . . We had sufficient light from the word of God for our proceedings."[84]

The English continued to pursue and destroy as many Pequots as they could find in what historian Francis Jennings described as "one long atrocity." Six hundred to seven hundred Pequots died in what the English called the "Mistick Fight." In Mason's view, "it was the Lord's Doings, and it is marvelous in our Eyes!" The final affront was that the "Pequots were then bound by Covenant, That none should inhabit their native Country, nor should any of them be called Pequots any more." The intent was to cause the erasure of their bodies and their culture, forever subsuming the Pequots into the "Moheags and Narragansetts," who took them as payment for helping in the English war.[85] "Blessed be the Lord God of Israel," Mason proclaimed, who "was pleased to smite our Enemies . . . [who would] give us their Land for an Inheritance."[86] By 1660, Capt. Leif Lion Gardener observed, only "remnants of the Pequot" lived in a town called Groton, where approximately forty Pequots lived on the useless "land reserved . . . [for] them" and where most of them, "mixed . . . with Negro and white blood," were even "more vicious and not so decent."[87] Their situation would remain marginalized, as Pequot William Apess observed in 1831 "a small remnant left from the massacre of the whites, who are now lingering in a miserable condition."[88] The Narragansetts who fought behind the English in the Pequot War were appalled by what had occurred. They came to Underhill afterward to commend the English on their victory "but cried Mach it, mach it; that is, It is naught, it is naught, because it is too furious, and slays too many men." From the Narragansetts' point of view, there was no honor in a war waged in this way.[89]

Lieutenant Gardener, reaffirming English ideas of exterminatory warfare, remembered that the Pequots queried him and his men before the Mystic battle whether "we did use to kill women and children." They wanted to know whether extermination was part of traditional English warfare or if it was unique to war with Native people in North America. Gardener declared that "they should see that hereafter." The Pequots then asserted after some thought that they too "can kill them as mosquetoes, and we will go to Connectecott and kill men, women, and children."[90] They never got the chance. According to the General Court of Massachusetts, the "right of conquest" and "revenge of innocent blood of the English" justified the wars against the Pequots. English law aligned with the desire of the settlers: to engage indigenous people in a type of warfare that allowed for the annihilation of men, women, and children living in the Massachusetts Bay and Connecticut regions.[91]

The fact that there was clear intent by the English to massacre the people within the Mystic River Pequot village demonstrates that a preexisting template for war was in place, challenging historian Adam Hirsch's assertions that this military culture was only prevalent during "actual warfare," that it occurred in a moment of passion.[92] Extermination was implemented and commonplace in colonial America. It was used by Europeans up and down the Atlantic coast as a strategy for the removal of indigenous people who stood in the way of "civilized progress."[93] The American way of warfare was no longer defensive. It was offensive; it became *the* way to clear the frontier of "barbarian savages," to make way for the civilized yeoman farmer and the future triumph of America's Manifest Destiny.[94]

The replication of the strategies used in the Pequot War continued well into the eighteenth and nineteenth centuries not only in New England and Virginia but also in emerging colonies such as New York, Tennessee, North and South Carolina, Louisiana, Florida, Ohio, and Pennsylvania.[95] This was certainly true in King Philip's War in Massachusetts, where, as Increase Mather pointed out, "many men, women and children were burned in their *wigwams*" and "Barbikew'd."[96] In fairness, both sides incurred astounding casualties. Several thousand English settlers lost their lives during King Philip's Pan-Indian effort to prevent the entire colonization of his land. Native people remember King Philip, or Pokunoket chief Metacom, as a "hero" who "died a martyr to his cause."[97] The best estimates suggest that three thousand to six thousand Native Americans were killed. Significant numbers of the Native Americans who eventually surrendered subsequently suffered enslavement. Most were sold to the West Indian plantation market, much to Increase Mather's pleasure, facilitating the near extinction of indigenous people in New England.[98]

English settlers in New England effectively propagandized that Native Americans should be condemned for their way of waging war.[99] Yet one must wonder at the dissemblance here. When Duke Holland, a member of the Wyandot tribe living near Detroit at the onset of the Revolutionary War, questioned a British order to kill "all the rebels," even the women and children, believing surely "it was meant that they should kill men only," he was told, "No, no . . . kill all; nits breed lice." Holland, however, rejected this idea. He recognized, no doubt, that this practice negatively affected his own people. Thus, honoring his own cultural traditions and the Law of Innocence, which forbade the killing or torture of noncombatants—women, children, and the elderly—he decided not to join the British military against the American patriots, nor did the sixteen tribes under him.[100]

After the Pequot War and King Philip's War, many woodland Native Americans were sold into slavery. Warfare practices encapsulated in New England codes of law were used as early as 1641 to affirm that bond slavery was lawful if the persons were "Captives taken in just warres." The crime of instigating warfare against the Puritan colonists, however, led to the decision that any Indians indulging in "hostile practices" should be removed "either to serve or be shipped out and exchanged for Negroes."[101] This same rationale was used in Virginia to justify Native American (and African) enslavement; but the collision of these ideas, just wars and the enslavement of Native Americans, was most pervasive in the Carolina region.

Carolinian Conquest and Native American Slaves

From the very beginning, English colonists engaged in warfare in South Carolina to foster Native American enslavement. Traders in Native American slaves followed a market-driven approach that was not only uniquely gendered but also attentive to age. As greater numbers of colonists settled the region, Native

Americans resisted the loss of their women, children, and land. They became an enemy who required not only subjugation through enslavement but also complete decimation and removal.

When King Charles II issued land grants to reward eight of his loyal supporters after his restoration to the throne in 1663, he also intended to monopolize the wealth that the eastern part of America had to offer. After the English removed the Dutch from the mid-Atlantic region and the provinces of New York, New Jersey, and later Pennsylvania and Delaware were established, Carolina became the southernmost region of settlement. White colonists, Charles II believed, would provide a buffer against the possibilities of Spanish and later French invasion. Thus, the English hoped to establish control over trade with the powerful Creek, Cherokee, Chickasaw, and Choctaw nations.[102]

Carolina's founding occurred just as the interest in buying and selling slaves in the colonies intensified. The region quickly surpassed the other colonies in the exportation of Native American slaves for use in other British territories and in response to the high demand for slaves in the West Indies. Exports of slaves exceeded imports in South Carolina until 1715.[103] Yet, according to plantation owner Robert Southwell, Carolina was particularly dependent on slave labor due to the difficulty of obtaining white labor, especially Irish labor. Apparently, the Irish feared returning to or becoming entrapped in labor agreements with the English that might echo their experience as unfree laborers in the West Indies after the massacres of Drogheda and Wexford.[104]

Eventually, as the Native American population along the coast diminished and as the demand for labor on the islands and in South Carolina increased, the colonists pushed farther into the interior. They encouraged Native Americans to fight each other and to betray previous alliances in order to find additional Natives for sale. Although slavery existed among southern Native Americans, they only enslaved "others" who were outside their clan. Slavery, however, took on a "new" dimension after Western contact, as did the Native American enslavement of prisoners of war.[105] Southern Native American nations—the Westos, Savannahs, Apalachees, Lower and Upper Creeks, Yamasees, Tuscaroras, and others—became deeply invested in the slave traffic. Much like the West African nations across the Atlantic, they too exchanged slaves for guns, powder, knives, hatchets, and rum.[106] Over time, the English in Carolina became more active in the sale of slaves than the English in any other colony.

In the first two centuries of English contact, many thousands of southern Indians became slaves. The exact numbers are not calculable because there are few extant records of their sale or export to the West Indies in the early colonial period. Native Americanist Alan Gallay estimates that thirty thousand to fifty thousand southern Native Americans were sold in the British slave trade from 1670 to 1715.[107] What we know for sure is that within fifty years of settlement, from 1663 to 1715, 50 percent of the southern indigenous population had disappeared due either to death, exportation, or enslavement.[108] Historian Gary Nash asserts that South Carolina was singular in its "naked exploitation of the indigenous people." Dr. Francis Le Jau, a missionary for the Society for the Propagation of the Gospel (SPG) in South Carolina, observed in 1712, however, that the intention of the English was more problematic than exploitation. Le Jau admitted that "we think to destroy the whole nation, that is kill the Men and make the women and children slaves, this is the way of our Warrs upon the like."[109]

Although Native women were also valued for their agricultural skills by Europeans, the enslavement of predominantly women and children in Carolina was to have the same effect as extermination. Since enslaved Native American women would not have children born within their own ethnic bloodline and raised within their own community, racial and cultural extinction would occur over time.[110] Not only were their descendants not viewed as indigenous people, many of the Native children in the slave system became categorized as Negro, reflecting Anglo ideas about race. A law passed in South Carolina in 1719 required that "all such slaves as are not entirely Indian shall be accounted as negroe."[111]

Former slave Susan Hamilton of South Carolina understood the implications of how Native Americans and Africans became a racially mixed community: "De white race is so brazen. Dey come here an' run de Indians frum dere own lan', but dey couldn't make dem slaves 'cause dey wouldn't stan' for it. . . . [D]en dey gone to Africa an' bring dere black brother an' sister. Dey say 'mong themselves, 'we gwine mix dem up en make ourselves king. Dats de only way we'll git even with de Indians.'"[112] Hamilton seems to suggest that racial mixture was another way that the English sought to conquer Native American peoples, an extension of a policy of cultural and racial extermination. She also appears to have an informed understanding of how Native Americans experienced enslavement as something they wouldn't stand for. Indeed, many Native Americans sent out of South Carolina as slaves were known to be "troublemakers and instigators."[113]

The low percentage of Native American children held in captivity also correlates with the fact that on the frontier, infants and very young children were seen as a nuisance to traders and others involved in the market for slaves procured through wars. Native slave traders also killed indigenous women and children in wars for slaves, although their deaths may not have been intentional, despite their position as "sustainers of life" by Native American societies.[114] Slaves who were children had little value to Europeans and were "generally perceived to be a liability" up until the end of the eighteenth century.[115] Native American slave babies and very young children were even more in jeopardy than were adults as casualties of war and in the commerce of human trafficking.

Indeed, the killing of children was widespread. Rev. John Heckewelder, a missionary for the Moravian Church who interacted extensively with the Lenni Lenape, related that a man he knew took the baby of a captive Indian woman near Detroit and "taking it by the legs dashed its head against a tree, so that the brains flew out all around." Mary Jemison, a white woman held in captivity by the Shawnee and later adopted by the Senecas, relayed in her narrative that a man named Ebenezer Allen, a Tory whose "cruelty was not exceeded by any of his Indian comrades," took an infant "and holding it by its legs, dashed its head against the jamb, and . . . after he had killed the child, he opened the fire and buried it under the coals and embers." Additionally, in Tom Quick's narrative, he "dashed out" the brains of a Native American infant to avenge the death of his father. Quick, an icon of American folklore, "thought it good policy to destroy the serpent while it was in embryo . . . [because] nits make lice!" In the massacre of Gnadenhutten, under the leadership of Col. David Williamson of the Pennsylvania militia, thirty-four Lenape and Mohican Indian children, along with twenty-two women and forty men, were killed by striking a mallet upon their heads. Heckewelder argued that these actions went unaccounted for because "it was no uncommon saying among many of the men of whom juries in the frontier countries were commonly composed, that no man should be put to death for killing an Indian; for it was the same thing as killing a wild beast."[116]

With a similar intent to decimate Native American populations through the subjugation and extermination of their women and children, in 1704 the former governor of South Carolina, Barbadian James Moore, and fifty other men led a coalition of Creeks, Yamasees, and Apalachicolas out to northwestern Florida, where he confiscated mostly Native American women and children to be sold as slaves. He went on to claim in a letter to the lords proprietors that "I did not make slave, or put to death one man, woman or child but were taken in the fight, or in the Fort I took by storm."[117] In his attempt to verify that what he did was legal in the context of a "just war" against the Indians, Moore admitted that he did indeed kill children.[118] Again, there were no consequences.

Killing women and children merely out of convenience also occurred. Along the Gulf Coast, South Carolinian traders organized a force of as many as six hundred, the majority Native American, to attack the Mobilien and Tome Natives in the Mobile region of French Louisiana in 1709. They managed to capture from twenty-six to twenty-eight women and children but eventually lost fourteen captives. The Mobilien and Tome men under siege went after the traders in an attempt to rescue their families. The traders then killed the rest of the women and children in their possession "in order to be more free to protect themselves."[119]

Although the English practiced a certain brand of exterminatory warfare, they were not different from the Spanish in their strategies of conquest in the Americas. The brutal depictions in Louisiana, the Carolinas, and Ohio echo details of the atrocities committed against Native Americans in Hispaniola described in Bartolomé de Las Casas's 1542 *Brevísima relación de la destrucción de las Indias* (*A Short Account of the Destruction of the Indies*). According to Las Casas, the Spaniards "forced their way into native settlements, slaughtering everyone they found there, including small children, old men, pregnant women, and even women who had just given birth. They hacked them to pieces, slicing open their bellies with their swords. . . . They grabbed suckling infants by the feet and, ripping them from their mothers' breast, dashed them headlong against the rocks." In another example, Las Casas writes that although some of the soldiers attempted "to save some of the children," others were not so merciful and "galloped about cutting the legs off all the children as they lay sprawling on the ground."[120]

Accounts of Native American babies suffering from a distinctly violent death are indicative of how vulnerable babies and young children of slave mothers were at a time when violence was unmitigated by law or custom. Native Americans experienced the trauma of the potential loss of their infant children to white violence. If we add the possibility that indigenous infants and very young children were slaughtered out of convenience as well, then the Native Americans' rationale for war against the colonists in the South would have been based on more than just unfair practices and ill usage by over-aggressive traders: it would have been for communal preservation.

The English fed a brutal, market-driven desire for slaves that resulted in the outbreak of the Tuscarora and Yamasee Wars in the 1710s. The barbaric treatment of their women and children, combined with the realization that no tribe was safe from enslavement, forced southern indigenous people to also mount a Pan-Indian effort to rid themselves of the ever-encroaching settlers. It was clear that the English sought to build a commercial empire without any regard for the formal agreements with Native nations that had previously existed.

The first initiative, the Tuscarora War, began in 1711 and ended in 1713 with either the death or the enslavement of the Tuscaroras. The fear of enslavement and greater numbers of German and Swiss settlers to the region at New Bern, North Carolina, brought with it epidemiological stresses and prompted the first altercation, in which 120 English and Swiss colonists lost their lives. For two years, an intense war between Anglos and Indians occurred, with several Indian nations fighting on the side of the British against the Tuscaroras with the expectation that they would profit in guns and plunder and perhaps finally defeat an old enemy.

Like some women in West African communities concerned with protecting themselves from becoming enslaved, even Tuscarora women engaged in combat. Their gender, however, did not protect them from being slaughtered. According to John Barnwell, an Assembly member from Colleton County and leader of the army raised by South Carolina to put down the Tuscaroras, "the enemy were so desperate, the very women shooting Arrows, yet they did not yield until most of them were put to the sword."[121] The casualties and losses were high for the English and the Tuscaroras, yet the demand for slaves in the Americas and the West Indies drove the war to its predetermined conclusion: four hundred Native Americans were killed, and a thousand Tuscaroras and their allies were sold into slavery.[122]

The Native American slave trade was at its peak when the Yamasee organized attacks at Port Royal, Charleston, and other South Carolina frontier settlements in 1715. Six percent of the white population, approximately four hundred settlers, died in the Yamasee conflict, which ended in 1718. A far greater number of members of the Pan-Indian alliance were killed or sold into slavery and shipped to the Caribbean.[123] Le Jau foretold the inevitable when he stated that although "peace will be try'd first with the Cherikees at least," the Indians, he understood, "must be all cut off Strange and Cruel Necessity!"[124] By 1730 the trade in Native American slaves from South Carolina had diminished significantly, and the Pan-Indian alliance had been destroyed. The calculated decision to rid themselves of all people in the colony viewed as Native Americans by law meant that British settlers could now focus on acquiring complete control over their African slaves.

English colonists came to America with a thorough understanding of how to use the tactics of exterminatory warfare after their conquest of the Irish in Europe. This type of warfare was then used to get rid of and then enslave the Native American populations in the Southeast and New England. The authority to do so was sanctified, the English believed, by Holy Scripture and by evolving definitions of race, which sustained already established theories of incompatibility between those who were white and those considered to be savages. Yet, colonists remained fearful of being treated barbarously—just like they had treated Native Americans and how southern Native Americans quickly learned to treat them. Thus, the template for how to deal with "unruly savages" remained fundamental to the colonists' strategies for survival in this supposed "New World." Early European efforts to make their African slaves cower in fear, however, were often not successful. As John Locke foresaw, living on the frontier involved a perpetual "state of war." Indeed, many West African slaves had their own notable history of what Europeans described as exterminatory warfare. They carried that history with them across the ocean via the Atlantic slave trade, causing white fear of yet another enemy who needed subjugation.

CHAPTER TWO

A "State of War Continued"
White Fear, Black Warriors

English philosopher John Locke predicted that West Africans who were compelled by force to become the slaves of Europeans and who understood that the "rights of freedom" pertained to them as much as they did to any other man would always be a threat to European colonists.[1] Indeed, some West Africans came from a culture where warfare prevailed to the extent that women, children, and old people were often the victims of war. The brutality exhibited by British colonists was matched by a ruthlessness that facilitated the African slave trade. And white colonists were well aware of how the people they brought across the Atlantic had become slaves. Thus, European dependence on African labor and the exponential increase in importations heightened white fear of a dangerous enemy whom they perceived had the potential to fight back ferociously—whereby Africans might dismantle the entire system and even possibly become the Europeans' masters.

The institution of African slavery in America emerged as a "state of war continued" between the English colonists and those who became their slaves. African slaves in America were not acquired through direct confrontations between "a lawful Conqueror and a Captive" but rather were purchased from African traders.[2] Subsequently, as third parties to West African warfare, Europeans held an arbitrary power over those enslaved that was never consensual.[3] In South Carolina, for example, the colonists had the power to kill and maim their slaves at any time. But slave masters knew that their dominance was never absolute. Whites, fearing the cataclysmic nature of African slavery, believed that bloodshed might be necessary in self-defense and in the control of a very large and highly militarized servile population.[4]

The reason that English colonists were so fearful of slave insurrections and ultimately black mastery had much to do with the fact that they knew that many West Africans had been warriors in their own countries. What white slave owners understood about their slaves' military past drove European obsessions about the possibility of a war between them and their African slaves.

How African Wars Supplied South Carolina with Slaves

Many of the Africans who became slaves in South Carolina were highly trained in war. A vibrant military culture had developed over the centuries in West Africa to meet the needs of European traders, pitting one African group against another in a struggle to either conquer or be conquered. Indeed, trade with European nations fostered a militarism that was both offensive and defensive. At the height of the slave trade, West African wars resulted in the loser becoming a captive who was sold, sacrificed, or retained within the conquering nation. In this age of warlordism, a period in African history that lasted from approximately 1600 to 1800, Africans were responding to the same lure for profits and power in Africa that drove English colonists in the American South to foment wars for slaves among Native Americans.[5] This warlordism, coupled with the heightened violence of the slave trade itself, produced Africans who were well trained in offensive and defensive warfare and subsequently sold into slavery in the South. Slaves in South Carolina came from the West Coast of Africa (Sierra Leone, the Bight of Biafra, the Congo, Angola, Senegambia, the Bight of Benin, and the Gold Coast regions), which had a distinguished military milieu that planters paid attention to.

Almost one-eighth of the slaves who came to South Carolina from the Windward / Ivory Coast and Sierra Leone / Liberia regions had been obtained through local wars there.[6] Prisoners of war included male soldiers as well as women and children, and because the trade in slaves had become central to the economies of various nations in Africa, they were all considered enemy combatants.[7] A fellow slave in South Carolina recounted his capture in Africa to ex-slave Charles Ball: "We were alarmed one morning, just at break of day, by the horrible uproar caused by mingled shouts of men and blows given with heavy sticks upon large wooden drums. The village was surrounded by enemies, who attacked us with clubs, long wooden spears, and bows and arrows. After fighting for more than an hour, those who were not fortunate enough to run away, were made prisoners. It was not the object of our enemies to kill; they wished to take us alive, and sell us as slaves." Although it is not possible to determine the region in which this event occurred, the people who captured the narrator were those "my protectors were at war with . . . a nation whose religion was different from ours."[8]

The English explorer Joseph Corry recalled a chief named Smart who commanded an extensive area of the Windward Coast (Ivory Coast) region, and "in one of his wars with his opposite neighbors and rivals," he began his attack "during the night to some of their towns, surprising them before they had arisen from sleep." Corry corroborates that the element of surprise became an

African tactic of war and that preying upon innocent people by marauding armies became commonplace.[9] West African people were well aware of the danger that the slave trade created for all nations, and this matrix of violence and enslavement forced some African leaders to develop sophisticated strategies to circumvent the capture of their people. This is evident in Corry's description of "Morrey Samba's town," which he describes as "one of the most regular built towns I have observed in Africa.... The town is surrounded by a mud wall, and . . . there are towers erected for the purposes of defence. The wall, with the towers . . . serve as a guard against any depredations of enemies, while it shelters the inhabitants from the effects of their arrows or musquetry."[10] The engineering of "walled and fortified villages" was an effective military strategy that West Africans used to protect themselves against enslavement, and it is strikingly similar to the one that South Carolinian plantation owner Col. John Barnwell depicts in his journal.[11] Barnwell was a general of the first militia regiment organized to fight against the Tuscarora, and he was highly active in the Native American slave trade in South Carolina. Leading five hundred men to defeat the Tuscaroras in 1712, Barnwell noted: "I imediately viewed the Fort with a prospective glass and found it strong . . . as Workmanship, having a large Earthen Trench . . . with 2 teer of port holes . . . & large limbs of trees lay confused about it to make the approach intricate. . . . [T]he enemy says it was a runaway negro taught them to fortify thus, named Harry, whom Dove Williamson sold into Virginia for roguery & since fled to the Tuscaruros."[12] It is possible that Harry was a soldier from the Sierra Leone region familiar with the ways of war, but even if he was not, he clearly transported West African indigenous practices in a way that was helpful to those Native Americans who were fighting against enslavement. European Carolinians no doubt benefited from these military skills as well.

West Africans from the coastal regions known as the Bight of Biafra and Bight of Benin also brought knowledge of the "arts of war" that English colonists would have been aware of.[13] The testimony of Olaudah Equiano, an Igbo who was born in Benin around 1745, informs us of the predatory nature of wars in this region and how enslavement was the motivation for much of the aggression between states. Yet, Equiano pointed out that a warlord had a lot at stake, because "if he prevails and takes prisoners, he gratifies his avarice by selling them; but if his party be vanquished, and he falls into the hands of the enemy, he is put to death; for, as he has been known to foment their quarrels, it is thought dangerous to let him survive."[14]

As was the custom, Equiano was trained as a youth in the "art of war: my daily exercise was shooting and throwing javelins." Interestingly, Igbo women were given military training as well. Equiano stated, "All are taught to use these weapons; even our women are warriors, and march boldly out to fight along with the men. Our whole district is a kind of militia." The constant drilling with "fire-arms, bows and arrows, broad edged swords, and javelins" was necessary because these communities were living under the constant threat of conflict induced by the slave trade.[15]

Equiano recalled one day witnessing a battle waged against his people, the Igbo, who were suddenly attacked: "There were many women as well as men, on both sides; among others my mother was there, and armed with a broad sword. After fighting for a considerable time with great fury, when many had been killed, our people obtained the victory." Although the purpose was to obtain slaves, many people, both men and women, were killed in the process, and Equiano noted, "Those prisoners which were not sold or redeemed we kept as slaves."[16] Igbo women fighting in wars might seem unusual, but there seems to be evidence that in the eighteenth century, Igbo women were encouraged to "fight along side their husbands in defense of their homeland" due to the diminishing population of able-bodied men.[17]

Yoruba ex-slave Joseph Wright, however, had a more troubling memory of the violence that slavery encouraged when his town of Ake in Nigeria was under siege: "The enemies satisfied themselves with little children, little girls, young men, and young women; and so they did not care about the aged and old people. They killed them without mercy. Father knew not son, and the son knew not the father. Pity had departed from the face of mothers. Abundant heaps of dead bodies were in the streets, and there were none to bury them. Suckling babies were crying at the point of death, and there were none to pick them up."[18] As it was with Native American slaves, certain limitations were placed upon those captives who were either too young or too old. And very few European slave ships carried infants or pregnant women across the Atlantic if they could help it. Thus, as Paul Lovejoy argues, very young children would have been a nuisance to African traders and others involved in procuring slaves through wars.[19]

Evidence of the killing of infants by traders can be found in the narrative of ex-slave Charles Ball. A South Carolinian slave from Africa recounted to Ball that when they were placed on the ships "the men who fastened the irons on these mothers, took the children out of their hands, and threw them over the side of the ship, into the water. When this was done two of the women leaped overboard after the children—the third was already confined by a chain to another and could not get into the water, but in struggling to disengage herself she broke her arm, and died a few days after."[20]

James Arnold, a ship's surgeon on board the African slaver *Ruby*, also affirmed that the barbarous treatment of babies in this region was fueled by the demand for slaves. When the ship banked at the island of Bimbe (located off the coast of present-day Cameroon), "a woman was brought out to us to be sold. As she had a child in her arms, the captain refused to take her and she was taken back to shore; but the next morning she was brought out again, this time without the child which had been killed the night before by the black trader in order to accommodate a sale of the mother."[21] As noted earlier, very young African children apparently had little value in the slave market and were "perceived to be a liability" up until the end of the eighteenth century.[22] Indeed, purveyors of slaves made it plain that they did not want any slaves beyond the age of forty and under the age of ten.[23] Ironically, this business model would have helped facilitate the continuity of African warfare practices, as many of the slaves who arrived in South Carolina and the colonies would have already received or been exposed to military training in their youth.

One of the largest groups of Africans deported to South Carolina with military skills came from Central Africa, from the Congo-Angola region to the island of Madagascar.[24] Using psychological methods of terror and rejecting any kinship loyalty among the general population, Imbangala warriors from the southern part of the Congo facilitated the enslavement of large numbers of Africans from West-Central Africa. Although the Imbangala enlarged their army with captured slaves, only uncircumcised boys, a ritual that identified those who were part of the opposing side's warrior class, received military training.[25] The Imbangala sold the rest as slaves, took whatever women they chose as wives, and killed the rest of the captives. Their rationale for doing so was probably based on the fact that by the eighteenth century lengthy civil wars would have produced a number of slaves who had military training and who were organized and efficient in the use of guns.[26] And as Equiano argued, this was not a population to leave behind, as they might entice others to rebel.[27]

Still, slaves from West-Central Africa and Madagascar were known to be captives who had military experience in their own countries. According to a slave from the Congo region named Adam, "His father, *Scindia Quante*, was a chief or captain under the king, and a great warrior, and had taken many people, whom he sold as slaves."[28] African American abolitionist, writer, and physician Martin R. Delany's paternal grandfather was a "pure Golah [Angolan]" who had been "a chieftain, captured with his family in war, sold to the slavers, and brought to America. He fled at one time from Virginia, where he was enslaved." He was caught and brought back from Canada to the United States, where "the fallen old chief afterwards is said to have lost; his life in an encounter with some slaveholder, who attempted to chastise him into submission."[29] A Maryland petition for freedom in 1796 by the descendant of "negro

Mary" sheds light on the nature of warfare and the politics of slave trading in Madagascar. The court noted that the people "of Madagascar make war upon each other for slaves and plunder; and they carry on the slave trade with Europeans."[30] The story of former slave Aunt Ciller validates this assessment by the court. Aunt Ciller knew that her father was a king "from the Island of Madagascar" who was brought from Virginia to South Carolina after the Revolution in 1783 by Capt. James Sims: "Her Daddy was taken prisoner in battle by another king, and instead of being beheaded, as was their custom, the king sold him and his family to a 'white-slave-trade-ship.'"[31]

In the Senegambia region, the slaves that Carolinian traders prized because of their expertise in rice cultivation were also warriors, as the peasantry who performed agricultural labor also received military training. As "warrior-cultivators," the Bambara in particular had a reputation for being skilled military men who captured huge numbers of captives in reoccurring wars for export from the Goree and Gambia Rivers.[32] Apparently, many Europeans often named all slaves whom they considered soldiers Bambara, which is the ethnic identification given to people from the greater Senegambian region. The true ethnic identity of the Senegambian people who ended up across the Atlantic, however, is Bamana (with their "warrior-cultivator culture" intact), and Bamana were known to have a rebellious nature.[33] Thus, the many Senegambians, Sierra Leonians, and West-Central Africans deported to South Carolina in large numbers heightened the fear among whites about their African slaves. Africans did not shed their experiences from their native countries during the Middle Passage; instead, they retained a warrior/military culture that had been formulated within their own nation.[34]

An account of the military culture of African slaves imported into South Carolina would be incomplete without mentioning the Gold Coast states (present-day Ghana) and the state of Dahomey (present-day Benin). These two regions offer perhaps the clearest examples of the violence and warfare employed in the acquisition of slaves. Although they would rank as a favorite of South Carolina traders, only small numbers of slaves procured from the powerful Gold Coast states of Bono and Denkirya were sold to Europeans prior to the eighteenth century. This was because, according to Samuel Brun, a Swiss surgeon on three Dutch voyages to West Africa, the victors of wars in that region "cut off all their enemies' heads, be they young or old, female or male: indeed they do not spare babies in their mother's wombs, just so that they bring home many heads and be considered mighty warriors." On another occasion, Brun noted that when he and his men supported the king of Sabou (Asebu) and his army, "Our people occupied the paths in time, so that no-one could escape. The three hundred Blacks then pounced quickly on the confident little mob and in two hours obtained three hundred human heads, the majority of which were of women and children; for the Blacks say it is better to strangle women and children than men, because then they will not reproduce quickly; and the children, if they came of age, would seek revenge."[35] The war tactics of Africans on the Gold Coast paralleled the brutal theories behind English warfare: because "nits make lice," women and children had to be killed as a means of eliminating future confrontations.

By the mid-seventeenth century, it was no longer necessary to kill captives of Gold Coast wars because of the surging demand for slaves by European nations. This Atlantic commerce also gave Gold Coast Africans access to guns and thus the military power to wage even more aggressive wars against their neighbors.[36] Casualties of war numbered well over 375,000 people from 1700 to 1750, and that number would double by the end of the century.[37] Gold Coast slaves were highly valued by South Carolinians for their tenacity at work and purported physical superiority to other slaves. Yet, slave owners also viewed them as "ferocious if angered, unmindful of danger, unwilling to forgive, but loyal if their devotion could be captured."[38]

Although few slaves in South Carolina came from Dahomey, every state in West Africa would have been aware of the most powerful slave-raiding nation in the region. Dahomeans were aggressively militaristic and innovative in their intentional inclusion of women as warriors. Through constant warfare, they had achieved great wealth as a people.[39] It was a nation much feared, and fear was part of the military strategy that Dahomeans used; their policy of extermination, King Kpengla explained, "makes my enemies fear me."[40]

Dahomeans used brutal "demonstration[s] of power" to illustrate their greatness in all military endeavors.[41] For example, despite the fact that the king of the Whydah nation (along the coast of the Bight of Benin) had already surrendered, the Dahomean army continued to kill five thousand Whydah soldiers and then held ten to eleven thousand more as captives for sale in the slave trade. Generally, after campaigns they would strip the dead and cut off their heads as trophies of war.[42] Additional evidence of this method of warfare appears in the narrative of Capt. Thomas Phillips, who recounts that he saw "nine or ten bags full of men, women, and childrens heads at a time brought to the king's town, when the soldiers return'd from ravaging."[43] King Adandozan, who would later be deposed in 1818, supposedly wrote a letter to England that was published in the *New York Weekly Magazine* in 1792. In it he challenged Europeans to not sit in judgment of how slaves were procured for the Atlantic market in Dahomey: "God made war for all the world; and every kingdom, large or small, has practiced it. . . . Did Weebaigah [a former king] sell slaves? No; his prisoners were all killed to a man. . . . Was he to let them remain in this country to cut the throats of his subjects? . . . [T]he Dahoman name would have long ago been extinguished, instead of becoming as it is at this day, the terror of surrounding nations."[44] Part of the political strategy that facilitated the control of their expansive empire was that Dahomeans offered protection to anyone within their borders, so that only Africans outside of the Dahomey nation ran the risk of being enslaved. To be sure, Dahomeans were known throughout West Africa for their callous extermination of enemy combatants and their ruthlessness in capturing slaves. They were also known among Europeans as the "Black Spartans" in the eighteenth and nineteenth centuries.[45]

Thus, West African slaves brought with them an understanding of warfare that was based on ideas of conquest, as well as resistance to the internecine conflict between slave-raiding nations. Europeans knew about African warrior traditions generally, and they knew that many of the enslaved retained military skills honed in various parts of West Africa.[46] For South Carolinians, this was a significant problem. It shaped their participation in the African slave trade and informed how they went about supplying the South Carolina market with slaves.

South Carolinian Knowledge of the Transatlantic Trade in African Slaves

South Carolina colonists were very attentive to the slave trade in West Africa. Many of them were not only slave owners but also slave merchants and ship owners involved in the lucrative and global business of slave trading around the world. The volatile nature of the slave market, however, made them concerned about the insurrections that frequently took place off the coast of Africa and across the British colonies. They also feared that the enslaved might threaten the security of South Carolina because of their military experiences in Africa. Hence, the colonists viewed Africans in America as dangerous adversaries who were poised to oppose their condition of bondage and who, given the right opportunity, might successfully win in a fight for their freedom.

Although African slaves were expensive in the seventeenth century, slaves made up one-fourth to one-third of the population in the first decades of English settlement in South Carolina, and three out of four were men. Many of the first British citizens who migrated from Barbados brought their slaves with them. By 1671 half of the settlers in South Carolina were from Barbados. Men like Sir John Yeamans, Thomas Drayton, Robert Daniel, Arthur Middleton, Stephen Fox, Richard Quintyne, Christopher Portman, and John Ladson had all emigrated with slaves from Barbados by 1679. They were given huge tracts of land in Carolina, whereupon these powerful men effectively planted the Barbadian model of colonial development in South Carolina, especially the plantation system.[47] Planters from other British colonies in the West Indies, including Jamaica, Antigua, and Saint Kitts, also settled with slaves, but the largest numbers of settlers were from Barbados.[48] Eventually, South Carolina had the largest number of Africans held by any colony, which was four times greater than the number held in Virginia.[49] The Native American slave trade had almost entirely dissipated by 1730, and the news of high prices and high demand drew large numbers of ships directly to the port of Charleston with Africans for sale.[50]

Colonial Americans involved in the slave trade were also attentive to the provenance of Africans brought to South Carolina.[51] Advertisements submitted by slave traders to the *South-Carolina Gazette* ran compelling bylines: "This day arrived from the Windward Coast of Africa . . . a choice Parcel of young healthy slaves" and "Whidah is esteemed to be the finest Country in Africa and Slaves from thence."[52]

Many slave merchants and plantation owners in South Carolina were from some of the wealthiest families in England. They worked hard at developing and maintaining potentially profitable partnerships in the resale of their human cargo.[53] Many slave merchants operating out of Bristol, London, and Liverpool (the latter the largest of the slave ports in England) had also lived in the Carolina colony for many years and therefore understood the needs of the planters.[54] The governor, Robert Johnson, appointed a council of some of the most respectable men involved in slave trafficking in the colony to assist him in managing the affairs of the region in 1731.[55] Among them were Joseph Wragg, a Londoner and leading slave dealer who owned a company in Charleston; John Guerard, the fourth largest slave trader in South Carolina, who was a partner with the English ship captain and merchant William Jolliffe; and James Crokett, who, although he returned to London in 1739, remained a Carolina merchant and retained a business relationship with slave trader Henry Laurens, who himself had consistent and extensive correspondence with slave-trading companies and ship owners all over the West Indies and in Liverpool, London, and Bristol. Laurens and other South Carolinians formed strategic partnerships with merchants across the Atlantic for the procurement of slaves once direct trade between Africa and South Carolina commenced in 1699.[56]

These men in England and South Carolina paid attention to the frequency of shipboard insurrections and wars in the various regions of Africa out of concern for their own business ventures.[57] From the first year that the Atlantic slave trade began in South Carolina, there were insurrections aboard the ships. Historian Eric Robert Taylor has documented 493 cases that occurred between 1509 and 1865, confirming that slave rebellions were "an ordinary occurrence" that plagued the African slave trade and provoked anxiety among the businessmen invested in it who knew, in their core, that these Africans would resist their captivity.[58]

In a scheme to protect their interests, investors and traders purchased "insurance" against insurrection. That they did so indicates just how tenuous and speculative the business of trading in human cargo was.[59] As Robert Norris, the captain of five slave ships with trading interests in Carolina, stated: "So far are the Whites from being accessary to these wars, as has been unjustly alleged; it is notorious, that the Europeans trading there, deprecate a war. . . . [T]rade is entirely suspended . . . and the term of their voyages is thereby protracted. . . . Hence arises an inevitable increase of expence, and an additional risk of sickness and mortality."[60] Norris might have added the risk of insurrection to his accounting, since European slave ships that remained along the coast of Africa were at great peril of experiencing the resistance of their captives. Because about half of all shipboard insurrections occurred when the vessels were still off the coast of Africa, many ship revolts may have occurred before the slavers were even fully loaded with slaves.[61] Such information increasingly shaped the business of purchasing slaves in the eighteenth century and alerted Europeans to the challenges they faced.

Indeed, South Carolina traders and merchants could ill afford not to be watchful of what transpired along the slave coasts of Africa and in the Caribbean islands, as news of an insurrection or war among nations could significantly affect their bottom line. Consequently, reports of slave uprisings on the islands of Jamaica, Barbados, Bermuda, Antigua, Saint Croix, Saint Kitts, Saint Thomas, and Saint John and aboard ships laden with Africans for sale circulated around the colonies and in the *South-Carolina Gazette*.[62] In 1729 a slave ship bound for South Carolina from the "Coast of Guinea" had "not got 10 Leagues on her Way, before the Negroes rose and making themselves Masters of the Gunpowder and Fire Arms, the Captain and Ships Crew took to their Long Boat, and got shore near Cape Coast Castle. The Negroes run the Ship on Shore within a few Leagues of the said Castle, and made their Escape."[63] According to another report in the *Gazette*, it was believed that the "negro traders" had instigated the uprising aboard a "sloop from Guinea": "A considerable Number of Negroes came off afterwards in Canoes, and endeavored to get on board, but were beat off. . . . About the same time the Slaves on board a Guinea-man belonging to Bristol, rose and destroyed the whole Crew, cutting off the Captains Head, Legs, and Arms."[64] Slaves rose on slave merchant Samuel Wragg's ship, the *Mary*: "[It was] drove ashore, plundered, and destroy'd in the River Gambia, by the Natives. . . . The Slaves rose, in the most barbarous Manner murdered the Ship's Crew, and obliged the said Captain and the Mate, Mr. David Donahew, to confine themselves in the cabin for 27 Days."[65] The slave ships from Bristol, the *Polly* and *Mercury*, were both "lost on the coast of Africa with a Cargo of Slaves." A captain on another slave ship from Bristol was also "attacked . . . and desperately wounded." But the captain, "rather than fall into the Hands of such merciless Wretches, when about 80 Negroes had boarded his Vessel, discharged a Pistol into his Magazine, and blew her up; himself and every Soul on Board perished." Laurens instructed his business partners to "remember to charge your Captain and others to be upon their guard constantly without discovering to the Negroes that they are so."[66]

Uprisings upon slave ships and in the West Indian colonies drew universal consternation, and they also made whites fear for their own safety. Robert Pringle, a prominent Carolina slave trader, wrote to his colleague Francis Guichard in Saint Kitts that he heard "of your being alarm'd for fear of an insurrection of the Negroes but hope their wicked Designs will prove abortive" in the attempted insurrection there in 1739.[67] Commissary Von Reck commented after meeting on board his ship with his "Excellency Robert Johnson Esq; and Mr. Oglethorpe," the former the sitting governor of South Carolina and the latter the founder of the colony of Georgia, that the slaves in Charleston were treated as if "they were a Part of the Brute Creation." According to Von Reck, this fostered an environment where Africans, "being thus used, [lay] amongst them a Foundation of Discontent; and they are generally thought to watch an Opportunity of revolting against their Masters, as they have lately done in the Island of St. John and of St. Thomas. . . . [A]nd it is the Apprehension of these and other Inconveniences, that has induced the Honorable Trustees for Georgia, to prohibit the Importation and Use of Negroes within their Colony."[68]

The *South-Carolina Gazette*'s extensive coverage of Jamaica's troubles signifies the anxiety that slaveholders had concerning the possible replication of these disastrous events of resistance in their own colony.[69] Indeed, the founder of Richmond, William Byrd II, speaking on behalf of many of the colonists in the Americas, argued that Parliament should consider ending the trade of "making merchandize of Our Fellow Creatures. At least the farther Importation of them in Our Colonys should be prohibited lest they prove as troublesome and dangerous everywhere, as they have been lately in Jamaica, where besides a vast expence of Mony, they have cost the lives of many of his Majesty's Subjects. We have mountains in Virginia too, to which they may retire as safely, and do as much mischief as they do in Jamaica."[70]

Although other South Carolina slave owners believed that "this Province cannot be well . . . managed and brought into use, without the labor and services of negroes and other slaves," what emerged in the beginning of the eigh-teenth century was a racial paranoia about the numbers of oppressed people in their midst and the possibility of Negro mastery.[71] White South Carolinians were presciently aware of the danger that African slaves represented to their community. The governor of South Carolina, John Gibbes, who had lived in the region for forty-eight years, told the Assembly in 1711 that because of the "large increase" in African slaves, he had observed that they were "beginning to exhibit a malicious disposition." He then urged members of the Assembly to consider increasing the white population of the colony for their own de-fense.[72] Yet, despite the fact that English settlers were becoming fearful of their growing slave population, they continued to view their dependency on Africans as a necessity.[73]

These fears had not always existed, however. Initially, blacks played a fun-damental role in the defense of the colony against any opposition to English settlement. In the early years, African, mulatto, and Indian slaves were re-quired to serve in the militia "toward the defence and preservation of this Province, in case of actual invasion," as colonists viewed "a great number of them" to be "trusty slaves."[74] Blacks served willingly in all capacities, as sol-diers against the powerful Creeks, Cherokees, Chickasaws, and Choctaws and in other conflicts with European nations such as Spain and, after 1699, France, and as drummers, messengers, and translators. Whites did not at-tempt to restrict the military service of slaves until 1712, around the time that South Carolina gained a black majority and after a notable rise in slave con-spiracies in South Carolina and other colonies.[75]

Africans may have agreed to fight against southern Native Americans be-cause they knew that indigenous people were paid by the English colonists to capture runaway slaves who attempted to reach Spanish territory.[76] At some point, however, the African and Indian communities must have ascer-tained that the European strategies of divide and conquer merely worked to strengthen European dominance in the region. The Goose Creek minister, Richard Ludlam, unequivocally stated it was the policy in South Carolina "for our present security to make the Indians and negroes a check upon each other lest by their vastly superior numbers we should be crushed by one or the other."[77] Still, Native Americans and Africans were not entirely at odds with each other even in the early colonial era in South Carolina.

For example, there is no doubt that black militiamen were instrumental on the side of the Europeans in both the Tuscarora and Yamassee Wars, but there were also significant collaborations among Africans and Native Americans who worked against South Carolina colonists in this period as informants and as soldiers.[78] Africans used their condition of enslavement and their employment in the Indian trade, where they learned Native American languages and customs, to create possibilities for their own liberation. A white Indian trader named Richard Smith was told that three runaway blacks had plotted with the Keowee people in 1751, telling them that "the white People was coming up to destroy them all." After the plot was discovered, some other slaves came to an elderly Keowee warrior and "told him that there was in all Plantations many Negroes more than white People, and that for the Sake of liberty they would join them" if they decided to go to war with the English.[79] African slaves clearly understood European tactics of war and the power of their numerical supremacy in the region.

Colonists were afraid, according to Lieutenant Governor William Bull, that "their negroes may . . . become their enemies, if not their masters," and that they would be "unable to withstand or prevent" slaves from taking over the region after a successful insurrection.[80] Sir Alexander Cuming chronicled that whites in South Carolina were constantly "in danger of the Blacks Rising up against them." And no doubt out of frustration that earlier policies put in place had been ineffective in keeping their African population from rising against them, council members of the South Carolina Assembly declared in 1739 that those enslaved were indeed an "intestine Enemy, the most dreadful of Enemies."[81]

The increased demand for African labor over the years only amplified the conditions that heightened white fear. The perceived restlessness of the slaves and the importations of ever larger numbers of Africans created the possibility in 1760 of fifty-seven thousand "intestine black enemies" insurrecting a real threat. The council reportedly only had six thousand white men ready for warfare.[82] Although whites exaggerated the disparity in numbers, they accurately captured the fear of insurrection. And matters only got worse in the decades that followed. In 1769, according to Lieutenant Governor Bull, there were eighty thousand Africans and forty-five thousand whites living in South Carolina because the number of slaves purchased had nearly doubled.[83] Between the years 1733 and 1785, 67,769 Africans were imported into South Carolina as slaves, the majority of them from Angola, the Congo, the Gold Coast, and Gambia.[84] And in anticipation of the end of the slave trade in 1808, traders purchased forty thousand more Africans in Charleston from 1804 to 1807.[85] Ironically, the merchants in Bristol, England, who were deeply invested as buyers and sellers in the trade acknowledged that South Carolinian fears of those enslaved needed redress and that because "South Carolina is overstock'd with blacks, in proportion to the number of white people . . . it must be allow'd that three independent companies . . . be serviceable to awe and terrify the slaves." They also, however, criticized South Carolinians for not "making proper laws and regulations to restrain the rich planters from keeping dangerous numbers of negroes," rather than expecting "the mother country" to pay for "a standing force to keep them in obedience."[86]

What white colonists feared most was their total annihilation in internecine warfare. If those enslaved had "an opportunity of knowing their own strength and superiority in point of number," stated missionary John Wikhead, the colonists felt certain that Africans would insurrect in order "to recover their liberty tho' it were the slaughter and destruction of the whole colony."[87] Another South Carolinian had similar concerns in 1720 that "ye whole province was lately in danger of being massacred by their own slaves."[88] Moreover, colonist John Brickell stated that because Africans were "a People of very harsh and stubborn Disposition . . . if the severest Laws were not strictly put in [place] against these People, they would overcome the Christians" and destroy "many Families."[89] According to an official British account of the colony in 1775, "massacres and insurrections were words in the mouth of every child."[90]

Nor were the colonists who envisioned their African slaves as dangerous adversaries complacent or dismissive about their familiarity with the ways of warfare. As the wealthy plantation owner William Byrd II in Virginia expressed, he was "sensible of many bad consequences of multiplying these Ethiopians amongst us." For those enslaved, as "descendants of Ham, [who were] fit to bear Arms . . . might with more advantage kindle a Servile War . . . and tinge our Rivers as wide as they are with blood."[91] The colonists in South Carolina, like Byrd in Virginia, also believed that Africans were accustomed to waging war, as the "Negroes that most commonly rebel, are those brought from Guinea, who have been inured to War and Hardship all their lives."[92] And although African warrior culture was not viewed ominously by this slaveholder, its continuity is also evident in the example of Gen. William Moulton, who was greeted in 1782 by shouts of joy upon his return to his plantation in Charleston by "the old Africans joined in a war-song in their own language."[93] Moreover, many of the advertisements for runaway slaves in the *South-Carolina Gazette* pictured them with a lance in hand after 1750, but by the 1760s, South Carolina colonists depicted Africans with the more potent weaponry of cutlasses and spears and as warriors in their notices of slaves for sale from across the Atlantic World.[94] English colonists in South Carolina had an acute understanding that the environment of master and slave, of domination and subjugation, was laden with the potential of danger and violence. Colonists understood that the methods of African warfare that facilitated the abundance of slaves for purchase in America did not fade away upon arrival to a new land.

European Understanding of African Methods of War

Indeed, Europeans had a long and studied history of being concerned about the military heritage of those enslaved. In the early eighteenth century, the English Parliament sought to determine whether African slaves were lawful captives or whether Europeans were responsible for instigating military confrontations for slaves. Ultimately, the debates about whether slaves were gotten from just wars or predatory wars only furthered a universal awareness of African military prowess in colonial America. Moreover, these discussions provide evidence that whites had a healthy fear of and respect for African soldiers.

According to abolitionist Thomas Clarkson, in the early years only those individuals directly involved in the market knew much about the African slave trade.[95] An outline for an investigation into the state of the slave trade by the Royal African Company (RAC), however, was reported out of committee on February 23, 1720. It proposed that Africans brought before their agents for sale should be asked questions, and the agents were to "make as strict an Enquiry as possible to find out what Sort of Country they came from. . . . What form of Government [did] they have? and in what manner Justice is exercised?" The RAC wanted agents to find out if Africans were "guided by written Laws, or Customs, or Absolutely by the Will of their Prince?" The most important information that the committee sought was, "How many fighting Men their Armys generally Speaking Consist of? Their manner of making slaves? Whether they become so by any other misfortune than that of being taken Prisoners in War time? And whether they have any other method of Trading for them than this of bringing them down to the Coast of Africa to Sell to the Europeans?" The RAC committee wanted "these Examinations to be very Carefully made and Sent over constantly with their Journals, for the Perusal and Information of the Royal African Compa."[96]

The fundamental purpose of recording this information was to ensure the continuity of the slave trade, yet these reports, held up as evidence that European culture was far different from the savagery exhibited by Africans, popularized ideas about African warfare. The proslavery proposition that evolved was that African captives sold into slavery would have otherwise lost their lives in warfare. The English also argued that slavery operated as a safety valve for the barbarianism practiced by African people, overlooking the horrific suppression by the English of the Irish in Europe and of Native Americans.

Although many of the reports claimed that Africans were brutal savages in warfare, which justified in British minds why slaves taken from that region were lawful captives, what is most apparent in many of the accounts is the British respect for the military capacity of the West African nations, their warrior chiefs, and their armies.[97] For example, Capt. William Snelgrave recounts of his travels in 1727 and 1734 that the Dahomey military "made, according to their barbarous Custom, a terrible Carnage of the People." It is worth noting that despite his harsh description, Snelgrave respected the king of Dahomey. He described him before this battle as "being a restless ambitious Prince." At other times, he called him a "great Man." Snelgrave also wrote admiringly about the king's soldiers, who were "marching in a much more regular Order than I had ever seen before, even amongst the *Gold Coast Negroes*; who were always esteemed amongst the *Europeans* that used the Coast of Guinea, the best Soldiers of all the Blacks."[98] Not only were Dahomean soldiers impressive, but apparently they surpassed the pristine reputation of the military men along the Gold Coast.

The warrior abilities of Africans from the Gold Coast region were even recognized by the eighteenth-century proslavery historian Bryan Edwards, who had the highest regard for the "Koromantyns," who were "heroic and martial." For Edwards, "the circumstances which distinguish the Koromantyn, or Gold coast, Negroes, from all others, are firmness both of body and mind; a ferociousness of disposition; but withal, activity, courage, and a stubbornness, or what an ancient Roman would have deemed an elevation, of soul, which prompts them to enterprises of difficulty and danger; and enables them to meet death, in the most horrible shape, with fortitude or indifference." He goes on to say, "Even the children brought from the Gold Coast manifest an evident superiority" in their aptitude for becoming warriors.[99]

Europeans also commented positively on West African military practices from other regions. John Hippisley, another English author on the slave trade in Senegambia and Angola, noted that in Africa by 1764, "the wars are infinitely less bloody than ours. Scarce any of the prisoners taken in battle are put to death, but are almost all sold, and brought to some part of the coast." From Hippisley's perspective (as an advocate of the slave trade), almost all the slaves that came from the Senegambia and Angola regions were prisoners taken in war, and many of them were soldiers.[100]

Mungo Park, the famous explorer, disagreed with Hippisley that African wars were less bloody, although he used the example of the Bamana in the Senegambia region to discuss all of Africa. He corroborated, however, that "every free man is accustomed to arms and fond of military achievements, where the youth, who has practiced the bow and spear from his infancy, longs for nothing so much as an opportunity to display his valour." Park also observed that there were two kinds of wars. The one in which war is previously declared, where the aggressor will "call out" his opponent, reminded him of the European method. The end result, however, was that victors gain captives of war, whom they carry off, although "the weakest know their own situation, and seek safety in flight." Noting the other "exterminating system" in the African trade, Park assessed that "such of the prisoners as through age or infirmity, are unable to endure fatigue, or are found unfit for sale, are considered as useless, and I have no doubt are frequently put to death."[101] Although Park uses the term "extermination" to describe the killing of women, children, and the elderly who were not fit for sale, these acts were not based upon tactics of war but rather in response to the European slave trade.

Many European Americans would have read about a courageous group of West African warriors who, with total unanimity, rejected their condition of enslavement as an outcome of war. An article printed in the *New York Magazine* in April 1796 recounts an attempted insurrection on Goree Island, during which "five hundred captives abhorring slavery more than any of their neighbors, after making themselves acquainted with the situation of the island and the fort, laid a plan for revolting." When asked the next morning by the commandant of the island if what he had heard was correct, "the two chiefs, without showing any signs of fear or terror, and without offering any excuse for their conduct replied boldly, that they intended to have put to death all the white men on the island, not through any hatred that they bore to them, but that no obstacles might oppose their flight, and prevent them from joining their young king, adding that they were all ashamed not to have died for him in the field of battle, with their arms in their hands; and that since their design had miscarried, they preferred death to slavery," after which the rest of the slaves cried out, "It is true, it is true."[102]

The published accounts of the lives of West African nationals, read by members of the RAC, the "Ten Percenters," the Privy Council, members of Parliament, plantation owners, and even those who had no interest in Africans as commodities, provided fodder for a growing anti–slave trade movement in England as early as 1735.[103] And religious groups and individuals living in America also condemned the rise in African warfare and the buying and selling of African slaves.[104] Over time, the Enlightenment philosophy of natural rights and the Great Awakening in America, which began in the 1730s, made necessary a clear rationale for why Britain should continue to participate in the African slave trade.[105]

Anthony Benezet, a Huguenot and notable American abolitionist living in Philadelphia, argued that Europeans had instigated the wars among African tribes, much as they had among Native Americans. Thus, Africans, through "hard usage" and because of burgeoning slave populations, "will always be a just cause of Terror: In *Jamaica*, and *South Carolina*." The exploitive and brutal nature of slavery created the warlike environment that whites took advantage of in order to justify their commerce in humans as lawful captives taken in a just war. It did not save their lives, as some argued.[106]

American religious leaders were at the forefront in broadcasting the way in which African slaves were both participants in and products of warfare. Evangelist George Whitefield wrote an open letter in 1739 to all white citizens of Maryland, Virginia, and the Carolinas, asking them if "it be lawful for Christians to buy slaves, and thereby encourage the nations from whence they are brought to be at perpetual war with each other."[107] The Quaker communities in Pennsylvania and New Jersey issued their position on the slave trade in 1754, asking, "How then can we, who have been concerned to publish the Gospel of universal love and peace among mankind, be so inconsistent with ourselves, as to purchase such as are prisoners of war, and thereby encourage, this anti-Christian practice; and more especially as many of these poor creatures are stolen away. . . . What dreadful scenes of murder and cruelty those barbarous ravages must occasion in these unhappy people's country are too obvious to mention." Eventually, those Quakers residing in Virginia, North and South Carolina, Maryland, and New York petitioned their own legislatures on this subject.[108] Alexander Hewatt, pastor of the Scotch Presbyterian Church in Charleston, argued that although "in war the conquerors were supposed to have a right to the life of their captives, insomuch that they might kill, torture or enslave them, as they thought proper," he challenged the European community's willingness "to vindicate the conqueror's right to murder or enslave a disarmed army."[109] By the end of the 1780s, public pressure forced King George III to command that the Privy Council establish another special committee "to take into their consideration the present state of the African Trade, particularly as far as [it] related to the practice and manner of purchasing or obtaining slaves on the coast of Africa." During the thirteen months in which the committee met, they printed and distributed 26,526 reports, written accounts of the parliamentary debates, and over 51,432 pamphlets or books on the issue of the African slave trade.[110]

Reports that supported the position that the slave trade positively served humanity, that espoused the "double argument of the humanity and holiness of the trade," or that claimed that the extermination of war captives was common were touted by "all the higher circles." Indeed, these were the reports that "the planters and merchants did not fail to avail themselves. They boasted that they would soon do away [with] all the idle tales which had been invented against them."[111] The Liverpool merchants and others invested in the continuation of the slave trade specifically used Dahomeans and their exterminatory method of warfare as evidence that the trade was actually a blessing. Dahomeans became the poster nation for why the slave trade ultimately served a positive good.[112] The ruthlessness and barbarity of African warfare were used extensively as a proslavery argument, even after the slave trade became illegal in 1808.

Although slave traders who testified acknowledged that these practices were not common among all African nations, they continued to trade with anyone who had slaves for sale. This market-driven approach was supported by the fact that African leaders made conscious decisions about how to retain their involvement in the global market for slaves. Writing about "the Cries of the poor Women and Children" who were beheaded as part of the ritual sacrificing of their enemies, William Snelgrave stated that he asked a Dahomean military man "why so many old Men were sacrificed in particular? He [the African colonel] answered, 'It was best to put them to death; for being grown wise by their Age and long Experience, if they were preserved, they would be ever plotting against their Masters, and so disturb the country; for they never would be easy under Slavery, having been the chief Men in their own Land. Moreover, if they should be spared, no *European* would buy them, on account of their Age.'"[113] The model of interdependent trade that evolved from the seventeenth through the nineteenth century between Europe and Africa was driven and facilitated by Europeans, but it was sustained by mutual consent.[114]

The European markets for slaves facilitated the exponential increase in the business of enslavement in Africa, but slaves taken in wars who had a wealth of life experience behind them would continue to be part of the military outcomes between African nations despite legislation ending the trade in England and America.[115] Additionally, an important aspect of African culture that Europeans talked about extensively was the volatility of military life and, despite their fears, their respect for African military abilities. They knew that Africans rejected enslavement and that, given the opportunity, they would fight to free themselves. As Rev. Hewatt told his fellow South Carolinians, "All men must confess, that those Africans, whom the powers of Europe have conspired to enslave, are by nature equally free and independent, equally susceptible of pain and pleasure, equally averse from bondage and misery, as Europeans themselves."[116]

Controlling African Labor

Thus, slavery was always a "state of war continued," because the supremacy of white power, at least in the colonists' minds, always remained insecure.[117] The consequential violence directed toward Africans in America was not driven by the desire for land and conquest but by the need for labor, which the Atlantic slave trade facilitated. Africans brought to South Carolina as slaves were essential to the development of the region, but they were always perceived to be dangerous resources of labor that would topple the colonial enterprise if they were not carefully controlled. Yet slave owners and the English colonial economy remained deeply invested in African slave labor. And, having already experimented with Native American slavery, South Carolinians believed that only extreme violence and judicially sanctioned performances of torture could keep their slaves at bay, making fear and the possibility of death a central feature of white mastery.

Despite the service that African slaves played in helping secure the colony, eventually colonists were fearful of "negroes and other slaves brought unto the people of this Province," because now, whites claimed, they were of "barbarous, wild, [and] savage natures." Unlike earlier times, these conditions of which Africans were "naturally prone and inclined" made it necessary for the people of South Carolina to enact legislation to "restrain the disorders, rapines and inhumanity" of those enslaved in order to secure the "safety and security of the people of this Province and their estates."[118]

The problem that the early settlers faced was that many African laborers simply ran away into the frontier, jeopardizing the stability of the region and making the deployment of heinous measures for colonial control appear necessary. When in 1712 the laws changed and slaves became chattel, or slaves for life, as did their children, the problem of Africans running away not only continued but also became more pervasive.

The laws enacted to address the problem of flight indicate the level of violence that the early colonists were willing to use upon those who they believed disrupted the system of chattel slavery. For the first offense, the penalty was a severe public whipping. But after the fourth offense, the slave, if he was male, was castrated, and if the slave was female, she was severely whipped and then branded on her left cheek with the letter R, and her left ear was cut off. For the fifth offense, the slave was either put to death or had one of his Achilles tendons severed. Not only would the runaway suffer, but also any "Negro" or slave who was found to have aided or encouraged the slave to run away would "suffer the pains of death" upon conviction.[119]

Some religious leaders in England (and only Le Jau in South Carolina) publicly rejected the South Carolinian law, in place for over twenty-five years, that required the castration of slaves as punishment for running away. They cited it as "an Abomination," especially if done outside the law or in the spirit of revenge, or "if he aimeth by it at his Slaves death." The Baptist Association in South Molton, in Devon, England, however, later reversed its position to conclude: "We apprehend, the Master, Acting according to the Law of your Province, in gelding his Slave, hath not committed any Crime, to give any

Offence to Any Member to break Communion with him in the Church; because we finde by Scripture, that 'tis lawfull to buy them. . . . And if lawfull to buy them 'tis lawful to keep them in order, and under government; and for Self preservation, punish them to prevent farther Mischief that may Ensue by their running away and [?] rebelling against their Masters."[120] The use of the word *gelding*, which is the term used for the castration of horses or mules in order to make them physiologically nonaggressive and docile, is important for what it signifies. The attitude of the master that slaves could be manipulated and controlled like animals is well documented. But the castration of runaway slaves in the colonial era seems to be suggestive of early experiments in social engineering.[121] It is also indicative of the difficulty slave owners had in getting Africans to submit to their will. In reality, Anglo-Americans could only fantasize that they could make the enslaved perform like animals, dependent docile slave creatures living only to serve their masters. Despite the brutal way whites sought to control the runaway slave population in South Carolina, Africans continued to resist enslavement.

By the 1720s African slaves comprised 65 percent of the total population of South Carolina, and in an effort to alleviate already existing tensions, regulations over slave mobility were established. The colonists believed that racialized laws that affirmed white mastery would curtail "any disorders Insurrections or Tumultuous Designs formed and carried on by any Negroes or other slaves."[122] White male patrols were responsible for keeping the province safe from slave rebellion, and legislation regulating what that entailed became more extensive. Slave owners wanted to know at all times where their slaves were and what they were doing. For example, in 1722 slaves were no longer allowed to be involved in "keeping and breeding horses, whereby they convey intelligences from one part of the country [and] carry on their secret plots and contrivances for insurrections and rebellions."[123]

Nevertheless, despite regulations, slaves continued to move about the province, threatening the security of the white community and the institution of African bondage. According to one colonist, who chose to remain anonymous: "The *stranger* had once an opportunity of seeing a Country-Dance, Rout, or Cabal of *Negroes*, within 5 miles distance of this town, on a Saturday night." Upon this occasion the enslaved formed "private committees," where they talked "in too low a voice, and with so much caution, as to not be overheard by the others." The European interloper observed, "Members of this *secret council*, had much the appearance of Doctors, in deep and solemn consultation upon life or *death*; which indeed might have been the scope of their meditations at that time." Moreover, slaves who were outlaws as fugitives and other slaves came freely to this event well equipped to make their escape if necessary: "Not less than 12 fugitive slaves joined this respectable company . . . 8 of whom were mounted on good horses. . . . The *Stranger* is informed, that such assemblies *have been* very common, and that the company has sometimes amounted to 200 persons." The cautious secrecy of these discussions should make it clear to everyone, the letter writer argued, that "whenever or wherever such nocturnal rendezvouses are made, may it not be concluded, that their deliberations are never intended for the advantage of the white people?"[124] Chastising the region's leaders in 1772 for not enforcing the slave laws of 1740, the "Stranger" feared that blacks plotted insurrections and the death of their white masters at these "meetings." Yet what this anonymous report also signifies is how the enslaved continued to contest their condition of bondage and to exert considerable control over their own lives, despite white efforts to curtail black freedom.

South Carolinians also implemented new regulations against gun usage by slaves in order to gain greater racial control over an ever-increasing number of Africans, over 90 percent of whom came directly from West Africa.[125] The termination of the slaves' usage of firearms, a change from earlier colonial times, is indicative of how serious the colonists were about the threat of their slave population rising in rebellion. Since the enslaved were now forbidden to carry or use firearms, patrols were instructed to "search for guns, pistols, swords, cutlaces [*sic*], lances, and other offensive weapons in negro houses." And the legislation required that "every master or head of any family" also "keep all his guns and other arms . . . locked up" or else face serious penalties.[126] Despite these laws, however, in his 1787 message South Carolina governor William Moultrie complained to the legislature that there were armed slaves "too numerous to be quelled by patrols" who were causing much trouble for the colonists in the region of Saint Peter's Parish.[127]

The prohibition against Africans playing drums in 1740 provides further evidence of whites' fears that their slave population could rise in violent confrontation. Now black people could no longer be found "using or keeping of drums, horns or other loud instruments, which may call together or give sign or notice to one another of their wicked designs and purposes."[128] Drums had long been associated with African rebellion in the European mind. The first laws established against drum usage occurred in Barbados. Sir Hans Sloane noted in 1689 that the slaves "formerly on their Festivals were allowed the use of trumpets . . . and Drums. . . . But making use of these in their Wars at home in Africa, it was thought too much inciting them to Rebellion, and so they were prohibited."[129] South Carolina waited a full forty years before enacting laws against drums based on their potential use for wars of insurrection. Yet in 1775, when colonists were fearful of British-inspired slave insurrections during the Revolutionary War, Charleston was reportedly filled with "the daily and nightly sounds of Drums and Fifes." Again, it appears that the legislation enacted did not exert complete control over the slave population in South Carolina, nor did it quell white fears.[130]

Indeed, the challenges of controlling an ever-growing African population in South Carolina were well known, and for many it required that slaves be abused nearly to death. Colonist John Brickell's observations support this in his claims to have "frequently seen them [slaves] whipt to that degree, that large pieces of their skin have been hanging down their backs." Yet despite the brutality, Brickell stated he had "never observed one of them shed a Tear, which plainly shews them to be a People of very harsh and stubborn Dispositions."[131] According to Benjamin Martyn, a Georgian who used South Carolina to demonstrate the problems of slavery, the first thing that white settlers had to do on the frontier where the population of Africans grossly outnumbered whites was to "secure herself [South Carolina] against them." Martyn believed that all slaves were "secret enemies . . . ready to join with her open ones upon the first occasion."[132] Johann Martin Bolzius, a German settler living in the Carolina region, argued that the ratio of whites to black slaves was a "dangerous disorder" that could lead to rebellion. Any Africans who fomented rebellion, however, would find themselves "punished in a very harsh and nearly inhuman way (which is not the way of the English), for example, slowly roasted at the fire." We know, however, that this was indeed the English way during the Pequot War, and similar brutal retaliation occurred during the aftermath of the 1712 and 1741 New York insurrection attempts.[133] Bolzius, like the colonists in South Carolina, believed that harshness was necessary, for if Africans "gain the upper hand in a rebellion they give no mercy, but treat the whites very cruelly." After all, he acknowledged, "eternal slavery to them as to all people is an unbearable yoke, and very harsh treatment as regards food and work exasperates them greatly. New Negroes therefore must be treated very carefully, for they frequently take their own lives out of desperation, with the hope of resurrection in their homeland, and of rejoining their people."[134] Both men were aware of the underlying problem. Martyn also noted that the antagonistic relationship between the black and white population was sustained by the fact that Africans were "fond of liberty just like white men, and he will struggle for it, when he knows his own strength, when he sees this is equal, at least very little inferior to his master's."[135]

The conundrum that faced those who needed labor to sustain their plantation economy and who needed to control a burgeoning population of nonwhite people was a serious one. African slaves were valuable because they brought with them skills in agriculture, animal husbandry, working with metal and wood, and masonry; as interpreters or "linksters" on the frontier; and in military service. Free and enslaved Africans who had skills were welcomed in those early years because "workers who were merely submissive and obedient would have been a useless luxury," which these new colonists could ill afford when so many of them had limited or no skills in agriculture or animal husbandry.[136] Nor were the colonists wrong in their perceptions that the slaves were restless, as the intensity of the plantation system led to an increase in slavery's brutality, which ultimately led to greater animosity and black rebellion.[137]

Informed about their slaves' artfulness at war, white South Carolinians grappled with what Africans made clear, that they would if they could fight for their freedom. The question was always whether colonists or Africans would win. Perceptions of this possibility changed over time depending on what was happening not only on the ground in South Carolina but also across the diaspora. The colonists' general lack of military training was very different from the experiences of many of their African slaves, and eventually the knowledge of this generated threats of unrestrained violence upon Africans in the New World.[138]

In truth, unlike with Native Americans, the colonists believed that they could not completely rid themselves of their African slaves, because they needed them. In a later debate over the importation of Africans in 1785, Charles Pinckney, a general in the American Revolution and a member of the Continental Congress, asked, "Was it not well understood, that no planter could cultivate his land without slaves?" Moreover, Pinckney argued, "this country was not capable of being cultivated by white men; as appeared on the attempt made by Georgia," and that "Negroes were to this country what raw materials were to another country."[139]

Ralph Izard, however, also a planter and the first senator from South Carolina, was not convinced that slaves would always remain invaluable. Izard imagined in a 1794 letter to Mathius Hutchinson what would happen if "the same horrid Trajedies among our Negroes, which have been so fatally exhibited in the French Islands" during the Haitian Revolution, were to occur in America. Izard predicted that the "proprietors of Negroes should themselves be the instruments of destroying that species of property" rather than see their slave population freed in South Carolina or in any other American colony.[140] Slave owners nevertheless made a calculated choice to perpetuate the institution of African bondage not only in South Carolina but also across the Atlantic World, and they used violence and the threat of death to sustain it.

Thus, whites' fears of African slaves' capacity to overwhelm them in any confrontation were not fantasies. Europeans understood what enslavement represented to Africans—that, as losers, they had been taken and removed from their own countries in the aftermath of warfare. This knowledge also heightened the colonists' fears that just as Africans were able to subjugate other Africans to their will, so might they be able to turn the tables on their white masters. Yet Europeans were poised to defend themselves and their insatiable demand for slaves in the New World. Although the lure of extraordinary profits generally protected the African slave population in South Carolina, exterminatory warfare was never completely off the table if those who were enslaved attempted to free themselves by force. White Americans knew that they had placed an enemy in their midst, an enemy procured to satisfy the ever-rising demand for African slaves, who continued to resist chattel slavery—who, after crossing the Atlantic Ocean, intended to effect total and unlimited warfare against a previously unknown adversary, white slaveholders.

CHAPTER THREE

"The Past Is Never Dead"

The Continuity of African and European Warfare Practices

Traditions of exterminatory warfare employed by the peoples of Europe and West Africa in their own countries reemerged around the African diaspora over the issue of black freedom and the institution of enslavement. Despite British efforts to control them, Africans who survived the Middle Passage were aggressive in their resistance to enslavement in the West Indies and American colonies and throughout the Revolutionary and post-Revolutionary era. Whites' fears of their destruction in a servile war shaped plantation owners' theories that only the severest and most traumatizing reprisals would keep the slaves from getting the upper hand and dismantling the entire system. Yet despite brutal retaliation, blacks continued to rebel, making white mastery over the enslaved seem elusive. European settlers knew that for Africans, as well as for themselves, "the past is never dead. It's not even past."[1]

Africans in the diaspora used their military backgrounds to foment insurrections and revolts across the Atlantic World.[2] They attempted to kill whites to free themselves and their families from enslavement, while whites enacted internecine violence against blacks to maintain or reinstate enslavement. The details of how bloody and terrible this violence became reveal that the enslaved were highly intelligent strategists who constantly challenged their condition of servitude for generations. As historian Vincent Harding articulated and scholar Manisha Sinha rightly confirms, these early freedom fighters were the first to call for and organize around the abolition of slavery. Indeed, black men and women were the originators of the nineteenth-century abolitionist movement.[3] From the slaveholders' perspective, enslaved Africans were endowed with considerable power to overwhelm them. Visions of black extermination evolved to become the option of last resort if a slave uprising was successful or if those enslaved refused to accept their condition of servitude. Denmark Vesey's attempted insurrection in 1822 demonstrates that African and European ideas of being at war with one another were ubiquitous. But what really concerned white slaveholders, what they really feared, was black freedom. The manifestation of those fears of a black revolution eventually occurred in Saint-Domingue and resonated throughout the African diaspora into the nineteenth century.

The Dangers of Black Resistance and White Reprisals

Closely read reports about slave insurrections occurring all over the West Indies and North America served as sober reminders to slave owners that many Africans remained well trained in the arts of war. This fueled an intense fear among whites of their enslaved black population that was as much a part of the legacy of America as slavery was. Europeans developed a "circular fallacy" that somehow it was inherently part of the Africans' nature, that it was the enslaved Africans' fault that whites feared their slaves, not the unnatural condition of servitude.[4] From slave trader Robert Norris's perspective, slaves brought their misery on themselves and because of this "are subject to correction, as a punishment for [their] own vices, and for the instruction of others."[5] The notion of correction, however, oversimplifies the conditions in which slavery existed. It was to the colonists a serious contest of wills, played out repeatedly across the Atlantic World with deadly and unpredictable consequences.

African tactics of warfare, very visible during the insurrections of those enslaved in the English colonies, generated the severity of white reprisals. Barbados, South Carolina's early trading partner, offers an excellent example of how Afro-Barbadians continuously rebelled for over a century despite the fact that they were tortured, worked to death, starved, whipped, and occasionally killed by whites who threw them into boiling vats of sugar. A combined effort in 1649 of white servants and slaves who were "so haughty in their resolutions, and so incorrigible" in their intention to "revenge themselves" or else die trying, led to the execution of eighteen of their leaders. Alleged to be a well-thought-out plan, their intention was to seize "their Masters, and cut all their throats, and by that means, to make themselves not only freemen, but Masters of the Iland."[6] The slave rebellion of 1675 had similar intentions, but according to Governor John Adkins, slaves from all over the island were organized with "a damnable design . . . to destroy them [whites] all." Governor Adkins admitted that he found the rebellion "far more dangerous than was at first thought, for it had spread over most of the plantations, especially amongst the Cormantin negroes, who are much the greater number from any one country, and are a warlike and robust people."[7] Accounts were published and distributed in all the English colonies, as many of the first settlers in South Carolina were from Barbados. There was also great comfort found in the reports that the "numbers of those that were burned alive, beheaded, and other wise executed for their horrid crime" eliminated further threats.[8] Of the seventeen who were found guilty, six were burned alive, and eleven were beheaded; the headless bodies were "dragged through the streets" and then "publicly burned." Twenty-five more slaves were executed, five committed suicide, and seventy were either deported or returned to their masters "after a savage flogging."[9] Still another insurrection plot uncovered in Barbados in 1692 in which the "slaves entered into a well concerted plan for exterminating the white inhabitants" led the South Carolina House of Assembly to propose a bill that year that "inhibited the Importation of such slaves as have been conserned in any plott in Barbados."[10]

Jamaican slaves also suffered hard usage under British colonialism, which resulted in their being "very troublesome" in their aggressive resistance to enslavement.[11] A Jamaican plantation owner wrote a report that circulated in the *South-Carolina Gazette* in 1734 that "our rebellious Negroes are to[o] numerous that they attack us everywhere, and are not afraid of our greatest Force. . . . About ten Days ago they attacked near 100 men, most Soldiers. . . . [M]ost of our people fled; we can get no body to stand before them."[12] What concerned Jamaican slave owners the most was that "we are at present more apprehensive of a *Civil War* than a Foreign War, and it is feared, if some effectual Means are not taken to reduce them [the slaves] they may in a Little Time render themselves stronger than the Force that can be sent against them. . . . The Number of Negroes on this Island are computed to be about Eighty Thousand, and the Whites not Nine Thousand, which strikes them all with a general consternation."[13]

The Maroons, slaves living in the hills of Jamaica, successfully fought against the British until they signed a treaty in 1739. Yet, as Sylviane Diouf argues, they did not just run away from their plantations and masters and fight against recapture. Maroonage represented a wholesale rejection of British culture. These West Africans did not want to assimilate; instead, they chose to coexist with Europeans on their own terms, with their own cultural traditions intact.[14] It is because of this that the formerly truant African slaves and their offspring were given freedom in perpetuity and semiautonomous governing of the Maroon towns of Trelawny, Saint James, Saint Elizabeth, and Saint George, all located within the interior regions of the colony.[15] The *South-Carolina Gazette*'s extensive coverage of the remarkable and troubling story of the negotiated truce in Jamaica signifies the intense concern that slaveholders had about the replication of this disastrous turn of events in their own colony.[16]

The British treaty with the Jamaican Maroon population did not resolve, however, colonists' fears of the rest of their African slaves rebelling. These fears were realized in 1760 when a slave named Tacky, "a Koromantyn Negro . . . who had been a chief in Guiney," led other enslaved Africans "carrying death and desolation" in their attempt to exterminate many of the residents of Saint Mary's Parish. But following African tradition, according to overseer Thomas Thistlewood, white plantation owners were warned ahead of time, as a "Col: Cudjoe Wrote to Col: Barclay & the gentlemen off this Parish a good While agaoa to warn the[m] off this that has happened."[17] Other warning signs, as well as examples of African warfare traditions, can be found in Thistlewood's observation that "at the beginning off the Rebellion, a Shaved head amongst the Negroes was the Signal off War." Amongst those who did so were some of the enslaved under Thistlewood's care, as that "very day Jackie, Job, Achilles, Quasheba, Rosanna, etc. had their heads Shaved."[18]

Nevertheless, "in one morning they murdered between thirty and forty Whites, not sparing even infants at the breast, before their progress was stopped." This "very formidable insurrection of the Koromantyn or Gold Coast Negroes . . . spread through almost every other district of the island."[19] In one district, "a negroe Carrying the Wooden Sword adorned with parrot Feathers (being the sign of union, in Some Part of guinea [Africa][),] was discover'd by a Capt: off a guinea Man, Who saw it Carrying in procession at Spring path, had the fellow Seized and he discover'd the affair." In all, the plan, according to Thistlewood, was that "Fire was to have been Sett to the Towns in many places at once, and all the Whites who Come [to] Extinguish them, are to be Murdered in the Confusion, Whilst the Estates Negroes engaged their Overseers, &c at the Similar time."[20]

Tacky was not the only leader: there were others who had significant military and leadership experience before becoming enslaved. According to Thistlewood, who may have gotten the information from John Cope, the owner of the Egypt plantation in Westmoreland Parish, "The Rebell Aguy was a hunter ffor his King in Guinea. Simon was one off the Said Kings Captains. . . . Wager alias Aponga, was a prince in guinea, tributary to the King off Dorme [Dahomey]: the King off dorme so Conquer'd all the Country ffor Miles round him. Aponga . . . He was Surprize'd and took prisoner when hunting, and Sold ffor a Slave, brought to jamaica & Sold to Capt: Forest. . . . Wager come to this Country 6 or 7 years ago."[21] The mission of Tacky, Cudjoe, Aguy, Simon, Aponga, and many other men and women insurrectionists was freedom.[22] In order to achieve that goal they intended to "kill all the Negroes they Can [who supported the whites] . . . fire the plantations thay Can, till they fforce the Whites to give them Free[dom]."[23] Besides those engaged in direct confrontation with the militia and troops, many others in the enslaved community participated in acts of resistance. They openly defied the rules and walked around "Without Ticketts." They refused to work in the fields and deliberately trampled on the sugarcane to "brak them." And they set fire to the symbols of their oppression, the plantations. Many of the enslaved had great faith in the rebel leaders, and they helped to dismantle the system of enslavement "in expectation off being free."[24]

Although "an old Koromantyn Negro, the chief instigator and oracle of the insurgents . . . administered the Fetish or solemn oath to the conspirators, and furnished them with a magical preparation which was to render them invulnerable," Tacky was eventually caught and decapitated.[25] Yet Thistlewood noted that "Col: Cudjoe's Negroes behved with great bravery." Even when the insurrectionists were tortured after capture, the enslaved Africans "never flinched, moved a foot nor groan'd or Cried oh." According to John Cope, "Cardiff, Who was Burnt at the Bay, told him and many others present that Multitudes of Negroes had took swear that iff they ffail'd off success in this rebellion, to rise again the Same day [in] two year[s] and advised them to be upon their guard."[26] Indeed, very few of the rebels willingly surrendered, and many instead committed suicide. The British militia "frequently came to places in the woods where seven or eight werc found tied up with whites to the boughs of trees, and previous to these self-murders, they had generally massacred the women and children" who had joined the rebel cause as cooks and porters.[27] According to Thistlewood, "The Dead Negroes in the Woods Smell like Stinking . . . oyl."[28] In the end, the enslaved killed sixty whites during the rebellion—but that number seems minuscule in comparison to the three to four hundred slaves who were killed or committed suicide, the one hundred slaves who were executed, and the five hundred slaves who were transported out of Jamaica in response to their suspected resistance to enslavement.[29]

Events in Antigua reported in the *South-Carolina Gazette* also aroused fears among South Carolinians about the militancy of their slave population. A report to the governor of Antigua, William Mathew, published by the *Gazette* in 1737 almost in its entirety, outlined an attempted insurrection that was led mostly by Africans from the Gold Coast (Coromantees) and by Creole slaves. A man named Court was the leader of the African contingent, and according to the report given to Governor Mathew, he was "of a considerable family in his own country, brought here at ten years of age." After growing up in Antigua, Court assumed the "title of King." The other leader, Tomboy, who was a Creole, along with Hercules, Jack, Scipio, Ned, Fortune, and Toney, made up the other half of the "negro conspiracy." The plan of the insurrectionists was that "three or four parties of 300–400 slaves were to enter the town and put the whites to the sword; forts and shipping in the harbour were to be seized," whereby "a new government was to be established when the whites were extirpated."[30] According to Billy Johnson, a free black, all whites were to be killed, because "it would be better if we had the country to ourselves."[31] In order to affirm solidarity in their effort to free themselves, oaths were taken: a person would drink "a health in liquor with grave-dirt and sometimes cock's blood infused, and sometimes the person swearing laid his hand on live cocks. The general tenor of the oath was to kill the whites."[32] Additionally, a "military dance" was done during the day

> of which whites and negroes not in the secret would be spectators yet ignorant of the meaning. It is the custom of Africa when a coromantee king has resolved on war to give public notice that the ikem-dance will be performed . . . the people forming a semicircle about him. The king then begins the dance. . . . When several have danced, the king dances again with his general and swears an oath to behave as a brave prince should or forfeit his life. If he is answered by three huzzas from those present it signifies a belief that the king will observe his oath.[33]

In the opinion of a confessant, "Tomboy was the greatest of generals." Not all the Gold Coast slaves supported the initiative, however, as "some of the coromantees, knowing that a war was intended, tried to stop the dance being performed," perhaps indicating their fear of white reprisals. It is also significant that an Akan ritual remained culturally intact despite the slaves' removal from their African homeland.[34] This evidence supports what historian John Thornton has argued with respect to Angolan and Congolese people: "Military dancing was a part of the African culture of war . . . as much a part of military preparation as drill was in Europe."[35] Indeed, it seems that not only Angolan and Congolese Africans but also Africans from many other ethnic groups performed military dances.

Because of the British discovery of their plot, eighty-eight slaves were put to death. Five were broken on the wheel, six were starved to death on gibbets, and seventy-seven were burned alive. Another forty-four slaves were sold away from the island of Antigua. Although no slave women were deported or executed, Judge Valentine Morris believed that African females had had a role to play in the rebellion and that they were complicit, because he sensed "by their Insolent behavior and Expressions [they] had the utter Extirpation of the Whites as much at heart, as the Men, and would undoubtedly have done as much Mischief by Butchering all the Women and Children."[36]

The continuation of African methods of war and white reprisals can be found outside of the British colonies as well. Evidence given after an attempted insurrection on the Dutch island of Saint Croix in 1759 indicated that the oath-taking practices performed in Antigua were pervasive throughout the diaspora. One informant told the judge that when making the oath to fulfill their plot, "French and Davis cut themselves in the finger in his presence, mixed the blood with earth and water, and drank it with the assurance that they would not confess to the conspiracy no matter what pain they were subjected to." A black woman taken up in an attempt to gather evidence about her husband, William's, involvement indicated that "the most binding oath that a Negro could take, was when he took earth from a dead Negro's grave, mixed it with water and drank it."[37] This conspiracy in Saint Croix resembles others within the British colonies in that after "setting the plantations on fire," the Africans purportedly planned on "killing or burning all whites who collected to put out the fires."[38] One does not have to wonder if the explicit details of the punishment that those accused received were similar as well. The husband of the "negress" above was "Wm. Davis, free negro, convicted by [testimony of] witnesses, and confessed. He cut his own throat. His dead body was dragged through the streets by a horse, by one leg; thereafter hanged on a gallows by a leg, and finally taken down and burned at the stake." Another description is that of "Franch, (or French) free negro, convicted by [testimony of] witnesses, but confessed nothing himself. He was broken on the wheel with an iron crowbar, laid alive on the wheel, where he survived 12 hours. The head was then set on a stake, and the hand fastened on the gallows." Finally, "Will, belonging to Soren Bagge, is convicted by [testimony of] witnesses, but made no confession. Was burned alive, lived in the fire 14 minutes."[39] These three examples demonstrate the high level of commitment that the decision to rebel required of those enslaved, as they clearly understood the expected and torturous outcome of failure. The torturing of dead bodies is also indicative of the level of violence that Europeans exerted in revenge against the enslaved and of their determination to deter any future efforts at liberation in the West Indies or in colonies such as South Carolina.

Internecine Warfare in South Carolina

White South Carolinians also had troubles controlling their slaves, and they knew that Africans had the capacity to organize and fight for their freedom as effectively as Europeans.[40] Indeed, South Carolinians had huge populations of saltwater Africans who had significant influence over the second and possibly third generations of country-born, or Creolized, African Americans as late as the end of the eighteenth century and the early decades of the nineteenth century.[41] The anxiety that large numbers of Africans engendered in the minds of white slave owners influenced how the institution developed in America.

Early recorded accounts of insurrectionary impulses in South Carolina indicate that aggressive resistance began in 1711, when "several Negroes [ran] away from their masters, and keep out, armed, and robbing and plundering houses and plantations, putting the inhabitants of this Province in great fear and terror."[42] Similar to how Native Americans were treated when they rejected British imperial policy, African slaves involved in a plot in Charleston in 1720 were brutally crushed. Almost one hundred slaves were burned and hanged for attempting to "destroy all the white People in the country." A letter sent to King George in 1721 relayed that "black slaves . . . were very near succeeding in a new revolution, which would probably have been attended by the utter extirpation of all your Majesty's subjects."[43]

In 1730 well-armed slaves involved in plotting their insurrection intended to meet for "a great Dance" and then descend upon Charleston to "rise and destroy" all the whites.[44] The "Chief of them, with some others" were stopped before they could execute their rebellion, but the ritual of dance and the assignment of leadership titles demonstrate how African military culture remained intact throughout the African diaspora.

South Carolina planters had the same concerns as Jamaican plantation owners about the numerical imbalance of slaves to whites in their own province, which made them feel vulnerable. Indeed, a man named "Mercator" published a letter to the editor of the *South-Carolina Gazette* in 1737 warning that "when it is considered that for the four years last past we have had imported 10,447 Negroes . . . I believe most People will agree with me . . . if some Method is not speedily taken to prevent this large importation of Negroes, it will . . . be of the most fatal consequences to this Province in many Respects to obvious to all thinking Men."[45]

As if fulfilling these predictions, the Stono rebellion in 1739 began with twenty African men, many of them Angolans, breaking into a store, where they acquired ammunition. These men would have been familiar with the use of arms either as slaves in South Carolina or as African soldiers from the Congo region, which was plagued by continuous intercontinental wars for power and control of the slave trade.[46] With Jemmy as their leader, approximately fifty rebels set about killing everyone living within the houses they passed on their way to freedom. For ten miles they killed men, women, and children, sparing just one man, an innkeeper who had shown kindness to his slaves.[47] After slaying twenty whites, they stopped in a field, where they began "dancing, Singing, and beating Drums to draw more Negroes to [join] them." Using the customs of African warfare to unite in battle those willing and those fearful of reprisals, these enslaved men demonstrated remarkable confidence in their ability to successfully reach their destination of Saint Augustine, Florida.[48] It has been suggested that because the South Carolina region was suffering from a smallpox epidemic and a potential confrontation with Spain, whites appeared distracted enough for the conspirators to determine that freedom was obtainable. They held onto these beliefs even after an equally large band of white militia suppressed their effort.[49] According to an account of the Stono rebellion, passed down orally for nearly two centuries, by the great-great-grandson of Cato, "Commander Cato speak for de crowd. He say: 'We don't lak slavery. We start to jine de Spanish in Florida. We surrender but we not whipped yet, and we' is not converted.' De other 43 say: 'Amen.' . . . He die but he die for doin' de right, as he see it."[50]

Much like what occurred in Jamaica, roughly one-third of the insurgent slaves remained at large after the initial confrontation on the field. It took an entire week before the bulk of them were captured and punished. Many were "put to the most cruel Death." It took another three years before the authorities found and killed one of the ringleaders. About sixty African slaves lost their lives in the aftermath, "some shot, some hang'd, and some Gibbeted alive."[51]

The reprisals, however, did not quell the possibility of another insurrection: in 1740 between 150 and 200 slaves planned to escape bondage after they seized Charleston. Repeating the model of the Stono rebels, this group intended to take weapons from a local storehouse in order to supply everyone with arms. One slave, Peter, told of their plot, however, and through entrapment, fifty bondspeople, ten each day, were hanged to deter the others from the crime of attempting to insurrect.[52] "So many Enemys to the Government" led the South Carolina legislature to put a duty on newly imported slaves in 1740 and to impose a hiatus on the importation of African slaves for three years.[53]

As blacks continued to foment insurrections, so did the determination of whites to suppress them. In 1816 Governor Williams ordered Maj. Gen. Youngblood to use the militia under his command to "either capture or destroy the whole body" of Maroons living in the swamps near the Combahee and Ashepoo Rivers whose "forces now became alarming, not less from its numbers than from its arms and ammunition with which it was supplied."[54]

These early insurrection attempts were wars waged by slaves for their own liberation. In each rebellion, slaves either claimed to be or attempted to engage in an armed struggle against those whites who they believed were *their* enemies, as the progenitors of racialized chattel slavery, a distinct form of bondage that African people rejected. Indeed, the successful insurrection in French Saint-Domingue at the end of the eighteenth century not only represented the determination of the enslaved to be free but also served as a harbinger of white colonists' greatest fears.

The revolution in Saint-Domingue was an inspiration to enslaved populations throughout the African diaspora and a horrific nightmare for white slave owners in South Carolina and across the Atlantic World. This beacon of hope, however, came at an astronomical cost for the enslaved Africans and the whites who lost their lives. The terror that ensued became a haunting example of the possibility of exterminatory warfare and black freedom, which struck fear in the hearts and minds of whites living among enslaved peoples across the Americas.

Like many other islands in the West Indies, Saint-Domingue, a French colony on the island of Hispaniola, had a large population of enslaved blacks. The first major effort of resistance there began in 1751 with François Mackandal, a Guinea African who attempted to unify the Maroon population with the intention of destroying slavery. Six years later, Mackandal was captured and burned at the stake. But by 1789 there were thirty thousand whites, twenty-eight thousand mixed-race people of color, and approximately five hundred thousand slaves, most of whom were African born, who provided the means for the first successful revolution to end enslavement in the Atlantic World.[55]

Vodou priest "Zamba" Boukman emerged as the leader of the revolution in Saint-Domingue that began in 1789, culminating in black freedom in 1804. Boukman, a coachman on the Clement plantation in Acul, organized large numbers of Maroons and plantation slaves. They took over the entire Northern Province, where the majority of the white elites lived, and by 1792 controlled over one-third of the island.[56] According to one anonymous source, the "vast project" was "the destruction of all whites except some who didn't own property, some priests, some surgeons, and some women, and of setting fire to all the plantations." This was necessary in order to make "themselves masters of the country."[57] A Creole soldier raised in France and fighting on the side of the French remembered that "one feared being slaughtered by one's servants. . . . [O]ne wept for a relative assassinated or exposed to the dangers of a war of extermination."[58] According to the account of M. Gros, a white lawyer taken captive, "those who believe in the false imprisonment and peaceable disposition of their negroes" were living in a fantasy land. Gros argued that "quite the reverse was their temper of mind: their whole intent was the entire annihilation of the whites."[59] Indeed, a Creole soldier admitted, "We were crushed by this war. One hundred thousand slaves in full revolt. . . . [T]heir musicians made a hideous din beating cauldrons—all this as an accompaniment to the accustomed shrieking of warring Africans."[60] In the end, the enslaved in Saint-Domingue destroyed many of the symbols of their oppression— hundreds of sugar, coffee, and indigo plantations—an oppression grounded in extreme violence and, as Laurent Dubois notes, "the threat of atrocity."[61]

Traditions of African warfare are evident during the capture and execution of a "negro whose regalia caused me to judge him to be one of the principle [sic] chiefs." Another soldier discovered that "on his chest he had a little sack full of hair, herbs, bits of bone, which they call a fetish; with this, they expect to be sheltered from all danger; and it was, no doubt, because of this amulet, that our man had the intrepidity which the philosophers call Stoicism." The continuity of African military traditions was not only observed by whites but also feared: "For the first time, I saw bows and arrows used; the latter fell about us like rain, and the fear that they could be poison did not cheer us."[62] Gros and other French colonists concluded, "We are now convinced of this grand truth, 'that the Negroes will never return to their duty, but by compulsion, or a partial destruction of them.'" Indeed, in Gros's view, who was made a prisoner of war by the black army, "the Negro women were infinitely worse, more hardened, and less inclined to return to their duty than the men," making enslaved women eligible for slaughter as well.[63]

For many planter elites, the massacre of so many white citizens demanded retaliation. Whites, denying that it had begun on both sides as an "exterminating war," believed that the "still steaming corpses seemed to demand that we take revenge for them."[64] According to one eyewitness, when whites overcame the black camps, it was terrible because "of the awful rage that had seized some of the inhabitants of Le Cap. . . . [S]ince men of color were their enemies, they wanted nothing less than to destroy all of them. . . . [T]wenty-eight Negroes and Negresses taken prisoner by our troops . . . were hacked to death. . . . [F]ifty Negroes were shot in trenches. . . . [T]wenty black brigands who had been captured were put on a boat and drowned in the sea. . . . Some Negroes and Negresses were shot at the parish house."[65] According to this Creole soldier's account, when his troops met with those enslaved, "we overcame them, and the camp was littered with the hacked remains of the victims."[66]

French soldiers thought that once they captured and killed Boukman the "brigands would sue for peace." Determined to regain complete mastery over the colony's African slaves, the French sought to denigrate the symbol of the slave insurgency's leader and instill fear among the rebels. They made a spectacle of "one of the most famous chiefs" by making their "entry into the town . . . [with] the head of Boukman on a pike."[67] Although this greatly unsettled many of "the brigands," black military leaders still remained in charge of their forces: "The chiefs went in mourning and ordered a solemn service to be performed . . . and caused a dance or *Calinda* to be held for three days."[68] The mulatto generals, Jean-François and Biassou, made an offer to negotiate an agreement for peace with the French, but they did not get a response. Gros's account tells us that it was then that Jean-François and "his counsel . . . unanimously decided to continue the war and complete the destruction of what remained, whether of the plain, or the mountains."[69] Their offer for peace was rejected by French Lieutenant Colonel Touzard because he believed that Africans were disposable: "The whites are more willing to lose all their remaining possessions and to annihilate the present race of rebellious slaves than to consent to a shameful agreement. . . . [T]he whites will have only a single aim: the complete destruction of the rebels and of their chiefs." Although Touzard understood that "the fate of all the Antilles, [was] threatened by this revolt," he foolishly underestimated the African and *gens de couleur* revolutionaries, whose actions, he believed, could "only bring them misfortune."[70]

The enslaved and mulatto forces were victorious in their battle for freedom after they nearly destroyed the largest city and busiest port in Saint-Domingue, Cap Français, in June 1793. French commissioners Léger-Félicité Sonthonax and Étienne Polverel aligned with free blacks and those enslaved in order to thwart the military efforts of Governor François-Thomas Galbaud, who refused to enforce an April 4, 1792, French law giving some citizenship rights to free people of color, generally the mulatto children of slaveholders, some of whom were landowners themselves with considerable wealth. The result was that by the end of 1793, Sonthonax had issued emancipation proclamations throughout French Saint-Domingue that ended slavery. One eyewitness recounted that "citizens of color . . . wonderfully aided by the blacks they had armed . . . were no longer men bent beneath the yoke of contempt and servitude; inspired by hatred and revenge, these men had thrown off their masks. No more truce between master and the slave in revolt. . . . [T]he spell was broken."[71]

Emancipation, however, occurred in the middle of the chaos of war, during which many white colonists were killed. The terrorized "whites, pale and frightened . . . asked each other what they ought to do, where they ought to go. . . . In the face of this pressing danger, some of them assembled . . . with the intent of reestablishing order and bringing back tranquility." But as the colonists made their way to Government House, "they were treacherously fired on by the mulattoes and blacks who were hidden there." A white woman was told by some blacks she knew that whites "had been killed in piles" during the night. Other whites heard blacks say as they sought to take over the city, "We should kill them all. The colony's got to be either all white or all black." Though Commissioners Sonthonax and Polverel successfully repelled Governor Galbaud's assault, the city of Cap Français burned for two weeks in 1793, and many white citizens were massacred. "When the fire died down somewhat," one white eyewitness reported, "I left . . . to return to town. . . . I found nothing but dead bodies: the streets were strewn with them."[72]

The atrocities committed by white colonists and by mulattoes and black slaves diminished significantly under Toussaint L'Ouverture's leadership. L'Ouverture's military accomplishments eventually enabled him, with the full support of the black and mulatto community, to restore order and proclaim that Saint-Domingue was free from French rule. A constitution established under L'Ouverture's guidance declared that Saint-Domingue had the right to self-governance, and it was the first European colony to become a sovereign black state in the Atlantic World. The price of independence would be high, however, and internecine warfare would again plague the island.

French monarch Napoleon Bonaparte was outraged that L'Ouverture would presume independence. Despite his assertions in 1799 to the "brave blacks" that "the French people alone recognize your freedom and the equality of your rights,"[73] Bonaparte sent his brother-in-law, Gen. Charles LeClerc, to Saint-Domingue to reestablish French rule. LeClerc was given secret orders to restore slavery as well. LeClerc and his successor, Governor-General Donatien-Marie-Joseph de Vimeur, vicomte de Rochambeau, were brutal in their attempts to defeat L'Ouverture's troops. Large numbers of blacks were murdered in order to, as LeClerc instructed, "inspire great terror."[74] In desperation because blacks continued to resist, however, LeClerc wrote Napoleon that "we must destroy all the Negroes of the mountains, men and women, and keep only children under twelve, destroy half of those of the plain. . . . [O]therwise it will never be calm." To LeClerc, the Africans in Saint-Domingue were now too corrupted by freedom to ever submit to enslavement, so the French would need to exterminate the adults and older children and then import new ones.[75] Although the French legislature recognized as "unfortunate that part of the human race is condemned by nature or social institutions to servile labor and slavery," the overseas colonies represented too much wealth and were too important to the industries that sustained the empire to not do whatever was necessary to recover Saint-Domingue. Men in the First Consul, merchants, and ship owners believed that "without our slave colonies, no more trade with Africa, no more way of increasing our fisheries . . . our agriculture and industry would decline, along with our East Indian commerce, our naval power would suffer. . . . All this would result from freedom for blacks."[76]

According to one American newspaper:

The French exercise[d] the greatest imaginable cruelties on the blacks which fall into their hands:—at St. Marcs, 600 of them were paraded and ordered to be disarmed; and because they resisted the measure, they were all massacred. The dead bodies of the negroes were seen floating on the water by American vessels coming out of the bite of Leogane. It was said, that every week a vessel took 100 to 150 negroes on board at Port-Republic, carried them to sea, stifled them in the hold with brimstone, and then threw the bodies overboard; and that a brig frequently took blacks on board at the Cape, went to sea, and in a few days returned empty.[77]

They also "executed officers *and* their families."[78]

Mulatto and black soldiers used similar tactics in order to thwart any attempt to reestablish slavery or French rule in Saint-Domingue. Toussaint L'Ouverture instructed Jean-Jacques Dessalines to "tear up the roads with shot; throw corpses and horses into all the fountains; burn and annihilate every-thing, in order that those who have come to reduce us to slavery may have before their eyes the image of the hell which they deserve."[79] Eventually, L'Ouverture was tricked into believing that French forces would work alongside his troops to keep the peace. The "Old African," as one plantation owner called L'Ouverture, was subsequently deported to France, where he died in prison. Nevertheless, after Dessalines betrayed L'Ouverture and joined the French army, he discovered that the French did indeed intend to reestablish slavery in Saint-Domingue as they had done in Guadeloupe. He then switched sides again and led his forces to "join their color" in the struggle against the colonial forces.[80]

Dessalines went on to fulfill the orders of devastation and destruction that both LeClerc and L'Ouverture had commanded against one another, only this time Dessalines told his black freedom fighters, "We don't need whites among us anymore."[81] French colonists once again assumed that after the arrest and capture of L'Ouverture everything would go back to normal: "When Toussaint was arrested it was suppose'd that war was finished."[82] They did not anticipate that Dessalines would galvanize his "indigenous army" by having them recall "the memories of slavery" and by invoking "stories of cruelties committed by certain white plantation owners." He effectively rallied the formerly enslaved population and "whipped up, their burning desire to get revenge for the worst treatment." According to one white captive's account, "Their unanimous cry" was that "you punished me, now I will punish you." Soon the "signal for a general massacre was given. . . . The whites of the canto . . . were soon pursued and collected from all over. Their brains, flying in all directions, stuck to the blood-spattered walls. . . . [P]erfidious balls struck old people and children without distinction." In the final months of what would become known as the Haitian Revolution, Dessalines made 1,436 white men of all description and rank leave their homes in Cap Français in 1804. Over the course of three days, Dessalines had them all killed, "their bodies thrown one above the other so as to form a mound of dead bodies." It was said that Dessalines had them murdered so that the "country negroes" could "look at their masters and no longer depend on them" and no longer fear being reenslaved by them. A "second wave of massacres" occurred in 1804 that was "aimed at white women and children."[83] Out of the thirty thousand whites who lived in the colony in 1789, approximately twenty thousand either lost their lives or were forced to flee the island.

Freedom, however, did not come without cost. More than 166,000 out of 500,000 enslaved Africans also lost their lives in the struggle.[84] The success of this servile insurrection in Saint-Domingue astounded Europeans. Dessalines, reclaiming the island's ancient aboriginal moniker, renamed it Haiti.[85] White reports about Dessalines described him as "ferocious, ignorant, and savage." But Dessalines's response was that the slaves had done nothing that Europeans had not already done to them. "Yes, we have rendered . . . war for war, crime for crime, outrage for outrage," and in doing so, Dessalines argued, "I have saved my country" from reenslavement and white violence.[86] Americans were especially troubled by France's willingness to grant freedom and civil rights not only to the mulatto population but also to those formerly enslaved as well. At that moment and as long as slavery continued in America, the Haitian Revolution served as a sober reminder of the powerful capacity of the African military forces that white Americans might face among their own slaves in rebellion. White fears were not without cause, as Dessalines did encourage those enslaved in Martinique and other parts of the African diaspora to rebel. And he incentivized ship captains to engage in helping those enslaved and other free people of color to escape white oppression by offering them "forty dollars for each black person" who was brought to the island of Haiti.[87]

Thus, the French refugees who fled to the mainland with their slaves, five hundred by 1793 and three thousand by 1816 in South Carolina alone, made many Carolinian colonists fearful of insurrections in their own communities.[88] They expressed strong concerns about "Frenchmen" escaping from Saint-Domingue who might "come to this country, who would fraternize with our Democratic Clubs," and who would therefore instigate a slave insurrection in America that would result in civil equality among the races and black freedom. Plantation owner Ralph Izard feared that because of the importation of slaves from this region, "the foundation of more serious troubles has [already] been laid in South Carolina."[89] For South Carolinian Mary Pinckney, the arrival of whites from Saint-Domingue with their slaves was indeed unsettling and "has given us a great deal of concern—We dread the future, and are fearful that our feelings for the unfortunate inhabitants of the Wretched island of St. Domingo may be our own destruction."[90]

The seeming inevitability of slave rebellions, based on nearly two centuries of Africans attempting to fight their way to freedom, plagued the minds of white colonists in South Carolina well into the nineteenth century. Certainly, Denmark Vesey's insurrection attempt in 1822 affirmed two things: despite the brutal exhibitions of power, whites still had trouble controlling their slaves, and future incidents of aggressive resistance and the threat of white extermination would continue to hover over the anomalous institution of chattel slavery in the American South.

Denmark Vesey's War

The endurance of African military culture, the pull of the African homeland, and black resistance to enslavement are apparent in Denmark Vesey's insurrection attempt in 1822, but so are white trepidations about a servile war in South Carolina.[91] Denmark Vesey's birth name was Telemaque. He was a free black carpenter who was born enslaved in Saint Thomas around 1767. While the plot of his insurrection is well known due to the transcript of the trial, sections of the document also describe African ideas of warfare that enslaved people brought with them from their ancestral homes. There is no way to ascertain whether all of the facts left as a record of the event are true,[92] as the courtroom was closed to outside spectators, which the prosecuting attorneys, Lionel H. Kennedy and Thomas Parker, argued had precedence in the insurrection trials in Antigua in 1736 and the "Negro plot" of 1741 in New York.[93] Yet the countless witnesses who testified to Vesey's plan to build large armies and acquire weaponry for the soldiers of those armies demonstrate his continuity with traditional African practices of warfare. There was also an Afro-syncretic adoption of the terminology "nits make lice" in alignment with the past exterminatory warfare practices of Europeans and some Africans.[94]

Like their West Indian predecessors, black South Carolinians worked at developing an army that replicated the forces in Saint-Domingue. Monday Gell confessed that he was "shown paper about the battle that Boyer had in San Domingue." And Rolla, Governor Bennett's slave, was told by Vesey, who had been sold by slave trader Capt. Joseph Vesey to a slave owner in Saint-Domingue, where he lived a short while, that "we must unite together as the Santo Domingo people did." Jack Purcell said Vesey was constantly reading newspaper articles to him about Haiti. Vesey, who could read and write in French and English, sent letters to Haitian president Jean-Pierre Boyer, a free mulatto who fought with Toussaint L'Ouverture in the early years, asking for his assistance. The letters were delivered to a ship's steward whose brother was a general in the army.[95] The South Carolina insurgents used the revolution in Haiti as a model to outline how they needed to organize, and continuous references to Saint-Domingue as the touchstone for what was to follow made it infinitely easier for Vesey and his leaders to articulate how a successful war would be waged.

Of particular interest is the idea of Africa as a liberator. Much like the Native American populations in the Southeast who formed pan-Indian alliances to maintain cultural unity and to protect their communities from the destructiveness of the Indian slave trade, black South Carolinians looked to their native land for assistance in freeing themselves. Bacchus, a slave belonging to Benjamin Hammet, along with a slave named Charles Drayton, consulted with an African named "old daddy" who was "marked on both sides of his face" about their plans to bring the "Country Negroes" down. They told him that "he must be in readiness" to "receive them" at the onset of the revolt.[96] Vesey asked to see an elderly Guinea slave named Peter, who agreed to join their effort.[97] Although there is no way to know what transpired, the fact that these consultations were mentioned suggests that "old daddy" and Peter may have retained essential experiences and wartime strategies from Africa that Vesey valued.

Vesey and his followers attempted to encourage participation by stating that Haiti and Africa were intimately involved in their struggle against enslavement. Rolla told a witness that "a large army from Santo Domingo and Africa were coming to help us." Another rebel warrior believed that once they "raised an army" and began the insurrection, soldiers from Africa and Haiti "would come over and cut up the white people."[98] The perception of kinship between Africans sold into slavery and Africans who facilitated the purveyance of slaves to the Americas remained. More deeply, perhaps, these affirmations of solidarity indicate a psychic need for Africa as a symbol of possibilities: Africa too, as a body of nations, would realize the strengths within its shores and end support for the expatriation and enslavement of its own people.

Other slaves had the more pragmatic view that the war they talked about "against the whites" was to be waged by them alone. Thus, they would need to be "making arms for the black people" so that they could achieve their goal of "slaying the whites." Some of the weaponry was to come from "some Frenchmen, blacks very skillful in making swords and spears, such as they used in Africa." Another witness said that a slave named Tom Russell who was a blacksmith "was making arms for the black people." A slave named Smart Anderson testified that he observed that "spear's were brought into Monday's shop," and Peirault, one of Vesey's main recruiters, admitted that he, a slave named Dean, and Vesey "met purposely to make a collection of spears," weapons used by African soldiers in the past. The organizers planned to obtain guns for their entire army once the insurrection began by seizing "the Powder Magazine and the Arsenal on the [Charleston] Neck" in South Carolina.[99]

Vesey and his team of leaders had been working for four years to organize large numbers of men. Denmark Vesey, Governor Bennett's slaves Rolla and Ned, Jack (Purcell), Peter (Poyas), Gullah Jack (Pritchard), and Monday (Gell) kept lists of all who agreed to join the effort. They recruited from as far away as Columbia and as close to Charleston as Goose Creek and Dorchester, where purportedly 6,600 slaves signed on to insurrect against their masters and where they divided their "regular army" across ethnic and regional lines. Monday Gell, an Igbo, was in charge of the "Ebo Company." Then there was the "Gullah Company," led by Jack Pritchard. The "French Band" was composed of slaves who spoke French and who "had been ready a long time." Finally, there were the "countryborn," or American-born (versus "saltwater," or African-born), slaves, who were not trusted by many members. Joe, the slave of Mr. Jore, stated that he "did not know how to trust countryborns," whereas Jack Pritchard boasted that he had no trouble with the countryborn joining because they all believed "he was a doctor" and were perhaps afraid of his using magic "charms" of conjure on them. As the leader of the Gullah Company, Jack was "their general" in the war. As part of his leadership strategy, he gave all his men charms of crab claws to put in their mouths and "parched corn and ground nuts" to eat prior to battle so that they would not "then be wounded."[100]

During the recruitment process, men took oaths much like the one used by African slaves in Jamaica, Antigua, and Saint Croix. All members were required to swear oaths of secrecy by standing and raising their right hand. Vesey, a saltwater African, asserted this was necessary so that they would "not tell if we are found out, and if they kill us we will not tell on anyone." Gullah Jack had his men eat a halfway-roasted fowl "as evidence of union." These oaths were to demonstrate serious commitment, and as the authors of the *Trial Record* noted, "not one of the leaders betrayed their associates; the companies of Vesey, Peter, Ned, Rolla, and Gullah Jack have escaped detection and punishment; with the exception of a few of Gullah Jack's band, who were discovered in consequence of one of his men, betraying those companions he knew, together with his leader." Yet the court grudgingly observed that Jack was to them a "savage who indeed had been caught but not tamed."[101]

The importance of secrecy had a long history in West African communities, especially among the Igbo in the Bight of Biafra region, the Ashanti/Fante of the Gold Coast, and the Yoruba and Dahomean of the Bight of Benin, as well as in the mandatory participation in the Poro (male) and Sande (female) societies in Sierra Leone and Liberia. The function of secret societies in Africa as political and social organizations and, importantly, as arbiters of justice assisted the collective organizing of African slaves in South Carolina.

And the amazing resilience of those leaders implicated in Vesey's insurrection attempt exemplifies how powerful cultural continuity was despite the oppressiveness of bondage. As historian Michael Gomez points out, "Some order and sense had to be fashioned out of New World disorder. To achieve this, the African antecedent was drawn upon, and in the process the African-based community began to see itself in heretofore unimagined ways."[102] Secrecy was the cornerstone of all insurrectionary attempts, and the continuation of military rituals practiced in Africa and the New World was reflected in the valuations given to honor and death.

Although Monday Gell testified in his confession that he was opposed to the idea, he avowed that everyone else agreed with Vesey's plan "in the murder of all." Their mission, similar to the tactics used by Europeans in, for example, the Pequot War, was to "set the town on fire in different places and as the whites come out we will slay them." It has been argued that Vesey found the ideas for his plan in the Old Testament, and the record indicates that passages from the Bible were used frequently in the meetings of the leaders to affirm that slavery was a sinful and immoral institution. In Vesey's view, fighting for their freedom as outlined by the Israelites was part of God's plan for black people, and Rolla recounted that this meant that "all should be cut off, both men, women, and children." Although some members confessed resistance at "killing ministers, women, and children," Vesey argued that "it was not safe to keep one alive, but to destroy them totally. . . . [T]he Lord has commanded it."[103] This evidence of Vesey's intent was repeated in another confessant's testimony that was given to a "Reverend Hall." Much like the English had done for centuries, Vesey seemed to use the idea that God commanded extermination as articulated in the book of Joshua to justify his actions.[104] Or perhaps Vesey used Joshua and the Old Testament to confound white theological interpretations, turning the tables on the spiritual hierarchy established by the planter class. Perhaps as the "new Israelites," Vesey and his followers were waging war against a people he believed were outside of God's covenant, thereby challenging slaveholders' claims to racial superiority and white notions that slavery was endorsed by Christianity at its core.[105]

Moreover, Vesey's affirmation that it was not enough to just kill white men and his usage of the European shibboleth of "what was the use of killing the louse and leaving the nit" flayed slave owners with their own historic rationale for killing children in Ireland and indigenous children in America.[106] Thus, Vesey signified his awareness of and attention to European methods of warfare that white South Carolinians no doubt would have preferred to remain invisible. Vesey boldly determined that "if you kill the lice you must kill the nits," because in his view whites were the ones who were uncivilized, as they kept black people enslaved against their will.[107] Yet the killing of women and children was also part of African traditions of war, as evidenced during the Atlantic slave trade. And so although Vesey may have appropriated European terminology to convince countryborn and saltwater slaves of the wisdom of his methods, his plan was also consistent with the type of exterminatory warfare practiced in some parts of Africa and in America.

Certainly, Vesey's usage of Old Testament scripture would have proved a valuable tool in winning the support of the over 1,848 black members of Charleston's Mother Emanuel African Methodist Episcopal Church.[108] Church leaders like Vesey, Peter Poyas, Ned Bennett, and Charles Shubrick used church gatherings as an opportunity to instruct other members about the revolutionary ideas contained within the Old Testament and the fundamentals of warfare.[109] Indeed, according to T. Hamilton, a black American living in Charleston at the time he called "the Reign of Terror," Vesey and Peter Poyas were successful because they were revered by the black community as religious martyrs for their "patriotic bravery" in leading the "determined revolutionary spirit of the slaves."[110]

Vesey and his followers may have rationalized his war against enslavement as part of God's commandments, but at the core of his strategy was the certain knowledge that if they proceeded in implementing their plans and were unsuccessful, retaliation would be severe, that "we should all have been destroyed."[111] They knew that success would only occur if they were able to escape from South Carolina and the American continent, which was the final stage of their plan.

Concerns over retribution must have been pervasive. Although a convicted slave named John was instructed by Monday Gell that "the *Northern Brothers* would assist them" in their insurrection, Gell also told them that "if they failed 'twould be no disgrace."[112] Amherst Lining, a slave acquitted of all charges against him, stated that although he was not involved in the insurrection attempt, he was concerned that "in the confusion, he would be in danger of losing his life whether he was engaged in it or not." Another witness expressed concerns over retribution, which focused on the responses of "the whites in the back country, Virginia, [who] when they hear the news will turn to and kill you all." William, a slave belonging to John Paul, made a concerted effort to protect the women out of fear that the justices were considering whether women should be charged. He begged, "You won't take up Sarah, for no woman knows anything about it."[113] Thomas Wentworth Higginson, with an eye toward this possibility, concluded in his analysis of the event that the conspirators "took no women into counsel,—not from any distrust apparently, but in order that their children might not be left uncared-for in case of defeat and destruction."[114] Yet we know that in the Dahomean and Igbo nations, women did serve in the military, did engage in warfare, and were also taken as captives of war.[115] Enslaved women also assisted on board in slave ship insurrections, so it is plausible that they might have been involved in insurrectionary efforts that occurred on land as well.[116] The court justices were aware that at least three black women, if not many others, knew about the rebellion and did not try to stop it. A slave named Edwin stated that "I have heard everybody, even the women say . . . that they wondered why Denmark and Monday Gell were not taken up." Sally testified against a slave named Jesse that he had told her that "all the white people would be killed." Another slave named Prudence said that she was "told a fort night ago about the plan." Then one of "Colonel Cross' wenches" said the head of the Mother Emanuel African Methodist Episcopal (AME) church, Rev. Morris Brown, knew all about it.[117]

Thus, the threat of a large-scale violent confrontation between blacks and whites was a real consideration. The dark prediction that Virginia whites would come and "kill you all," and the slaves' subsequent careful protection of black women and children, evidences an awareness of that reality. The fact that enslaved and free blacks attempted to rebel anyway only affirms their determination to be free and that slaves and whites were locked in a never-ending contest of wills that ultimately made them fearful of one another.

Indeed, the white community was traumatized by the fact that some witnesses testified, probably in exaggeration, that an army of nine thousand was ready to commence warring against the whites of South Carolina on Sunday, July 16, 1822.[118] The subsequent trial lasted for five and one-half weeks, long enough for South Carolina officials to charge 131 blacks. One white child described the executions as "a sight to strike terror in the heart of every slave."[119] This youth's observations were not off the mark, as Justice William Johnson wrote to Thomas Jefferson that "you know the best way in the world to make them tractable is to frighten them to death."[120] Yet all references to the affair within the white community were silenced out of fear that "something further of the same nature" might come to pass. No day of prayer, no day of "public thanksgiving" was deemed appropriate despite Rev. Richard Furman's assertions that "Divine Interposition has been conspicuous; and our obligations to be thankful are unspeakably great."[121] Anna Johnson believed that "our own God has saved us from horrors equal if not superior to the scenes acted in St. Domingo." Indeed, she claimed, "There is a look of horror on every countenance."[122] Mary L. Beach wrote that she "heard it remarked by several that all confidence in them [the enslaved] now is forever at an end!"[123]

Yet at the same time, many South Carolinians recognized in private that

Vesey's plot was "a good plot—an excellent plot."[124] They said that his "plan denoted a fine military tact and admirable combination" and that the leaders "met their fate with the heroic fortitude of Martyrs."[125] Others said that Vesey and his men "were *true* warriors—Not a single Woman knew a word of their plan."[126] Indeed, the owner of several of the insurgents and the governor of South Carolina, Thomas Bennett, defined Vesey's insurrection attempt in the lexicon of American Revolutionary action in remarks to then South Carolina congressman John C. Calhoun: "It ought to excite no astonishment with those who boast of freedom themselves, if they should occasionally hear of plots and desertions among those who are held in perpetual bondage. Human beings, who once breathed the air of freedom on their own mountains and in their own valleys, but who have been kidnapped by white men and dragged into endless slavery, cannot be expected to be contented with their situation. White men, too, would engender plots and escape from their imprisonment were they situated as are these miserable children of Africa."[127]

Proslavery writer and Charleston editor Edwin Holland noted that there had been a pattern. The attempted insurrection in 1816 in Camden, South Carolina, was motivated by just such "wild and frantic ideas of the rights of man, and the *misconceived injunctions and examples of Holy writ*." Clearly, Holland believed that Vesey's organization was different: it represented a political movement, a radical challenge to established authority, a racialized opposition to the existing order. He revealed that the recent insurrection attempt was more than just rowdy heathens trying to start trouble: "Let it never be forgotten" that "our Negroes are truly the *Jacobins* of the country; that they are the *anarchists* and the *domestic enemy*; the *common enemy of civilized society*, and the barbarians who would, IF THEY COULD, become the DESTROYERS *of our race*."[128]

Still, Holland clung to the idea that if a war did commence, black people would lose, evidencing that both blacks and whites had similar ideas that no doubt created a volatile atmosphere in the South that was thick with fear: "The struggle, it is true, might be a bloody and awful one; but it would be limited to a very short period. A few hours would decide the conflict and the *utter extermination* of the black race would be the inevitable consequence. In such an event, it would be difficult to discriminate. The innocent, as well as the guilty; would alike fall a sacrifice to the vengeance of violate humanity."[129] Perhaps Holland felt confident about his threats against rebellious blacks because he was familiar with the federally sanctioned action against Native Americans in the Battle of Horse Shoe Bend, commonly called the Red Sticks Massacre, led by Andrew Jackson in 1814. In this nationally celebrated event, nine hundred Creek Indians were killed, the largest death toll of any Anglo-

Indian war.[130] Or perhaps Holland was really speaking to an audience of whites who viewed Vesey's actions as a warning that one day God would "raise up a Toussaint, or a Spartacus, or an African Tecumseh to demand by what authority we hold them in subjection" in order to let them know, from the South's perspective, how disastrous that would be.[131]

Despite these warnings, whites' fear of the African slaves in their midst remained as indelible in 1822 as it had been in the colonial era. Slaves were now executed for things that they had previously only been whipped for.[132] There were calls for strengthening and the further development of the military in South Carolina; a special guard of 150 men was established to protect Charleston. Lawyer and plantation owner Robert J. Turnbull went ahead and organized a voluntary militia outside the purview of government regulation in 1823 for the protection of the port city as well.[133] The South Carolina legislature required that any free black sailors, cooks, or stewards employed on board ships be kept in jail until the ship's departure; male slaves were no longer able to hire out their time; free black males over the age of fifteen had to have a guardian; free blacks not living in the state for more than five years had to pay fifty dollars per year in order to remain in South Carolina; and no slave could be brought in from the West Indies, Mexico, South America, or north of Washington, D.C.[134]

Harking back to earlier European American accomplishments in war, the members of the Charleston court told the ten convicted conspirators that the "plot [was] so wild and diabolical . . . [that it] would have probably resulted in the destruction and extermination of *your race*."[135] The past was not dead. Slavery was just, and the racialized privilege of redemptive warfare belonged to white Americans who would respond to the "great law of nature," which was "self preservation."[136] Whites knew that blacks understood total warfare from every perspective: how it was used against Native Americans to take away their land, how it was used by European Americans to sustain their power, how Old Testament Israelites had used it to ensure that their nation would remain free, and how Africans used it first to enslave their own people and then as a strategy for liberation in America.

Africans brought across the Atlantic strategies of warfare that were used in procuring slaves for sale; the enslaved then used these strategies in their efforts to free themselves. British colonists, having fashioned their own templates of war, were determined to thwart any insurrectionary attempts with a callous ruthlessness intended to make the enslaved dread white retaliation. Yet Europeans knew from experience that many Africans had carried their African military heritage unambiguously across the Atlantic Ocean. Thus, the institution of enslavement was always pregnant with the possibilities of an internecine war. Although Vesey's rebellion and all the other insurrections that took place from the colonial to the early national period (with the exception of the Haitian Revolution) were not successful, they do reveal what both sides believed was at stake, what they believed was required in effectively fighting for or in obstruction of black freedom. The potential of exterminatory warfare would continue to be part of the slave-owning/slave-resisting lexicon well into the antebellum era. Never did it waver in its intended ferocity and prophecy of doom for the slave or as a strategy of liberation amongst blacks in America, that is, until 1831, when the trauma that the black community experienced after Nat Turner's insurrection in Virginia effectively changed the way the enslaved approached resistance to bondage in America.

CHAPTER FOUR

The Abridgment of Hope
After Nat Turner

Although traditionally Nat Turner's insurrection in 1831 has been viewed as a momentous event for white Virginians, it was equally traumatic and certainly more transformative for the black community in the slaveholding South. Laws set in place to curtail servile insurrections did not stop the enslaved from continuing to attempt to free themselves. And Nat Turner's rebellion, in his attempt to do what insurrectionists had done elsewhere, was such a moment. In response, whites living in the South, which had become much more militarized than in the colonial era, allowed unchecked retaliation to ensue. The vigilante violence experienced by the black community, enslaved and free, was meant to send a message. The message was that any future attempts to dismantle a system of labor that white southerners had grown to depend on would be suppressed with an overwhelming use of force. Indeed, the large numbers of volunteers, militia men, artillery companies, assistance from neighboring states, troops provided by the federal government, as well as the two warships ready to engage at a moment's notice, signified that Virginia was ready for all-out war.[1]

Nat Turner's insurrection was the moment that whites always feared, and they did what they warned they would do in response. Indeed, the heightened threats of racial extermination and interminable retaliation after Turner's attempted revolution forced a re-visioning of the black community's strategies of resistance, strategies that were culturally specific to Africans in North America. The enslaved had experienced brutal and torturous reprisals before, but the retribution that they remembered after Turner's insurrection was far broader and more widespread. This created traumatic and transhistorical memories for black communities throughout the South that shaped future strategies of resistance and abolition. Turner's insurrection made plain how a war between the races would play out for both sides, not only for innocent African American men, women, and children, enslaved and free, but also for whites in the South and the North.

Gen. Nat Turner

About seventy miles from Richmond, a man named Nat Turner attended a barbeque during which he arranged with six other men—Henry Porter, Hark (or Hercules) Travis, Sam and Will Francis, Nelson Williams, and Jack Reese—to take back what they knew belonged to them in the first place: their freedom.[2] On August 21, 1831, these seven men put into action what they had been planning for months and what Nat Turner had been dreaming about for years. In the beginning, all went according to plan. Between sixty and eighty blacks joined Nat's army as it passed from one house to the next, beginning in the Cross Keys region of Southampton, Virginia. They gathered ammunition, guns, and money as they went along. At each house they enlarged the army of slaves, who, now masterless but not leaderless, readily followed orders to divide themselves into groups so that they could quickly achieve their purported goal of "killing all the white people."[3] They managed to remain united for over forty-eight hours, killing sixty-one whites before the insurrection was suppressed.[4]

Nat Turner's insurrection caused a frenzy of fear and excitement among the citizens of Virginia. Every white person, male and female, was concerned with where Nat's army planned to strike next. They wanted to know whether Nat had communicated with other slave and free communities outside of Southampton and how many insurgents (as whites called them) there actually were.[5] Ex-slave Ella Williams, who lived in Saint Petersburg, Virginia, reported that her mistress "come drivin' up in de carriage jus' screamin' to beat de ban'. 'De niggers is riz,' she yelled. 'De niggers is resurrected, an' dey's killen all de white folks.' Marsa Charlie come runnin' out wid his gun an' he say, 'where is dey?' Den she say, 'Down in Southampton County.' An he say, 'Aw I thought dey was in dis county,' and he took his gun back in de house cause Southampton County musta been hundreds miles fum us."[6]

There were rumors that large numbers of slaves were planning to participate in Turner's rebellion. Some reports stated that there might be as many as 150 slaves riding on horseback, while other reports speculated that the number was 800, with two or three white men as leaders. U.S. troops and the militia from Norfolk, Nansemond, and Princess Anne Counties were all told to search the entire Dismal Swamp region. It was believed that between two and three thousand fugitive slaves were there amongst the colonies of Maroons, who were accustomed to waging the kind of guerrilla warfare that Nat intended and who were organizing in preparation to join him in his revolution.[7]

White residents of North Carolina, whose border was less than fifteen miles from the Cross Keys region, were particularly concerned that the "banditti" were heading for their state to join those enslaved already organized to insur-rect.[8] Soon, a story circulated throughout the nation that two thousand slaves had killed all of the white residents and overtaken Raleigh. That sequence of events did not happen, but there was supposedly an insurrection plot that included the counties of Duplin, Sampson, Wayne, New Hanover, and Lenoir. The twenty-four men who were in the process of organizing it were discovered only because a free black man told the authorities of their plan. In South Carolina and Georgia, similar types of rumors generated similar hysterical responses.[9]

The Root and Consequences of Servile War

Nat Turner's organized insurrection in 1831 had serious ramifications for both enslaved and free African Americans. His war against the institution of slavery was much like other insurrectionary attempts in that the simple objective was freedom from enslavement. Yet no other servile insurrection on American soil generated as much fear and retaliatory violence as did Turner's. The reason, simply put, was that he successfully implemented his battle plan of waging unlimited warfare against a significant number of slave-owning men and their families, half of whom were women and children. Turner challenged white manhood and white supremacy at their core. Yet the number of black people who lost their lives due to the white rage that ensued curiously remains unknown.

Nat Turner's insurrection, like Denmark Vesey's insurrection and earlier insurrections in the West Indies, was motivated by visions of liberation. Turner waged war against what he believed was an ungodly institution and against those who believed in the rightness of his oppression. As Turner, a "Baptist preacher and exhorter on the plantation," purportedly confessed, he knew "by the signs in the heavens . . . I should arise and prepare myself and slay my enemies with their own weapons."[10] The abuse and suffering that marked chattel bondage motivated those who were enslaved to believe that they were right to attempt to fight for their freedom. Former slave J. H. Banks argued that if a slaveholder "takes my liberty, he endangers his own. This is the law of consequences ordained by God, and firmly incorporated into his moral system."[11] Indeed, according to family lore, Turner was "driven to desperation by the repeated whipping of his aged father, who was growing too weak to do the hard work expected of him on the plantation, and by the repeated insults to Nat Turner's aged and high spirited mother."[12] Reputed to be of "royal African blood," Turner's mother, known as "Nancy of the Nile," was abducted by slave traders in northern Africa and was sold to Benjamin Turner in 1799. She was often whipped, as she would not submit to enslavement, or what she termed "the dark days of slavery."[13] Nancy recounted to Turner and his children her remembered experiences of Africa, "of the happiness of the family in Africa, before they were captured . . . of the comfortable home along the beautiful river, of the flocks and herds, the fruits, the crops, the circle of loyal and contented friends." Thus Nancy, an "olive-complexioned" and "queenly-looking black" woman, may have laid the foundation for Nat Turner's discontent and rejection of the institution, as well as "his noble character" and "love of his people."[14]

Since slavery, as ex-slave William Thompson put it, was "cousin to hell," the boundaries protecting women and children, much as they had been in Denmark Vesey's insurrection, were intentionally erased as a strategy of war.[15] The nephew of Hark Travis related that Nat believed he had received a message from God, telling "him to start the fust war with forty men." To a man as deeply spiritual as Turner, this revelation meant that none of the enemy, even children, should remain alive, especially the child who was legally his owner: "When he [Turner] got to his mistress' house he commence to grab him missus' baby and he took hit up, slung hit back and fo'h three times. Said hit was so hard fer him to kill dis baby 'cause hit had bin so playful setting on his knee and dat chile sho did love him. So third sling he went quick 'bout hit—killing [the] baby at dis rap."[16] For Turner and his men, slaying all the whites in their path regardless of age or gender was a tactic of war that would serve a particular objective. According to the *Richmond Enquirer*, when Turner was examined by the magistrates after his capture, "he said that indiscriminate massacre was not their intention after they obtained foothold, and was resorted to in the first instance to strike terror and alarm. Women and children would afterwards have been spared, and men too who ceased to resist."[17]

Turner was not the only one with designs to free those enslaved. Not that Turner's leadership was in doubt: former Virginian slave James L. Smith identified Nat Turner as the "captain" in a war "to free his race." Yet Smith distinguished Turner as "*one* of the slaves who had quite a large army," indicating that perhaps there were others who shared Turner's aspirations.[18] And Turner's goal, according to a slave owned by plantation owner William Brodnax, was to reach the free states, where they would galvanize other blacks to return to the South to liberate the rest of "their brethren."[19]

It must have seemed to those enslaved in 1831 that Turner's strategy was their only hope. Insurrection must have seemed the only way to liberate the entire black community from a callous socioeconomic structure that sustained the economic interests of the elite few and the social interests of the masses. Enslaved Hardy Edwards, who initially thought that the British had massacred white Americans, said that it "ought to have been done long ago—that the negroes had been punished long enough."[20] As convicted slave Ben indicated, Nat Turner's insurrection was an attempt to destroy an institution, to destabilize it, in the hopes of creating something new. After hearing that the "negroes" were "killing the white people," Ben said to another slave, named Sam, "Did not I tell you there would be war?"[21]

Although the insurrection appears to have only involved slaves from Southampton, the court proceeded to call witnesses from other nearby counties to ascertain if any slaves outside the province seemed to know about Nat's plan. The court found credible the testimony of a sixteen-year-old girl who stated that she had heard the plans for insurrection discussed among her master's slaves and those of a nearby neighbor almost eighteen months before the massacre occurred. The court convicted as many as nine people on her unsupported testimony.[22] Nat Turner, however, remained at large.

By August 28 the U.S. troops and militia from various counties had arrived and restored order, whereupon a North Carolinian newspaper reporter stated, "The white people commenced the destruction of the negroes."[23] The *Richmond Enquirer* had already predicted that "these wretches will rue the day on which they broke loose upon the neighboring population, is most certain. A terrible retribution will fall upon their heads—Dearly will they pay for their madness and their misdeeds."[24] Susan Selden of Norfolk described the state of affairs in Virginia this way: "Nothing to be heard but the firing of arms . . . and nothing to be seen but uniforms & warlike looking men."[25] On September 27 John Hampton Pleasant, the senior editor of the *Constitutional Whig*, noted: "The people are naturally enough, wound up to a high pitch of rage. . . . [I]t is to be feared that a spirit of vindictive ferocity has been excited, which may be productive of farther outrage, and prove discreditable to the country. Since Monday, the insurgent negroes have committed no aggression, but have been dodging about the local swamps, in parties of three and four. They are hunted by the local militia with great implacability, and must all eventually be slain or made captive."[26] The commanding officer, F. M. Boykin, felt it necessary to publish a letter assuring the residents that it was safe for them to come home, and he lamented the sorrow that they felt. Included in this letter, however, is a reprimand: "It is with the most painful sensation, that the Commanding Officer has to [illegible] upon the conduct of any citizen . . . that any necessity should be supposed to have existed, to justify a single act of atrocity. . . . But he feels himself bound to declare, hereby announces to the troops and the citizens, that no excuse will be allowed for any similar acts of violence."[27]

But the violence against black people did not cease. The unrestrained bloodshed that the southern black community experienced after Turner's insurrection exemplifies what a race war would inevitably evolve into, proving that the verbalized threats of extermination were neither abstractions nor mere bluster. Moreover, the slaughter and terrorizing of blacks shows how destructive racialized ideas of self-defense and retaliatory violence can be when the power to define them as such lies with the state. Militia member Robert S. Parker observed, while traveling with the Murfreesboro Company, the Governor Guards, and other vigilante forces, that the "negroes are taken in . . . and executed everyday."[28] Ex-slave Allen Crawford related that when the U.S. soldiers met at the Cross Keys they built "log fires . . . and every one that was Nat's man was taken bodily by two men who catch you and hol yer bare feet to dis blazing fire 'til you tole all you know'd 'bout dis killing," even if you "don't know nothing."[29] On September 24 southerner S. B. Ebbons wrote that he met a man on a stagecoach who had witnessed blacks who were taken prisoner being tortured and generally treated in a "barbarious manner. Their noses and ears cut off, the flesh of their cheeks cut out, their jaws broken asunder and then set up as a mark to shoot at!!! If a black was found out of doors, after dark, without a pass, he would be immediately shot down."[30] Three weeks prior, the *Constitutional Whig* reported that it also had evidence that there had been a "slaughter of many blacks, without misconduct, and under circumstances of great barbarity." The newspaper had apparently interviewed one man who admitted killing between ten and fifteen people in retaliation for the massacre of whites. The *Whig* felt "compelled to offer an apology for the people of Southampton, while we deeply deplore that human nature urged them to such extremities. Let the fact not be doubted by those whom it most concerns, that another such insurrection will be the signal for the extermination of the whole black population in the quarter of the state where it occurs." In its final analysis of the Southampton insurrection, the *Whig* noted that the lessons from this event should not be forgotten. Whites needed to be ever vigilant and secure in their position of power, and blacks needed to understand that "20 armed men would put to route [*sic*] the whole negro population, and we *repeat* our persuasion, that another insurrection will be followed by putting *the whole race to the sword*."[31]

These words were no idle threat, as white former resident Mr. Robinson confirmed that "there [was] not a Virginian . . . whose mind would revolt at any cruelty, however atrocious, of which the blacks might be the object." According to Robinson, a country doctor stated that he "assumed that the blacks were not men, and that they ought all to be exterminated. 'They had declared war first,' he said, 'let them be hunted like wild beasts.'"[32] Moreover, the idea that all slave owners valued the lives of their slaves is perhaps troubled by one woman, "a pious Methodist," who said "she would willingly cast her own slaves into the street, there to be shot, provided others, who had slaves, would agree to do the same."[33] Ultimately, even though Robinson helped put down the insurrection in Southampton, he was run out of town after being severely whipped for merely stating that "blacks, as men, were entitled to their freedom, and *ought* to be emancipated."[34]

Northerners and their newspapers also expressed their concerns over the plight of black people after Turner's efforts to destroy the institution. The *Liberator* reprinted countless articles that affirmed that the violence experienced by blacks in the aftermath of Turner's rebellion was "of a more savage and blood-thirsty character, than any which have occurred in this country since its early conflicts with the savages, with the single exception of Gen. Jackson's barborous massacre of the Indians, after he had gotten them into his power, at the Horse Shoe Bend."[35] Northern ideas about black people being at serious risk fostered the belief that southerners were poised to "give over a whole race of two million of human beings to butchery and destruction."[36] It was therefore, as former Virginian Robinson believed, "necessary for the people of the non-slaveholding states to interfere and save our country from the disgrace of adding to the horrors of slavery the crime of destroying hundreds upon thousands of those who are only guilty of conspiring, as did the founders of our republic, to obtain their freedom."[37]

Black Fear and the Abridgment of Hope

We have yet to come to terms with the legacy of Nat Turner.[38] Was he a rogue killer, a revolutionary, a mass murderer, or a martyr for his people? Slave owners had the freedom to identify the terms of engagement—that Turner was waging a servile war—but we should not allow slave-owner interpretations to continue to have a monopoly on the emotional, cognitive, and spiritual meaning that such a conflict engendered. White people knew that they had the upper hand politically, socially, and economically, and the law of the land was on their side.[39] One-sided violence is "deeply terrifying," especially when experience and rumor have taught that "you do not count."[40] The "active fear" of the slave, who believed that nothing stood in the way of his or her annihilation, cannot be fully understood unless we bring to light how white threats of racial extermination after Turner's insurrection figured into the thoughts of the enslaved.[41] Black people knew what they were up against: Nat Turner's insurrection put everyone, men, women, and children, at risk, and the cost to the entire black community was untenable.

The aftermath of Turner's insurrection had serious ramifications for many

African Americans. The old ex-slave Charity Bowery testified that during the time of the "old Prophet Nat," black people could not even express religious sentiment out loud for fear that "low whites would fall upon any slaves they heard praying, or singing a hymn . . . kill[ing] them before their masters or mistresses could get to them." Religious expression apparently reminded white southerners of Turner's divine visions of freedom. In her interview with abolitionist Lydia Maria Childs, Charity lamented, "The brightest and the best was killed in Nat's time. The whites always suspect such ones."[42]

This harassment of the black community extended well beyond the region of Southampton County and Virginia. Former slave Harriet Jacobs stated that the Turner insurrection threw her town of Edenton, North Carolina, into utter chaos. According to Jacobs, poor whites in the community took advantage of the situation to inflict unrestrained violence against the community of color:

> Those who never witnessed such scenes can hardly believe what I know was inflicted at this time on innocent men, women, and children, against whom there was not the slightest ground for suspicion. Colored people and slaves who lived in remote parts of the town suffered in an especial manner. In some cases the searchers scattered powder and shot among their clothes, and then sent other parties to find them, and bring them forward as proof that they were plotting insurrection. Every where men, women, and children were whipped till the blood stood in puddles at their feet.[43]

Affirming Charity's experiences, Jacobs, as did other former slaves, remembered that it was the slaveholding class that ultimately served as protector for many blacks, as they became concerned that they were losing too much of their slave population to the violence inflicted by poor whites against blacks.[44] Mrs. Colman Freeman, a free black woman also from North Carolina, remembered, "The white people that had no slaves would have killed the colored, but their masters put them in jail to protect them from the white people" and as a way, whites believed, to protect "themselves of being killed."[45] In Norfolk, Virginia, ex-slave George Teamoh noted that a white woman helped to protect the people of color in his community. Still, he recalled the trauma he experienced: "The persecutions of 1832, when colored people of this State were slaughtered as sheep for the shambles, had brought me into serious doubt as to the existance of an omnipresent, as well as an all creating Being, still with a lingering hope mingled with despair, and a mind, floating as it were into empty space, I hoped on, in the midst of hopelessness."[46] Trauma, as defined by literary scholar Michelle Balaev, "refers to a person's emotional response to an overwhelming event that disrupts previous ideas of an individual's sense of self and the standards by which one evaluates society."[47] In their written acts of remembering, Bowery, Jacobs, and Teamoh attempted to place in the public sphere the emotional and psychological terror they experienced during the violence that ensued.

To be sure, Nat Turner's insurrection attempt was weighted with significance and held serious meaning for black people everywhere. Even as far away as Philadelphia "the intense interest depicted in the face of my mother and her colored neighbors; the guarded whisperings, the denunciation of slavery" led to intense disappointment, black abolitionist Mifflin Gibbs recalled, and "the hope defeated of a successful revolution affected my juvenile mind and stamped my soul with hatred to slavery."[48] Yet the intentional exclusion of any account of Nat Turner's rebellion also seems clear in some of the slave narratives written during the antebellum era. One marker of trauma that surrounds the aftermath of Turner's insurrection is the "conspiracy of silence," where, anthropologist Aaron Denham argues, an "explicit or unstated taboo forbids the asking about or discussion of trauma."[49]

For example, Rev. Noah Davis was born into slavery in Madison County, Virginia, and served as a house servant in Fredericksburg. In his detailed account of the months preceding, during, and after the Turner rebellion, Davis never once mentions the chaos that plagued the black and white community in Fredericksburg at the time. His frequent references to reading and carrying the New Testament versus the Bible seem deliberate, suggesting an attempt to disassociate himself perhaps from any knowledge of Old Testament theology or wars for liberation.[50] Davis's reference to the date of September 19, 1831, a time when violence against the black community was most virulent, as the point in which he became "baptized, in company with some twenty others," seems important for what it potentially says about his state of mind. Perhaps the fact that Davis made no mention of Turner, the insurrection, or the intense retribution that blacks, as well as the black church, faced indicates that despite Davis's attempts to obfuscate his anxiety about what happened, it had serious meaning for him even many years later.[51]

This explanation seems plausible, as the timing of Davis's religious conversion experience in 1831 was similar to that of Henry Box Brown's in Richmond. Brown stated that he did not know why whites suddenly began to whip, hang, and "cut down with swords" any slaves in the streets after dark. His master explained that the sudden intensity in violence was because some "slaves had plotted to kill their owners." Brown recalled, "About this time, I began to grow alarmed respecting my future welfare. . . . I thought perhaps the day of judgment was not far distant and I must prepare for that dreaded event." After "praying for about three months," Brown asked his master if he could join the Baptist Church, which he got permission to do.[52] Unlike Davis, Brown does relate how horrible the post-Turner retribution was for the black community, but even he limits the traumatic experience to only a few pages of his narrative.

Bethany Veney's narrative is another example of how the memory of Nat Turner is conspicuously absent from the memoir of a slave growing up in Virginia. Veney would have been a young adult at the time of Nat Turner's rebellion, and yet she makes no mention of it.[53] It is possible that in the western part of Virginia where she was enslaved there was not as much anxiety and violence directed toward the black community at the time. Yet Veney's silence seems odd. The evidence indicates that whites in the west were just as vested in asserting control and as full of fear of their black population as those slaveholders living in the tidewater and eastern regions. Indeed, the governor of Virginia, John Floyd, claimed that he got requests for arms from everywhere, as "the alarm of the country is great in the counties between this and the Blue Ridge Mountains."[54]

Veney, however, did reveal what it was like for free blacks living in Virginia. She observed when she was hired as a cook for blacks working on "the pike" that was under construction in the 1830s that "the [free] negroes were a rude set, as might be expected; for at that time they were the one class despised by everybody. They were despised by the master-class, because they could not subject them to their will quite in the same way as if they were slaves, and despised by the slave-class, because envied as possessing a nominal freedom, which they were denied."[55] Slaveholders particularly targeted free blacks after Turner's rebellion because they believed that blacks not in bondage unsettled those still enslaved, making white mastery insecure. Moreover, much of the discourse among elected officials after Turner's insurrection centered on how to get rid of free blacks or terrorize them into leaving Virginia. Although Veney does not mention the Turner insurrection, she does give evidence of the climate of heightened animosity that existed at the time.

The majority of slave narratives from Virginia and throughout the South that were collected during the mid-1930s as part of the New Deal Works Progress Administration (WPA) Federal Writers' Project also do not mention Nat Turner at all or claim to never have heard of him or any insurrection attempts. In many of the WPA narratives of Virginia slaves and those from other southern states, the interviewers' list of questions apparently included whether the ex-slave had ever heard of Nat Turner.[56] Too often, the answer was that the ex-slave did not "remember anything about the Nat Turner Rebellion, and never heard anything about it."[57] Some ex-slaves deliberately deflected the question by stating something like, "I don't know nobody in that rebellion" or "we never had any slave up-risings in our neighborhood."[58] One woman claimed that she "never knowed about uprisings till the Ku Klux sprung up."[59] Out of all the published extant copies of Virginia WPA narratives only four interviewees mention Nat Turner by name, and all of these accounts were given to interviewers of color.[60] It is probable that some black people in the South may not have known about Nat Turner's plans or that an insurrection took place on August 21, 1831. It is highly doubtful, however, that they did not know about or experience, in some form or other, the retaliation fed by white paranoia that occurred afterward.

Nevertheless, there was not complete silence during the antebellum era about the retribution experienced after Nat Turner's rebellion. Although Harriet Jacobs, Box Brown, and Charity Bowery stand out as exceptions to this claim, there were a few others. In a letter to Jacobs, Lydia Maria Childs told her to add more detail to her chapter on Nat Turner.[61] Jacobs, who was born a slave in Edenton, North Carolina, around 1813, complied by detailing how violent the aftermath of Nat Turner's rebellion was for her and the rest of the enslaved and free black community. She noted that in town "towards evening the turbulence increased. The soldiers, stimulated by drink, committed still greater cruelties. Shrieks and shouts continually rent the air." And although "the wrath of the slaveholders was somewhat appeased by the capture of Nat Turner," for two months black folks, particularly those who "lived out of the city . . . [suffered] the most shocking outrages . . . committed with perfect impunity. Every day for a fortnight, if I looked out, I saw horsemen with some poor panting negro tied to their saddles, and compelled by the lash to keep up with their speed." Jacobs also noted that during this time, black women were victims of rape by roving bands of white men who at night "went wherever they chose among the colored people, acting out their brutal will. Many women hid themselves in woods and swamps, to keep out of their way. If any of the husbands or fathers told of these outrages, they were tied up to the public whipping post, and cruelly scourged for telling lies about white men." Everyone was alarmed and lived in fear of the violence inflicted upon the black community Jacobs recounts, "the consternation was universal."[62]

Moses Grandy would have been forty-eight years old during what he called "the time, called the time of the Insurrection . . . when the whites said the colored people were going to rise, and shot, hanged, and otherwise destroyed many of them" in Norfolk, Virginia. Grandy stated that although he did not suffer personally he clearly was traumatized: "The soldiers were seizing all the blacks they could find. . . . I could see the jail, full of colored people, and even the whipping post, at which they were constantly enduring the lash."[63] This slave narrative also depicts how dangerous religious expression was, and Grandy, who never says Nat Turner's name, stated that

> after the insurrection which I spoke of before, they were forbidden to meet even for worship. Often they are flogged if they are found singing or praying at home. They may go to the places of worship used by whites; but they like their own meetings better. My wife's brother Issac was a colored preacher. A number of slaves went privately into a wood to hold meetings; when they were found out, they were flogged, and each was forced to tell who was there. Three were shot, two of whom were killed and the other was badly wounded. For preaching to them, Isaac was flogged, and his back pickled; when it was nearly well, he was flogged and pickled again, and so on for some months; then his back was suffered to get well and he was sold.[64]

Grandy goes on to say how slaves lived in constant fear, and, affirming Bethany Veney's assessment, he noted that "free negroes are liable to great cruelties. They have their dwellings entered, their bedding and furniture destroyed, and themselves, their wives and children beaten. . . . There is nothing which a white man may not do against a black one, if he only takes care that no other white man can give evidence against him."[65]

The facts of traumatic experiences, psychologist Pumla Gododo Madikizela argues, are often filtered through considerable concern by others over their accuracy, but in these narratives the "facts of the traumatic experience are written on the victim's body and heart and remain an indelible image of what the victim suffered." Memories of internecine violence and fears of extermination became "embedded in the emotional scars" that millions of victims of enslavement carried with them not only in the South but across the African diaspora. The black community dealt with the aftermath of Nat's insurrection as best they could, but African Americans were not able to talk or write about what happened from their perspective, to name those who were guilty of causing the trauma in their lives, which would have helped in the healing process.[66]

As a free person of color, Mrs. Colman Freeman made the decision to leave North Carolina after Nat Turner's insurrection because of the violence directed against her and her family. Freeman stated that when "they came into my mother's, and threatened us—they searched for guns and ammunition; that was the first time I was ever silenced by a white man. One of them put his pistol to my breast, and said, 'If you open your head, I'll kill you in a minute!' I had told my mother to hush, as she was inquiring what their conduct meant. We were as ignorant of the rebellion as they had been. Then I made up my mind not to remain in that country. We had to stay a while to sell our crops: but I would not go to church there any more."[67]

While enslaved in a small community in eastern Virginia, Fields Cook wrote that he "was a boy about the time of nat Turners insurrection who had better never been born than to have left such a curse upon *his* nation I say that he had better never been born."[68] By intertwining the extreme, yet divinely ordained, suffering of Job from the Bible with the aftermath of Turner's insurrection, Cook, a preacher, medical practitioner, and eventual candidate for Congress in 1869, places that ordeal within the larger context of the struggle between good and evil—between slaves and slaveholders. In the biblical story of Job, slavery is wrong, and in the end, God promises those who are faithful that he has the capacity to humble those with great physical power when he decides to.[69]

Cook marked the Turner rebellion as transformative for the black community, as the curse that black people experienced after Turner's open battle for liberation. To be sure, for Cook, the curse upon "his nation" was the curse of white persecution and chattel slavery, not a curse upon blacks as a people or a condemnation of what Turner did as sinful. And although Turner might have regretted the destruction of people of color that ensued after the insurrection, Cook suggests that Turner's divinely ordained mission dictated that the suffering of the African American community would serve a higher purpose.[70]

In Cook's account, African Americans continuously faced life-and-death struggles after Turner's insurrection. As a teenager, when Cook was put into the fields for the first time, he stated, "I had to comply with the old saying work little pig or die." Cook also described how frightened many Afro-Virginians were: "[They] could not sleep at nights for the guns and swords being stuck in our windows and doors to know who was here and what their business was and if they had a pass port and so forth and at that time a colored person was not to be seen with a book in his hand. . . . [M]any a poor fellow burned his books for fear."[71] Cook believed that "we poor colored people" did not deserve the persecution and subsequent white violence.

The enslaved community most traumatized during the aftermath of Turner's insurrection, however, was Nat Turner's family. According to Gilbert Turner, Nat Turner's son, because Turner "had fought for and demanded his freedom . . . as befitted one made in the image of God," his wife, children, and "everyone with a drop of Nat Turner's blood must be shackled and sold into the far South." Gilbert, approximately nine years old at the time, witnessed that "the fury of the master class was let loose on the helpless Negro men, women, and children alike." Particularly traumatic to Gilbert was that he saw his "black-haired and dark faced" mother, whom he called Fannie, get whipped, but "Gilbert knew that he must not cry out, and he hoped and prayed that Melissa [his two-year-old sister] would not sob, as he knew that the usual custom of slave auctioneers with colored babies, when they began to cry and become troublesome and thus interfere with the progress of the sale, was to grasp them by both heels, and to dash their brains against the lintel of a door."[72]

Gilbert's account of slave life and his description of the killing of slave babies by white slave owners are supported by and remained indelible in the minds of other people enslaved across the South. One ex-slave recounted that his uncle from Virginia told him how "they used to take a child out and sling it up against a tree and sling its brains out."[73] An anonymous slave from Culleoka, Tennessee, rebuked similar behavior of one slave master she knew by saying: "I never saw as many dead babies in my life as I did on his farm. . . . I actually saw old man F. walk through the field and, seeing a baby crying, take his stick and knock its brains out and call for the foreman to come and haul off the nasty, black rat. . . . This is one reason I believe in a hell."[74] Another slave from Mississippi said that "slavery is one of the greatest curses that ever was. . . . [K]illing babies—I have seen one with its brains dashed out against a red oak tree. Tired of carrying it, its mother being in the gang, and troubled with it, as any man would be, they put it out of the way."[75] The pervasiveness of the violence directed toward enslaved babies is in the account of ex-slave Angie Boyce from Indiana. When Angie was a baby, she and her mother were put in jail as runaways, even though they were free. An Irish woman "threatened to bash its [Angie's] brains out against the wall if it did not stop crying." Angie's mother, Margaret, stayed up all night to keep the woman from carrying out her threat to kill Angie.[76]

Other enslaved people also remembered American slave traders killing slave babies.[77] Ex-slave Parthena Rollins recalled that a young mother of a baby was up for sale, but because the trader did not want the child, he would not buy the woman. So the owner "took her away, took the baby from her, and beat it to death right before the mother's eyes, then brought the girl back for sale without the baby, and she was bought immediately."[78] Fannie Berry of Virginia recalled that when women with young babies were sold off, "as soon as dey got on de train dis ol' new master had train stopped an made dem poor gal mothers take babies off and laid dem precious things on de groun' and left dem behind to live or die."[79] Former slave L. M. Mills recounts that he knew of a woman in Glasgow, Missouri, who along with her two-month-old baby was sold away from her husband. When she was unable to keep herself from crying about being separated from her husband, Mills said the slave driver "snatched her little baby from her and threw it into a pen full of hogs. That sounds like a strange story, but I saw it."[80] Indeed, infants were often disposable to white slave owners because they were "worthless" as "productive laborers."[81] Much like what had happened to Native American children, enslaved people knew that black babies were subjected to brutal and barbaric treatment by whites well into the nineteenth century.

Gilbert's little sister was sold to slave traders out of the state of Virginia, then to a slaveholder in Alabama, and then to one in Texas, ultimately ending up returning to the area of Northampton, North Carolina, as the property of Marcus W. Smallwood. Her name had changed to Mary Eliza, and she lived in fear throughout her life, hiding her true identity as the daughter of Nat Turner out of "fear of reprisal." Yet she did tell her story to her son, formerly enslaved Dr. John Jefferson Smallwood, who would commit his entire career to combatting racism and encouraging uplift "in spite of all the atrocities that the Negro had been subjected to."[82]

Clearly, many of the enslaved did know about Turner's actions, and many no doubt revered him for what he attempted to do. Fortunately, there is evidence that Turner's legacy remained part of and was sustained by oral tradition—that Turner was indeed a folk hero. George H. Burks, a lawyer in Indiana, wrote a lecture in 1890 proclaiming that Turner was a martyr who was "hanged and murdered because he dared to speak in behalf of liberty and for no other cause was he murdered." In his speech, Burks argued in support of Fields Cook's analysis, that Turner laid the groundwork for John Brown, the Civil War, and the efforts of Abraham Lincoln, and because of this, "Nat Turner's object was successful." Finally, Burks concluded, "Nat Turner is not dead. He lives in the hearts of those who love freedom and liberty."[83]

Lucy Mae Turner learned the story of her grandfather Nat Turner, a "tall, poetic, masterful, ambitious reddish-black young slave," from her father, Gilbert Turner, who was only able to reclaim his surname after relocating to Ohio after the Civil War. "His voice still echoes in my ears, telling the story of slavery," Lucy Mae remembered, and she learned that as a young man Gilbert "thought many times of the struggles and sacrifices of his father." Gilbert knew that his father was "a leader among his people" who taught "them that slavery was intolerable, and was an institution doomed for destruction." Most importantly, Gilbert relayed to Lucy that "Nat Turner was a slave who stood for supreme, great brotherhood. Where men did not each other buy." And it was not just her father who thought this way. In her home, Lucy remembered that "exslaves would sit by the open fireplace of evenings and go through the story of slavery from Nat Turner's insurrection to the assassination of Abraham Lincoln."[84]

The memorializing of Turner as a hero is also evident in the testimony of ex-slave Daniel Goddard, who indicated that "the Nat Turner insurrection in Virginia and the Vesey uprising in Charleston was discussed often, in my presence, by my parents and friends." Goddard, who was an infant during the Civil War, recalled that most former slaves knew about Nat Turner and other acts of resistance across the black Atlantic: "I learned that revolts of slaves in Martinique, Antigua, Santiago, Caracas, and Tortuga, was known all over the South. Slaves were about as well aware of what was going on, as their masters were. However the masters made it harder for their slaves for a while."[85]

Harriet Jacobs was also inspired by the memory of Nat Turner. When Jacobs determined that she had to make her escape from slavery and the sexual advances of her young mistress's obsessed father, Dr. James Norcom, she went to the grave site of her parents: "As I passed the wreck of the old meeting house, where before Nat Turner's time, the slaves had been allowed to meet for worship, I seemed to hear my father's voice come from it, bidding me not to tarry till I reached freedom or the grave. I rushed on with renovated hopes."[86] It seems significant that for Jacobs, her father's instructions came from a godly place whose memory was tied to the revolutionary Turner.

Although only a few former slaves in the Virginia WPA narratives were willing to admit any knowledge of Turner's insurrection, some ex-slaves living outside of Virginia did recall being told about Nat Turner. Indeed, the WPA narratives of ex-slave Anna Washington from Clarendon, Arkansas, and slaves from other communities illuminate how the oral tradition of storytelling may have helped to sustain Turner's memory across the South. Washington, whose mother and father were slaves in Virginia, claimed, "I heard my pa talk about Nat Turner. He got up a rebellion of black folk back in Virginia. I heard my pa sit and tell about him." Emma Turner, from Pine Bluff, Arkansas, whose mother was born in Virginia, says she "heard her talk of the Nat Turner Rebellion but I never did see him." Rev. Frank T. Boone, a free black born in Nansemond County, Virginia, who was also living in Arkansas at the time of his interview, stated that "I have heard the 'Nat Turner Rebellion' spoken of. . . . I think the old people called it the 'Nat Turner War.'"[87]

Due to Virginia's robust participation in the internal slave trade, stories about Nat Turner and his rebellion traveled across the Deep South. And these memories, carried by those enslaved, were passed on to future generations as examples of how black people had indeed contested their condition of servitude and oppression. Cornelia Carney remembered that Turner became part of the slave vernacular—a particular way of being that African Americans clearly valued and named as culturally relevant to their own formulations of resistance and similar to the trickster, Brer Rabbit, in *Uncle Remus' Tales*: "Niggers was too smart fo' white folks to git ketched. White folks was sharp too, but not sharp enough to git by ole Nat. Nat? I don't know who he was. Ole folks used to say it all de time. De meanin' I git is dat de niggers could always out-smart de white folks. What you git fum it?"[88]

These transmissions of black history might have additionally served as lessons to the black community. Stories about rebellions like Nat Turner's would remind those enslaved of the scope of white retaliation when blacks waged wars of liberation against their oppressors: they were cautionary tales of the potential ramifications of black-white conflict in America and rationales for supporting certain strategies of uplift over others. An examination of the number of attempted insurrections throughout the South from 1832 up to the Civil War shows that the number of those enslaved who were convicted or even accused is extremely small compared to the nearly four million African Americans living in America by 1860.[89] In fact, of the twenty-five insurrections or conspiracies listed in historian Herbert Aptheker's careful study of slave rebellions between 1835 and 1860, only nine of the attempted revolts could be defined as large in scale, involving at least forty to several hundred slaves.[90] Several of the reported insurrections or conspiracies were not attempts to engage in warfare at all. In six events, all in the 1850s, the enslaved were attempting to run away en masse to some place where they could be free. Of the twenty-five attempts by blacks to rebel in the twenty-five years after Turner, only one incident was recorded in which arms were found among the enslaved.[91] Therefore, the vast majority of slaves did not attempt to insurrect after 1832, and the reason they did not can be found in the testimonies of those who understood slavery firsthand.

Former slave Lunsford Lane lets us know that in Virginia, he and his fellow slaves were "aware of our utter powerlessness" in stopping the "wrongs endured by themselves or friends." They also understood that "any attempt at resistance would bring certain and immediate destruction." Affirming that the memories of the aftermath of Nat Turner's rebellion remained indelible, Lane recalled that "we had seen the attempt fail, and we were not anxious to put our necks in the halter." Lane noted that for whites, ideas of commoditization aligned with the "calamity" of racial annihilation, and the discernment of what had happened after Nat Turner seemed to figure prominently within this former slave's psyche.[92] Slave owners made it clear that black people were mere chattel that could be worked to death, and if an insurrection was attempted, all blacks, whether they were guilty or innocent, would be killed.

Black men and women, enslaved and free, did not need any more examples of white retaliation to let them know that, ultimately, they did not matter. As one female ex-slave put it: "You know white folks would just as soon kill you as not, and you had to do what they said" if you wanted to stay alive.[93] Mom

Ryer Emmanuel was given a similar accounting of slavery by her mother: "I say, 'Ma, if dey been try to beat me, I would a jump up en bite dem.' She say, 'You would get double portion den.' Just on account of dat, ain' many of dem slavery people knockin bout here now neither, I tell you. Dat first hide dey had, white folks just took it off dem. I would rather been dead, I say . . . 'Ma, yunnah couldn' do nothing?' She say, 'No, white people had us in slavery time.'"[94]

Indeed, reliving the memory of "cruelties occasioned by this [Nat Turner's] insurrection," former Virginia slave Henry Box Brown confirmed that slaves made a calculated choice not to insurrect after 1832:

> It is strange that more insurrections do not take place among the slaves; but their masters have impressed upon their minds so forcibly the fact, that the United States Government is pledged to put them down, in case they should attempt any such movement, that they have no heart to contend against such fearful odds; and yet the slaveholder lives in constant dread of such an event . . . the fierce yells of an infuriated slave population, rushing to vengeance.
>
> There is no doubt but this would be the case, if it were not for the Northern people, who are ready, as I have been often told, to shoot us down, if we attempt to rise and obtain our freedom. I believe that if the slaves could do as they wish, they would throw off their heavy yoke immediately, by rising against their masters, but ten millions of Northern people stand with their feet on their necks, and how can they arise?[95]

Nat Turner's insurrection exposed for both sides how antebellum ideas of a race war and extermination would perhaps play out not only in the southern mind but also among those living in the North.[96]

We do not know the number of black people who lost their lives in the aftermath of Nat Turner's insurrection. Although the Auditor's Office lists only nineteen slaves executed and twenty-one slaves deported from August 21 through December 31, 1831, for the entire state of Virginia, this number cannot be an accurate accounting of the total loss of life.[97] Estimates of over one hundred have been suggested, and, based on observations of blacks who lived during the 1830s, in "one day 120 Negroes were killed."[98] These numbers only take into account the region of Southampton. The total number, which would include blacks from all the southern states, was undoubtedly much higher.

After Turner's insurrection, blacks in the North came under siege as well. Antiblack sentiment expressed in race riots predated the Nat Turner rebellion, but the number of incidents increased exponentially, from 20 incidents between 1820 and 1829 to over 115 incidents between 1830 and 1839.[99] In Providence, Rhode Island, a riot broke out in September 1831 when a mob of between seven and eight hundred whites, most of them sailors, destroyed nearly all the homes of the black community in response to rumors that blacks had insurrected in North Carolina and had taken over the city of Wilmington.[100] Black abolitionist Frederick Douglass noted that in Saint Michaels, Maryland, a mob threatened him and other blacks for establishing a Sabbath school in 1833, and "one of this pious crew told me, that as for my part, I wanted to be another Nat Turner: and if I did not look out, I should get as many balls into me, as Nat Turner did in to him." These sorts of threats appear commonplace, as Douglass also claimed that "the feeling was very bitter toward all colored people in Baltimore, about this time, (1836,) and they—free and slave—suffered all manner of insult and wrong." He recalled that when he was working on the docks in Baltimore as a ship's carpenter, the white carpenters began to "talk contemptuously and maliciously of 'the niggers;' saying, that 'they would take the country,' that 'they ought to be killed.'"[101]

In Philadelphia some white men determined that the black population within that city was dangerous and that northern free blacks must have collaborated with Turner in planning his insurrection. A proposal was put forth seeking to have the state government expel not only any newly arriving black settlers but also the existing free black population. Abolitionist James Forten and other leaders of the black community tried to defend themselves against the accusations that they had aided Turner in his rebellion, but the tide of emotion was such that no words could appease those white Philadelphians who were focused on getting rid of a people they viewed as dangerous. When the *Julius Pringle*, a ship hired by the American Colonization Society (ACS) to transport newly freed blacks from North Carolina to Liberia, stopped in Philadelphia for some repairs in 1832, an armed mob quickly gathered to repel any attempts made by the black passengers to disembark, as it was rumored that they were part of Nat's army. The ship was forced to quickly leave port and make its repairs farther down the coast at Chester.[102]

In 1833 and 1834 antiblack riots broke out in New York City, Philadelphia, and New Haven, Connecticut, affirming that some whites in the northern white community were just as opposed to the idea of black freedom as whites in the South. Black people in the North and South experienced an escalation in racial violence, making Nat Turner's war against slavery a pivotal moment for the black community and the nation long after the dust had settled in Southampton, Virginia.

Nat Turner's insurrection represented an organized attempt to dismantle a system that had become even more oppressive over time, one in which violence and the possibility of death remained fundamental tools for sustaining white mastery. In the aftermath of the insurrection, black people experienced the trauma of unspeakable persecution, which for many remained either too painful or too dangerous to fully articulate for posterity. And yet the abridgment of hope articulated above, and the curtailment in the belief in a Haitian model of liberation working in America did not mean that black Americans lost their need to be free. It suggests, rather, that the slave and free community came to see that a Haitian-style revolution was unachievable, that as a strategy, it would never result in freedom. Whites clearly sent a message that black people understood: whites would win any war of liberation that blacks might wage, even if it meant death to the entire black community. These ideas were grounded in historical precedence. Indeed, they were rearticulated in didactic fashion by the Virginia legislative body in 1832 in its attempt to assure the public that no other incident like Nat Turner's war of liberation would ever occur again.

CHAPTER FIVE

"In the Hands of the Master"
The Virginia Debates

When political theorist Alexis de Tocqueville surveyed the southern states of America in 1832, he observed a pervasive sense of "conflict between the white and the black inhabitants of the Southern States of the Union." He noted that this "danger . . . however remote it may be, is inevitable" and that it "perpetually haunts the imagination of the Americans." Tocqueville discerned that in the North, people talked incessantly about the possibility of a violent struggle, but for those in the "Southern States the subject is not discussed." While it may be true that southerners did not discuss with him what he called the "tacit forebodings of the South," they did discuss quite openly and in great detail the possibility of "open strife" with each other during that year's Virginia Debates.[1]

As a formative event in southern history, the Virginia Debates mark the point when the trope of interracial warfare obfuscated even gradual emancipation legislation and when ideas over the racial composition of America, frontier justice, and the indefinite rights to property were debated and then formalized. Despite Governor John Floyd's requests, Virginia legislators, who claimed that the debates were a "feast for the soul," used the potential of exterminatory warfare to justify why slaves should remain in bondage and to restrict the freedoms of free blacks.[2] What emerged in January and February 1832 as a solution to "this damning curse of slavery" was the triangulation of the idea that black people had three choices in America: remain enslaved, be colonized, or die in a war between the races.[3] Although southerners asserted that the enslaved were no longer a threat to white mastery, Turner's rebellion heightened white fears of black people as the enemy, and complete abolition without removal was henceforth never under consideration in Virginia.

Governor John Floyd's Case for the Necessity of Removal

Governor John Floyd pressured Virginia delegates to enact legislation for the colonization of free blacks and to gradually emancipate the enslaved because he feared that antislavery ideas circulating within and outside the state would bring about another servile war. Included with his annual message were incendiary documents that supported his belief that all blacks living in Virginia were a threat to the white community. In one instance, Floyd blamed antislavery outsiders for Nat Turner's insurrection. He also accused free blacks in Virginia of conspiring with the enslaved. Ultimately, it was the persistence of white fear of Virginia's black population that convinced Floyd of the need for the gradual abolition of slavery.[4]

Thus antiblack sentiments resonated in Governor Floyd's annual message to the legislature on December 5, 1831. He wrote at length about the necessity for a revision of state laws to ensure the subordinate status of African Americans in Virginia. He specifically asked for the allocation of funds for the removal of free blacks, since they encouraged and abetted insurrections and "seek to excite a servile war; a war, which exhausts itself in the massacre of unoffending women and children on the one side, and on the other, in sacrifice of all who have borne part in the savage undertaking."[5]

Governor Floyd believed that many whites, as evangelical participants in the early nineteenth-century revival known as the Second Great Awakening, were responsible for Turner's rebellion by their encouragement of egalitarian ideas and their promotion of the religious instruction of blacks. According to Floyd, northern preachers and laymen used Christianity to teach slaves that they had a right to be as free as whites, and this information helped motivate Turner to plan an insurrection. Although the governor allowed that their involvement might have been unintentional, southern women were also responsible for the revolt, as some women in their benevolence had taught "negroes to read and write" as an act of piety. Governor Floyd was also concerned with the activities of nonreligious types, "Yankee peddlers and traders" who taught slaves that they were equal and therefore encouraged insubordination.[6] In reality, beginning in the eighteenth century, black people themselves insisted that literacy be part of their conversion to Christianity and spiritual education. Over time, African Americans became more independent religiously, and Virginia became a breeding ground for black leadership.[7] Floyd was convinced that "every black preacher in the whole country east of the Blue Ridge" knew about Nat's plans.[8]

It was literacy, Floyd warned, that enabled black preachers to read to their congregations the inflammatory pamphlets of "Walker, Garrison, and Knapp of Boston." Black church leaders then circulated these "incendiary publications," which inspired the "fanatical preacher" Nat Turner.[9] Indeed, the writings of black abolitionist David Walker fostered intense concern among whites when the Virginia House of Delegates was informed in January 1830 that thirty copies of *Walker's Appeal* had been intercepted en route to Thomas Lewis, a free black living in Richmond. The delegates confiscated a letter Walker sent to Lewis instructing him to disseminate the pamphlets "to those who can *pay for them*,—and if there are any who, Cannot pay for a *Book* Give them *Books* for nothing."[10] The Virginia legislature discussed the letter and the content of Walker's message behind closed doors. Surprisingly, other than the recovery of all but ten of the pamphlets, nothing was done to counteract his invocation.[11] Worried about the barrage of antislavery material written by Walker, Garrison, and his coeditor, Isaac Knapp, the Virginia legislature banned whites from teaching blacks to read and write and forbade blacks to gather for educational purposes five months before Turner went to war, on April 7, 1831.[12] It was not until after Turner's rebellion, however, that Floyd became convinced that "the plans as published by those Northern presses were adopted and acted upon by them."[13] The writings of Walker must have been particularly disconcerting to whites, as Walker had proclaimed, "We must and shall be free I say, in spite of you. . . . And wo, wo will be to you if we have to obtain our freedom by fighting."[14]

Floyd, having carefully preserved *Walker's Appeal* in his papers, no doubt read his message of revolution.[15] Walker predicted that although things did not start out that way, the evolution of the slavery system had predetermined that things would end violently: "God will show the whites what we are yet. I say, from the beginning, I do not think that we were natural enemies to each other. But the whites have made us so wretched, by subjecting us to slavery, and having murdered so many millions of us in order to make us work for them . . . that there can be nothing in our hearts but death alone for them." Yet Walker cautioned the black community, particularly the enslaved community, to "read the history particularly of Hayti, and see how they were butchered by the whites, and do you take warning."[16]

In Walker's view, frontier justice and the law of self-preservation applied to African Americans as well. He instructed those enslaved to embrace these principles, outlined by whites to justify colonization and enslavement, in their fight to become free. But "if you commence, make sure work—do not trifle, for they will not trifle with you—they want us for their slaves, and think nothing of murdering us in order to subject us to that wretched condition—therefore, if there is an *attempt* made by us, kill or be killed . . . and believe this, that it is no more harm for you to kill a man, who is trying to kill you, than it is for you to take a drink of water when thirsty." In prophecy, Walker advised them that "the person God shall give you, give him your support and let him go his length, and behold him in the salvation of your God. God will indeed, deliver you through him from your deplorable and wretched condition. . . . I charge you this day before my God to lay no obstacle in his way, but let him go."[17]

Floyd was particularly angry with the editor of the *Liberator* and founder of the American Anti-Slavery Society, William Lloyd Garrison, who Floyd believed wrote "with the express intention of inciting the slaves and free negroes in this and other States to rebellion and to murder the men, women and children of those states." In the aftermath of Turner's insurrection, Floyd warned that if the invasion into their "ultra states rights" by men from other states did not cease, repercussions would be severe, for "the law of nature will not permit men to have their families butchered before their eyes by their slaves and not seek by force to punish those who plan and encourage them to perpetrate these deeds."[18]

Floyd's opinions about the negative impact of northern antislavery influences on slaves like Nat Turner were supported by information he acquired about black abolitionists from a traveler to Philadelphia. In his letter to the governor, John Patton quoted for several pages the minutes from the first annual black abolitionist convention held in Philadelphia in June 1831. Although Patton only looked at the convention minutes briefly, he was able to identify in his letter black participants from ten participating states. He specifically noted that white participants, including Garrison, Benjamin Lundy, and Arthur Tappan, were in attendance. Although the convention's "great object . . . is not distinctly stated—but so 'shadowed forth' as to make its darkness visible," Patton felt sure that this meeting was against the interests of the southern states. The convention of free blacks, including one delegate from Virginia, resolved that the Constitution sustained their rights to full citizenship, and they mandated the reiteration of this information at every gathering. The Fourth of July was to be set aside for fasting and prayer in order to affirm the idea that one day the "almighty God" would "intervene on our behalf—that the shackles of slavery may be broken—and our sacred rights obtained." Patton beseeched the governor to share this information with the legislators, who he knew were presently in session discussing the issue of gradual emancipation and slavery.[19]

Floyd no doubt believed that the information he received about black abolitionists confirmed they were conspiring to disrupt slavery in the South. Patton attested to the fact that "it had been for sometime known in Virginia that there had been during the last summer a convention of the Free negroes of the United States, by delegates—who assembled at Philadelphia. But so far as I am informed, the character and the objects of that assembly have not been known in our state." The idea that a group of free blacks was asserting the right of all blacks to be free "throughout the United States" clearly concerned Virginians. Evidence linking two free blacks from Fredericksburg as elected officers of the convention did nothing to calm white fears about future trouble. One of these men was supposedly "the same individual to whom—a seditious and insurrectionary letter which was picked up in the market place at Fredericksburg—during the last summer or fall was directed."[20]

Particularly worrisome to Floyd must have been a letter written by a former Virginian slave living in Boston who claimed that the enslaved population would continue to rebel and kill whites even after Nat Turner was apprehended and executed. A black man named Nero sent a letter to Jerusalem in Southampton County, Virginia, which was then forwarded to Governor Floyd in the fall of 1831, claiming that there would soon be another slave insurrection. The letter, merely addressed to "sir," foretold of a vast conspiracy of northern blacks leading southern slaves "to avenge the wrongs and abuses the Slaves have received in the United States." According to Nero, these northern blacks had "no expectation of conquering the whites of the South States"; their purpose was purely "revenge for the indignities and abuses received." They would then make their escape as the "Non-Slaveholding States . . . and Haiti offers an asylum for those who survive the approaching carnage." Nero assured Floyd that they had established accomplices from the free states who were willing to support those who were "willing to hazard their lives in defence of our common rights." The members of this secret organization purportedly "pledged ourselves in a goblet made of the skull of a slaveholder." Moreover, the writer of this letter did not believe slaveholders' threats of "exterminating the black population," for "you are to[o] inert to do without them." Nero taunted them to go ahead: "We defy you; do your best—we ask no favors—spare neither age nor sex, for we assure you that we shall not—that you shall destroy every vestage of a slave is what we desire."[21]

On the intended apocryphal "day of carnage" there would be a "promiscuous slaughter of [white] women and children." Nero claimed they had recruited men who "can perform deeds of death and destruction that would have made a Cortes or Pizarro relent, a Red Jacket sympathize, or a Tecumseh weep. Would to Heaven, we could enlist the Indians of Georgia in our common cause—and we are not without hopes that we shall." The possibility of enlisting Native Americans in the liberation of those enslaved would have hit a nerve. Southerners like Governor Floyd were well aware of the fighting potential of another perceived enemy that the South had yet to conquer. Moreover, to Floyd, Nero's letter affirmed that slave unrest was generated by outside influences, especially since Nero implicated many northern African Americans when he claimed, "There are people in Boston, N. York, Philadelphia and Hartford who know more of the circumstances of the late insurrection than any Slave holder in Virginia or North Carolina."[22]

Although dismissive of the ultimate results of the actions of this secret organization of northern blacks, Nero nevertheless laid out in clear terms an idea that many African Americans would not have supported when he claimed: "We prefer to see every person of colour headless, and their 'heads on poles' if you please than to see them servants to a debauched and effe/min/ate race of whites. O my blood boils when I think of the indignities we have suffered, and I long for the scene of retribution; and at that day let there be no more whining about cruelty and above all let there be no sympathy expressed for the 'poor deluded blacks' who may fall in your battle." Nero asserted that members of his group represented the slave and free populations, "three hundred thousand men" who vowed that death was desirable over slavery. The evidence left by those formerly enslaved and free, however, suggests otherwise.[23] Of course, what Nero described did not occur. Nor does there appear to be any indication that the enslaved were intent on dying for the cause of revenge and retribution. And perhaps northern blacks had their hands full fending off antiblack sentiment and the race riots occurring in their own communities.

Finally, it was white fear and the continued demand for arms from across the state that made Floyd fixate on the gradual abolition of slavery. Floyd wrote in his diary, "The alarm of the country is great in the counties between this [Southampton] and the Blue Ridge Mountains. I am daily sending them a portion of arms though I know there is no danger as the slaves were never more humble and subdued."[24] The governor hoped that after viewing the evidence he presented of how antislavery fanaticism had infiltrated their state, the legislators would vote gradual emancipation into law. Floyd envisioned forced migration, meaning that in due time all blacks would be removed from Virginia. His plan was to "drive from this state all free negroes and to substitute the surplus revenue in our Treasury annually for slaves, to work for a time upon our Rail Roads etc etc and these sent out of the country . . . as the first step to emancipation." He did not think that slavery was immoral but rather that slave labor was an impediment to the growth and economic development of Virginia.[25] His conceptualization of Virginia as a free "white" society, however, was not new. Floyd was following a theoretical vision that had begun to coalesce in the days of the early Republic.[26] Floyd never publicly announced his support for gradual emancipation; rather, he championed it privately in his diary and to those in the House of Delegates who were in his inner circle.[27]

The Dangers of Emancipation and Servile War

For white Virginians, Nat Turner's revolt was so significant that it initiated a profusion of petitions to end slavery through gradual emancipation, as well as calls for greater restrictions on the lives of slaves and free blacks. The speaker of the House of Delegates established a select committee to review the gradual emancipation petitions, many of which asked for the "removal of a race irreconcilably antagonistic to ours."[28] A serious discussion then occurred within the House over what legislative action Virginia should take. Should the state follow the path of the northern states and abolish slavery gradually, or should Virginia remain part of an economic system that had made many men wealthy and powerful? Many legislators agreed with Governor Floyd and those petitioners who believed that gradual emancipation was necessary, but they also believed that the large black population in Virginia was dangerous, making a war between the races inevitable. Others, while rejecting emancipation because it infringed on their rights to their property, saw gradual emancipation as especially dangerous. They feared it would only inspire the desire for immediate emancipation among those still enslaved and thus another servile war like Nat Turner's and ultimately black extermination. Slave owners claimed that "the very breath" of those enslaved "is in the hands of the master," yet at the same time all agreed that the "feeling of security [was] gone forever, destroyed."[29]

Immediately after Floyd's message was delivered to the House of Delegates, Speaker of the House William O. Goode of Mecklenburg selected a committee to consider proposals relating to "insurrectionary movements." These proposals were then taken up by the legislative delegates in what would become known as the Virginia Debates.[30] Of the thirteen members appointed to the Select Committee on the Coloured Population, the conservatives, who were from the eastern quarter of Virginia, constituted 76 percent of the voting strength. Goode appointed William Henry Brodnax of Dinwiddie as chair of the select committee.[31] Although the division amongst the legislators appears wide, those who genuinely feared the potential for slave rebellion and those who feared losing their property were united about the danger that slavery posed to the white community.[32] Where they differed was in whether the solution to that danger would be colonization, enslavement, or extermination.[33]

Petitions that requested that slaves be immediately emancipated *postnati* and then colonized so as to restore their rights and, most importantly, to secure the "peace, prosperity, and happiness" of white Virginians provoked fierce debates between factions.[34] Goode, as well as Charles S. Carter of the northern Tidewater region, asserted that the duties of the select committee did not extend to discussing the issue of emancipation. The committee should focus only on the issue of free blacks and their removal from the state of Virginia.[35] Chairman Brodnax, who was a moderate and a colonizationist, disagreed. He argued that slavery was part of the larger question that they needed to address, since the job of the committee was to respond to those Virginians who now lived in constant fear that another insurrection might occur at any time. After much discussion, the debate over slavery began in earnest among members of the entire House.[36]

Committee and House delegates who supported gradual emancipation argued that slavery had an ill effect on the population of the states where it existed and that slavery was a dangerous institution that needed to be eliminated from Virginia. House member Moore believed that slavery was responsible for the decline in population growth in Virginia among whites, while the black population steadily increased. In order to check this gain, Moore stated, there must be an "immense emigration" of blacks "from it" through gradual abolition, for "the time has come, when emigration [to Virginia] must be confined almost exclusively to the white population."[37]

For many delegates, what really made slavery a threat to Virginia society was the "overflowing black population" that would inevitably lead to violence and war between the races.[38] Those members from the western section of Virginia who advocated gradual abolition did not want any of the black population currently residing in the eastern part of Virginia to be sold or forced into their region.[39] They feared that if slavery did spread throughout Virginia, it would "become more unmanageable—we do not wish it to extend beyond the convenient reach of legislative remedy—we do not wish it to overspread that part of your State . . . rendering its eradication, in any other mode than that of the sword, utterly and forever hopeless."[40]

Even legislators who opposed emancipation had some questions about the future safety of the institution. Conservative delegate Robert Powell of Spotsylvania believed that something had to be done to address the evil of slavery and the growing population of African Americans. For him, reiterating the concerns of gradual abolitionists, it was an issue of "self-preservation" and the fact that the slaves, in his calculations, would outnumber the whites ten to one. Indeed, Powell believed that the struggle for freedom manifested in Southampton would become "a common occurrence, and the historic muse of Virginia, be fated to weep, often to weep over similar catastrophes. Sir, whatever the results of the convulsive struggles may be, whether they eventuate in the attainment of their object, by this ill fated people, or whether, as to me there seems little doubt, they result in their utter extermination, at the point of the bayonet; in either event, their history will be written in characters of blood."[41]

Virginia legislators were not the only ones worried that the large numbers of African slaves in America might lead to a race war. The increase in the black population in North America due to the expansion of slavery farther south troubled many whites across the nation. From 1790 to 1830 the number of enslaved in America grew by 188 percent. The number of slaves increased from 697,624 to 2,009,043, while the white population increased 232 percent, from 3,172,006 to 10,537,378. Of particular concern was the fact that during this same period, the number of freed African Americans rose by 437 percent, from 59,557 to 319,599. Although nationally the number of white Americans increased by a substantial number in forty years, for a country that viewed itself as Anglo-European in origin and culture, the increasing number of people of African descent was problematic. In Virginia, where the white population increased by only 57 percent, compared to the 60 percent increase of the enslaved population and the whopping 268 percent increase in the number of free blacks from 1790 to 1830, demographic trends deepened Anglo-American fears of servile insurrections or, worse yet, a war of extermination between the races.[42]

Thus, at the center of the issue facing the House of Delegates about whether to maintain blacks in slavery or emancipate them was the question of just how dangerous the slaves were to the white community and the plausibility of a servile war. Gradual abolitionist Samuel M'D. Moore of Rockbridge reflected: "What must be the ultimate consequences of retaining them among us. To my mind, the answer to this enquiry must be both obvious and appalling. It is, sir, that the time will come, and at no distant day, when we shall be involved in all the horrors of a servile war, which will not end until both sides have suffered much; until the land shall every where be red with blood and until the slaves or the whites are totally exterminated." Moore had no doubts that the enslaved would continue to fight for their freedom, and he knew what type of warfare would be waged: "From what we know of human nature generally, and from what we hear of the spirit manifested by both parties in the late Southampton rebellion, it is very evident that such a war must be one of extermination, happen when it will."[43] Many Virginia legislators feared that "a Nat Turner might be in every family, that the same bloody deed could be acted over at any time and in any place, that the materials for it [slaves] were spread through the land and always ready for a like explosion." It was because they considered blacks as an "alien element in . . . our civil society" that Virginians held the "suspicion" that slaves were "extremely fanatical, and therefore always dangerous," a view that was "eternally attached to the slave himself."[44]

They were dangerous, delegate James M'Dowell argued, because slaves by nature loved freedom, because they were men who understood the world around them: "Take the slave in his general relation to ourselves, and you cannot regard him otherwise than as man,—having the capacities and resentments of man, both indeed repressed but both existing." In M'Dowell's view, "the love of liberty come[s] to us with life. . . . [Y]ou may . . . debase and crush him [the slave] as a rational being . . . and the idea that he was born free will survive it all." Indeed, the "idea [expressed during the debate] that the slave . . . can be so attached to his master and his servitude as to be indifferent to freedom . . . is wholly unnatural."[45]

The idea that "a death struggle must come between the two classes in which one or the other will be extinguished forever" was something delegate Henry Berry of Jefferson agreed was inevitable. In Berry's view, however, Virginians had nothing to worry about, because he felt confident that "we have the power to crush any such effort [insurrection] at a blow. I know that any such effort on their [the slaves'] part, at this day, will end in the annihilation of all concerned in it; and I believe our greatest security now, is in their knowledge of these things—in their knowledge of their own weakness." The problem, Berry stated in agreement with M'Dowell, was that no matter how many laws were enacted and no matter how ignorant whites attempted to keep those enslaved, the idea of freedom was all around them.[46]

A few plans for the emancipation of the slaves were brought forward despite eastern conservatives' attempts to block all discussion of the subject. When Representative Charles James Faulkner asked that the select committee present a resolution of gradual emancipation to the House, he knew it would have little effect on his own livelihood. Faulkner, who was from a northwestern county bordering Maryland, was the owner of one slave. The gradual emancipation proposal that Faulkner suggested to the committee was that slave owners would have the right to compensation for their existing slaves, but they would forfeit the potential for future profits from their slave's increase. Easterners immediately tabled the proposal.[47]

Thomas Jefferson Randolph, the grandson of Thomas Jefferson, offered a counterproposal to Faulkner's for gradual emancipation *postnati* and recommended that Congress look to Virginia voters to decide if they supported his plan. Randolph was not concerned, however, that his plan for emancipation did not mean freedom for blacks in Virginia. In Randolph's plan, the state would mandate that slaves born after 1840 would be free, whereupon after slave males turned twenty-one and females eighteen, they would work for the Commonwealth of Virginia to pay their passage to Africa or some other place outside of the United States. Slave owners would receive compensation for their existing slaves from the state, or they could sell them in the Deep South slave markets. Thus, they would forfeit the part of their property rights contained in the potential for their slaves to reproduce and increase naturally. All slaves born before 1840 who remained in Virginia would remain enslaved for twenty-eight years from the time at which the legislature passed the act emancipating them. Colonization would cost the taxpayer nothing, as the slaves would work off their own passage over the course of their remaining time in bondage. Those slaveholders who chose to sell their property out of state could of course keep the entire profits made from their sale, which solved the problem posed by those looking for or needing full compensation for their slaves.[48] The introduction of this proposal inspired a serious and eventually heated debate over property rights. Members of the House of Delegates were especially concerned that Randolph insisted that any legislative act for emancipation be put before their constituents for approval.[49]

Most legislators rejected Randolph's proposal of gradual emancipation because they viewed it as an invasion upon their lawful rights to their private property. They believed that Randolph's proposal was unconstitutional, and they argued that any emancipation plan had to overcome the difficult question of how the state could legislate over slave owners' exclusive right to own or sell their slaves. Since the state of Virginia had no authority to exercise eminent domain in the expropriation of slaves without the consent of the planter class, allowing the people of Virginia to vote on a plan for gradual emancipation was unconstitutional. *Postnati* emancipation directly challenged the conservative planters' Lockean notions of absolute rights to their property ensured by the Fifth Amendment of the Constitution. Moreover, Congressman Bruce argued, the increase of the slaves as property had always been "recognized by the civil law, and runs through all our statutes, from the earliest period of our colonial existence." This right to "children born of slaves" had first been defined by common law, and if the children of female slaves after 1840 became the property of the state, "it must be at once acknowledged, that they are either persons or property, for there is no third class to which they can be assigned; not being property, then, they must be persons." They would not be persons, however, Bruce stated, because now the state would own what plantation owners called their property as defined by the Constitution, as well as their increase until they could be removed to a foreign country. The Randolph proposal was therefore egregious and oppressive, Bruce declared.[50]

At the heart of their argument regarding property rights was Virginia's deep investment in the internal African slave trade.[51] As early as the seventeenth century, Virginia was the dominant provider of slaves to the other southern states. By the 1830s, and after the closing of the Atlantic African slave trade in 1808, the demand for more slaves in the Deep South made the commoditization, the trade in enslaved black people, lucrative for Virginian slave owners and the merchant class. Improvements in infrastructure, the building of railroads and canals, and the usage of slaves for these works and in factories revived even greater interest in slave labor within eastern Virginia. The high demand for male slaves, who were a scarce resource, according to one planter, made the prices for a single slave jump 25 percent: from $400 to $500 by 1832. By 1837 the price had risen to $1,100 for a prime field hand. If the prices of slaves continued to rise, as they did, and if there was a shortage of the preferred male slaves from ages twelve to eighteen, as there was, then it is no wonder that slaveholders were overanxious to protect what appeared to them a flourishing market.[52]

Other congressmen, however, noted that the species of property that legislators claimed in slaves was troubled by how slaves came "into this country," since they were not acquired, as John Locke defined, by "a lawful Conqueror and a Captive." Slaves in America were acquired "by strategies of war, and the strong arm of the conqueror: they were vanquished in battle, sold by the victorious party to the slave-trader who brought them to our shores." Congressman John Chandler challenged the method by which "ancient authors" claimed one could become a slave by asking, "If warriors had no absolute right to the person of his captive, may there not be SOME DOUBT whether the Virginia planter has an unqualified one[?] . . . The truth is, that our ancestors had no title to this property in the first place."[53]

Not able to come to any consensus on the issue of property rights, the House also resisted calls for gradual emancipation because some members believed it would actually inspire revolution amongst the slaves. Speaker of the House William Goode wanted to make the legislature's position on the subject of emancipation clear to the press and the community as quickly as possible. He therefore argued that the question of emancipation should be eliminated from consideration.[54] The state had no money to compensate slave owners, nor did the state have money to pay for their removal, so why waste time talking about something that could not happen? Goode was particularly concerned with the fact that open discussion might encourage slaves to assert their rights to be free and therefore further endanger whites: "They would naturally reason, if a few desperadoes in Southampton, by a few murders, produced such a sensation and such a disposition, what may not be achieved by numbers and combination?"[55] Slaves, Goode warned, were not as they had been portrayed, an "ignorant herd of Africans" who had no interest in the outcome of this discussion. They were an "active, intelligent class, watching and weighing every movement of the Legislature with perfect knowledge of its bearing and effect." If the committee continued this discussion, Goode asserted, it would be a signal to the slaves that Nat Turner's actions had inspired Congress to enact laws to emancipate them. It would strengthen their belief that by creating havoc and "fear" they could advance their own freedom.[56]

Many legislators agreed that the discussions they were conducting could have dangerous ramifications, but they predicted a disastrous outcome for the black community: "If *one insurrection* has been sufficient to secure the liberty of *succeeding* generations, might it not be inferred that *another* would achieve the freedom of the present? I know, Sir, that such an inference would be delusive. I know that the result of any insurrection in Virginia for centuries to come, must be, the extermination of its perpetrators; and often repented, the total destruction and annihilation of the slave population." The gradual emancipation scheme would precipitate a race war, and because of the envisioned outcome, it would financially ruin the majority of the slaveholding class, legislator James H. Gholson argued, and "uncalculated millions" would be lost.[57]

Outlining a scope of retribution that was not theoretical but rather reflected what had already been and continued to be enacted against African Americans after Turner's insurrection, most legislators agreed with Congressman Thomas Marshall: "No plan of general insurrection could be carried into successful operation" because of the scope of retaliation and because of the "dread of punishment prompt, awful, and universal; involving alike the innocent and guilty in its sweeping and sanguinary course." Marshall had to admit, however, that the possibility of a servile insurrection was unsettling, for "all men are affected by dangers which are unseen, but known to exist." Indeed, the "minds of men are commonly most disturbed by dangers which do not appear."[58]

William Brodnax, a general in the Dinwiddie County militia who helped put down the Turner insurrection, however, vowed that should blacks attempt "a few more Southamptons, . . . whites with moral, intellectual, and scientific advantages would annihilate the whole race."[59] Blacks could never "exchange conditions with us." Moreover, Brodnax argued, the possibility of a "negro legislature" envisioned by Congressman Rives was ridiculous: "So far from overwhelming the whites, conquering the country, overturning our political dynasty, and usurping the seats of legislation, *the very act of their imbodying, would be the immediate signal for their annihilation.*" There was not "a human being in the region," Brodnax argued, who did not believe that "it will be the *blacks* themselves, and not the whites who must fall in such a struggle."[60]

In order to avoid such a cataclysmic event, Brodnax, an avid supporter of the American Colonization Society, offered a compromise proposal that was essentially a replica of the ACS model. Brodnax proposed first the systematic colonization of Virginia's free blacks and then, eventually, its slaves through voluntary emancipation. Through the efforts of the ACS, a thirty-two-cent tax levied on each white resident, and the annual revenue of $275,000 a year from the sale of public lands, approximately six thousand freed blacks could be relocated in Africa each year. The ACS had a long history in Virginia, and many believed that Brodnax's moderate proposal was the answer they were looking for. It also refocused their attention toward Governor Floyd's previous assertions three weeks earlier of the necessity of removing free blacks.

Colonization as the Final Solution

The colonization proposals made by the Virginia legislature for the removal of black Virginians in 1832 reflected a long history of inherited ideas about the disposability of black bodies in America.[61] Although some scholars tend to view colonization as a humanitarian endeavor, in this case, coercion through vigilante violence was the method of enforcement that the legislature discussed at length and then executed through extralegal means.[62] Colonization was the process by which both the threat of premature death and the removal to Liberia, an African state specifically founded to serve as a homeland for freed slaves, became reality for African Americans, enslaved and free. The seriousness of these ideas is affirmed by free black Theodore Wright, who remarked that "immediately after the insurrection in Virginia, under Nat Turner, we saw colonization spreading all over the land; and it was popular to say the people of color must be removed. The press came out against us, and we trembled . . . we despaired. . . . [T]hat was a dark and gloomy period."[63]

Across the nation, many whites viewed colonization as the solution to the danger of blacks living in America and a war between the races, and they had done so for at least three decades.[64] Perhaps one of the most active champions of colonization in the nineteenth century was the Presbyterian minister Robert Finley from Basking Ridge, New Jersey. Finley was largely responsible for the influential gathering of prominent men who responded to calls from across America for something to be done with what many believed was a dangerous population living in their midst. To address what liberal elites termed "the negro problem,"[65] the ACS was founded in Washington, D.C., on December 21, 1816.[66] Although others before him made similar statements regarding the colonization of free blacks, Finley's assumptions were widely accepted: "Everything connected with their condition, including their color, is against them; nor is there much prospect that their state can ever be greatly ameliorated."[67] The cofounders and signers of the ACS constitution in 1816 included many notable Virginians. One signer was congressional representative John Randolph of Roanoke Plantation in Charlotte County. Randolph, a descendant of one of the oldest families in Virginia, was known as one of the greatest orators for the proslavery South. John Taylor of Caroline County, Virginia, a political writer and politician in the U.S. Congress for many years, also signed the ACS constitution. So did George Washington's nephew Bushrod Washington of Westmoreland County, who became the ACS's first president.

Contained in Finley's widely read pamphlet, *Thoughts on the Colonization of Free Blacks*, were ideas of racial strife that the ACS founding members used to formulate their initiative to rid the country of its black population. In this document, Finley laid out why blacks and whites needed to be separated and why it was best that blacks be removed from the American continent. His reasoning was simple. First, the presence of black people demoralized whites and made them lazy. Second, racism among whites was "too deep rooted to be eradicated." Third, blacks felt and acted, and therefore remained, inferior in their own minds, even when they were free, because they were reminded of their past servitude while they lived amongst their former masters. Slavery would never end, Finley believed, as long as so many whites believed it "to be unsafe to encourage the idea of emancipation," and colonization provided the answer for those who wearily searched for how to put an end to "all this [slavery]."[68]

Finley's pamphlet also made clear that the resettlement of enslaved and free blacks within U.S. territory was a bad idea because of his certainty that it would lead to a war between the races. He saw in "an independent settlement of people who were once our slaves" that "there might be cause of dread, lest they should occasionally combine with our Indian neighbors, or with European nations who have settlements adjacent to our own, and we should have them for our enemies." Moreover, the close proximity of a free colony of blacks would encourage slaves to run away and "escape to a land where their own race was sovereign and independent." Word would spread about the free territory and would make those who remained in slavery "uneasy in their servitude." If, however, blacks were removed to Africa, Finley argued, "we should have nothing to fear from their becoming our enemies. Removed far from our sight, our contempt of them, produced by their situation, and by long habit confirmed, would gradually die away."[69]

Finley was also concerned that blacks be removed so that racial amalgamation would not occur, which would inspire the demand for social equality and thus conflict between the races. "It can scarcely be doubted that slavery has an injurious effect on the morals and habits of a country where it exists," Finley argued. "Could they be removed to some situation where they might live alone, society would be saved many a pang which now is felt, and must in course of time be much more sensibly felt from the intermixture of the different colours."[70] Many Anglo-Americans envisioned that if blacks were emancipated and not removed, the inevitable intermixing of the races would lead to a race war and the extermination of African Americans.[71] Thus, the logic ran, thwarting the possibility of racial amalgamation and the growth of a multiracial America was an act of benevolence central to the issue of and the necessity for developing a plan for the removal of black people.[72]

When committee chair Brodnax proposed colonization, he shared the ACS's views of the necessity of blacks' removal and the impossibility of blacks ever gaining full citizenship in America. Even though the Virginia legislature recognized that the enslaved were no longer African, "this [America] is their home—their birth-place."[73] Nevertheless, Brodnax argued that in Virginia they would remain a "distinct and degraded caste" and would never be truly free. The "middle ground" of colonization was a more productive position than that of either the conservatives or the abolitionists. Brodnax believed that, under Randolph's proposal, plantation owners would be inclined to sell their slaves rather than liberate them.[74] Under Brodnax's plan (which took up the assumptions that Thomas Jefferson laid out in 1787),[75] white labor would become available to replace black labor so that "the vacuum produced by the withdrawal of portions of our colored population, would soon be filled again by emigrants of our own color, from other quarters of the world."[76] Yet Brodnax also knew that the colony of Liberia was too underdeveloped to accommodate the six thousand slaves annually that he suggested would relieve Virginia of its entire population of free blacks in ten years.[77]

Other members of the committee and House of Delegates who supported colonization echoed Finley's fears of interracial sex. Congressman Moore argued that since the slaves were incapable of being virtuous and moral in their condition, the "demoralizing influence of the indiscriminate intercourse of the sexes among our slave population" corrupts the entire society of Virginia. The dangers and "dissolute habits of a large number of our citizens, especially of the very poorest class, is too notorious to be denied, and the cause [slaves] of it is too obvious to be disputed."[78] For Moore and other legislators who supported gradual emancipation, this dangerous disruption of racial boundaries between poor whites and blacks made it an imperative that blacks, when freed, be removed from the state of Virginia.

Southern abolitionist Charles Faulkner, however, challenged Brodnax's colonization plan because it "deals too much in contradictions, and seeks too fancifully to reconcile impossibilities." It would not resolve the issue of ensuring who would win in a war between the races. Many in the Virginia House of Delegates, Faulkner stated, believe that "something must be done," and if something was not done, they "concede that one race or the other must be exterminated." Note that "the gentleman from Campbell, (Mr. Rives)," Faulkner posited, believes that "the throats of all the white people will be cut—No, says the gentleman from Dinwiddie [Brodnax]—'The whites cannot be conquered—the throats of the *blacks* will be cut.'" If this was the case, Faulkner declared, the "supreme law of society" demanded more than Mr. Brodnax's plan of postponement to halt the growth of slavery and its "further march to the west."[79] It demanded that whites "relieve the country of their [slaves'] presence as promptly and efficiently as . . . our resources will permit. We stand in a relation towards them, not as absolute masters, but of fiduciaries." Indeed, "if this immense negro population were now in arms—gathering into black and formidable masses of attack—would that man be listened to, who spoke of property? . . . I think I am then borne out . . . that we should be justified *now* in removing this class of our population." For if extermination was to be the result of an ensuing race war, Faulkner asked, what would the colonization of first free blacks and then afterward the gradual emancipation of those enslaved do to prevent it?[80]

Archibald Bryce Jr., who also supported gradual emancipation, suggested that the delegates look to the Brodnax proposition of colonization as a "first step" toward the rectification of the dangerous possibility of a servile war. Bryce believed the question of removing slaves would have to wait until there was more public consensus about it. The colonization of free blacks would demonstrate to the world that Virginia intended to end slavery. When the state was able to tackle the challenge of removing so large a population of undesirable inhabitants, some legislative body in the future would do so.[81] This proposal was so similar to that of Brodnax that they were combined to form the Brodnax-Bryce compromise. Discussions regarding emancipation opened up anew, only this time the discourse became angry and heated. Abolitionists like Mr. Marshall of Fauquier also called for the immediate abolition of slavery and asserted that slaves would no longer be dangerous if they were removed.[82] Still, the Brodnax-Bryce proposal passed narrowly and was attached to the committee report, which stated that emancipation was possible through colonization and that although the issue of slavery was unresolved, it remained open for legislation.[83]

Ultimately, colonization conflated two of the possible outcomes discussed over the course of the debates: removal and death. When the committee met again on February 7, 1832, their agenda was to "discuss the bill for the removal of Free persons of Colour from this Commonwealth" and the means by which that could occur.[84] Which blacks were willing to go to Liberia, which slave owners were manumitting their slaves for the purpose of removal, and whether free blacks could be made to leave Virginia by compulsory means were all questions that remained unanswered. For Brodnax, who continued as chair of the select committee, the pressing question was whether the "legislature would or would not adopt a coercive plan" to remove free blacks, because "no gentleman, who forms a component of this committee . . . can believe that the free negroes of Virginia are, in truth, willing to be removed from the United States." Furthermore, Brodnax asked, "Who has not observed the proceedings of the great meeting of free negroes last summer in Baltimore, and that they are not only utterly opposed to emigration themselves, but are making exertions to dissuade all others of the same class, throughout our country?"[85] More than likely, because compulsion was something that the ACS had always categorically denied was part of its philosophy and because of the suspicions of the black community, Brodnax "wished the name of the Colonization Society might be forgotten until this legislation had got through its action on the question."[86]

Brodnax concluded that since he knew of no free blacks who were willing to go, "sooner or later the free negroes will be *forced* to leave the state."[87] Other members thought that they could use "moral" force, harnessed through severe laws that restricted blacks' "existing privileges" and the will of the white community through lynch clubs and similar types of vigilante organizations to "induce their removal." A few members thought that there were some blacks willing to go voluntarily, and their willingness would allow for the "responsibility of coercion to fall upon the shoulders of others." Brodnax did not agree: "Depend on it, force must be resorted to in some way."[88] According to formerly enslaved Virginian Moses Grandy, Brodnax was correct. He believed that free blacks did not want to go to Africa: "America is their home: if their forefathers lived in Africa, they themselves know nothing of that country." The problem, as Grandy saw it, was that "none but free coloured people are taken there: if they would take slaves, they might have plenty of colonists. Slaves will go any where for freedom."[89]

Central to the delegates' argument for colonization was that there was nothing to protect the black community from violence and "adoption of a compulsory principle" because Virginia laws did not protect the rights of blacks. According to Brodnax, "Free negroes have many *legal* rights and privileges in Virginia, but no *constitutional* ones—they are not citizens, or members of the body politic." Disregarding Brodnax's lengthy assertions on the morality of being "frank, and magnanimous, to . . . declare to all these people what it is you really intend in the first instance," the Virginia House formally rejected ideas of colonizing free blacks through coercion.[90] It adopted instead Congressman John C. Campbell's plan for the voluntary colonization of free blacks and manumitted slaves. Eventually, the Senate indefinitely postponed the House plan for colonization, as members could not agree on who should finance the removal of blacks from Virginia.[91]

Yet the ACS, despite the inability of Virginians to legislate on the issue of colonization, still had the largest shipment of black emigrants ever assembled in 1832. And Virginia was the biggest exporter, apparently undeterred by Liberia's known inability to sustain so many new settlers. Although in previous shipments the number of free blacks departing for Africa through the ACS had been small, in 1832 the number of free blacks emigrating out of the South dwarfed the number of emancipated slaves.[92] This push for expatriation occurred despite the fact that mortality rates in Liberia were extremely high, reaching almost 50 percent from 1820 to 1843, and white and black Americans knew this.[93] And when Joseph Mechlin, the colonial agent in Monrovia, warned that malaria and the rainy season currently made preparation for large numbers of new settlers impossible, the ACS went forward anyway and commissioned three shipments of black emigrants after Turner's rebellion in 1831 and 1832. Out of almost 350 people, 291 were free African Americans who left Virginia aboard the *James Perkins* in December 1831, and another 171 blacks from Virginia left on the *Jupiter* in May 1832. In July of that same year, 39 emigrants left from Virginia and Washington, D.C., and 89 North Carolinians left for Liberia on the brig *American*.[94] Ultimately, white Virginians cared little about whether blacks survived in Africa or not. According to Mechlin's carefully kept records, of the 1,449 emigrants who arrived in Liberia between 1831 and 1833 looking for freedom from oppression, 21 percent of them died from malaria alone.[95]

The spectacle of extralegal violence, murder, and harassment after the Southampton affair continued to generate candidates for emigration, and this, William Brodnax stated, allowed those who claimed to object to physical coercion to remain blameless:

Many of those [blacks] who have already been sent off, went with *their avowed consent*, but under the influence of a more decided compulsion. . . . I will not express, in its full extent the idea I entertain of what has been done, or what enormities will be perpetrated to induce this class of persons to leave the state. Who does not know that when a free negro, by crime or otherwise, has rendered himself obnoxious to the neighborhood, how easy it is for a party to visit him one night, take him from his bed and family, and apply to him the gentle admonition of a severe flagellation, to induce him to *consent* to go away. . . . [T]he gentleman from Southampton will put me right, that of the large cargo of emigrants lately transported from that county to Liberia, all of whom *professed* to be *willing* to go, most of them were rendered so, by such severe ministrations as those I have described.[96]

Indeed, acts of violence against the black community were rife after Nat Turner's insurrection. And the shipload of free blacks coerced into leaving Southampton for Liberia were aboard the *James Perkins*, which was filled beyond legal capacity.[97]

Blacks who continued to reside in Virginia after the Virginia Debates experienced the severity of legislative action intended to protect the white community from any future servile wars.[98] For example, African Americans were no longer able to preach at religious meetings or meet at night for such purposes unless in the company of their slave owner or mistress. Ex-slave James Lindsay Smith remembered that "when Nat Turner's insurrection broke out, the colored people were forbidden to hold meetings among themselves." These restrictions were put into place, Smith stated, so that blacks could not plot "some scheme to raise an insurrection among the people."[99] In the final analysis, the legislature did nothing to loosen the chains of bondage for those enslaved in Virginia. Rather, it seems that the rhetoric of the Virginia Debates functioned more as a rationale for the greater violence and oppression waged against all people of color, slave and free. Proslavery ideology was well served by these discussions, and one example of how this event was canonized in the antebellum era can be found in the writings of Thomas Dew.

Thomas Dew, a professor at the College of William and Mary in Virginia, was asked by Governor Floyd to present what was described as a scholarly view of both sides of the issue.[100] Dew questioned whether "two distinct races of people now living together as master and servant, [could] be ever separated" so that the latter would have "rights, to an equalization with the whites." With little ambivalence, Dew declared that they could not. Reaffirming the inevitable outcome of the debate, he stated that "every plan of emancipation and deportation which we can possibly conceive, is totally impractical."[101]

Dew revisited old ideas about war and slavery to explain why the institution was not only lawful but also necessary. He argued that slavery saved Africans from African extermination and made wars on the continent of Africa more mild. Dew took on African precepts of justice in arguing that as a "commutation of the punishment of death," slavery served a positive good. Dismissing those who questioned slave owners' rights to those held in bondage, Dew used the definition of just wars cited by Dutch jurist Hugo Grotius, which allowed that "the law of nature permits prisoners of war to be killed, so the same law has introduced the right of making them slaves."[102] In the instance of Nat

Turner, his actions were not virtuous and were informed by "the passion of re-venge," as this, Dew argued, was what savages do, unlike Europeans: "When polished nations have obtained the glory of victory, or have acquired an addi-tion of territory, they may terminate a war with honor. But savages are not sat-isfied, until they extirpate the community which is the object of their hatred. They fight not to conquer, but destroy. The desire of vengeance is the first and almost the only principle, which a savage instills in the minds of his children." The remedy for these savage wartime practices, Dew contended, was slavery. Slavery was the element that changed the "nature of the savage" as it facilitated the "taming of man," making blacks "fit for labor" and Western civilization. The slave "generally loves the master and his family," and because "blacks are as much civilized as they are in the United States," the white population had little to fear of another insurrection like Nat Turner's ever accomplishing "such fell deeds" as the wholesale "murder of men, women, and children." Dew op-timistically predicted that even in the next century, in 1929, and based on the latest census, whites would retain control of and power over the black race and be even "much more secure from plots and insurrections."[103]

Indeed, in Dew's opinion, the mistake that America had made with Native Americans was that whites should have enslaved all Indians to save them from extermination:

A great number of Indians within the limits of the United States would have been saved, had we rigidly persevered in enslaving them, than by our pres-ent policy. . . . They have rapidly disappeared, as the pale faces have advanced. Their numbers have dwindled to insignificance. . . . The President of the United States [Andrew Jackson] now tells you, that their removal further to the West is necessary. . . . [T]o remove them is all we can now do for them. . . . Our popu-lation will again, and at no distant day, press upon their borders—their game will be destroyed—intoxicating beverages will be furnished to them—they will engage in wars, and their total extermination will be the inevitable conse-quence. The *handwriting* has indeed appeared on the *wall*. The mysterious de-cree of Providence has gone forth against the red man—his destiny is fixed, and final destruction is his inevitable fate.[104]

Dew's linkage of the plight of Native Americans with his assessment of the future of black people in America is telling. As he further concludes, "Slavery, we assert again, seems to be the only means that we know of, under Heaven, by which the ferocity of the savage can be conquered . . . by which, in fine, his nature can be changed."[105] Indeed, Dew's positing that African Americans and Native Americans were essentially savages incontrovertibly places both groups at risk for annihilation. It also further validates the apprehensions that black people had about whites not using force to resettle them in Africa.[106] Laying out the historical model for how Americans dealt with those whose warlike ability predisposed them to elimination, Dew's message was clear: the freedom given to Native Americans was a disastrous mistake, and if Virginia chose to emancipate its African American slaves, that freedom would ultimately lead to their extermination.

Anxiety about internecine warfare and the inability of white southerners to accept the existence of a large free black population shaped the dialectic over emancipation in the Virginia Debates in 1832. Colonization, as the only solution to getting rid of all the free blacks in the state, was complicated by the fact that black Virginians did not want to go to Africa. The issue of how to control a large population of enslaved and free blacks was resolved by ideas of force and violence and by loud assertions of a potential war between the races. Yet, although many Virginia delegates claimed that any challenge to slavery would result in a war of extermination, one that they were determined that blacks would lose, they never intended for any such escalation to occur, because a prolonged servile war would not have sustained slavery—it would have ended it. Unfortunately, the fear that permeated the white community was left with no redress, and the backlash, the vigilante violence that ensued after Nat Turner's rebellion, attempted to compensate for that. Indeed, the Virginia Debates functioned as a tool to let black Virginians know that their lives were in jeopardy as individuals and as a community. For as the committee chair, William Brodnax stated, the "negroes know very well what is going on. Will they not see your debates?"[107] Thus, despite Turner's war for freedom, things got worse for those blacks enslaved and free in the South. Even more troublesome was the fact that instead of trending toward abandoning the institution as the Founding Fathers predicted, many slaveholders sought to expand it. Nearly two decades later, southerners debated whether to supply the expansion of slavery with newly imported African slaves by reviving the African slave trade.

CHAPTER SIX

Would Have to "See His Blood Flow"
Reopening the African Slave Trade

The quest to reopen the African slave trade caused vigorous debate among proslavery southerners in the 1850s. Some politicians were concerned that the reestablishment of the trade would create sectional tensions, perhaps even disunion. The states on the border of the slave South argued that the effects of an increase in the slave population would negatively influence the price for goods and slaves. The need for more labor and the perceived erosion of political power, however, inspired several southern men to call for the repeal of federal laws that prohibited them from purchasing slaves directly from Africa. Their argument was that since the nation upheld slavery morally and politically and recognized it socially as a domestic institution, legislation restricting the African slave trade was improper. What was the difference, they asked, between buying slaves in America versus buying them from Africa, Cuba, or Brazil?

Despite these assertions, many white southerners believed that the importation of slaves directly from Africa, rather than through other markets, would result in black and white violence and, inevitably, black or white extermination. Even though they remained unsure about their American-born slaves, white southerners nevertheless argued that new Africans would disrupt the institutional practices of paternalism and the master-Sambo relationship that they claimed existed.[1] What the discussions over reopening the foreign slave trade reveal is that the idea of a war between the races was very much in play in the decades before the Civil War commenced, and these visions of violence would remain central to proslavery and antiblack ideology. These debates were also of great concern to African Americans, and they deliberately taunted Anglo-Americans by encouraging white fear of a race war.[2] Thus, Anglo-American fears of the enslaved and newly imported African slaves must be added to the list of factors for why the foreign slave trade movement ultimately failed.

The Pro–Slave Trade Perspective

Those who supported reopening the African slave trade understood that in reality the slave trade had never ended. Practically every European nation was searching for a cheap, exploitable, and disposable labor force, and the foreign African slave trade continued to fulfill that need throughout the antebellum era and beyond.[3] Southerners, well aware of the reemergence of an international trend that championed the exploitation of Africans and other peoples of color for their labor, believed that reopening the slave trade would be good for Africans and, with proper oversight, good for the nation. The brutality and cruelty and the substantive increase in African mortality from the illegal business of acquiring Africans for slaves encouraged southerners like Virginian George Fitzhugh to reason that "if it be right to prohibit the slave trade, it must be wrong to increase it, and aggravate its cruelties . . . worse, still . . . to multiply its horrors."[4]

In light of the protracted participation of and fantastic wealth made by nations around the world from the continued commerce in African slaves, some southern men were serious about the viability of reopening the foreign slave trade in America.[5] Former Alabama congressman William Yancey argued: "If it is right to raise slaves for sale, is it not right to import them? . . . If it is right to buy slaves in Virginia and carry them to New Orleans, why is it not right to buy them in Cuba, Brazil, or Africa and carry them there? . . . If it is not wrong to hold slaves, and to buy them and sell them, it is right in morals, and under the Constitution which guarantees the institution, that we should buy them in whatever place we may choose to select." Yancey concluded by questioning why anyone would want to pay $1,500 for a slave when he could purchase him for $600 in Cuba or go to Africa and pay $60.[6]

Some southerners felt sure that they had support for reopening the foreign slave trade in the North because it would be especially good for those involved in the manufacturing and mercantile industries.[7] Virginian George Fitzhugh understood that white northerners also benefited from the cotton produced from slave labor in the South. Slaves provided the factors of production that drove the New England economy, which in turn supplied the markets of the world. The slave trade would also benefit northern white wage laborers. Recent reports about the conditions in Africa and Europe indicated that people were "starving for want of food, employment, and a market." The rising demand for products made from slave labor would increase production and reduce prices. Increased production would occur through the employment of white laborers, who would then benefit from cheaper manufactured goods. Fitzhugh went on to say, "But were the slave trade renewed, there is no doubt that the North would on the whole reap much the larger share of advantages and profit. This trade would render the Union indissoluble."[8]

An age-old idea that continued to have currency among white southerners for or against the trade was that slavery actually benefited African people as well. No one could dispute that in Africa "slavery is the common condition of that country," South Carolinian lawyer and newspaper editor Leonidas Spratt and others harangued, and "to the captive of the savage there are no alternatives but death or slavery." From his perspective, slavery and the reopening of the slave trade "save[d] to life and usefulness" the African from "the barbarities of savage warfare."[9] Proslavery South Carolinian Edward Bryan stated that indeed the slave trade elevated the African, which justified whatever cruelties existed. Of course, cruelty "abounds in every human institution," but those opposed to the importation of new Africans, Bryan argued, should reflect on the fact that there had been less cruelty in the slave trade before its legal abolition. Bryan believed the inhumanity of the Middle Passage could simply be alleviated with care. In any case, the harshness of the current trafficking in African slaves "should not condemn uses, they rather should be reformed by a good regulation of the uses" of slave labor.[10] The faulty reasoning of Spratt and Bryan and the sophistry of George Fitzhugh that northern abolitionist William Seward and his cohorts should consider "whether this memorable, universal, and time-honored trade, be not an operation enjoined and demanded by the higher law" were deceptive arguments used by many southerners.[11]

Nevertheless, it was no secret that those involved in the illegal slave trade inflicted the most inhumane and barbarous cruelties upon their African captives. Slave traders, concerned with getting as many Africans on board ship as they possibly could, anticipated that roughly one-third of their cargo would die as they crossed the Atlantic and another one-third would die after arrival.[12] Unlike the days before abolition, where the mortality rate was approximately 14 percent, traders packed their ships with Africans, sometimes with as many as 750 in a vessel only one hundred feet long. Captives would have to sleep in spoon-like fashion, and the ships reeked with the stench and filth of death and disease.[13] The slaves, who were mostly male and now, in large part, children between the ages of ten and fifteen, arrived dazed and emaciated. They were dehydrated to the point that, according to Dr. Jose E. Cliffe, an American citizen who participated in the African slave trade, they appeared to be mere skin and bone, with "eyes like boiled eye of a fish." Two other English women witnessed nearly the same atrocities on a captured slaver in Kingston, Jamaica.[14] When reaching deck to disembark "they all rushed, like maniacs for water, as if they grew rabid at the sight of it."[15] Another informant noted in 1829 that generally slaves were unable to stand up straight after being confined in a space that for adults averaged five feet, six inches long, sixteen inches across, and two feet high during the long voyage across the ocean. Children, it was believed, withstood the torturous journey better than adults, and traders especially favored boys between the ages of eight and twelve.[16] Their smaller stature enabled more bodies to be committed to the ever-diminishing space allowed.[17] Yet these children, with their stomachs distended from starvation, suffered as much as adults, which the nearly 150 percent mortality rate—from seizure to Middle Passage to landing—indicates. As John Leighton Wilson estimated, in order for slaveholders to have 100,000 African slaves available for purchase, slave traders needed to start with 250,000 captives.[18]

At times, the enslaved were deliberately killed during this illegal period of the transatlantic slave trade. It was not uncommon for slaves to be cast overboard if slavers thought that their law-breaking activity had been detected. They sometimes threw away as many as five hundred at one time, whereupon, as a commander of a British cruiser observed, sharks, which Herman Melville called the "invariable outriders of all slave-ships," proceeded to eat the still "shackled negroes."[19] If the Africans were believed to be too sick to survive reaching the "fattening pens," many of them were cast overboard. Traders did so in order to avoid the ten-dollar import duty that the Brazilian government, for example, charged ships for entering and landing slaves at its ports.[20] At a slave depot called Gallineos, two thousand slaves were reportedly murdered because English cruisers blocked the ability of African traders to get them aboard the awaiting slave ships. Finding "it impossible to embark them," they "beheaded the whole number, placing their heads on poles stuck in the beach saying—'If you will not allow us to make profit of prisoners we take in war, we will kill all.'"[21]

Nor was it unusual for large numbers of Africans to die on recaptured vessels. According to the "Sierra Leone Report," issued by a committee in 1830 at the behest of the House of Commons in London, one-sixth to one-half of all the captives on board slave ships taken by cruisers of any nation died before ever landing due to the additional five weeks that it took for them to reach Sierra Leone in West Africa.[22] In these "floating pest-houses," the death toll skyrocketed. Over 13.4 percent, or 6,700 of 50,000, African captives died on their way to Sierra Leone by 1830. In the case of the recaptured Portuguese vessel *Progresso*, 39 percent of those on board ship died before landing in Cape Town, South Africa, in 1843.[23] The large number of deaths led some observers to believe that from a "humane point of view" the recaptured African was "infinitely worse off than if permitted to pursue his original destination."[24]

The statistics above, however, do not take into account the starvation and often reenslavement that recaptured Africans experienced once returned to their "homeland." In American naval officer Robert Schufeldt's opinion, as benevolent as the intentions of the American Colonization Society might have been, landing recaptured Africans in Liberia often meant either certain death or reenslavement.[25] Unfortunately, the recaptured slaves generally belonged to various tribes that differed in language and custom and with whom they might have been enemies. From Rev. Pascoe G. Hill's perspective, "the capture" of a slave ship was "an event far more disastrous to the slave than to the slave dealer," as it was an "unintentional aggravator of their miseries."[26]

Violence, or what abolitionist Sir Thomas Buxton called the "whole sale murder" of Africans, reached its highest level when the enslaved attempted insurrections. According to the deposition of one crewmember aboard the American vessel *Kentucky*, an attempted slave rebellion resulted in forty-six men and one woman out of five hundred slaves suffering gross mutilation. They were hung high in the air by their necks and then shot, after which "the legs of about a dozen were chopped off" to save the loss of the irons around their ankles. When some of "the feet fell on deck," great "sport" was made. The woman was shot and thrown overboard still alive, whereby she "was seen to struggle some time." After this, twenty more men and six women were severely flogged. All of the women died, and the men, suffering the rest of the passage, would "groan and sob with the most intense agony," the skin "where they were flogged, putrified."[27] Thus, the illegal continuation of the African slave trade facilitated the death of hundreds of thousands of Africans, making a mockery of the much-celebrated laws to end the trade by the Revolutionary generation in 1808. Southerners used these facts to support their paternalist argument that legalizing the African slave trade would save African lives and reduce the brutality that currently existed because it operated without formal regulation.

The revival of the slave trade, some southerners argued, would also serve as an instrument for positive good by enabling the expansion of slavery and by protecting black Americans from a race war and extermination. A Dr. Van Evne wrote in 1853 on what he described as "the mighty negro question," the "greatest question of modern times." He concluded that the expansion of slavery was essential to the survival of the southern way of life and that the enslavement of Africans was "a normal or natural condition, and it must therefore always exist so long as the white and black races are in contact." The "Negro," as "a drug in the labor market," had always been a necessity until blacks had to compete with white immigrants. The superiority of white labor benefited the North and those regions where black labor was unprofitable, yet the South provided the necessary safety valve for blacks in America. The extension of slavery ensured the well-being of blacks because of virulent racial prejudice in "free" society. If slavery was not able to expand, the pressures of survival would lead whites to destroy black populations wherever limited opportunities for their employment existed. The British writers and northerners who argued that slavery was an evil did not understand that freedom, because of "the physical necessities, the absolute overwhelming pressure of hunger," would "impel them [blacks] to crime, robbery, insurrections, to violence and blood." Freedom, in Van Evrie's view, was "certain to end in [their] complete and total destruction. There can be, or there need be no doubt or uncertainty on this point. . . . [T]he cry of no more slave States, or no more extension of slavery is tantamount to no more room of the blacks, and *death to the negro.*" Van Evrie concluded, "The deluded fanatic, when . . . opposing slavery extension, is not only warring against the higher law, but doing all he can to exterminate the very race that he professes to labor for."[28] Leonidas Spratt affirmed these sentiments in his proposal for reopening the foreign slave trade at the Southern Convention in Vicksburg, Tennessee. He claimed that if the South failed in asserting its power and the socioeconomic order of its section, and "if we bend . . . to the requisitions of another people . . . [then] with subjugation comes a war of races, hand to hand, that will not end while a remnant of the weaker race remains."[29]

Many white southerners believed that Britain's real intent was to cause a servile war in the country's relentless push to end the foreign slave trade. In southerners' view, Britain's efforts to enforce the laws against slave trading were contorted by a larger vision to end slavery in America. Abolition was a "well-conceived scheme of self-aggrandizement" to create "the same failure in Brazil, Cuba and the U.S. and the reduction in productive capacity" as currently existed in England. By creating a trade equilibrium among competing nations, England would be able to regain its market share of the world's commercial trade that it held before emancipating its own slaves. Accordingly, Governor James H. Adams of South Carolina reasoned that England's secret intention was "to sow further dissensions between the Northern and Southern sections of the Union, with the hope of dissolving their compact under circumstances calculated to ensure a series of civil and servile wars."[30]

Southerners remained certain that if emancipation did occur in America as it had in the British Commonwealth in 1832, it would be a disaster leading to black annihilation. Blacks would return to "savageism and negroism." The "abolition of slavery and the total extinction of the negro, is the same thing in fact," Van Evne argued.[31] Slaveholder James Henry Hammond of South Carolina had already formalized these ideas in 1845. Historicizing the mechanisms in place that ensured control over the African race, Hammond prognosticated: "Let the story of our British ancestors and the aborigines of this country tell the sequel. Far more rapid . . . would be the catastrophe. . . . [T]he African race would be exterminated or reduced again to slavery."[32] An article in the *Staunton Vindicator* confirms that these ideas remained salient by proffering that emancipation would be disastrous because it would undermine the sociopolitical function that African labor provided: "If African labor is evil, the North and the civilized world have extracted an immense and incalculable good out of it. This may be said not only of the whites, but of the blacks also. . . . Emancipation is not only the destruction of African labor, but the extermination of the Negroes themselves."[33] The idea of freedom for black Americans was equally troubling to southerner W. W. Wright, who argued that if abolitionists incited an insurrection, it would end in the "bloodshed and probable extermination" of those enslaved.[34] Slavery and the African slave trade stymied both international and national aggression; but without the economic benefits derived from this form of labor, people of African descent would become valueless to the nation and therefore inexorably dispensable.

Pro–slave trade advocates had clear ideas about how to maintain control over an enlarged slave population, however, and they dismissed concerns that reopening the slave trade would dangerously affect white people in the South. Southerners had no intention of allowing the black population in the South to increase disproportionately, nor did they believe those who argued that if more Africans were brought to America, "our institutions will therefore languish, and a contest of some sort [would] spring up between . . . [Africans] and the white race."[35] Instead, Leonidas Spratt envisioned that slaves would extend beyond the present boundaries of the South into "the whole broad plain from the Mississippi to the Pacific. Nor even without this, do we see the reason to dread a density of population. Slaves can be as dense as freemen; the discipline will be greater; the order will be greater; the economy of resources will be greater."[36] Unlike the colonies of Britain and France, where absentee ownership of plantations still prevailed, African Americans lived alongside their masters, a situation that most Europeans and northern Americans eschewed. Spratt, like most southerners, however, believed that "while so unequal, there is no reason why these races may not come together . . . unless it can be inferred that the stronger was intended to exterminate the weaker, as it has crushed out the Indian on this continent."[37] Mississippian Henry Hughes, in taking up this question, argued: "The African slave trade can, by no possibility realize in the South an over powering disproportion of blacks to whites."[38] Hughes also envisioned a racial hierarchy that would regulate the expansion and racial composition of those enslaved:

> If the African slave trade shall be reopened, all Mexico, all Central and South America may be reckoned as wild land. Nor is that all; they may be esteemed not only uncultivated but unpeopled lands. For their population is either pure blood or mixed. But if mixed blood, extinction by degeneration or sagacious and benevolent extermination for the purity of races is a certainty and perhaps an ethnical duty. But if pure blood, they are either Caucasians, Africans, or Indians. As to Caucasians, there are virtually none. As to Africans, they will be elevated into slavery to prevent, amongst other atrocities, that of sexual amalgamation. And as to pure blooded Indians, they will not be civilized, and therefore must, directly or indirectly, be benignly slaughtered.[39]

In the debates about reopening the slave trade, some southerners ultimately counseled patience, since "the whole civilized world was discussing the question" of how to exploit African labor in new ways.[40] According to Wright, who did not support reopening the African slave trade, Europeans made claims of African wage labor being superior to slave labor, but often wage labor only escaped the responsibility and name of slavery. Indeed, civilized nations, Wright observed, "are exterminating the human race . . . in most cases literally kidnapping or purchasing those whom they transport as free. In the case of the African negro emigrants this is now universally acknowledged."[41] While the American South was able to increase its slave population ten to one, all the other nations around the world were "destroying the lives of negroes, Coolies, Chinese, and Portuguese with frightful rapidity."[42] Thus, at the Southern Convention in Montgomery, Alabama, Mr. Preston of Virginia proffered that perhaps it was impolitic for southerners to create divisions among themselves when "England and France were endeavoring to establish systems of labor like our own, differing only in name[.] Let us rather wait."[43] Southerners knew that England was making apprentices out of Africans seized from slave ships, and this fact was proof to some of them that the slave trade needed to be "renewed legally and actively." According to Wright, England imported to its colonies 14,784 immigrants from Africa between 1848 and 1855.[44] The accounts of Rev. Hill verify that it was Britain's "authorized practice to apprentice negroes brought to the Cape in prizes [recaptured slave ships], as servants or farm-labourers, for the term of six or seven years, according to their age."[45] In light of this practice, Roger Pryor of the Virginia House of Delegates argued, the South should be strategic in taking up this question, as "England with her coolies, and France with her apprentices . . . [show] gradual amelioration in sentiment upon this subject. We should bide our time, and not, by this public action, give our institution an irretrievable recoil. . . . Allow things to go along smoothly."[46] From the African American perspective, southerners were right to feel confident, as in their view, "the proposition to reopen the African slave trade [was] daily growing in popularity in the South," while at the same time northern and southern "opposition . . . [was] becoming feebler every day."[47]

White Fear and the Law of Might

Southern opposition to the slave trade movement resonated not only with fears of a growing African and African American population but also with the same anxiety about slave rebellions that had plagued whites in the past. Slave owners argued that although they had complete mastery over their American slaves, newly imported Africans would resist enslavement and therefore disrupt the slave South, making violence again necessary. Some southerners believed that increasing the numbers of African slaves would make their states more susceptible to northern abolitionist interference. Nevertheless, whether advocating for or against reopening the foreign slave trade, many slave owners confidently concluded that they could control inferior people with superior force, or if compelled, they would get rid of them entirely. African Americans were presciently aware of the seriousness of the debates over whether to reopen the foreign slave trade, no doubt because the ideas of a race war and black extermination permeated the discourse. Black leaders also understood that many whites feared a violent confrontation between the races. African Americans used what Frederick Douglass claimed became part of a broader strategy for black liberation, namely, scare tactics: "Now the next best thing, if we cannot make them love us, is to make them fear us."[48] Thus, to heighten white fear of servile unrest, many African Americans wrote and published predictions that violence would indeed ensue with the importation of more African slaves, as the greater numbers of people of African descent would facilitate a successful servile war. They also intentionally stoked white fears in the hopes of protecting Africans within Africa from becoming the victims of an increased trade in African slaves.

Many white southerners were against reopening the African slave trade because they feared American blacks and African slaves would wage a servile war against them. To bring in new Africans, "a teeming population of barbarians," Henry Washington Hilliard of Alabama believed, would make the South the slave market of the world, and a disproportionate number of Africans to whites could only lead to cataclysmic events like those in "St. Domingo and Hayti."[49] Moreover, an enlarged population of African slaves, Roger Pryor argued at the Southern Convention in Montgomery, Alabama, would make slave owners become cruel: "It would create a new grade of slavery and create in the slaves we already have a feeling of superiority that we should avoid."[50] The South would be overrun by savages "who have yet to learn that treachery and bloodshed are wrong" when directed toward their masters. Similarly, legislator James Johnston Pettigrew of North Carolina stated that if the South were to "reopen this floodgate of impurity . . . all that we have accomplished in a half century would be lost . . . and a new night would descend; the very ignorance by which they would be incapacitated for a grand scheme, would urge them to outrages . . . for an unknown tongue would afford convenient means of concealment."[51] Slaveholders had not forgotten that African slaves came with a military past, and they were not keen on perpetuating the cycle of bloodshed and fear that marked the colonial period.

That was not to say that the domestic slave population was ignorant of their strength, Pettigrew argued, but that they had been educated to fear white power. The black slave saw in the white sheriff "not an individual man, not the leader of an armed posse, but the representative of the latent force of a whole society."[52] Mississippian Walter Brookes and others at the Southern Convention in Vicksburg, Mississippi, agreed with Pettigrew that the present population of slaves had attained a certain level of education, that "spirit-of-obedience which rendered them so peculiarly fitted for a state of slavery." However, if the slave trade were to be reopened, Brookes argued, "the condition of the slaves would be put back two hundred years, and the condition of white men would be put back too. Every semblance of humanity would have to be blotted out from the statute-books, and the slaveholder . . . [would become] a bloody, brutal, and trembling tyrant." Brookes also believed that if the price of slaves were to become nominal, as envisioned, planters would find it "profitable to work their slaves to death, because they could replace them by others."[53]

Some southerners opposed reopening the slave trade because they knew that it would not be easy to impress their brutal system of control upon Africans who were accustomed to personal freedom. The African, Pettigrew argued, "whose ancestors have delighted his youth with tales of war and resistance to control, [who grew] up with this sentiment strong in his breast," would not easily accept white mastery.[54] The presence of these Africans would force the institution of slavery into a backward trend of "visible exhibitions of power," because Africans would never peaceably submit to the commands of their owners. Violence would become necessary: the African would have to "see his blood flow" before the South would be secure again from insurrection and a race war. From "a mere military point of view," Pettigrew argued, it would be a serious mistake to reopen the slave trade.[55]

Although slaveholders were concerned about the influence of African military traditions, they acknowledged that they remained fearful of American blacks as well. According to one columnist in the *Franklin Repository*, the real danger that "fire-eaters," or extremist proslavery politicians, ignored was the complete Africanization of the southern states if the tables should be turned: "Is it not astonishing that the simpletons who urge so strongly the propriety of repealing the laws of Congress which pronounce the Slave-trade piracy, cannot see that they are preparing for themselves the most horrible doom imaginable? The slave-holders of the South are now almost afraid to go to bed without a revolver under their pillows for fear their darkeys will rise in the night and inflict retaliatory vengeance upon their self constituted owners—their unfeeling task-masters. Then why do they insist upon increasing the danger?" The article goes on to say that "the only way that slavery is upheld now, or ever was, is by brute force—the law of might," exposing that the paternalistic vision of peace and tranquility between master and slave, of patriarch and "Sambo," was never more than an illusion.[56]

Slave-owning men understood that newly imported Africans could become a problem to the South, but clearly blacks in America *remained* a problem to whites' security despite the rhetoric. Virginia slaveholder Edmund Ruffin acknowledged that northern abolitionists, especially those like John Brown, martyred at Harpers Ferry, Virginia, in 1859, had effectively reached the slave masses, causing discontent; and Ruffin admitted, "Negro slaves probably would generally rebel, and free themselves and seize on their masters' property, if perfectly assured of success." Ruffin was adamant, however, that a successful insurrection could never happen again, and even if it were initially successful in execution, like Nat Turner's rebellion, it would be suppressed quickly. From "a military aspect," Ruffin said, "nothing could be more fruitless, feeble or contemptible than a negro insurrection, even with all the aid . . . by northern philanthropy. These general truths are recognized by every southerner. Yet, when an alarm of insurrection comes, with all the usual uncertainty, every head of a family at once thinks of the possibility of the near vicinity of the outbreak, and of all that are precious to him being the victims."[57] Southern whites remained haunted by the possibilities of slave unrest. Validating what Thomas Jefferson acknowledged in 1787, they wondered "whether the slave may not as justifiably . . . slay one who would slay him?"[58]

Many southerners were not as confident as Ruffin: they remained fearful that by reopening the African slave trade they would only increase the everpresent potential of a slave rebellion and the possibility of white defeat.[59] Although the author of an article signed "A Florida Farmer" recognized that Africans "would produce dangerous discontent," he was also concerned that abolitionists would intentionally import large numbers of African slaves, train them to "render the slaves we have dissatisfied," and then send them down south to be sold. These same northerners would also aid the slaves in a "general insurrection and massacre. The white people would be butchered, as they were in St. Domingo."[60] Senator H. S. Foote of Tennessee agreed that the potential for northern involvement was problematic, especially if an antislavery Republican won the next presidential election, and then "we shall have enough to do to take care of what slaves we have, without importing a horde of wild Africans to corrupt them, and thereby add to our domestic troubles." Foote projected what would happen if new states admitted to the Union created a majority in Congress with enough votes to legislate against slavery: "Will not ourselves and our children have sufficient trouble to manage the native population, without sending for thousands, and perhaps, millions, of Africans to add to our cares? If we repeal the laws, as asked for, the North will enjoy the exclusive benefit, while we shall have to bear its burdens. . . . [T]he proposition is too monstrous to be mentioned for a moment."[61]

The South's preoccupation with the possibility of servile war was based on real fears, but it also was supported by a pervasive acceptance of violence as a core social experience. In the 1850s southerners vehemently denied that slavery was a military liability or a problem to the white community. By 1860 the South viewed itself as the "fountainhead of martial spirit" in America, perhaps in response to taunts from abolitionists that slavery weakened southerners militarily and regionally. Historian John Hope Franklin argued that white southerners believed in their ability to win any battle, and they "were not being merely theatrical, although they had their moments of sheer acting." Ultimately, however, southerners knew that they still had not oppressed their current slave population completely, and subjugation was a synonym for what Franklin calls the "violence [that] was inextricably woven into the most fundamental aspects of life in the South and [that] constituted an important phase of the total experience of its people," especially after the Mexican-American War.[62]

Thus, the opposition's arguments that reopening the slave trade would jeopardize the "entire security and harmony" of the South was loudly and confidently proclaimed as absurd by many of its supporters by the end of the 1850s. Untruthfully, Leonidas Spratt claimed that the slaves that first came to America were not an "explosive mixture," and there were fewer whites then than now and far greater opportunities for disorder and plunder. Therefore, "we see no reason for believing the negroes would be more savage now than they were at the earlier period," but even if this were so, "there are securities of order here which exist in no other form of society." By that, Spratt meant that the slave owner was the conservator of his own power, giving him the authority to punish without restraint. It was legally permissible for slave owners "to crush the germ of insurrection," making it impossible for slaves to successfully rise against their masters.[63] Even Pettigrew, who did not support reopening the trade, admitted, "We Suck in rebellion or obedience with our mother's milk. . . . Perhaps no nation on the globe is more highly tempered, restless, excitable and violent in resistance to illegitimate authority, than the inhabitants of these Southern States."[64] And Henry Hughes argued, "Even if the servile population should have the desire and knowledge for a rebellion, they would not have the ability. Ability to rebel is nothing more than war ability. Arms, ammunition, provisions and discipline are powers of war, and the negro race want and must want all these. But if they had the ability to rebel, their subjugation and entire extermination would be but a day's bloody toil."[65]

In light of these views, paternalism and the "doctrine of reciprocity" were never palpable factors in the slaveholding South. Clearly, white southerners understood that native-born African Americans and African-born slaves had not accepted their condition of servitude. Indeed, American liberal-republican ideology, which concluded that slaves did not want freedom, that they chose their condition of enslavement by not rebelling, is fallacious.[66] Threats of death and the possible extermination of black men, women, and children were always present. It is fair to say that throughout the African diaspora, the ownership and purchasing of slaves never elided with the supposed paternalist spirit of "love" for "those who[m] they made to suffer." Nor did "slaveholders display all the qualities of ordinary humanity" toward those enslaved. Indeed, in the case of a war between the races, Africans in America had no reciprocal rights to accept or expect from the slaveholding South or the nation.[67]

Yet the very idea of a bloody confrontation is what African Americans used in their attempts to hopefully unsettle and dismantle the proposition to reopen the African slave trade. African Americans knew that despite the rhetoric, many antebellum slave owners remained fearful of their slave population, and these fears significantly shaped their opposition to reopening the foreign trade in slaves. Of course, with the power of the federal government behind them, slave owners in the South were prepared to act if necessary to protect their property and to defend their families. But black leaders did their best to convince white southerners that the importation of new African slaves was a dangerous idea.

African Americans were well aware that the illegal trade in foreign slaves continued in Africa and America with impunity. Black abolitionist John B. Russwurm reported from Liberia that although it was thought that the slave trade had ended in 1808, "nothing is more erroneous, as the trade was never carried on with more vessels nor with greater vigour than it has been for the last two years. Even now [1830], as I am writing, slavers are within forty-four miles of the colony at Cape Mount."[68] Black editor and scholar Martin R. Delany wrote in 1849 that Cuba was the "great channel through which slaves are imported annually into the United States. . . . Into this island are there annually imported more than fifty thousand slaves, expressly for the human market, and being contiguous to the United States, vessels from Baltimore, Washington city, Richmond, and other American slave-markets . . . sail to the isle of Cuba under the pretext of touching by Havana for trade." The traders then "purchase a full cargo of slaves, sail to New Orleans where they are sold out to the highest bidder, at the slave market there, from whence they are taken to all parts of the South."[69] An illiterate yet highly intelligent fugitive slave named John Brown recalled that he was "quite sure" that even in 1855, "the slave trade [was] carried on between the Coast of Africa and the Slave States of the American Union." Brown knew of at least five hundred "Saltbacks," or slaves directly from Africa, who lived on Zachariah Le Mar's Savannah plantation sometime between 1830 and 1834 and that "new ones were constantly brought in." These Africans, who lived in Georgia with Brown, could not speak English that well, yet they were very much a visible part of his community.[70] Formerly enslaved Charley Barber stated that both his parents were from Africa, where

> they was 'ticed on a ship, fetch 'cross de ocean to Virginny, fetch to Winnebora by a slave driver, and sold to my marster's father. Dat what they tell me. When they was sailin' over, dere was five or six hundred others all together down under de first deck, of de ship, where they was locked in. They never did talk lak de other slaves, could just say a few words. . . . It was 'ginst de law to bring them over here when they did, I learn since. But what is de law now and what was de law then, when bright shinny money was in sight? . . . Yes, sir, my pappy and mammy, was just smuggled in dis part of de world.[71]

Ex-slave Paul Singleton recounted how the brutality and murder of African slaves by American slave traders became folkloric among African Americans living along the Altamaha River in Darien, Georgia: "Lots uh time he [his father] tell me annuddah story bout a slabe ship bout tuh be caught by revenoo boat. Duh slabe ship slip tru back ribbuh intuh creek. Deah wuz bout fifty slabes on bode. Duh slabe runnahs tie rocks roun duh slabes' necks and tro um ovuhbode tuh drown. Dey say yuh kin heah um moanin an groanin in duh creek ef yuf goes deah tuh-day."[72]

Thus in the decade between 1850 and 1860, many African Americans believed that if they did not respond aggressively to the call to reopen the African slave trade by stoking white fear, all would be lost, and the enslaved would face interminable bondage. The possibility of the United States increasing the slave population with newly imported African slaves was a serious step backward for blacks in America, and readers of the *Provincial Freeman*, the black newspaper in Canada, *Frederick Douglass' Paper*, the *Liberator*, and the *National Era* noted that the idea was growing in popularity in the South. Initially, African American leaders did not take the movement seriously. They believed that "the idea of reviving the slave trade . . . [was] very silly . . . that . . . no candid mind will believe that it is seriously entertained in the South."[73] Yet there was concern, as abolitionists noted at a meeting of the Western Anti-Slavery Society in Salem, Ohio, in 1854, about the "repeated avowals in leading Southern newspapers of a design to reopen the inhuman traffic." And they asked "every friend of freedom" to renew their efforts to persevere on behalf of the antislavery movement.[74] By 1857 the *Provincial Freeman* reported that should any "conflict of State and Federal authorities arise" over the importation of African slaves, "it cannot be doubted that it will be decided in favor of the South, and that the slave trade would be formally established under the principles of the Dred Scott decision."[75] Finally, in a call to action, one anonymous source noted, "The myriads of our fellow-men in Africa, marked as future victims of a hellish trade, are voiceless. Who, then, standing up before this nation and the whole civilized world, shall protest, in the name of God, and in behalf of our common humanity, against the consummation of this astounding crime? Who, but we, the free colored inhabitants of these United States?"[76]

Determined to protect Africa from further European exploitation, many black leaders did their best to encourage whites to remain fearful of increasing the African population in America by predicting that blacks would win in an internecine war between the races. Black abolitionist Dr. James McCune Smith, in a provocative essay, has his fictional character Fly envision that if southern whites did reopen the African slave trade, the Congo war cry, *Canga li,* used during the Haitian Revolution, which "transformed indifferent and heedless slaves into furious masses [would] . . . ring in the interior of Africa."[77] Fly further taunted southern slaveholders that this Haitian model of resistance against enslavement as a result of reopening the slave trade would occur in America as well: "I go in for extending the area of Slavery, for the renewal of the African slave-trade. Let them import a million a year; then in six years . . . these six millions of 'children of the sun,' restless under the lash, and uncontaminated, unenfeebled by American Christianity, may hear in their midst 'Canga li,' and the affrighted slave owners, not stopping to count their 'people,' will rush away North faster than they did from St. Domingo."[78] In another article, an unknown author prophesied that reopening the African slave trade would force poor whites to leave the South out of fear that the renewed trade would "precipitate the horrors of a negro insurrection." States like South Carolina would became "Africanized." The author warned that "agitators of that measure" would be "wise to read the handwriting on the wall before it is too late."[79]

Although black abolitionist William Wilson believed that "this reopening of the African slave trade has . . . become a fixed fact," he was confident that it would ultimately bring "great numerical and physical strength . . . to Anglo-Africans from this source" and therefore the success of a servile war in securing black freedom. Wilson, who wrote under the pseudonym Ethiop, hoped to arouse white fear by further arguing that African Americans should not "wear sad faces at the prospect of this reopening of the slave-trade; but as load after load, and gang after gang, fresh turned loose, go clanking their chains through the land. Let us listen," as the increased numbers would facilitate black success in "a hand-to-hand struggle." And there would be no turning back, Ethiop taunted, "when the final day does come, as come it must. . . . [I]t may then be with the Anglo-African a question of numbers on this continent. . . . [I]t may be with him [the enslaved] . . . not merely the question of his liberty, but entire indemnity for the past, full security for the future, and the most perfect and fullest equality for all time to come." Despite slave owner claims that Africans were only "fit for slaves," Wilson reminded both whites and African Americans that Africans had also "been shown fit for good soldiers in any hour of need."[80] In an editorial in 1860, black abolitionist Thomas Hamilton warned that although secession would mean that nothing stood in the way of southerners reopening the African slave trade, the result of South Carolina seceding from the Union and the "renewal of the African slave trade" was that an "insurrection of the slaves must follow," because now the "slaves, knowing or believing that no Northern army will come down to interfere, will raise the arm of rebellion."[81]

Black leaders may have seen advantages to an increased population of newly imported African slaves, but in reality, their biggest concern was that reopening the slave trade would mean that slavery was more secure than ever. Moreover, despite the arguments made for forceful resistance by some black leaders, most black abolitionists remained presciently aware of the danger of such actions. Nevertheless, African Americans used fear to taunt slaveholders into rejecting reopening the African slave trade, hoping in the midst of hopelessness to render the idea of greater numbers of African slaves—of black warriors—too frightening a proposition to ever make real.

Although the slave trade ended officially in the United States in 1808, most Americans knew that the trade in African slaves continued and that it was perpetrated in the most barbarous manner and with little regard for the lives and the simple humanity of those Africans held as captives. Ultimately, the rally around the importation of African slave labor set the stage for future ideas about black labor and black disposability. Yet fears of a race war and black or white extermination if whites brought in newly imported Africans also concerned many slave owners. White southerners certainly had misgivings about importing large numbers of Africans, but they were also anxious about the growing population of American blacks, who, in whites' minds, threatened their self-induced sense of security. African Americans, well aware of the debate over whether to reopen the slave trade in America, did their best to stoke white fear. Although both African Americans and southerners used fear to influence the outcome of the debate, only one side espoused the kind of violence that specifically included extermination—to envision the possible necessity of killing not only men but also women and children. Despite their apprehensions that victory in such an event would not come without cost, pro–slave trade southerners continued to embrace their vision of maintaining black labor in bondage. Southerners continued to believe that blacks in freedom would create a race war and violence, while blacks in bondage would not. These ideas would be tested, however, by the efforts of white abolitionists like John Brown, who invaded Harpers Ferry in the belief that the black community should wage war upon slavery.

CHAPTER SEVEN

John Brown's Mistake

The Power of Memory and
the Dangers of Violence

When white abolitionist John Brown first plotted to terrorize the South, he may have believed that the black community was ready to join him in carrying out his vision of a slave revolt throughout the South. Brown seized the United States Federal Arsenal in Harpers Ferry, Virginia, on October 16, 1859, because for him, "slavery was a state of war, and the slave had a right to anything necessary to his freedom."[1] Most blacks, however, did not know what Brown's plans actually were—they did not know all of what he really intended to do. Some blacks did give Brown their support for what they understood would be "Railroad business on a somewhat extended scale."[2] For many other blacks, however, despite Brown's dissemblance, using forceful means to help the enslaved escape through the Underground Railroad was viewed as a mistake and was unlikely to succeed. Nevertheless, Brown attempted to seize Harpers Ferry in order to arm those slaves he hoped to encourage to run away from neighboring plantations. The fugitives would then be able to flee to the free states or Canada or remain as part of an armed force to help Brown and his men hold the Allegheny Mountains as a sanctuary of freedom. Brown wanted to replicate this model throughout the South. Brown failed.

A popular perception is that if Brown had had more support from blacks, his plan could have succeeded. But the lack of black participation in Brown's insurgency in Harpers Ferry was deliberate: blacks and whites had not forgotten nor gotten rid of their anxiety about a potential war between the races. Indeed, the aftermath of Brown's invasion into Harpers Ferry verifies that the concerns black people had about racial violence and their fear of black extermination were legitimate. Brown's operation was founded upon certain assumptions girded by white nineteenth-century notions of masculinity that sanctified violence if a person's rights were trampled upon. Therefore, Anglo-Americans could not respect people, in this case black men, if they were unwilling to fight for their own freedom.[3] Yet black men had their own ideas about manhood, which did not sanction exposing the black community, particularly black women and children, to violent retribution. Brown's invasion of Harpers Ferry did unsettle the institution of slavery in the South, but it was enslaved and free blacks who suffered the consequences of Brown's actions.

Black Fears of Extermination in the 1850s

It was not unreasonable for John Brown to initially assume that he had support from the black community to use force to liberate those enslaved. After decades of failed efforts to end slavery in the southern states and to acquire for themselves civil liberties in the North, blacks enslaved and free faced an uncertain future. A rhetoric of black militancy emerged in response to a waning belief that William Lloyd Garrison's methods of moral suasion would end slavery. Federal laws favoring slaveholders in the southern states continued to circumscribe the lives of all blacks in America. There was a pervasive sense of doom that fostered a growing commitment to forceful resistance among the free black community that also extended to the slave. Although the black community was in a "militant mood" after 1852, for the most part, suggestions by black abolitionists to begin "the formation of military companies for the defense of the state or nation" were responses to the heightened animosity of American whites toward free blacks in the North and South.[4] In many ways, black challenges to slavery trumpeted an endorsement of violent confrontation, and inculcating fear of the possibility of slave insurrections was a strategy that black abolitionists used frequently in the decade preceding the Civil War. Yet upon closer examination, for the majority of black leaders in America, the use of force by slaves against slaveholders in the South continued to be equated with catastrophic results.

Indeed, most blacks believed that resistance on the part of those enslaved in the form of insurrection would only end in their destruction. According to Canadian immigrant and black abolitionist Henry Bibb, an enslaved man knows that "public opinion and the law is against him, and resistance in many cases is death to the slave, while the *law* declares, that he shall submit or die."[5] Solomon Northup, a formerly free traveling musician from Saratoga Springs, New York, was sold into slavery on a plantation in Louisiana. While there, Northup related, "such an idea as insurrection . . . is not new among the enslaved population of Bayou Boeuf. More than once I have joined in serious consultation, when the subject has been discussed, and there have been times when a word from me would have placed hundreds of my fellow-bondsmen in an attitude of defiance. Without arms or ammunition, *or even with them*, I saw such a step would result in certain defeat, disaster and death, and always raised my voice against it."[6] Another Canadian immigrant, pastor and editor Samuel Ringgold Ward, warned those free blacks who talked of using force in the 1850s that the "sword" or "physical force [is] right enough . . . when it can be successfully wielded, but unwise and suicidal in the case of so few against so many."[7] Despite the rhetoric, Frederick Douglass acknowledged, "We cannot but shudder as we call to mind the horrors that have marked servile insurrections—we would avert them if we could . . . because the overthrow of that tyrant would be productive of horrors."[8]

After a purported insurrection attempt in December 1856, the accounts of brutal and deadly retribution by those enslaved living in Dover, Tennessee, confirm such apprehensions.[9] According to a former slave living in Tennessee at the time, "Out at Hillsman's iron work they have shot niggers and chopped their heads off, and stick their heads on poles and throw their bodies in the river. They did everything they could think of. (During a period of fear of slave insurrections)."[10] One former slave stated, "I didn't know I was a slave until once they cut darkies heads off in a riot. They put their faces up like a sign board. They said they was going to burn niggers up by the hundreds. I have heard a heap of people say they wouldn't take the treatment what the slaves took, but they woulda took it or death. If they had been there they woulda took the very same treatment."[11] Another former slave confirmed that "in 1856 they whipped more colored people to death because they thought the colored people were fixing to rise."[12] According to the *Clarksville Jeffersonian*, the enslaved feared "a general and indiscriminate slaughter." One resident noted that some slaves had taken five to six hundred lashes before confessing anything. The *Jeffersonian* editor asked that "fearful and terrible examples should be made in every neighborhood where the crime can be established, and if necessary, let every tree in the country bend with negro meat. . . . We must strike terror, and make a lasting impression."[13]

Nor would free blacks be exempt from violence or the possibility of extermination. Ward, a fugitive slave from the Eastern Shore of Maryland, told his fellow "Beloved Brethren" who are free that he believed that despite white attempts to pass "compulsory laws for your removal . . . you will never be removed as a mass, by force or favor. . . . [T]he destiny of any peoples . . . is almost invariably wrought out . . . on their native soil. This is true," Ward stated, "even where that destiny is extermination."[14]

Benj S. Bebee, a free black from Massachusetts, prophesied that because extermination remained a real possibility in 1852, freedom in his opinion was unachievable in America. Bebee stated, "A mutual fear and prejudice exists between the two races engendering that spirit of antagonism which must ultimately turminate in the entire extirpation of the weaker race. If I could cause my voice to be heard from the Atlantic's raging billows to the calm bosom of the pacific I would warn (them) my people of the disasterous fate that awaits them and their posterity."[15]

This was not mere hyperbole, as northern whites in New York threatened to exterminate blacks in a race war in 1851. According to Frederick Douglass, some whites in Rochester threatened that black abolitionists would be responsible for a race war if they attempted to resist the recapture of fugitive slaves after the Fugitive Slave Law of 1850 was enacted.

> It has been observed that colored persons are pricing and buying fire arms . . . with the avowed intention of using them against the ministers of the law, in our city. . . . Whether what our correspondent apprehends be fully justified by the facts or not . . . let the negroes buy as many revolvers as they please—but they may rest assured that the first one that is used by them against our citizens, will be the signal for the *extermination* of the whole negro race from our midst. If they wish to provoke a war of the races by re-enacting the bloody scenes of Christiana . . . let it be known at once, that our people may be prepared for the enemy.[16]

According to Douglass, there were "at least" two northern presses in Rochester looking to encourage white violence with "utterly preposterous" charges like these against the black community.[17]

In 1856 the first female African American editor, Mary Ann Shadd Cary, who also immigrated to Canada from Wilmington, Delaware, noted that extermination remained a threat to blacks in America in her assessment of what would happen if a war ensued between Britain and the United States. In America, Shadd Cary argued, "the colored man is both hated and feared, despised, and respected, ridiculed and praised. . . . He must either take the side of his oppressor and oppose his benefactor, or declare in favor of the latter, and bring down upon his own head, the dreadful ordeal of an extermination massacre. The extermination of the whole colored race in the United States."[18]

Shadd Cary also wrote about the deadly consequences of slave insurrections for free black communities in the South: "The papers contain daily accounts from the Sunny South, of Insurrections and rumors of Insurrections, of wholesale terror, hanging, flogging to death etc." Although Shadd Cary did not dismiss "as unreasonable" the view that insurrections concentrated in one area might "afford relief to the fettered millions," she believed that it would inevitably result in a massive immigration to Canada. As "signs multiply daily indicating the approach of troublesome times . . . the effect of this horrible state of affairs . . . *flogging men to death without trial or the slightest pretext or proof of guilt* upon the nominally free colored man of the South, will be very sad—almost too intolerable to be born[e]. . . . As soon as the Spring opens therefore large numbers are anticipated."[19]

The threat of violent retribution in response to imagined or real insurrection attempts caused many of the enslaved to flee in terror as well. Shadd Cary stated that "the Underground Railroad Cause has suffered to some extent on account of the rumors of Insurrections and as the numbers escaping . . . are not as numerous as they were [in 1856] last year this time. . . . A resolute young woman . . . stated that about 40 had fled from her neighborhood recently and that the balance had fully resolved to leave in the Spring at all hazard. Whether they [the enslaved] will succeed or not of course remains to be seen."[20]

The northern black community well understood the danger of forceful resistance. At a black abolitionist convention in Massachusetts in 1858, antislavery speaker Charles Remond, who was born free into an elite family in Salem, Massachusetts, called for an address to be written to the enslaved telling them to organize an insurrection in the South. Rev. Josiah Henson, the founder of the Dawn settlement for fugitive slaves in Ontario, Canada, immediately challenged him. Henson stated that because "he [Henson] didn't want to see three or four thousand men hung before their time, he should oppose any such action. . . . If such a proposition were carried out, everything would be lost. Remond might talk, and then run away, but what would become of the poor fellows that must stand? . . . [T]hey had nothing to fight with at the South—no weapons, no education." Mr. Troy from Windsor, Canada, stated that he "wanted to see the slaves free, for he had relatives who were the property of Senator [Robert] Hunter, of Virginia; but he knew no such step as was now proposed could help them at all. He hoped the Convention would vote the thing down." Convention delegate Capt. Henry Johnson stated, "It was easy to talk, but another thing to act. He was opposed to insurrection. . . . If we were equal in numbers, then there might be some reason in the proposition. If an insurrection occurred, he wouldn't fight." Remond's motion lost. It was noted that the debate calling for a slave insurrection was "by far the most spirited discussion of the Convention."[21]

After decades of failed efforts to end slavery and civil inequalities, blacks, enslaved and free, continued to face an uncertain future that was fraught with their potential destruction and possible extermination. The question, then, is why Brown, a colleague and friend to many black abolitionists, would attempt to initiate a slave insurrection in the South? Perhaps Brown failed to realize that the rhetoric of violence used by the black abolitionist community was merely patterned after national trends that used fear as a strategy, as historian Benjamin Quarles has argued, and that the discourse was without substance.[22] While Quarles's analysis is true to some extent, Brown did know, as did the black community, that violence and black extermination were still real threats to those enslaved in the South and to those blacks living in the North. The evidence suggests that Brown was well informed by the end of the 1850s that the black community North and South would have been unwilling to instigate a violent uprising of the slaves. His insistence on going ahead anyway with his insurrection plans points toward his style of leadership, as well as his and other white radical abolitionists' racial assumptions.

Romantic Racism and the Ethos of White Manhood

By the 1840s the shift toward scientific racism, which argued that differences in people were biological, had fostered the development of racial assumptions about Europeans, Africans, and their diasporic counterparts.[23] Nineteenth-century ethnologists such as Charles Caldwell, Josiah C. Nott, and Samuel G. Morton questioned whether there was an inherent hierarchy in the different races, and, if so, if the lower or inferior races could become equal or civilized like the higher races of man, namely, the Anglo-Saxon race.[24] White southerners embraced the supposed modern scientific theories that claimed that peoples of African descent were racially inferior and could not become civilized, as these theories supported the institution of enslavement. These imagined ethnological differences were also couched and accepted by nineteenth-century northerners, however, and their acceptance of these ideas has been described as "romantic racialism," which attaches, at some level, positive value to ideas its subjects would have deemed offensive (i.e., that blacks were childlike or docile). The ethnic chauvinism of northern humanitarians was a form of racism that, despite historical evidence to the contrary, sought to rationalize and glorify Anglo-Saxon aggression.[25] John Brown and the six men who supported him financially and organizationally (Franklin Sanborn, Theodore Parker, Samuel Gridley Howe, Rev. Thomas Wentworth Higginson, Gerrit Smith, and George Luther Stearns) held "common social assumptions" about enslavement and black people that united them to Brown's cause.[26] Their racist ideas about black men informed how they went about attempting to disrupt slavery in the South and why Brown, despite objections from the black community, went forward with his plans.

The six men who supported Brown, known historically as the Secret Six, believed that "slave violence would destroy" slavery.[27] They shared the belief that a slave insurrection would demonstrate that black men were men and, therefore, illegitimately held in bondage. More importantly, all six members "felt that a willingness to fight for freedom was the core of Anglo-American political, social, and economic life" and that an "insurrection would be the slave's first step toward assimilation of a value system that emphasized individualism" and thus, as François Furstenberg points out, make them "worthy of freedom."[28] An insurrection would change white attitudes about the black race. It would encourage a core set of values among blacks that were quintessentially Anglo-American.

The Secret Six, however, had concerns about Brown's assertions that the black population in the South would join him in a massive insurrection, because they did not believe that the enslaved would fight their oppressors.[29] Secret Six member Theodore Parker's lack of faith was based on his romanticized belief that "the African is the most docile and pliant of all the races of men." Parker attempted to rewrite the history of enslavement by stating that the African race, unlike the Caucasian, "has so little ferocity: vengeance . . . is exceptional in his history. In his barbarous savage, or even wild state, he is not much addicted to revenge; always prone to mercy . . . so little warlike. Hence is it that the white men have kidnapped the black, and made him their prey."[30] The notion of the African race being weak and helpless, almost effeminate, is directly opposite to what some southerners knew to be true: many Africans were and had always been great warriors. Parker goes on to state that it was because the "African is not very good with the sword and the Anglo-Saxon is something of a master" that antislavery societies had not advocated using force. If blacks had been able warriors like white men, Parker argued, "the stroke of an axe would have settled the matter long ago. But the black man would not strike."[31]

The notion that black men needed white men to lead them into battle was pervasive among the Secret Six and their allies. James Redpath, a close friend and supporter of Brown, believed that the "Underground telegraph," which linked the enslaved to each other on "hundreds of plantations," would facilitate a "formidable insurrection directed by white men."[32] Although Thomas Higginson was the only one of the six who held that African slaves were warriors, he believed that because of slavery, the African had lost "what he had once been and what he may be again."[33] It is clear, however, that other white supporters of Brown did not entirely believe these prevailing ideas. John Henry Kagi, Brown's advisor and second-in-command, wanted to participate so that he could be "directing and controlling the negroes to prevent some of the atrocities that would necessarily arise from the sudden upheaval of such a mass as the Southern slaves."[34] Kagi is talking about atrocities against whites, demonstrating that despite the prevailing ethos of what I call romantic racism, he nevertheless held assumptions that the ferocity of black men in battle would need to be controlled.

Brown and other white radical abolitionists discounted the atrocities that the black community would face if they were to initiate an insurrection in the South. Brown stated that "it would be better that a whole generation should pass off the face of the earth—men, women, and children,—by violent death" than live without full freedom. Brown also believed that black men lacked the manly ideal or black manhood, which aligned with prevailing notions of white romantic racism. Brown stated: "When they stand like men, the nation will respect them. . . . [I]t is necessary to teach them this." In his serial essay, *Sambo's Mistake*, Brown lectured to black men that they were wrong to expect "to secure the favor of whites by tamely submitting to every species of indignity, contempt, and wrong, instead of nobly resisting their [whites'] brutal aggressions from principle, and taking [their] place as men, and assuming the responsibilities of a man, a citizen, a husband, a father, a brother, a neighbor, a friend,—as God requires of every one."[35]

James Redpath expressed similar sentiments that rebuffed the consequences of black extermination: "I dismiss the argument that we have no right to encourage insurrections. . . . [I]f all the slaves in the United States—men, women and helpless babes—were to fall on the field . . . if one man only survived to relate how his race heroically fell, and to enjoy the freedom they had won, the liberty of that solitary negro, in my opinion, would be cheaply purchased by the universal slaughter of his people and their oppressors."[36]

Northern white men were not the only ones to condone the death of children and genocidal violence for the sake of liberty and freedom—white women did also. Harriet Beecher Stowe, author of *Uncle Tom's Cabin*, claimed that she was certain that there was not "a mother among us all . . . who could ever be made to feel it right that that child should ever be a slave, not a mother among us all who would not rather lay that child in its grave."[37] When white abolitionist Lucy Stone visited fugitive slave Margaret Garner a few years later, Stone "told her that a thousand hearts were aching for her, and they were glad that one child of hers was safe with the angels." Garner's "only reply," as an enslaved woman who murdered her infant child after being recaptured by her owner in Ohio, "was a look of deep despair—of anguish such as no word can speak." From Stone's point of view, Garner's actions were quintessentially American:

I thought the spirit she manifested was the same with that of our ancestors . . . the spirit that would rather let us all go back to God than back to slavery. . . . Rather than give her little daughter to that life, she killed it. . . . That desire had its roots in the deepest and holiest feelings of our nature—implanted alike in black and white by our common Father. With my own teeth would I tear open my veins, and let the earth drink my blood, rather than wear the chains of slavery.[38]

White radical abolitionist calls for using violence as a way of asserting black manhood drew upon a long history. It was a history defined by violence, central to how Europeans colonized America and how, from their ethnological point of view, Anglo-Americans became the superior race. If, as Parker believed, blacks had been better fighters, then enslavement would have ended long ago. It was a matter of who was stronger, who was willing to fight to the death for the sake of liberty and freedom, to end what Parker called "this Crime against Humanity."[39] The black community was well aware of the racism that questioned their courage and ability to fight without white leaders. They had, however, their own understanding of manhood and freedom.

The Power of Black Manhood over Romantic Racism

By the end of the 1850s, African Americans were at the forefront of creating their own solutions to ending slavery and achieving full freedom in America. In doing so, they asserted their own ideas, which were also prevailing European notions, about the protection of their women and children in violent conflict. Some black leaders in response to challenges by white men trumpeted superficial endorsements of insurrections. Most blacks, however, continued to believe that an insurrection would be catastrophic because they knew that the rules of standard warfare did not apply to them. They were cognizant of what happened to Native Americans and thus worked to forge a different path, hoping for a different outcome than that which they perceived had happened to aboriginal people in America. Yet blacks in the 1850s constantly had to defend their decision not to encourage those enslaved to use force as a strategy for liberation.

Black abolitionists, well aware of the negative discourse condemning black manhood, contested what they viewed as northern liberal-republican propaganda, which argued that slaves did not rebel because they were happy, they were too oppressed, or they lacked courage. In an editorial, Douglass noted how the value of nonviolence as a strategy had changed and how it was currently used against the black community to support white prejudice:

> That submission on the part of the slave, has ceased to be a virtue, is very evident. . . . [I]nstead of being set to the credit of the poor sable ones, [it] only creates contempt for them in the public mind, and becomes an argument in the mouths of the community, that negroes are, by nature, only fit for slavery; that slavery is their normal condition. . . . This approach must be wiped out,

and nothing short of resistance on the part of colored men, can wipe it out. Every slave-hunter who meets a bloody death in his infernal business, is an argument in favor of the manhood of our race.[40]

Although Douglass urged fugitive slaves to resist recapture, he did not call for an insurrection of those enslaved.

Solomon Northup argued that slaves were just as invested in becoming free as white men were, but they intentionally kept these ideas to themselves. The enslaved had "secret thoughts" that they "dare not utter in the hearing of the white man." Moreover, whites like Brown were not correct in thinking that the enslaved would not fight. Northup argued: "They are deceived who flatter themselves that the ignorant and debased slave has no conception of the magnitude of his wrongs. They are deceived who imagine that he arises from his knees . . . cherishing only a spirit of meekness and forgiveness. A day may come—it will come . . . when the master in his turn will cry in vain for mercy."[41]

The abolitionist and fugitive slave Rev. John Sella Martin argued that the idea that black men were not good warriors capable of fighting for their freedom espoused by whites like Parker was absurd. Martin asserted that the history of warfare in America demonstrated that these assumptions were false: "I know very well that in this country, white people have said that the negroes will not fight; but I know also, that when the country's honor has been at stake, the dire prejudice that excludes the colored man from all positions of honor, and all opportunities for advancement, has not interfered to exclude him from the military."[42] Whites like Brown and the Secret Six might claim that blacks made poor soldiers, Martin argued, but the participation of blacks in the military throughout American history proved that this theory was without foundation.

As New York abolitionist James McCune Smith saw it, the problem was that "our white brethren cannot understand us unless we speak to them in their own language; they recognize only the philosophy of force. They will never recognize our manhood until we knock them down a time or two; they will then hug us as men and brethren. That holy love of human brotherhood which fills our hearts and fires our imagination, cannot get through the—in this respect—thick skulls of the Caucasians, unless beaten into them."[43] In McCune Smith's view, many white Americans had lost faith in the strategy of nonviolence. They had no other vision of how the end of slavery would occur but for blacks to fight against whites as their oppressors.

For most black Americans, however, facilitating a slave insurrection across the South would have been antithetical to *their* understanding of manhood.

Protecting their families was of singular importance to free and enslaved black men. According to John S. Jacobs, Harriet Jacobs's brother, "To be a man, and not to be a man—a father without authority—a husband and no protector—is the darkest of fates. Such was the condition of my father. . . . The knowledge that he was a slave himself, and that his children were also slaves, embittered his life, but made him love us the more."[44] The former slave Andrew Jackson of Kentucky recalled that this concern extended to black women as well: "Although my master seemed to regard a female slave little better than a beast, nature taught me to consider the impropriety of her treatment, and I could not endure it. Whatever men may think of us, we are not destitute of the feelings of men."[45] Black abolitionist and author Rev. James C. Pennington revealed that "they [black men] are also conscious of the deep and corrupting disgrace of having our wives and children owned by other men . . . who have given us no flattering encouragement to entrust that of our wives and daughters to them."[46] Pennington, who was enslaved in the western part of Maryland before running away to Brooklyn, New York, goes on to say that another "evil of slavery that I felt severely about" was that he witnessed overseers who "seem to take pleasure in torturing the children of slaves, long before they are large enough to be put at the hoe, and consequently under the whip."[47] Fugitive slave Henry Bibb said that the abuse of his infant child led him to escape to find "a better home" for his family.[48] And as much as Lucy Stone may have sided with Margaret Garner's actions, one must not overlook Margaret's "deep despair" at having killed her child.[49] According to her husband, Robert, he would have stopped her. Robert "saw that his wife had cut the throat of her girl Mary, three years old, from ear to ear . . . and was making a dash at his boy Samuel. He sprang to his rescue, calling on her to desist and received part of the blow himself."[50]

Moreover, the nexus of unfettered retribution and resistance to enslavement linked the black community to Native Americans who fought back fiercely against white encroachment. The near annihilation of Native Americans provided an important example to the black community of what they might experience as racialized others in their own struggle for freedom. Austin Steward recollected that he met up with an old Indian in making his escape to freedom. When "the kind-hearted old Indian repeated to me the story of his wrongs, it reminded me of the injustice practiced on myself, and the colored race generally. . . . I have often wondered, when looking at the remnant of that once powerful race, whether the black man would become extinct and his race die out, as have the red men of the forest; whether they would wither in the presence of the enterprising Anglo-Saxon as have the natives of this country."[51] William J. Wilson, black abolitionist and editor of the *Anglo-African*

Magazine who used the pseudonym "Ethiop," wrote an essay entitled "What Shall We Do with the White People?" in which he also seemed concerned that what happened to Native Americans would happen to black Americans:

> They [white people] came to this country in small numbers and began upon a course of wrong-doing. The Aborigines were the first victims. They robbed them of their lands, plundered their wigwams, burned their villages and murdered their wives and children. Thus, they advanced, until now they have almost the entire possession of the continent.... We find room enough for us [blacks] in this country ... yet they would elbow us off what we possess, to give them room for what they cannot occupy. We want this country, say they, for ourselves alone.[52]

Frederick Douglass argued: "The negro is sometimes compared with the Indian, and it is predicted that, like the Indian, he will die out before the onward progress of the Anglo-Saxon Race. I have not the least apprehension at this point ... with the negro. There is a vitality about him that seems alike invincible to hardship and cruelty. Work him, whip him, sell him, torment him, and he still lives, and clings to American civilization."[53]

Black people, Dr. John Rock claimed, were "often insulted with the assertion, that if we had the courage of the Indians or the white man, we would never have submitted to be slaves."[54] Rock, an African American physician and lawyer in Boston, pointed out that those who believe that slaves should rebel against their masters were not looking at the reality of the situation, because "for a man to resist where he knows it will destroy him, shows more foolhardiness than courage." For Rock, it was clear that "nothing but a superior force keeps us down," the same force that had decimated Native American people. Those "white Americans [who] have taken great pains to prove that we are cowards," white men who say that they would fight if they were in the slaves' place, Rock argued, are not being honest, especially knowing the "true character of the Anglo-Saxon race."[55]

Observations about the plight of Native Americans by black Americans shed light on the black community's objectives and fears, in that they hoped to abolish slavery *and* to remain alive in America. Black men loved their wives and their children. The thought of engaging in an unwinnable war with whites in the South was just not an option that most black men viewed seriously. If nothing else, enslaved and free men could protect their wives and children from suffering any violence emanating from their own actions. And many in the black community did forewarn John Brown that arming slaves to enable them to escape or arming them to insurrect against their enslavement would not create the outcome of transforming the slave South that he envisioned.

John Brown's Plan from the Black Perspective

Thus, despite the opinion of whites, blacks overwhelmingly rejected John Brown's plan to arm those enslaved in the South and thereby "rous[e] the nation."[56] As black entrepreneur Edward V. Clark argued in a meeting at the Zion Church in New York City about the use of force, "the principle of dying before your time is much better in theory than in practice. . . . [Y]ou see it would be a loosing [sic] game, you see clearly we lose."[57] Although Brown might have believed at the onset that he had the support of a few members of the black community, he could not have believed that most supported his efforts. Nor could he know that the enslaved supported his ideas at all, as he intentionally did not adequately inform them. Indeed, Brown's penchant for secrecy and perhaps even deceptive practices of telling different stories about what his mission was to be would become highly problematic for him. Whether Brown changed his plans at the last moment or kept secret his real intentions will never be known. For the black community, arming the enslaved to run away or to insurrect was fraught with risk. Whichever version Brown chose to present to them, many blacks assessed that Brown would face insurmountable challenges that they astutely believed he was not prepared to overcome.

When Brown "unfolded his plan" to abolitionist Henry Highland Garnet nearly two years before Harpers Ferry, Garnet rejected it. According to Rev. J. Sella Martin, a fugitive slave from Alabama, Garnet told him tactfully, "Sir, the time has not come yet for the success of such a movement. Our people in the South are not sufficiently apprised of their rights, and of the sympathy that exists on the part of the North for them; our people in the North are not prepared to assist in such a movement in consequence of the prejudice that shuts them out. . . . The breach between the North and the South has not yet become wide enough."[58] Whether Brown told Garnet, a fugitive slave from Maryland, of his intention to incite an armed slave insurrection and seize the armory at Harpers Ferry is unclear. But he may have, since Brown helped pay for the publication of Garnet's famous speech "An Address to the Slaves of the United States," in which Garnet advocated forceful resistance in 1848.[59] Yet Garnet specifically did not call for an insurrection in his address.[60] For although Garnet cited Nat Turner as a patriot who followed in the footsteps of the "martyr" Denmark Vesey, he told the enslaved not to follow their unsuccessful strategy of violence in liberating themselves from enslavement. Garnet set the actions of Turner and Vesey apart from what he advocated in his address by stating that he did not advise the enslaved to use the approach of those "noble men" who had tried to "blast the trumpet of freedom" to no avail.

An often-missed but important aspect of Garnet's speech is his unambiguous warning: "We do not advise you to attempt a revolution with the sword, because it would be inexpedient. Your numbers are too small, and moreover the rising spirit of the age, and the spirit of the gospel, are opposed to war and bloodshed."[61]

Garnet's biggest concern was whether northerners would aid the enslaved in the South in any confrontation between blacks and whites. He insisted that the enslaved would need to know with certainty that northern assistance was forthcoming in order for them to participate, something that Brown repeatedly argued as unnecessary. Brown had to realize that he could not guarantee that the northern states would support those enslaved fighting for their freedom and that the North would not intercede at the behest of the South.

The black community found proof of the continuing alliance between the North and the South in the passing of the Kansas-Nebraska Act in 1854, which effectively repealed the 1820 Missouri Compromise. Congress, motivated by industrial expansion and plans for a transcontinental railroad, allowed for the territories of Nebraska and Kansas to determine the status of slavery when they were admitted as states to the Union. As the Free-Soilers and proslavery citizens of the North fought each other over the issue of slavery, the Republican Party was born. The newly formed party, however, refused to take up the issue of civil equality for free blacks. Equally disturbing to black abolitionists was the party's position on slavery, which allowed slavery to remain where it existed. Republican support for colonization was also troubling to the black community, as calls for black removal continued to have salience among northerners and southerners alike. And the *Dred Scott* case in 1857, which determined that black people were not citizens and therefore held no constitutional rights in America, also signaled the rise of antiblack sentiment in America. Thus, there was reasonable uncertainty in the black community about the noninterference of northern states in suppressing any organized confrontation between master and slave, essential in any legitimate call for action from Garnet's point of view.

When Frederick Douglass found out that Brown intended to capture Harpers Ferry, he also rejected the plan because it would be dangerous to the black community. Douglass told Brown that "to me, such a measure would be fatal to all engaged in doing so. It would be an attack upon the federal government and would array the whole country against us." Douglass discovered that Brown "had completely renounced his old plan, and thought that the capture of Harper's Ferry would serve as notice to the slaves that their friends had come, and as a trumpet to rally them to his standard." Incredulous that Brown thought he would be successful, Douglass recalled: "I looked upon him with some astonishment, that he could rest upon a reed so weak and broken, and told him that Virginia would blow him and his hostages sky-high, rather than that he should hold Harper's Ferry an hour." Douglass admitted that over the years "once in a while" Brown "would say he could, with a few resolute men, capture Harper's Ferry, and supply himself with arms belonging to the government at that place, but he never announced his intention to do so. . . . I paid little attention to such remarks." Nevertheless, during Brown's meeting with Douglass in Chambersburg, Pennsylvania, they talked "long and earnest . . . Brown for Harper's Ferry, and I against it; he for striking a blow which should instantly rouse the country, and I for the policy of gradually and unaccountably drawing off the slaves to the mountains, as at first suggested and proposed by him."[62] According to Douglass, "The taking of Harper's Ferry was a measure never encouraged by my word." In his view, he was "ever ready to write, speak, publish, organize, combine, and even conspire against slavery, when there is a reasonable hope for success." To take on something "so wild and rash as this," as Brown's plan, was not Douglass's style.[63] Late nineteenth-century civil rights activist and scholar W. E. B. Du Bois noted that Douglass "knew, as only a Negro slave can know, the tremendous might and organization of the slave power. . . . Only national force could dislodge national slavery. As it was with Douglass, so it was practically with the Negro Race."[64]

Charles H. Langston, a leader of black supporters of Brown in Cleveland, expressed that he was against Brown's plan to capture Harpers Ferry. Langston did not think that Brown had enough men to succeed.[65] At Harpers Ferry, although he had hoped for more supporters, Brown had only twenty-one men, sixteen whites and five blacks. Statistically, Harpers Ferry would have been the least plausible place to begin an insurrection in the South, as there were not many slaves living in the six counties around the town. The 1860 census data show that there were 115,449 whites, 9,891 free negroes, and 18,048 slaves in the area, most of whom lived in the southern part of Maryland and Virginia. In Harpers Ferry there were nine whites for every one black person, slave or free.[66] Langston later acknowledged that he had the "deepest sympathy with the Immortal John Brown." However, Langston couched his view of the wrong-headedness of a slave insurrection by stating that to not view Brown as a hero would be "in my opinion more criminal than to urge the slaves to open rebellion," which was what Brown intended. Langston also noted that after Harpers Ferry, the South saw "in every colored man the dusky ghost of Gen. Nat Turner, the hero of Southampton," a repercussion with potentially deadly consequences.[67]

By 1859 Rev. Jermain W. Loguen's enthusiasm had also faded away, and he was no longer willing to participate. According to John Brown Jr., one of Brown's two sons who participated in Harpers Ferry, Loguen was now luke-warm toward "our cause."[68] Loguen's lack of support would have disappointed Brown, as Loguen's call for violent action in his published letter to Frederick Douglass and his participation in aiding the fugitive slave Jerry's rescue in Syracuse, New York, had inspired Brown to seek his help.[69] Formerly enslaved in Tennessee, Loguen professed in 1853, "I believe that slavery has yet to be done with, whether by agitation or bloodshed. I sometimes think that I care not which. . . . I have an old grey mother, and sisters, and brothers, all in slavery at this time. . . . I would . . . rather today hear them swimming in blood and nobly contending for their rights, even at the cost of their lives, than have them remain passive slaves all the rest of their days."[70] These were just the sorts of sentiments that would have appealed to Brown, but this singular espousal urging internecine violence at the cost of his family's lives was mere rhetorical speech inspired by the Fugitive Slave Law of 1850. Loguen's biography in 1859 indicates that he had extremely close ties with his family, especially his mother: "I value my mother, brother, and sister . . . more than my own life."[71] And he made consistent references to his "dear mother and sisters and brothers," whom he intended to see liberated from enslavement: "I mean to embrace you again, mother."[72] Loguen certainly did not want his family to die in violent conflict against their enslavers, as Brown might have thought. But Loguen would have supported the idea of facilitating the escape of greater numbers of those enslaved, and thus he introduced Brown to Harriet Tubman, giving Brown access to the black community in Chatham, Canada, in 1858.

Since the fall of 1857, Loguen had been actively engaged in and a leader of the Underground Railroad in Syracuse, New York. Loguen "devoted himself wholly to this humane work" and was responsible for shepherding hundreds of fugitive slaves "to Canada or to places of safety on this side of the St. Lawrence" River.[73] Again, we cannot know which plan Brown told Loguen, but by the time Brown was ready to invade Harpers Ferry, Loguen had found a different strategy, one with which he could "advance the movement . . . where he could do something for humanity."[74] Thus, the three black men apparently closest to Brown—Douglass, Loguen, and Garnet—did not support him. Nor did they intend to participate in Brown's plan for attacking Harpers Ferry in order to instigate an insurrection.[75]

Although Brown "strenuously" insisted that no women were to be told of his plan, Mary Jones, the wife of black abolitionist John Jones, knew all about it and was against it as well. Brown and Douglass stayed at her house in Chicago many times in 1858. As an active participant in the Underground Railroad, Mary had some knowledge of the slave South, and she "told Mr. Jones

I thought he [Brown] was a little off on the slavery question and that I did not believe he could ever do what he wanted to do. The next morning I asked him [Brown] if he had family." Mary's attempt to prod Brown to think beyond the men he hoped to recruit suggests that she had serious doubts about the viability of Brown's plan and concerns about what might happen to the women and children caught in the middle of his battle against slavery: "I thought to myself, how are you going to free them?" Her husband, John, a prosperous black tailor and Underground Railroad conductor, held a similar opinion. When Brown dropped by their house "he would talk about slavery and say what might be done in the hills and mountains," but Mary recalled that her husband "told him that he did not believe his ideas would ever be carried out."[76]

Chicago's leading Underground Railroad conductor, George DeBaptiste, also believed Brown's plan would fail. Although DeBaptiste's obituary cited him as a supporter "who helped arrange the plan" for Brown's insurrection in Harpers Ferry, DeBaptiste actually "disapproved" of Brown's scheme. DeBaptiste wanted Brown instead to plant gunpowder, whereupon "fifteen of the largest churches in the South would be blown on a fixed Sunday." DeBaptiste, a free black man born in Fredericksburg and living in Richmond, Virginia, in the 1830s, cited "the Nat Turner insurrection in 1831, by which fifty-three white lives were lost," as his model of what was required to shake up the South. It was the cost of white lives that led "the next Virginia legislature to consider a bill for the gradual emancipation of the slaves, which lost by only two votes." Brown, however, objected to DeBaptiste's plan "on the score of humanity . . . the intention being not to shed blood unless it became absolutely necessary." For DeBaptiste, Brown's plan did not go far enough. And this, DeBaptiste prophesied, would "perhaps cause the loss of a million lives before the troubles likely to ensue were ended."[77]

When Brown went to Chatham to recruit men for his effort, some black and white Canadians thought that Brown's plan was doomed to fail as well. To enable the enslaved to "take [their] liberty and to use arms in defending" their right to do so was risky business that required not only the will but also the means.[78] After meeting with Brown in April 1858, Martin R. Delany called and helped organize a convention to introduce Brown to the broader antislavery community. Brown believed that Canadian blacks were different from northern free blacks or those still enslaved in the South who, according to him, were afraid to fight.[79] Yet his distinctions were false ones, as many of the men Brown talked to were fugitive slaves who also had sufficient experience with the South to know whether Brown's scheme would be successful.[80] There was some support for the idea of instigating a massive runoff of enslaved people, but there was no consensus during the Chatham convention or within the broader black and white communities that Brown's plan was a good one. For starters, two powerful white members of the Canada West community "declined to attend." George Brown, the highly influential editor of the *Toronto Globe*, and Rev. W. King, the founder of the Buxton settlement, just south of Chatham, "doubted the wisdom of Brown's plan." Perhaps King's support and "influence would have been of weight with his colored friends and former pupils," but black Canadians questioned the viability of Brown's plan on their own.[81]

During one of the Chatham meetings, the black members in attendance "discussed the chances of the success or failure of the slaves rising to support the plan proposed," and gun shop owner and former slave James Monroe Jones remembered evidence of their skepticism. Jones recalled that he "expressed fear that he [Brown] would be disappointed because the slaves did not know enough to rally to his support. The American slaves . . . were different from those of the West India Island of San Domingo, whose successful uprising is matter of history, as they . . . were not so overawed by white men."[82] The Saint-Domingue revolution was the model that Brown studied in making and developing his plan; ironically, it was a revolution led by blacks. First and foremost, Jones was concerned that Brown insisted on keeping the enslaved in the dark up until the last minute. Clearly, Brown did not understand, according to fugitive slave William Wells Brown, that slaves viewed "every white man as an enemy."[83] Indeed, J. Sella Martin argued that the enslaved "have learned this much from the treachery of white men at the North, and the cruelty of the white man at the South, that they cannot trust the white man, even when he comes to deliver them."[84] Second, the ratio of whites to blacks in the slave South and the nation made insurrections implausible as a strategy for blacks in Canada. Jones went on to say that "one day in my shop I told him how utterly hopeless his plans would be if he persisted in making an attack with the few at his command." Brown made it clear to Jones, however, that he was ready to "sacrifice himself," as did Jesus Christ.[85]

According to James Jones, some convention members questioned whether the time was right for "making the attack. . . . Some advocated that we should wait until the United States became involved in war with some first-class power; that it would be next to madness to plunge into a strife for the abolition of slavery while the Government was at peace with other nations." Again, Brown dismissed the concerns of black leaders. It is important to point out, however, that members attending the Chatham convention were not concerned about whether Brown should take over the federal armory at Harpers Ferry. According to Jones, there was no mention of taking Harpers

Ferry, as "John Brown never, I think . . . communicated his whole plan" to the Chatham convention.[86]

Martin Delany also affirmed that those participating in the Chatham convention did not know of Brown's plan to invade Harpers Ferry. According to Delany, "The idea of Harper's Ferry was never mentioned or even hinted. . . . Had such been intimated, it is doubtful of its being favorably regarded."[87] Nevertheless, Delany supported the idea of a slave runoff to Kansas, which Brown proposed, and he, along with thirty-four other black men, signed Brown's "Provisional Constitution for the Proscribed and Oppressed People of the United States" and his "Declaration of Liberty."[88] Convention members only heard what was contained in these two documents, as Brown had been unable to secure copies for distribution. The length of the documents made it impossible for those attending the convention to engage with the specifics of it.[89] It is significant, however, that Delany was adamant that the preamble, which acknowledged that blacks were at risk of extermination, stand "as read":

> Whereas slavery, throughout its entire existence in the United States, is none other than a most barbarous, unprovoked and unjustifiable war of one portion of its citizens upon another portion—the only conditions' of which are perpetual imprisonment and hopeless servitude or absolute extermination. . . . Therefore, we, citizens of the United States, and the oppressed people who, by a recent decision of the Supreme' Court, are declared to have no rights which the white man is bound to respect . . . ordain and establish for ourselves the following Provisional Constitutional and Ordinances, the better to protect our persons, property, lives, and liberties, and to govern our actions.[90]

Still, Delany did criticize Brown's plan of assisting slaves to escape the South. Although Delany made many comments that were positive, he "objected to many propositions favored by Captain Brown, as not, having the least chance of giving trouble to the slaveholders, except the fortification at Kansas." Delany's questions aggravated Brown to such an extent that he challenged Delany's manhood. Brown "sprang suddenly to his feet, and exclaimed severely, 'Gentlemen, if Dr. Delany is afraid, don't let him make you all cowards!'" Having already heard Brown describe all free black men in the North as cowards because "blacks are afraid of the whites," Delany chastised Brown, stating, "There exists no one in whose veins the blood of cowardice courses less freely; and it must not be said, even by John Brown of Ossawatomie."[91] Despite Brown's attempts to get Delany personally involved in his scheme of helping the enslaved run away, Brown was unsuccessful. Delany had written a serial fictional essay entitled *Blake* that advocated violence. Perhaps Brown read it, as it was published in the *Anglo-African Magazine* from January to July in 1859. But it was fiction, "imagined solutions" to no doubt stoke white fear.[92] Delany and many other emigrationists at the convention already had other plans and were involved in Delany's "African Exploration movement; which he had been developing prior to his meeting Captain Brown." Indeed, Delany was in Abbeokuta, West Africa, researching the possibility of a black American settlement there when he heard about "the Harper's Ferry insurrection."[93]

Although Harriet Tubman recounted that Brown told her he did not intend "to destroy property, nor to hurt men, women or children, but to fetch away the slave when they could," she did not join Brown either.[94] Tubman, known as the Moses of her people because of her success in helping at least two hundred slaves escape from the South, impressed Brown.[95] At their first meeting, which Loguen arranged in Saint Catherines, Canada, Brown called her "General Tubman" out of respect for her legendary leadership. However, in much the same way that southerners viewed female abolitionists as women who "unsexed themselves" because of their work in the public sphere, Brown called Tubman a man. Brown wrote in his letter to his son, John Brown Jr., "Harriet Tubman booked on his whole team at once. He (Harriet) is the most of a man."[96] Just as they invented the idea of "Sambo" to represent all black men, white men constantly stereotyped black women, and Brown's reconfiguration of Tubman's gender is a conspicuous example.[97] Indeed, Tubman was "proud of being a black woman," and Brown's erasure of Tubman's womanhood by using masculine pronouns to describe her as an intelligent, courageous woman who was worthy of respect was an experience shared by black female abolitionists Sojourner Truth and Frances Harper as well.[98] Nevertheless, despite the sincerity of Brown's platitudes, there is no evidence that Tubman committed to recruiting black Canadians for Brown, nor did she attend the Chatham convention. Furthermore, there is no evidence that Tubman herself intended on participating in his initiative in Harpers Ferry.[99]

It is reasonable to conclude that Tubman, a spiritually gifted and sophisticated strategist, foresaw the failure of Brown's plan. Tubman told Loguen that she dreamed about Brown before ever seeing him in Saint Catherines and that in her dream "a great crowd of men rushed in and struck down the younger heads and then the head of the old man. . . . This dream she had again and again." Tubman had a premonition that Brown and his two sons would be killed. Therefore, it is highly doubtful that she seriously entertained involving herself in what she must have perceived would end in failure.[100]

The reluctance of black Canadians to join Brown in the South does not mean that blacks in Canada were unwilling to engage in violent confrontations with slave owners. John H. Hill signified in his letter to William Still, a leading force in the Underground Railroad in Philadelphia, that those southerners who talked of reclaiming their slaves from Canada should think again. Hill, a fugitive slave living in Toronto, forewarned slaveholders that "they had better keep their side for if they comes over this side of the lake I am under the impression they will not go back with something that their mother borned them with. . . . I know of someone here . . . [who] wants to retaleoate upon his persecutor. . . . [P]eople here would kill them."[101] Rumors that there were three black companies from Buxton, Chatham, and Ingersoll making their way down to Detroit to join Brown, however, were without foundation. At best, there were a few Canadian immigrants making their way South to assist Brown when the Harpers Ferry raid occurred.[102]

As the only black Canadian participating in the Harpers Ferry raid to escape alive, Osborn Anderson joined Brown without knowing what he really intended to do.[103] According to Douglass, Anderson met with him after the raid and told him that Brown "was careful to keep his plans from his men, and that there was much opposition among them when they found what were the precise movements determined upon; but . . . like good soldiers were agreed to follow their captain wherever he might lead."[104] This account is corroborated by John Brown Jr., who claimed that in "the early part of September, 1859," he and his father "had many earnest discussions as to the feasibility of making the attack at Harper's Ferry,—which plan was not known to any of us until after our arrival at the Kennedy Farms. All of our men, excepting Merriam, Kagi, Shields Green, and the colored men (the latter knowing nothing of Harper's Ferry), were opposed to striking the first blow there."[105] According to Charles Tidd, "All the boys opposed Harper's Ferry, the younger Browns most of all. In September it nearly broke up the camp."[106] Brown became depressed at the opposition of his men and subsequently resigned so that they could choose a new leader, whom Brown vowed to "obey." Within "five minutes, he was again chosen as the leader, and though we were not satisfied with the reasons he gave for making our first attack there, all controversy and opposition to the plan . . . ended."[107] Thus, blacks in the North and in Canada could not have known about Brown's Harpers Ferry plan, just as they asserted afterward, because Brown's own men did not know about it until after they arrived at the Kennedy farm in Maryland.

After the Harpers Ferry raid occurred, those still enslaved in the South related similar assessments of and concerns about Brown's plan. It would seem that Brown's penchant for secrecy may have diminished the ability and willingness of those blacks he did recruit to participate. Consider the testimony of Antony Hunter, a slave who asserted that there were large numbers of enslaved blacks ready and organized to join Brown from the Harpers Ferry area. When asked why blacks did not join Brown at Harpers Ferry and help him, Antony retorted, "Cos we was afraid. De culled people's been cheated so offen by de white folks, dat when dey struck de blow too soon at de Ferry, we was 'fraid we was goin' tar be cheated." Moreover, their decision ultimately not to join Brown seemed based on a different understanding of what was to occur. Antony and the rest of the "folks" were troubled that "Mr. Brown an' his men . . . was killin' de white an culled folks" and that if they showed themselves in support of such an event, they would then be killed or sold. Apparently, Brown's men had instructed them to be ready to join him on Monday, and "we'd wait in de mountains back ob de Ferry, till Mr. Brown gabe de word an' den all hurry dar ter jine him." If the enslaved could have "beliebed in de white men being true" and if Brown had stuck to the appointed day instead of beginning Sunday evening, Antony claimed, "many . . . would hab fought fur him till all was killed."[108] Again, that the enslaved viewed "every white man as an enemy" was commonplace, according to fugitive slave William Wells Brown.[109] Apparently to counteract any interference from northern whites, Henry Bibb stated, white slaveholders "told the slaves to beware of the abolitionists, that their object was to decoy off the slaves and then sell them off in New Orleans. Some of them believed this, and others believed it not."[110] That Brown did not take the time to gain the slaves' confidence and cooperation was a serious mistake.

Without information, it was impossible for those enslaved to know if Brown was truly engaged in an effort that would end in their freedom. In J. Sella Martin's opinion, if it was Brown's intent not to shed any blood, then

> this was one of the faults of his plan. In not shedding blood, he left the slaves uncertain how to act; so that the North has said that the negroes there are cowards. They are not cowards, but great diplomats. When they saw their masters in the possession of John Brown, in bonds like themselves, they would have been perfect fools had they demonstrated any willingness to join him. They have got sense enough to know, that until there is a perfect demonstration that the white man is their friend—a demonstration bathed in blood—it is all foolishness to co-operate with them. . . . So it was not cowardice, nor their craven selfishness, but it was their caution, that prevented them from joining Brown.[111]

Thus, if Brown's real intent, as Tubman understood, was merely to "attract the attention of the country and to strike for freedom" without actually achieving freedom for those enslaved, he could do so without them.[112]

Yet, according to slaves like Harrison Berry, tactics like Brown's did not help their cause, because the strategy of agitating the slave owners into confrontation was wrongheaded and dangerous. Berry claimed that the enslaved experienced greater oppression because of antislavery efforts.[113] Living in Georgia, Berry offered his assessment of the futility of rebellions like Brown's, thus demonstrating the seriousness with which the slaves viewed the threat of their demise: "I can imagine that I see gibbets all over the Slave-holding States, with negroes stretched upon them like slaughtered hogs, and pens of lightwood on fire! Methinks I hear their screams—I can see them upon their knees, begging, for God's sake, to have mercy. I can see, them chained together by scores, and shot down like wild beasts. These are but shadows to what would have been done, had John Brown succeeded in his plan of getting up a rebellion among the Slaves."[114]

Berry made one other argument that contested Brown's claims that death would be a better fate for those enslaved. Berry stated it was not their destiny to kill themselves off as a race; instead, "if it be so that the children of Israel were enslaved, for the express purpose of saving much people alive, how much more might it be possible that the Slaves of America are enslaved to save many Africans alive?"[115] Berry rightly imagined that the history slaves made was in their ability to stay alive, so that they too as a race of oppressed people might contribute to the future of African people everywhere.

Looking at Brown's plan from outside the black community, some whites not only shared their assessment but also understood why blacks perceived Brown's plan to be flawed and dangerous to those enslaved. One southern Republican argued that it was a "fatal mistake to infer that the negroes have no desire to be free, because they remained passive at Harper's Ferry. They knew their own strength too well in that vicinity to rush upon destruction." The writer noted that the idea of a grand runoff of slaves, however, was plausible and would not necessarily have required Brown's leadership: "They are . . . the class of slaves from whom we should least expect an effort at insurrection. They are on the border of the Free States, and it would be much easier and safer to liberate themselves by running away than by revolting."[116] Indeed, during the 1840s and 1850s, the enslaved organized several, albeit unsuccessful, massive runoffs to freedom across the South.[117] Abolitionist Lydia Maria Childs lamented in a letter to her friend Mary Stearns that she honored "Brown's motives; but he made a great mistake; a *very* great mistake. The efforts may be favorable to freedom in the long run; but it is impossible to foresee the consequences."[118] Black people, enslaved and free, knew what the consequences would be for instigating an insurrection, which is why some free blacks were only willing to support Brown's plan of running off slaves to free territory. African Americans "knew the slave system." And they rightly predicted that any direct confrontation to disrupt slavery in the South would create a new reign of terror, heightening fears of a race war and the slaughter of black people everywhere.[119]

The New Reign of Terror: The Aftermath of Harpers Ferry

It took less than thirty-six hours for the Virginia militia and federal troops to capture and arrest John Brown in Harpers Ferry. Hours before Brown's capture, there were reports of white mobs "one thousand to two thousand strong" roaming the streets of Harpers Ferry looking for anyone who might have been involved in John Brown's insurrection.[120] Fear was as palpable among whites in the area as it was within the black community. White slaveholders responded swiftly. The black community was terrorized, and some were even killed. As far as white southerners were concerned, not only was John Brown a traitor to the nation, but by attempting to incite violence among the enslaved he was also a traitor to the white race. Black Americans, foreseeing what would come, did their best to protect themselves.

Although Brown embraced the possibility that he would end up sacrificing his life and that of black Americans for his cause, he did so with the expectation that standard military rules of engagement would apply. Brown complained to Captain Sims, the commander of a Maryland militia, that "his men had been shot down like dogs while bearing a flag of truce; [Captain Simms] told him *they must expect to be shot down* like dogs, if they took up arms in that way." When Brown cried out for quarter in surrender, he was apparently unaware of how white southerners waged war on those who engaged in slave insurrections, even if they were white. Two other white men, John E. Cook and Edwin Coppoc, also had similar impressions about what their fate would be in participating in Brown's plan. When "both addressed the Court, denying that they had any knowledge of Brown's intention to seize the Ferry until the Sunday previous . . . [t]hey expected to be punished, but did not think they should be hung."[121] Their understanding of what punishment they would face would have been accurate if they had been merely helping the enslaved run away. The penalty that whites and blacks generally suffered for that crime was imprisonment. Attempting to lead those enslaved in insurrection usually meant death. Cook and Coppoc were executed, as was Brown, but Brown did not shirk from responsibility for his actions, nor did he back away from the idea that the annihilation of black people would be better than the continuation of enslavement: "I believe that to have interfered as I have done . . . I did not wrong but right. Now, if it is deemed necessary that I should forfeit my life for the furtherance of the ends of justice, and mingle my blood with the blood of my children, and with the blood of millions in this slave country whose rights are disregarded by wicked, cruel, and unjust enactments, I say let it be done."[122]

Although Brown testified that he was not attempting to instigate an insurrection, southern whites believed that he was, which would have led to a war between the races. Edmund Ruffin, a Virginia planter and writer, assessed in his diary that "the great mass of the people of the north . . . do not entirely condemn the attempt to excite insurrection of the slaves, with all the unspeakable atrocities and horrors which would attend even their partial success. Their complete success, in establishing their freedom, even with all the aid of our northern white *brethren*, is utterly impossible. . . . [R]enewed & extended attempts of this kind may produce a war of races, to be terminated only in the extermination of the blacks, & ruin, with their victory, to the whites."[123] Journalist David Hunter Strother reported that it was Brown's plan to "overthrow the Government of the United States and the Anglo-Saxon race in the South." Strother further claimed that he had heard Brown state that "he had entered Virginia for the purpose of making war on the white race, determined to kill all who opposed his views."[124] Certainly, Strother may have misinterpreted what Brown said, if he heard him say it at all, but he was not alone in believing that unlimited warfare was what Brown intended.

Governor Henry Wise of Virginia wrote in his message to the Senate and State Assembly that Brown's purpose was to force the enslaved "to fight to liberate themselves by massacreing their masters . . . combining with Canadians . . . for the purpose of stirring up universal insurrection of slaves throughout the whole south."[125] In a private letter to white abolitionist L. Maria Childs, ultimately published in the *New York Tribune*, Wise described Brown's "attempt" as one that "whetted the knives of butchery for our mothers, sisters, daughters and babes."[126] White southerners, invoking memories of what happened during other slave insurrections, retained an infinitely old understanding of what was at stake during this sort of warfare. And regardless of whether Brown believed that arming the enslaved would result in a massacre, he seemed willing enough for that level of violence to ensue. Indeed, southerners shared the black community's fears of how such actions might play out. One woman's chastisement of Childs for her willingness to care for Brown in prison demonstrates how resilient the idea of exterminatory warfare remained for many white southerners: "You would soothe with sisterly and motherly care the hoary-headed murderer of Harper's Ferry! A man whose aim and intention was to incite the horrors of a servile war—to condemn women of your race . . . to see their husbands and fathers murdered, their children butchered, the ground strewed with the brains of their babies."[127]

Clearly, whites remained fearful of their slave population despite the claims of Governor Wise and other southerners that the enslaved did not have any desire to rise in rebellion.[128] In fact, whites were "wild with terror." According to Osborn Anderson, who provided important testimony in his *A Voice from Harper's Ferry*, he saw white men, women, and children "fleeing" from what they believed was "their doomed city."[129] Concerns over whether Brown's ideas had reached slaves beyond Harpers Ferry created overwhelming panic, especially among women: "At the time of the John Brown affair," *Harper's Weekly* reported, "Governor Wise told us that Virginia matrons living miles and miles away were beside themselves with terror."[130] Another report observed that "local whites were heavily armed even in daylight."[131] Someone from Petersburg, Virginia, reported that "the panic has seized all classes of the people. . . . If five or six negroes are seen talking together, they are speedily magnified by rumor into a hundred, armed with pitchforks and scythe blades."[132] These rumors, based on imagined fears of slave insurrections, were pervasive. According to Col. Robert W. Baylor, commander of troops at Harpers Ferry, after returning from "the Maryland side of the river," where there were reports that there were "disturbances still occurring," another "alarm was occasioned by a gentleman . . . riding into town in great haste, stating that he saw firing and heard the screams of the people, and that a large number of insurgents had collected and were murdering all before them. Forthwith Col. [Robert E.] Lee . . . proceeded to the spot. . . . [T]he alarm . . . proved to have been false."[133]

White fear about the enslaved population insurrecting after Brown's invasion at Harpers Ferry caused "universal alarm" in many other parts of the South.[134] Plantation mistress Ann Agnes Coe expressed trepidations that she claimed were "fears entertained by many" in South Carolina that "the northern abolitionist will not rest until they bring upon the South all the horrors of a *servile war* nothing but such scenes as was witnessed at St. Dominge will ever satisfy those wild fanatics."[135] These fears are affirmed by another slave-owning woman in South Carolina, who stated, "We tremble in our own homes in anticipation and expectancy of what is liable to burst forth at any moment—a negro insurrection. . . . Not a night passes that we do not securely lock our field servants in their quarters. . . . Our planters and owners of slave property do not allow their servants to have any intercourse with each other, and the negroes are confined strictly to the premises where they belong."[136] William S. Pettigrew wrote from Plymouth, North Carolina, that "the people [were] . . . ready to slaughter the negroes indiscriminately." Pettigrew went on to say that in his opinion, "in case of a panic on the subject of insurrectionary designs the negroes are in much more danger . . . than the whites are from the negroes."[137] Indeed, if the slaves were emancipated due to the "intermed-dlings" of the "Abolitionist" and the "new recruits of John Brown," Judge John Townsend of South Carolina claimed,

> there will be a general uprising among the whites of all classes to drive them out of the country. Thus will commence that war between the races, which every reflecting mind perceives to be inevitable, where an inferior and degraded race has been *forced up*, by foreign interference, to an equality with their former master race. In such a war . . . [h]orrible tragedies may be enacted in a few neighborhoods; but it must soon terminate in the indiscriminate slaughter of the negros, by the tens of thousands and hundreds of thousands, until they shall be either exterminated, or driven out of the country.[138]

Brown's insurrectionary attempt galvanized white animosity, and "rage had taken the place of . . . alarmed surprise."[139]

Thus, the panic of whites in the South resulted in the black community being terrorized and tortured. According to Pastor Charles White's account of the affair, "The negroes about Harper's Ferry were terribly alarmed. . . . We have patrols out every night." White managed to save the "slave of Mr. Al-stadt" from "being randomly murdered." The "fellow stated that he had orders from the Captain of Charlestown Company," yet "so enraged were the multitude that it was with difficulty they were restrained from hanging and shooting several [slaves] on the spot."[140] Osborn Anderson observed that they sent "poor whites . . . to do the safe but cowardly judicial murdering afterwards." Anderson footnoted at the end of his narrative that it was "more like a great hunting scene than that of a battle."[141]

Many blacks were killed in the aftermath of Harpers Ferry. According to a Harpers Ferry mill worker named Kindle, "many of the negroes . . . ran for the river and they were shot." Another source noted that "in surrounding towns there were several deaths of slaves blamed on overreaction of slaveowners due to Brown's raid."[142] In Somerset County, Maryland, after an alarm sounded of an impending insurrection at a prayer meeting, white citizens went out and scoured the neighborhood looking for slaves in revolt but could not find one black person. The next night, a patrol was organized, whereupon they went about searching the huts of all the free negroes, until finally they found one man in his hut and then shot him to death.[143]

The murder of innocent blacks was not limited to the Harpers Ferry area. According to another report, "So terrible was the alarm created by that trumpery attempt" among whites that "down on the Gulf shore negroes whose behavior had attracted attention were imprisoned, whipped, and even shot by scores."[144] Johnson J. Hooper of Montgomery, Alabama, told Virginian Edmund Ruffin "of much that had not entered the newspapers, in which indeed there has been very little said, either of statement or comment. . . . No doubt there are gross exaggerations of the facts, & probably many innocent negroes may suffer for the guilty . . . [but] discoveries have been made in different parts of Alabama—and that the infuriated inhabitants have in sundry cases executed summary vengeance (or justice, if not mistaken) on the detected culprits, white and black."[145]

Certainly, newspaper editors may have not been able to separate whether fears of the enslaved rising were "real or imaginary," but they did not exaggerate the violence and trauma that blacks experienced at the hands of whites.[146] In Alabama, slave owners went "from plantation to plantation, taking up and whipping slaves without cause."[147] Evidence of an insurrection plot was "extorted" from one slave after "the application of eight hundred lashes to his back."[148] Another female slave received similar treatment until she was "ready to confess anything to escape the lash."[149] In Texas, fears of slave insurrections caused what is considered "one of the greatest witch hunts in American history."[150] In response to what southerners called the "Texas Troubles," or the "John Brown Foray in Texas," many innocent slaves were hanged after the outbreak of several fires in the region.[151] As far as one southern correspondent was concerned, "it is better for us to hang ninety-nine innocent (suspicious) men than to let one guilty one pass. . . . Such is the universal sentiment of this community, and soon must and will be of the entire South." When the supposed plot to "poison as many people as they could . . . to burn the houses and kill as many women and children as they could . . . and then kill the men as they returned home" was uncovered, hundreds of blacks were arrested and examined.[152] Three men, Cato, Sam Smith, and Patrick, were lynched by a mob for supposedly being the leaders of this thwarted insurrection in Waxahachie, Texas. Afterward a resolution was passed, and "every negro in the county" was whipped.[153] Across northern and central portions of Texas, "about sixty-five of negros . . . were hung or burnt, as to the degree of their implication in the rebellion and burning."[154] In Natchez, Mississippi, during the campaign for the presidency in 1860, "two slave men were overheard repeating what their masters said, that if Lincoln was elected he would free all the slaves, . . . and they declared that if this was true they would go to the Yankees and help to free their nation." Rumors then circulated that there was going to be an insurrection in "that part of the State," and "all slave men or boys who were overheard to pray for freedom, or to say anything indicating a desire to be free, were marked." A large group of over one hundred white men organized to compel confessions from "all these marked slaves and then to hang them. . . . Many negroes were dragged out of their cabins or yards without knowing the cause, stripped, tied to the whipping-post or taken to the calaboose, and given as many lashes as could be endured. . . . Some hundreds were thus hanged in the edge of the city, and on an adjoining plantation." According to abolitionist Laura S. Haviland, the total number of slaves executed was 209, but she was "told by a number of persons, both white and colored, that there were over four hundred tortured to death in this reign of terror."[155] Whatever the actual number was, clearly blacks throughout the South were under siege. They were tortured, terrorized, and lynched without cause long after Brown's execution at Harpers Ferry.

Many slaves were also sold to the Deep South states as a result of the Harpers Ferry insurrection, the thing that enslaved people dreaded most because of the brutal working conditions there. In Harpers Ferry, the majority of the enslaved worked in the mills, but in the 1850s, declining productivity made their labor less in demand.[156] Thus, in order to reduce the risk of any future insurrectionary attempts, slaves "who were suspects, unruly, or turbulent" were sold at reduced prices in Maryland and Virginia.[157] Slaves were also sold off in South Carolina: "Negroes are selling at enormous prices not withstanding the later outbreak at Harper's Ferry."[158]

Free blacks in the South did not escape the white backlash either. Rev. Thomas W. Henry fled from Baltimore because of a reference to him in a letter in John Brown's possessions. Henry, formerly enslaved for twenty-two years, stated that after Harpers Ferry, a "Black Person could not leave the city of Baltimore unless he was vouched for by some responsible white person."[159] White southerners closed black churches not only in Virginia but also in South Carolina, and "other gatherings [were] prohibited" as well.[160] In Georgia a law was passed that "free negroes wandering or strolling about or leading an idle, immoral . . . course of life, shall be sold into slavery."[161] Former slave Bethany Veney remarked that "after John Brown made his invasion into Virginia; the excitement that followed made it unsafe for any one who sympathized with or defended him to be seen in any Southern State."[162] Perhaps the increase in blacks escaping from the South reported by northern abolitionists was motivated, as Mary Ann Shadd Cary observed, by terror as well as by the thirst for liberation.[163]

That the black community lived in terror in the aftermath of Harpers Ferry is also evidenced by events in the northern states. In making his escape from the South to return to Canada, Osborn Anderson stopped at the home of "William Goodridge, a seasoned fugitive slave abetter" in York, Pennsylvania, which "produced great fear and consternation in the Goodridge family. Goodridge ordered him away from the house."[164] According to Annie Brown,

John Brown's daughter, Anderson's father also "drove him away from his door with threats of having him arrested and sent back to Virginia . . . and called him all manner of vile names for what he had done."[165] Apparently, the black community was aware that there was "an indictment against him. . . . [T]he government officials," black abolitionist Charles Langston stated, "live only to hunt '*niggers*' and guard the interests of the peculiar institution." In secret, members of the Fugitive Aid Society in Cleveland, Ohio, "rushed forward to take him [Anderson] by the hand, and to rejoice that he had the good fortune to escape Virginia's bloody halter." But out in the public sphere, Anderson was a pariah. He told Annie Brown when visiting Brown's grave in North Elba, New York, in 1860 that he "dreaded to go back and into the world where he would be so friendless and alone."[166] He was friendless because blacks who had nothing to do with Brown's insurrection lived in constant fear. Black seamen from the North were now at risk of being abducted from ships docked in southern ports and sold into slavery.[167] Douglass, in fear of apprehension by federal authorities, fled to Canada.[168] Free blacks feared the long hand of southern white violence in the North just as they did in the South, leading John Rock to conclude that "the whole country has entered into a conspiracy to crush him [blacks]; it is against this mighty power that he is forced to contend. Some persons think we are oppressed over in the South: this is a mistake. We are oppressed everywhere on this slavery-cursed land."[169]

In the aftermath, blacks nevertheless continued to fight for the liberation of the enslaved and used Brown and his martyrdom to advance a nonviolent approach in resolving what they saw as the inevitable confrontation between the North and South over slavery. At an antislavery gathering, H. Ford Douglass, a fugitive slave from Virginia, claimed that in order to end slavery, "We must do as John Brown did, not necessarily in the *way* he did it, but we must labor with the sure determination to effect, in some way, the complete overthrow of slavery. I am not an advocate for insurrection. I believe the world must be educated into something better and higher than this before we can have perfect freedom, either for the black man or the white."[170] Harriet Tubman expressed deep admiration for Brown in his efforts to end slavery, calling his death a "second Crucifixion." Yet she was adamant that violence was not part of his vision in ending slavery. According to Tubman's grandnephew Harkless Bowley, Tubman told him, "It was not John Brown's idea to murder the white people but to stir the slaves so as to attract the attention [of the] country and to strike for freedom."[171] Nevertheless, Frederick Douglass, addressing Bostonians on Brown's contributions to the abolitionist movement, argued that violence had indeed been "the John Brown way." Douglass reasoned that the antislavery movement could use Brown and the fear that his actions generated throughout the South to its advantage. At the same time, abolitionists could continue with the nonviolent strategy of assisting slaves in making their escape: "We must . . . reach the slaveholder's conscience through his fear of personal danger. We must make him feel that there is death in the air about him . . . that there is death all around him. We must do this in some way. . . . The negroes of the South must do this; they . . . must make them feel that it is not so pleasant, after all, to go to bed with bowie-knives, and revolvers, and pistols, as they must. . . . Every slave that escapes helps to add to their discomfort." Despite the rhetoric, Douglass was not calling for an organized South-wide insurrection but rather for the instability that the possibility of one could cause: "I know that all hope of a general insurrection is vain. We do not need a general insurrection to bring about this result. We only need the fact to be known in the Southern States generally, that there is liberty in yonder mountains, planted by John Brown."[172]

While most blacks revered and admired Brown for his martyrdom, some also linked his efforts at Harpers Ferry with those of Nat Turner and other black freedom fighters in order to rally northern sentiment on the issue of slavery. Osborn Anderson argued that what Brown attempted to do was quintessentially African American, that white men were not the only ones who fought and died for freedom. Anderson began his narrative by claiming:

> There is an unbroken chain of sentiment and purpose from Moses of the Jews to John Brown of America . . . to the untutored Gabriel, and the Denmark Veseys, Nat Turners and Madison Washingtons of the Southern States. The shaping and expressing of a thought for freedom takes the same consistence with the colored American—whether he be an independent citizen of the Haytian nation, a proscribed but humble nominally free colored man, a patient, toiling, but hopeful slave—as with the proudest or noblest representative of European or American civilization and Christianity. . . . Nine insurrections is the number given by some . . . whether correct or not. . . . Gabriel, Vesey, Nat Turner, all had conference meetings; all had their plans.[173]

Anderson stressed that Brown's insurrection should be viewed as a "progressive," an "elevated" version of what had occurred in the past—that what Brown did was not new.

John Rock also placed Brown and Turner on the same moral footing, as the "only events in the history of this country which I think deserve to be commemorated . . . the organization of the Anti-slavery Society and the insurrections of Nat Turner and John Brown."[174]

The editor of the *Anglo-African Magazine*, Thomas Hamilton, also reflected on Nat Turner and John Brown after Harpers Ferry and made comparisons between the two freedom fighters. Where Turner and Brown differed was that in Turner's method of warfare, used historically by both blacks and whites, he "could only see the enfranchisement of one race, compassed by the extirpation of the other; and he followed his gory syllogism with rude exactitude." John Brown, Hamilton argued, was not attempting to exterminate white people, as Brown believed that "the freedom of the enthralled could only be effected by placing them on an equality with their enslavers." As a white man not eligible for enslavement, Brown "in the very effort at emancipation" was "moved with compassion for tyrants as well as slaves, and seeks to extirpate this formidable cancer, without spilling one drop of Christian blood." Hamilton went on to suggest that Turner was a greater threat to the South than Brown ever was because of his leadership, his determination, and his condition of being oppressed: "Had the order of events been reversed—had Nat Turner been in John Brown's place at the head of these twenty one men, governed by his inexorable logic, and cool daring, the soil of Virginia and Maryland and the far South, would by this time be drenched in blood, and the wild and sanguinary course of these men, no earthly power then could stay." Hamilton challenged his readers to think deeply about the fact that there were "a hundred Nat Turners. . . . So people of the South, people of the North! . . . choose ye which method of emancipation you prefer—Nat Turner's or John Brown's?"[175]

John Brown's detachment from the lived experience of blacks made it impossible for him to foresee that his capture of Harpers Ferry would inevitably end even more violently than he imagined. Unlike during the 1960s civil rights movement, when nonviolence was favored among whites for its shining example of moral refinement, blacks in the 1850s had to defend their decision not to use force as a strategy for liberation. Brown and other radical abolitionists, however, believed that armed resistance was the only way to gain the respect of white Americans. Who was most at risk in his willingness to dismiss the potential of a race war and black extermination seems very clear. Black Americans in the United States and Canada knew that arming large numbers of slaves would be perceived by the South and North as an act of insurrection requiring state and federal military action. It would jeopardize the lives of innocent men, women, and children in what blacks viewed would be an unwinnable war. Yet, importantly, Brown's miscalculations emanated from his "head," not his "heart."[176] And this the black community well understood, using his name, as well as Nat Turner's, as a symbol of where America's moral conscience should be on the issues of freedom and equality. Ideas about black freedom and the inevitability of a race war between blacks and whites, however, remained unchanged in the southern mind, coming out in full relief during the Civil War and post–Civil War years.

CHAPTER EIGHT

Making "Hell for a Country"
The Civil War and Post–Civil War Era

The Civil War, even in the beginning, was at its heart about blacks in America and the institution of slavery, making the issue of a war between the races more relevant than ever before. South Carolina was the first southern state to secede from the Union, and two of its reasons for withdrawing from the Union stand out: hostility to the institution of slavery expressed by nonslaveholding states and the federal government's waning commitment to protecting the South from a servile war. These two significant causes of the Civil War, resting under the umbrella of states' rights, centered on what had historically given substance to the ideas of race war and black or white extermination, namely, the issue of slavery, as well as the freedom of African Americans. This was true for the Union side as well. It was politically more beneficial for the Union to dissemble what caused the fracture between the states rather than admit that everything the South claimed about northern hostility and dwindling support was true. Many black Americans distrusted Abraham Lincoln's lack of commitment to the abolition of slavery and his proposals to colonize former slaves. Yet Lincoln admitted to a group of African American clergy who met with him in the White House in August 1862: "But for your race among us there could not be a war. . . . [W]ithout the institution of slavery, and the colored race as a basis, the war would not have an existence."[1] Indeed, as Frederick Douglass pointed out, in the federal government an "attempt is made to conceal . . . the real cause of the rebellion."[2] Unfortunately, the Lincoln administration's unwillingness to honestly confront the issue of slavery as the cause of the war and the consistency of federal efforts to reunify with the southern states allowed for greater violence and uncontested assertions that with emancipation would come the extermination of African American people.

The ramifications of the outbreak of hostilities between the North and South were not lost on those enslaved in the South. They saw the war as the opportunity *they* had been waiting for. Now that the federal government supported the abolition of slavery and was willing to send in northern troops on their behalf, African Americans were ready and willing to fight for their right to be free. The enslaved were hopeful and optimistic that this was their moment, when their dream of liberation from centuries of oppression would finally materialize. Thousands of enslaved people fled to Union lines seeking protection in the first months after the fall of Fort Sumter in April 1861, and by the war's end, over five hundred thousand African Americans had freed themselves across the South.[3] But their active participation in their own liberation did not come without cost. Confederate soldiers deliberately sought to intimidate the noncombatant populations of the black community in their attempt to stem the flow of what Union soldiers termed "contraband of war," a term used for property. Renewing a strategy used for centuries, Confederate soldiers brutally killed many African Americans under the policy of no quarter for black soldiers, and they also killed women and children with equal fervor. This sort of violence did not end after the Civil War. The continued exhibitions of racially motivated and inchoate acts of brutality traumatized many black Americans and made them fearful that white southerners intended to carry out what they had threatened to do for centuries. They had only to look around the nation, to the West, and, indeed, to their own communities to determine that the threats were real, threats that greatly concerned the black community well into the next century.

A Most Uncivilized War

Once the Civil War commenced, aside from both sides being consumed about who would ultimately win the war, white Americans intensely engaged in discussions about what was to be done with the enslaved if they were freed and whether there would be a race war ending in black extermination. The same triangulation of choices that emerged during the Virginia Debates for African Americans emerged during the Civil War: remain enslaved, be colonized, or face extermination. But now another option was included, which was slavery by another name. For African Americans, freedom remained at the forefront of why they invested in the war by walking away from their masters and by their willingness to fight and die if necessary for what they knew was their inalienable right, to be free. At the beginning of the war, former slave Henry Wright remembered, "All the slaves grew hopeful and glad of the prospect of being set free."[4] According to another former slave from Tennessee, "They just expected [their] freedom" to be the result of the Civil War.[5] White southerners responded to the emancipation of those enslaved and their subsequent service as soldiers, however, with acts of brutality that they rationalized not only as a tactic of war but also as a means of retaining control over what they still viewed as their servile population.

According to Frederick Douglass, the first option discussed in the North and South by whites during the Civil War to resolve the "Negro problem" was that slavery would remain a fixed institution in America. Only now the nation would "reduce the whole colored population to slavery." This idea, however, lacked plausibility in the climate of the free-labor discourse among whites that was so pervasive during the middle of the nineteenth century. As Douglass stated, it would have meant that "the slaveholder would then be the only really freeman of the country. All the rest would be either slaves, or be poor white trash," whose liberty would never be safe from a "class of tyrants."[6]

In the second and newest scenario of the future of newly freed blacks in America, southerners envisioned a labor system where they would "retain them as slaves in fact." As Douglass saw it, they would be free in name only, they would be made "a degraded caste" by not "conferring equal rights" upon them. This vision was particularly dangerous to the black community, argued Douglass, because "it would . . . lacerate and depress the spirit of the negro, and make him a scourge and a curse to the country. Do anything else with us, but plunge us not into this hopeless pit."[7]

Colonization continued to be seriously entertained as another possible solution to the "Negro problem" during the Civil War, "a singularly pleasing dream" to white Americans. Douglass noted, however, that "even if we could consent to the folly of sending away the only efficient producers" in America, it would not occur, because of the costliness of the present war.[8] Yet for Suzie King Taylor, an enslaved woman from Savannah, Georgia, who ran behind Union lines, the first year of war "was a gloomy time for us all" because of this very issue. As contraband in a camp on Saint Simons Island in Georgia, Taylor, her uncle, and her seven siblings were told that "there was going to be a settlement of the war. Those who were on the Union side would remain free, and those in bondage were to work three days for their masters and three days for themselves. . . . [W]e [the contraband] were to be sent to Liberia." Taylor stated that when asked whether she would prefer to go back to Savannah or go to Liberia, she stated that she hoped to go back to Savannah "by all means." Nevertheless, Taylor remained concerned that she would be sent to Liberia: "We did not know when this would be, but were prepared in case this settlement should be reached. However, the Confederates would not agree to the arrangement, or else it was one of the many rumors flying about at the time."[9]

They were not merely rumors, as Abraham Lincoln made several propositions to resettle contraband outside of the nation as part of his proposal for reunification with the South.[10] Lincoln vigorously asserted as early as 1861 and throughout the war that it was necessary for the good of the nation to remove blacks from the American South, as Lincoln believed that the two races, blacks and whites, could never live together peaceably.[11] African Americans overwhelmingly rejected these assertions, and Lincoln's position on colonization brought about a serious level of concern about and even distrust of his administration.[12] These ideas also fueled the administration's reticence to enlist black regiments. In black abolitionist Alfred M. Green's opinion, "The longer the government shirks the responsibility of such a measure the longer time she gives the rebel government to tamper with the free colored people of the South, and prompt and prepare their slaves for shifting the horrors of Saint Domingo from the South to the North."[13] Historian and college president Bishop Daniel A. Payne, after meeting with Lincoln and other black leaders, wrote that to him there was a "crisis upon us" because "the opinions of the government are based upon the ideas, that white men and colored men cannot live together as equals in the same country; and that unless a voluntary and peaceable separation is effected *now*, the time must come when there will be a war of extermination between the races."[14] If the president as head of the federal government thought that blacks and whites could not live together, where would support for the African American community's right to full citizenship come from once slavery was abolished?

The final solution of a race war, which clearly concerned Lincoln, was also Douglass's greatest concern. The *New York Times* noted that newspapers in border states like Maryland were prognosticating that "emancipation . . . would be no philanthropy to the negro: his fate was extermination."[15] Another article in the *Times* expressed concern that if emancipation was "carried into effect, the blacks remaining intermixed with the whites . . . will induce a war of extermination." Thus, "enfranchised blacks," that is, free blacks, had to be moved "west of the Mississippi river; in the States of Arkansas, Louisiana (West) and Texas," while all the rebels would be "driven from the Slave states west of the Mississippi into those of the east of it." By gathering all the blacks in the nation into one region, "it will place the blacks where their future deportation—in part or in whole—will be the most convenient" and prevent their extermination. To do nothing would "cause an animosity on the part of the South . . . that five generations would not see obliterated, and which would be placed in the category of the deeds of Cawnpore," a particularly brutal altercation of internecine warfare that occurred between British and Indian rebels in 1857, ending in the slaughter of hundreds of women and children.[16] Commenting directly on these ideas, Douglass was emphatic about what many blacks continued to fear and what Americans talked about incessantly during the Civil War: "The white people of the country may trump up some cause of war against the colored people, and wage that terrible war of races which some men even now venture to predict, if not desire, and exterminate the black race entirely. They would spare neither age nor sex." But Douglass was quick to denounce such prospects: "But is there not some chosen curse, some secret thunder in the stores of heaven red with uncommon wrath to blast the men who harbor this bloody solution? . . . Such a war would indeed remove the colored race from the country. It would fill the land with violence and crime, and make the very name of America a stench in the nostrils of mankind. It would give you hell for a country."[17]

The prevailing threat of a war between the races did not deter slaves who emancipated themselves and African American soldiers, who knew that they faced serious danger. Some northern Democrats, according to free black George E. Stephens of Massachusetts, attempted to scare him from enlisting in the Fifty-Fourth Massachusetts Regiment by sharing what they knew to be true: "Every one of them that the rebels catch will be hanged, or sent into the Indigo mines, or cut up into mincemeat, or quartered and pickled, or spitted. . . . [W]hat good is it going to do the colored people to go fight and lose their lives?" Yet Stephens called upon African American men not to be discouraged from enlisting in the Union army by such dire warnings or by their understandable skepticism about the sincerity of Lincoln's commitment to African Americans. Stephens argued that these "copperheads" had no idea of how powerful the call from "Heaven, as with a voice of thunder, calls on you to arise from the dust, and smite with an avenging hand the obdurate, cruel, and relentless enemy and traitor . . . whose life and sacred honor are pledged to wage an interminable war against your race."[18] When Union general Benjamin Butler asked some colored officers in New Orleans if they thought their men would fight, they responded by saying, "General, we come of a fighting race. Our fathers were brought here slaves because they were captured in war, and in hand to hand fights, too. We are willing to fight." Within one day in August 1862, two thousand black men were ready to enlist in the "first regiment of colored troops ever mustered into the services of the United States during the War of the Rebellion." Yet they too did not take their enlistment lightly or without calculation, as indicated by their response to Butler's query as to why they had not already "struck a good blow somewhere for their freedom." One man responded by asking the general: "If we colored men had risen to make war on our masters, would not it have been our duty to ourselves, they being our enemies, to kill the enemy wherever we could find them? And all the white men would have been our enemies to be killed?" General Butler answered, "I don't know but what you are right. . . . I think that would be a logical necessity of insurrection." To which this former slave replied, "If the colored men had begun such a war as that, General, which general of the United States army should we have called on to help us fight our battles?" To which Butler wrote, "That was unanswerable." What was clear to Butler, however, was that "in a very short time three regiments of infantry and two batteries of artillery were equipped, drilled, and ready for service. Better soldiers never shouldered a musket. They were intelligent, obedient, highly appreciative of their position, and fully maintained its dignity. They easily learned the school of the soldier."[19] This training would come in handy, as African American men, formerly enslaved and free, faced considerable peril in fighting against the Confederates, who viewed their participation as an act of servile war.

Indeed, white southerners were emboldened during the Civil War to act upon the ideas of black extermination in their establishment of the policy of the black flag, or no quarter on the battlefield. This policy did not acknowledge the surrender of black soldiers and the white officers who led them. It also allowed for the murder of newly freed slaves or contraband of war found among them. According to a letter addressed to a Union officer, Maj. Gen. Samuel R. Curtis, by a Confederate officer, Maj. Gen. Thomas H. Holmes, "Ordinarily when civilized and Christian nations are belligerents no special settlements of any rules of warfare would seem requisite," but Lincoln arming the slaves had changed all that. Slaves with arms, in the white southerner's mind, put white women and children at risk, and "it cannot in such a situation be expected that we will remain passive, quietly acquiescing in a war of extermination against us, without waging a similar war in return."[20] From the perspective of Jefferson Davis, president of the Confederacy, Lincoln's Emancipation Proclamation, which freed all those enslaved in the Confederate states, removed any possibility of a "reconstruction of the old Union." Rather, it "has established a state of things which can lead to but one of three possible consequences—the extermination of the slaves, the exile of the whole white population from the Confederacy, or absolute and total separation of these states from the United States." Indeed, in Davis's opinion, which was republished in *Douglass' Monthly*, the slaves were "doomed to extermination."[21] Lincoln's Emancipation Proclamation may have stoked white fear that a race war and servile insurrection were imminent, but there is no evidence of blacks harming white women and children during the Civil War. There is evidence, however, that southern whites ruthlessly murdered not only countless African American soldiers but also black women and children.

The Confederacy used the Emancipation Proclamation to rationalize its military strategy of extermination, of brutally murdering black Americans across the South. Southerners hoped that waging exterminatory warfare would intimidate those enslaved and free from joining with or seeking protection from the Union army. For example, according to one escaped slave, several blacks were hanged without trial under the suspicion that they were organizing those enslaved to insurrect. Proof of their intent was that copies of the published Emancipation Proclamation "were found in their possession." According to the report, the knowledge that "such a proclamation has been made is well-known among all the negroes, and it produced the most startling effect. The terror of the whites is beyond description. Apprehensions of a re-enactment of the Nat Turner horrors are felt to an alarming extent." In response to the unfounded fears that blacks were set upon massacring whites and to repudiate the possibility of black freedom, "seventeen negroes were promptly taken out . . . and hung. It is said that the negroes of the different counties . . . are all engaged in the conspiracy for a general insurrection."[22] Allen Parker, a former slave who served with the United States Navy, heard a slave owner warn another slave that "if the south were successful they would kill all the negroes that ran away."[23] Although Allen and his friend Joe were not deterred by this prophecy, as they chose to believe that the South would not win, many runaway slaves were killed to send the same message of intimidation. The *Liberator* reported in 1863 that twenty unarmed Negro teamsters were shot and killed because they were wagoneers for the Union forces. Eighteen black men and boys serving as cooks and cabin boys on the captured Union steamer *Harpeth Shoals* were "tied and taken to an open field . . . and deliberately shot down in cold blood."[24] Then there is the example of troops from Texas under Col. William Henry Parson murdering the refugees attached to the federal supply train in northeastern Arkansas. According to a Wisconsin soldier, William De Loss Love, "The rebels, now that resistance had ceased, took possession of the Camp, and with the most fiendish barbarity murdered many negroes, both men and women."[25] Similar actions against unarmed runaway slaves took place in April 1864 during the Battle of Marks Mills, Arkansas, where, according to Lieutenant Pearson, Rebel soldiers admitted to him that "they had killed eighty odd negroes men women & children."[26]

The most highly publicized example of Rebel atrocities during the Civil War, however, took place at Fort Pillow in the western part of Tennessee. Fort Pillow, overlooking the Mississippi River sixty miles north of Memphis, had been nearly empty until the arrival of over six hundred troops, some traders, two hundred contraband, and the families of the soldiers. Two hundred and forty-six of those soldiers were African Americans sent by Gen. Stephen A. Hurlbut to secure the fort for trading purposes and to ensure that the federal forces were free to navigate the Mississippi without obstruction. Unfortunately, the soldiers and their leaders were ill prepared for a Confederate siege upon the fort on April 12, 1864. Hurlburt would later claim that he never received the orders from Union general William Tecumseh Sherman to abandon the fort in January 1864.[27]

When the rumor spread like wildfire that Confederate lieutenant general Nathan Bedford Forrest was on his way to attack the fort, many women, children, and some sick blacks were put on board a barge pulled by the gunboat the *New Era* to seek shelter at a place named Coal Creek. The more than two hundred women and children who were at Fort Pillow as contraband of war did not make it onto the barge, however, and they ran into the brush along the river's edge, hiding in the massive tangle of driftwood.[28]

Once the battle commenced, Forrest, with over fifteen hundred Confederate troops, took illegal advantage of a cease-fire, and his men leaped over the fort's garrison wall in a solid mass, crying, "No quarter!" The stunned Union troops, recognizing that the battle was now over, threw down their weapons and made a mad dash down the steep and slippery side of the bluff, all the while hearing the Rebels yelling again and again, "No quarter!" and "Kill the damned niggers; shoot them down!"[29] The Confederates had placed a regiment of cavalry to block off the escape of the Union soldiers, and all of them who could either raised their arms in surrender or continued running toward the Mississippi River.[30]

Almost all of the Union troops, black and white, who had made it to the water's edge ended up dead or nearly so. According to Acting Master William Ferguson of the U.S. steamer *Silver Cloud*, there were "unmistakable evidences" that a "massacre" had occurred. Bodies were left with gaping holes, some soldiers were "bayoneted through the eyes," some had their "skulls beaten through," other bodies were found with "hideous wounds as if their bowels had been ripped open with bowie-knives." With cold-blooded barbarity, the Rebels continued to shoot and kill those who surrendered, as well as those who attempted to hide "behind logs and under the brush" for protection, showing how "persistent was the slaughter of our unfortunate troops."[31] Union soldier Daniel Stamps certified that the next morning he saw "negroes who were wounded, and had survived the night, shot and killed as fast as they could be found."[32]

Black women and children were not exempt from slaughter. According to Union soldier William J. Mays, "2 negro women and 3 little children" were murdered after a "rebel stepped up to them and said, 'yes, God damn you, you thought you were free, did you?' And shot them all. They all fell but 1 child, when he knocked it in the head with the breach of his gun. They then disappeared in the direction of the landing, following up the fugitives, firing at them wherever seen."[33] Two other formerly enslaved women were shot down, and "their bodies were thrown into the river after the place was taken."[34] Union surgeon Horace Wardner received a "young negro boy, probably sixteen years old, who was in the hospital there sick with fever, and unable to get away. The rebels entered the hospital, and with a saber hacked his head, no doubt with the intention of splitting it open. . . . He was brought here insensible, and died yesterday."[35] Elias Falls, cook and private in the "colored" infantry, testified that there were others and that he was informed that the Rebels killed "two women and two children" who were also sick in the hospital at Fort Pillow.[36] Another African American soldier, Thomas Adison, testified that Confederate soldiers shot two "little children not more than that high (holding his hand off about four feet from the floor)" whose names he recalled as "Dave" and "Anderson."[37] Colored infantryman Manuel Nichols also witnessed a "little boy belonging to company D" being "shot . . . down."[38] Three young boys who helped with the breastwork were also murdered, "lying in the water, with their heads out; they could not swim. They begged them as long as they could, but they shot them right in the forehead." George Shaw, a former slave who had enlisted in the Union army at Fort Pillow, was perturbed by the fact that from hardly ten feet away he could see that the "boys" were "not more than fifteen or sixteen years old. They were not soldiers."[39]

The Rebels also set houses, the hospital, and the commissary located at the bottom of the bluff on fire, deliberately burning alive the many injured Union soldiers placed inside them. Ransom Anderson, a former slave from Mississippi who enlisted in the army when the city of Corinth fell into Union hands, testified that he heard the Union soldiers' "hallooing" screams, but they could not escape, because the doors were "barred with one of those wide bolts."[40] Contraband Jacob Thompson stated that he also saw the Rebels nail "black sergeants to the logs and set the logs on fire. . . . [They] drove the nails right through their hands."[41]

Out of six hundred men, three to four hundred men lost their lives. The Confederates gathered up the remaining black troops as prisoners and made them "pull the artillery, whipping them at the same time in the most shameful manner" as if they were beasts.[42] According to the congressional report, "At least three hundred were murdered in cold blood."[43] In the end, approximately 62 black prisoners, most of them severely wounded, were all that was left of the 246 combatants in Companies A through D of the Sixth United States Colored Heavy Artillery division and Company D of the Second United States Colored Light Artillery division.[44] It is not possible to assess how many black women and children lost their lives, but clearly many were killed. The Confederacy praised Forrest for his actions, calling it a "brilliant campaign . . .

a campaign which has conferred upon its authors fame as enduring as the records of the struggle which they have so brilliantly illustrated."[45]

In commenting on Fort Pillow, African Americans noted, "We know that, when we enlisted, threats had been made, and we expected them to be fulfilled; and this butchery is not a new thing to us—we have had experiences before to-day. With slaveholders this is only *an act on a grander scale*."[46] For many black soldiers, the phrase "remember Fort Pillow" would be their rallying cry for the remainder of the war.[47] Rev. Henry McNeal Turner, serving as chaplain to the First U.S. Colored Troops, recalled that at the Battle of Petersburg in Virginia, African American soldiers "and the rebels were both crying out—'Fort Pillow!' This seems to be the battle-cry on both sides. . . . [O]nward they went, waxing stronger and mightier every time Fort Pillow was mentioned." When the Rebels attempted to surrender, "some few held up their hands and pleaded for mercy, but our boys . . . with few exceptions" killed them.[48] For Turner, while he understood why the black soldiers showed their adversaries no mercy, he still opposed behavior that he recognized was

> highly endorsed by an immense number of both white and colored people . . . that is the killing of all the rebel soldiers taken by our soldiers. True, the rebels have set the example, particularly in killing the colored soldiers; but it is a cruel one. . . . Such a course of warfare is an outrage upon civilization and nominal Christianity. And in as much as it was *presumed* that *we* would carry out a brutal warfare, let us disappoint our malicious anticipators, by showing the world that higher sentiments not only prevail, but actually predominate.[49]

It is important to point out, however, that indiscriminate acts of violence against people of color during the Civil War were pervasive across America and not just in the South. Certainly, Chief Justice Roger B. Taney's decision in the *Dred Scott* case in 1857 helped to encourage ideas that African Americans were disposable and could never be part of the fabric of American life.[50] Thus the exclusion of blacks as citizens in America left them relatively unprotected by law when violence ensued, regardless of their status as free people.

In the North, the Democratic Party, led by elite white southerners, the northern aristocracy who profited from slavery, and those determined to sustain white supremacy in America operated to ensure the subordinate status of African Americans through the indoctrination of a burgeoning immigrant population. Democratic newspapers and presidential candidates, like Stephen A. Douglass, used the race card to stoke fears of black emancipation among white workers. In Democratic political clubs, they used pamphlets, poems, and songs to effectively galvanize an antiblack sentiment that would eventually turn deadly. For example, in 1863 a collection of poems and songs was published in minstrel style to be used in Democratic club meetings. Democrats warned that if African Americans were to become free through Lincoln's Emancipation Proclamation, white Americans, especially white women and children, would be in danger. One poem called "De Serenade" harks back to the Haitian Revolution as a touchstone to rouse white fear of black freedom:

> *Oh de Sangomingo darkeys had a standard which dey bore;*
> *Twas a pretty little baby's head, all dripping in its gore!*
> *And if we undastand aright de President's Proclaim,*
> *He tells de Dixxie niggers dey may go and do de same! . . .*
>
> *Oh, de Sangomingo darkies, dare old Massa took and tied.*
> *And den dey got de handsaw and sawed 'em till they died!*
> *And after dey had sawed 'em till dey sawed away dare lives,*
> *You may bet dey had a good time a kissin' ob dare wives!*
> *And if we understand him,*
> *Mass Linking makes proclaim,*
> *Dat de niggers down in Dixie*
> *Have a right to do de same!*[51]

Another song entitled "Fight for the Nigger" has a particularly effective stanza:

> *Moreover, if you're drafted, do not refuse to go,*
> *You are equal to a nigger and can make as good a show;*
> *And when you are in battle to the Union be true,*
> *But don't forget the darkey is as good a man as you!*
>
> > *Fight for the nigger.*
> > *The sweet-scented nigger,*
> > *The wooly-headed nigger,*
> > *And the Abolition Crew.*[52]

This sort of rallying of the forces was no doubt quite effective, especially among the Irish. Upon arrival in America, Irish immigrants faced significant discrimination due to the rise in nativism, a sociopolitical movement that opposed foreigners who nativists believed would not assimilate into American society for religious or cultural reasons. Ethnic bigotry placed the Irish at the bottom of the social hierarchy, hardly above African Americans, whom the Irish were in competition with for jobs. Northerners stoked white fear to nurture and maintain ideas of white supremacy and to incite racial violence against black Americans during the Civil War. And the idea of a war between the races, which played out on the battlefields of the South, was played out in northern cities where African American communities prospered.

For example, during the Detroit riot, which began on March 6, 1863, many race-based acts of violence were perpetrated against black men, women, and children. Instigated by Lincoln's call for new recruits to the Union army and after the trial of a fair-skinned black man named William Faulkner, who was wrongfully convicted of raping two girls, one white and one black, hundreds of immigrants, young men and boys, some "apparently not over ten years of age," many of them Irish and some German, swept into black neighborhoods and terrorized the community.[53]

According to several African American sources, the organized mob went down Beaubien Street "yelling . . . and crying kill all the d——d niggers." Free black Thomas Buckner heard another "ruffian" claim, "If we are got to be killed up for niggers then we will kill every nigger in this town." Even white females "were heard crying, kill them." Eventually the mob came upon a black-owned cooper shop, and "they made a rush upon the house in which were . . . [three] women and [four] children. . . . The [five] men in the shop [which was attached to the house] seeing this, rushed out of the shop into the house to protect the women and children. . . . The women and children were dodging from one room to another to escape the stones." Two African American men, Louis and Solomon Houston, remembered that "then the mob set the shop on fire . . . and soon it was in flames! The mob then surrounded the house in every direction, as if determined to burn up the property and all the men, women, and children that were therein."[54]

William Jones, an African American who was visiting Detroit from Canada, remembered the "women crying for mercy's sake to let them out, for already a part of the roof of the house had fallen; but no entreaty, no appeal for sympathy moved the mob . . . determined to burn them all up. . . . We then made an attempt to force our way out of the house . . . but was met by United States soldiers and others, with stones, bricks and billets of wood." In making their escape, "a helpless babe was torn from the arms of its unprotected mother, and in her presence kicked and buffed until life was almost extinct." Old people were subject to violence as well, as seventy-nine-year-old Richard Evans was shot in the head, and eighty-year-old "Father" Ephraim Clark, sexton at the local African Methodist Episcopal church, was badly beaten.[55]

Former slave William Webb, who was working in Detroit at the time, recalled, "A great many colored people were fleeing out in the country where I was, and some came to the house where I was stopping to get shelter, both men and women. . . . We put a guard around the place, so that if they saw any people coming, to give the alarm. We sat up and watched all night. . . . I came into the city next day to see what damage they had done. The colored people were very scarce. . . . I found that some had run over into Canada, and some of them had run into the woods."[56]

The black community knew that the mob action was "in harmony with Democratic feelings" and that the refusal of Detroit politicians to compensate them for their losses, "estimated at fifteen to twenty thousand dollars," was due to the fact that "Detroit is a Democratic city." An anonymous author noted that there was "but one thing the colored man knows, that the class of men of the same politics as those South are doing the mobbing North; so they are not only ready to suffer, but to die in the cause that promises over three millions of their race liberty. Whatever . . . the rage of the enemies of freedom may be!" Yet for one eyewitness named Mr. Dale, it was "most revolting, to see innocent men, women and children, all without respect to age or sex, being pounded in the most brutal manner."[57] In a sermon given to his church congregation, Rev. S. S. Hunting elaborated on what was perhaps the emerging spirit of African Americans, as well as that of white Americans, across the nation:

> The threat is made, that "if the course of things" . . . the elevation of the negro in moral, intellectual and social endowments, "shall not be arrested," the recent riot "is but premonitory of an uprising which will leave no resting place for the negro in the States of the Northwest." Now, let it be distinctly understood, that the attempt to exterminate the negro will bring extermination to certain classes of their enemies. . . . This negro hatred is what blinded the eyes of the nation, and threatens future calamity if it is not checked and overcome.[58]

Four months later, African Americans were traumatized by similar yet heightened acts of racial violence in the New York draft riot on July 11, 1863.[59] Although attempts were at first made to "stand and resist the attack . . . being overpowered by superior numbers, they broke ranks and scattered" as best they could.[60] Indeed, according to African American sources, "All were slain, either while in the peaceful pursuit of their honest, though humble vocations, providing for their families, or while endeavoring to escape from the hands of their destroyers." One African American wondered, "Why should they hurt me or my colored brethren? We are poor men like them." This man, over sixty-three years old and a whitewasher by trade, was left to die on the railroad tracks with a broken arm and a battered face. According to one woman, "Not less than one hundred colored people fled" from her neighborhood of Sullivan Street.[61] And they did so for good reason. According to another African American woman, Mrs. Statts,

At 3 o'clock . . . the mob arrived and immediately commenced an attack with terrific yells. . . . In the next room to where I was sitting was a poor woman, who had been confined with a child on Sunday, three days previous. Some of the rioters broke through the front door with pick axes, and came rushing into the room where this poor woman lay, and commenced to pull the clothes from off her. Knowing that their rage was chiefly directed against men, I hid my son behind me and ran with him through the back door, down to the basement. In a little while I saw the innocent babe, of three days old, come crashing down into the yard; some of the rioters had dashed it out of the back window, killing it instantly. . . . Fearing we should be drowned in the cellar, (there were ten of us, mostly women and children, there) I took my boy and flew past the dead body of the babe, out to the rear of the yard, hoping to escape with him . . . but here, to our horror and dismay, we met the mob again; I, with my son, had climbed the fence, but the sight of those maddened demons so affected me that I fell back, fainting, into the yard; my son jumped down . . . to pick me up. . . . As they surrounded us my son exclaimed "save my mother, gentlemen, if you kill me." "Well, we will kill you," they answered . . . and armed with a crowbar . . . deliberately struck him a heavy blow over the head, felling him like a bullock to the ground. (He died in the N. Y. hospital two days later.) I believe if I were to live a hundred years I would never forget that scene.[62]

As Mrs. Statts ran for her life, she was caught by another mob, which "beat me severely."[63]

Attempts to kill African American children seem to have been pervasive in the New York draft riot. Although the matron and superintendent of the Colored Orphan Asylum managed to save all "230 children between the ages of 4 and 12 years in the home at the time of the riot" by removing them to the police station, the mob deliberately went there to seek them out. Subsequently, "the main buildings were burned . . . the shrubs uprooted. . . . All was destroyed."[64] Former slave James Lindsay Smith recalled, however, that "a sweet babe was brained while holding up his little arms, and smiling upon his murderers. Many little children were killed in this manner."[65] Frederick Douglass also claimed that during that same "bloody uprising" in New York, the mob "spared neither age nor sex; it hanged negroes simply because they were negroes, it murdered women in their homes, and . . . it dashed out the brains of young children against the lamp posts."[66]

Douglass noted that the "mobs at Detroit, Chicago, Cincinnati, and New York" were evidence of "the unconquerable aversion of the Irish towards the colored race . . . that the Irish people are among our bitterest persecutors." It was "in one sense . . . strange[,] passing strange, that they should be such." Douglass, quoting the Irish activist Daniel O'Connell, knew that the "history of Ireland might be traced like a wounded man through a crowd—by the blood. The Irishman has been persecuted for his religion about as vigorously as the black man has been for his color." Knowing this to be the case, Douglass was perturbed by the violence of Irishmen upon black Americans, stating that "there is something quite revolting in the idea of a people lately oppressed suddenly becoming oppressors, that the persecuted can so suddenly become the persecutors."[67]

Racialized and gendered warfare also occurred out west in 1864 in a region of the Colorado Territory during what became known as the Sand Creek Massacre. According to an interpreter and special Indian agent to the military, John S. Smith, one hundred families of Cheyennes and six or eight lodges of Arapahos who were known to be "friendly Indians" were massacred on November 29, 1864, by U.S. troops under the leadership of Col. John M. Chivington. Of the 500 Native Americans, based on Smith's calculation of "five to a lodge," approximately 250 were killed, and more than half of the dead were women and children. According to Smith, women and children were slaughtered "indiscriminately," and "I saw the bodies of those lying there cut all to pieces, worse mutilated than any I ever saw before; the women cut all to pieces . . . scalped; their brains knocked out; children two or three months old; all ages lying there, from sucking infants up to warriors."[68] A soldier who protested the attack of Cheyenne chief Black Kettle's village to no avail and was still ashamed that he "was in it with my Co. Col. Chivington" acknowledged that what Smith testified to was true, that he saw "a squaw ripped open and a child taken from her, little children shot while begging for their lives."[69] The massacre lasted for six to eight hours. Years later, a veteran, Dr. T. P. Bell, recounted the events of that day, and when he was asked, "But how about the children, doctor?" Bell "smiled grimly" and stated that he and the other soldiers were told just before the charge began, "Boys, remember that nits make lice." Bell went on to state that "we all seemed to feel the same way."[70]

Significantly, the *Liberator* aligned the Sand Creek Massacre with the massacre of African Americans in the South by juxtaposing the paper's exposé of "The Chivington Massacre" above an article entitled "Awful State of Affairs in Alabama," which described the murder of black men, women, and children.[71] Only people of color experienced exterminatory warfare during the Civil War. Although over 750,000 soldiers, white and black, died in this war, the deliberate killing of noncombatants, namely, women and children, was unique to African American and Native American communities. Concerned at the war's end that now many black men were both armed and trained, Lincoln stated,

"I fear a race war," ignoring the fact that there had already been a war between the races going on, a war of extermination that would continue to be waged against the black community.[72]

The Post–Civil War Years

Race-based acts of violence continued for many years, long after the Civil War ended. Whites in the North and the South continued to talk about black extermination and a war between the races as inevitable. Black people found themselves caught relatively unprotected in the subsequent undeclared war that southerners waged against people of color residing within their communities. In an attempt to restore the supremacy of the white race, black people were treated as if they were disposable and not essential to the South or the nation. These ideas fostered the continuation of exterminatory practices toward African American men, women, and children during Reconstruction that lasted well into the twentieth century.

Emancipation destroyed the rituals of domination and subordination between southern blacks and whites. The newly freed men and women possessed a pervasive attitude of defiance, and this worried plantation owners, who complained to federal officials about their fears of black freedom.[73] African Americans, no longer intimidated by their former masters, demanded new economic and social relationships. Their assertive actions negated all of the earlier proslavery rhetoric that those enslaved were docile children incapable of taking care of themselves and their communities. Freed men and women engaged in the formerly unlawful act of educating themselves and their children with such intensity that it was widely regarded as phenomenal when it outpaced poor whites. Additionally, blacks fully immersed themselves in the political process throughout the South. Prior to the Civil War, registration had not been necessary in order to vote, but blacks soon mastered what was required of them as free citizens.[74] They reclaimed their families, became property owners, and built their own churches, schools, hospitals, political organizations, and businesses with a fervor that was unprecedented.

Thus, for most southerners, it was the elevation of African Americans to an equal or, as many feared, superior status to whites that would cause a race war to ensue after the Civil War ended. In Georgian writer Eliza Frances Andrews's view, unless labor and race relations returned to their former conditions, "the fanatics who have caused the trouble" will "force the negro in their rash experiments to justify themselves for his emancipation," making direct confrontation inevitable. Andrews believed that because of this pressure on southern whites, "eventually the negro race will be either exterminated or reduced to some system of apprenticeship embodying the best features of slavery."[75] Mary Jones, the wife of Rev. Dr. Charles Colcock Jones, also believed that circumstances in the South were dire for African Americans. In her religious prophesizing, Jones predicted that "with their emancipation must come extermination. . . . I feel if ever we gain our independence there will be radical reforms in the system of slavery as it now exists. When once delivered from the interference of Northern abolitionism, we shall be free to make and enforce such rules and reformations as are just and right."[76] These women were writing privately in their diaries, but they were also perhaps echoing public sentiment.

This idea that a "war between the whites and blacks of the South is probable" was reported in several newspapers by the end of the Civil War. According to one paper, the view "widely prevails throughout the South. It was an universally accepted axiom there, long before the rebellion, that emancipation would result in one of two things—either amalgamation or extermination."[77] Another paper noted that "already we hear from many quarters the prophecy that the whole black race in this country is doomed to extermination."[78] In Alabama, a newspaper reported that "some planters even boast that they could manure their lands with the dead carcasses of negroes." Commenting on the lack of federal intervention, the article went on to say that "if negroes can be shot down daily in garrisoned towns where the authorities are unable to stop this state of things, it is very reasonable to suppose that this brutal work is carried on more extensively where the blacks have no protection. This wholesale murdering of human being[s] is, we fear, the practical working of the conspiracy to exterminate the colored race."[79] According to the *Milwaukee Daily Sentinel*, another southern newspaper warned that although it had "a great solicitude for the welfare of the colored men . . . in the event of the negroes securing the elective franchise a war of races will ensue which will result in the extermination of the race."[80] It was this kind of talk that concerned American author and diplomat C. Edwards Lester of New York, apparent in his open letter to Governor James Lawrence Orr of South Carolina:

> When men talk so idly of a war of races which would end in the annihilation of the negro in the South . . . they are using language far more dangerous . . . than they did when they declared that if Slavery or the Union were to perish the Union should be the victim. . . . What then shall the South do to make the best of her position? She can neither get rid of these four millions of people nor exterminate them: both are impossibilities. The nineteenth century is not going to allow four million of people, who have committed no crime to be swept from the face of the earth.[81]

African Americans were not so confident, as they believed that southern whites were determined to show that they meant what they said, that they would exterminate African Americans in order to reaffirm white supremacy. According to Robert Hamilton, Thomas Hamilton's brother, also a black abolitionist and now editor of the *Weekly Anglo-African*, because African Americans had fought on the side of the Union, "the scheme is now . . . to exterminate the negro." He also noted that the "virus of negro hate" had always been conjoined with the "mania of eternal negro slavery." Southerners had not reconciled with the outcome of the Civil War and the subsequent destruction of the institution of slavery, and now the "rebel hates the negro because he has thrown off *his* yoke and become free" and because "he defeated the object and the aim of the rebellion." Indeed, Hamilton argued, the hatred was so severe and "their jealousy of their former slaves is such that they would rather see everyone of them blotted out of existence, than to see them free." What concerned Hamilton was that "this feeling is shared by thousands at the South who have not been slaveholders. The shocking barbarities now suffered by the colored people at the South affords a solemn lesson for the Government." Hamilton called on Congress not just to take his word for it but to do something to protect blacks in the South from white vengeance: "We trust that Congress will ventilate when it meets, and let the country and the world know if there is a conspiracy to institute a massacre, or to reestablish slavery at all hazards."[82]

The conspiracy to massacre African Americans of which Hamilton warned seemed to begin almost immediately after the Civil War. For example, there were reports from Clark County, Alabama, in 1865 that "men are hanged for saying they are free, and tied hog-fashion, and thrown over in the river and drowned. Women are shut up in chicken-coops, and thrown in the river. All these things are done, and no person to protect them." According to a teacher from the Northwest Freedman's Aid Commission in Mobile, Alabama, "One hundred and thirty three dead bodies were counted in the woods, five bodies were seen floating in the river. . . . Women and children killed, and then boxed up and thrown into the river." One black man, who had his ears cut off by former Rebel soldiers, was told by them that "five thousand of them had formed a clan to kill every negro that they could without detection; that if the negro was to be free, he should not live in this country; that the tariff that the government has established for wages was too small for a man to live on; therefore, in order to obtain more, the negroes must be banished, so that they could get higher wages."[83] According to Inspector General Col. Charles F. Johnson, during the riots in Memphis, Tennessee, the city recorder, John C.

Creighton, called for the "whole sale slaughter of blacks." In a speech he delivered on May 1, 1866, Creighton urged the "crowd of police and citizens" to continue to "prepare and clean out every damned son of a bitch of a nigger out of town. . . . Boys, I want you to go ahead and kill every damned one of the nigger race and burn up the cradle."[84] The fact that a city official urged violence gave the white crowd a license to kill: "During the night the Negroes were hunted down by police, firemen and other white citizens, shot, assaulted, robbed, and in many instances their houses searched under the pretense of hunting for concealed arms, plundered, and then set on fire, during which no resistance so far as we can learn was offered by the Negroes. . . . All crimes imaginable were committed from simple larceny to rape and murder. Several women and children were shot in bed. One woman (Rachel Johnson) was shot and then thrown into the flames of a burning house and consumed."[85]

African Americans were well aware not only of the danger that freedom engendered but also that the desire to drive the "whole negro race out [of] the country" was at the heart of white violence against them during the post–Civil War years.[86] Martin R. Delany, fearing that talk of colonization would fuel southern ideas of black extermination, wrote a letter on July 21, 1866, to James Lynch, editor of the *Christian Recorder*, entitled "Letter on President Warner of Liberia." In his letter, Delany chastised President Daniel Bashiel Warner, the third African American president of Liberia, for his public comments suggesting the removal of southern blacks from America. For Delany, there was real danger in even discussing the idea: "Does President Warner know, that the commencement of such an act of national injustice is itself a barbarity that might lead to *extermination*, a much cheaper and by far easier method of ridding the nation of this people!"[87]

Over time, as ideas about a race war continued to preclude absolute freedom in the South, Delany became concerned about the possibility of national support for a war between the races and black extermination. In a letter to Douglass in 1876, Delany reveals that his fears of extermination were real: "The eye of the whole North and West being already turned in this direction, and their minds made up, and the first occasion of a murmur of a conflict of races, and the whole country will rise up and rush to arms with such force and power. . . . Extermination will be their theme. Their watch-word, 'Every Negro in the grave!' . . . When our race, shall only be remembered among the things of the past!"[88] Delany's inclusion of the "West" no doubt reflected the fact that the U.S. military was now in the western part of America executing a doctrine of destruction and extermination on Native American people. President Ulysses S. Grant issued a sharp yet heartfelt warning to Native Americans in the West, stating that they had only one choice in 1873: either allow themselves to be brought "under the benign influences of education and civilization," or face a "war of extermination."[89]

Aside from federal policy and the Sand Creek Massacre, Delany might have also been referring to the Camp Grant Massacre in 1871. Out of the 125 Arivaipa Apaches killed by a large party of Anglo-American merchants, Mexican American ranchers, and Tohono O'odham from the San Xavier del Bac Mission, only 8 were men. The camp, Lt. Royal Whitman recalled, was found "burning and the ground strewn with their mutilated women and children." These Apaches were not the instigators of anti-American aggression or uncivilized members of society, as President Grant portrayed all Native people in his proclamation. Instead, Whitman believed that Americans would "drive them into a hopeless war of extermination."[90] Moreover, the national outrage at Gen. George Armstrong Custer's death during his confrontation with the Sioux Indians at Little Bighorn on June 25, 1876, incited many Americans across the country to call for unrelenting warfare against Native Americans and for their complete extermination.[91] Delany seems to imply that black Americans might be next. Given the racial strife that existed in the South, his implications were certainly justified.

During Reconstruction, black men organized themselves across the South into trained military units to fight against rising white forces like the Ku Klux Klan. For many former slaves during the postwar years, "things were mighty tough for us."[92] From 1865 to 1869, fifteen hundred African Americans were lynched in the South.[93] According to Richard Taylor, the son of President Zachary Taylor and the brother-in-law of Confederate president Jefferson Davis, between the assassination of President Lincoln in 1865 and 1869, "The entire white race of the south devoted itself to the killing of negroes. . . . Thousands upon thousands were slain. . . . [S]uch was the ferocity of the slavedrivers, that unborn infants were ripped from their mothers wombs. Individual effort could not suffice the rage for slaughter. . . . Thus 'Ku-Klux' originated, and covered the land with a network of crime."[94] Many blacks, like those in Bennettsville, South Carolina, carried weapons with them at all times and patrolled the streets to prevent attacks from the Klan. The problem was most pervasive in counties where many blacks owned farms and where the population was racially mixed. Thousands of blacks left their homes every night and took to the forest, as, according to the testimony of former slave Essic Harris, they feared for their lives once darkness fell. Yet Harris went back into his house "because I could not leave my children there to be killed." Harris knew what the Klan was capable of, as the family of another black man, named Anthony Davis, had been nearly killed when "they whipped him and shot at his children." The children and their father survived, but the Ku Klux Klan had "wounded them."[95] African American Republican congressman Richard Cain of South Carolina surrounded his house with armed men, as he and his family lived under the constant threat of violence.[96] Republican officials attempted to calm the tension between blacks and whites by urging black militias to cease their defensive counterviolence, but times had changed, and black men were no longer willing to be victims at the hands of whites. According to former slave William Henry Rooks, the violence that groups like the KKK and others exhibited against the black community was "about equalization after the freedom."[97] Indeed, according to Eli Coleman, they were determined "not [to] let the negro exert his freedom." In this old ex-slave's view, "the white man he thought we ought to still work for them like we did during slavery time. . . . It is still that way, son, to this day with some white people."[98] While recognizing the very legitimate reasons for the state of unrest existing in the South, for Delany the problem was that if "this great divergence and extraordinary estrangement . . . [f]rom whichever side it comes . . . [is] not permanently checked, my race can have but one terminal destiny, political nonentity and race extermination."[99]

By the end of Reconstruction in 1877, many Republicans in Congress believed that the "Negro question" had been resolved with the passing of the Fifteenth Amendment, and they no longer wished to pursue national involvement in southern affairs. Northerners in both parties felt that, as was the case with newly arriving immigrants, it was up to blacks to create their own future in the American marketplace. Congress's laissez-faire approach to the freedmen hurt Reconstruction efforts, giving space for racial violence to continue.

Many black leaders confirmed that the possibility of extermination or reenslavement remained a considerable threat to the black community for the rest of the century, especially after the civil rights cases brought to the Supreme Court in 1883 nullified the Civil Rights Act of 1875, which argued that Congress did not have the constitutional authority to regulate acts of discrimination committed by individuals or organizations.[100] For example, Dr. Henry McNeal Turner, a bishop of the African Methodist Episcopal Church and an emigrationist, wrote in 1883, "That decision [the nullification] will either put the Negro back into national politics, where his status will be either fought over again, or drive him out of the country, or result in his extermination." Turner also referred to the period of time between 1873 and 1883 as "the reign of blood and slaughter."[101] T. Thomas Fortune, a journalist and editor of the *New York Age* and *New York World*, wrote in 1884 that the Republican Party had "betrayed its trust in permitting thousands of innocent men to be slaughtered without declaring the South in rebellion. . . . No: it is time that the coloured voter learned to leave his powerless 'protectors' and take care of himself." Fortune also made it clear that from his perspective, "a people in whom the love of Liberty is in-born cannot be enslaved, though they may be exterminated by superior force."[102] Frederick Douglass stated in 1886, "Sometimes I have feared that, in some wild paroxysm of rage, the white race, forgetful of the claims of humanity and the precepts of the Christian religion, will proceed to slaughter the Negro in wholesale, as some of that race have attempted to slaughter chinamen, and as it has been done in detail in some districts of the Southern States." Apprehensively optimistic, Douglass concluded, "The future of the Negro therefore is, that he will not be expatriated nor annihilated."[103] Newspapers like the *Weekly Age-Herald* prophesied, however, that the education and uplift of the African American population had made things worse between the "two races." And because "there seems to be ever increasing signs of a race war in the South," blacks should be removed in order to avoid the inevitable conflict.[104] W. E. B. Du Bois reflected, however, that it was only due to the efforts of those Americans who helped the freedmen to improve their condition through education that blacks were not "reenslaved or exterminated in an unequal and cowardly renewal of war."[105]

Activist and journalist Ida B. Wells also noted the racial animosity embodied in the increased violence toward blacks in 1895, as there had been more than "a thousand lynchings in ten years." Wells called it an "unprecedented slaughter of human beings."[106] Another leading activist, Mary Church Terrell, argued that black women feared being lynched just as much as black men. For Terrell, it was not white fears of social equality or immorality among blacks that caused the "hanging, shooting, and burning [of] black men, women and children in the United States." It was "race hatred . . . and lawlessness." "Lynching," Terrell stated, "must still be regarded as the legitimate offspring of slavery," as is the "actual enslavement of negroes . . . under the peonage system of Alabama and Mississippi, and the unspeakable cruelties to which men, women, and children are alike subjected."[107]

The inaccurately named "race riots" that took place in Wilmington and Atlanta also affirm that mass violence threatened the black community. The appellation of "race riot" is inappropriate because it ignores how these events were tied to a history of one-sided mass violence that was not episodic but rather continuous and entrenched.[108] Although classified as race riots, these events signified a shift from the *petite guerre* strategy, whereby two sides fight each other, to blacks merely fighting back in self-defense against an organized effort to exterminate them in their communities. And much as it had during the pre–Civil War days of slavery, the federal government weighed in on the side of the oppressors of black people.[109]

According to Rev. J. Allen Kirk, one of the ministers forced to flee the city, the purpose of the "bloody Riot in Wilmington, North Carolina," in 1898 was "to remove all . . . able leaders of the colored race." To that end, an organized mob of white citizens "went from house to house looking for Negroes that they considered offensive; took their arms they had hidden and killed them for the least expression of manhood." Black lawyers, physicians, clergymen, merchants, businessmen, and property holders were the citizens most at risk. Kirk and other ministers in Wilmington were forced by the mob to "go around the city with them and ask the colored people to be obedient to the white people and go in their homes and keep quiet. This was a great humiliation to us and a shame upon our denominations."[110]

But Kirk also noted the death and trauma in the ensuing chaos, during which "thousands of women, children and men rushed to the swamps and there lay upon the earth in the cold to freeze and starve. The woods were filled with colored people. The streets were dotted with their dead bodies. A white gentleman said that he saw ten bodies lying in the undertakers office at one time. Some of their bodies were left lying in the streets until the next day. . . . [S]ome were found by the stench and miasma that came forth from their decaying bodies under their houses."[111] Letters from blacks living in Wilmington were sent to President William McKinley's office, begging the government to intervene and provide the black community with federal protection. In a letter that began "Please send relief as soon as possible or we perish," one woman outlined how "the Companies from every town came in to kill the negro. There was not any Rioting Simply the strong slaying the weak. . . . Oh, to see how we are Slaughtered, when our husbands go to work we do not look for their return. . . . [T]hey tried to slay us all. To day we are mourners in a strange land with no protection. . . . I cannot sign my name and live. But every word of this is true."[112]

Blacks all across the country, outraged by what happened in Wilmington, organized massive protest meetings. At one of the largest meetings, held in New York City under the leadership of T. Thomas Fortune, there was a call for an amendment to the Constitution that would allow the federal government to intervene when states failed to protect citizens threatened by mob violence. Unfortunately, President William McKinley was not motivated politically to interfere with states' rights issues, since he sought to solidify a renewed sense of national unity between the North and South resulting from the Spanish-American War. McKinley's reluctance to call for federal troops to intervene in a timely manner established a precedent that future presidents would follow.[113] As a result, men like Fortune told the black community to be ready to fight back, as he sensed that "the negro is on the verge of a greater crisis than any of former times." Fortune stated that he believed "in the law, but if the law can afford us no protection then we should protect ourselves, and if need be die in the defense of our rights as citizens."[114] Other black men, like the Honorable George H. White, argued in the North Carolina House of Representatives, "Should not a nation be just to all of her citizens, protect them alike in all their rights, on every foot of her soil? . . . [D]uring the last thirty-five years . . . fully 50,000 of my race have been ignominiously murdered by mobs, not 1 percent of whom have been made to answer for their crimes in the court of justice." White held up as an example "the miserable butchery of men, women, and children in Wilmington N.C. . . . who had committed no crime, nor were they even charged with crime," in the hope that Congress would act.[115] Allen Kirk, however, counseled "the Negro race to refrain from threats and highhanded talking. . . . [T]ry by all means to keep the peace that is necessary to our *existence* in this country."[116] These differing approaches had little effect on the lives of the black community in North Carolina, and subsequently over one thousand black residents left Wilmington that year rather than live in fear. Those who remained in North Carolina chose survival as their form of resistance.

African Americans in the Atlanta massacre—a better description than race riot—also had concerns about the possibility of their extermination in 1906. According to educator and activist William Pickens, "White politicians talked race-war; Georgia white newspapers urged and inspired race war" to avenge the purported rape of southern white women.[117] Pickens noted that the editor of the *Atlanta News* claimed that it was these "vicious blacks" who were "sounding the doom of their race. . . . [W]hat else can white men do except to make war to the bitter end against the black devils who continue to attack defenseless white women? . . . The men of this community will stand it no longer. They will begin a warfare on the black race. . . . The blacks will be destroyed, annihilated, completely vanquished if they do not stop these crimes." But J. Max Barber, editor of the *Voice of the Negro*, refuted these claims: "The only Reign of Terror . . . in the South is the menace of . . . lawless white men." Indeed, Barber argued, "The black woman is the woman who is in real danger and is really left without protection in the South." Barber also believed that the Atlanta massacre was led by an "organized mob . . . [a]s the mob chased and killed all the colored people it could in the heart of town. Then it attacked the street cars, the cabs and even the Pullman cars in search of Negroes." As was the case in the Wilmington massacre, Barber noted that "no soldiers could be had on the scene until the mob had done all the damage it cared and that for quite a while even the police did not intervene."[118] The coroner's office refused to hold an inquest. Ten thousand black men were arrested in 1906, and one-half of all black males in Atlanta were forced into convict labor. Over one thousand men, women, and children left Atlanta permanently, feeling absolutely terrorized about what had taken place.[119] The *Atlanta Constitution* reported that the massacre would only end if blacks stopped causing "TROUBLE" and only if they were able to stop other blacks from bothering white women; otherwise, whites would "BRING ON A WAR OF EXTERMINATION."[120] Another letter to the *Atlanta Georgian* editor proclaimed, "Let the war of extermination begin."[121]

Fears about black extermination remained rife within the black community, and the two thousand African Americans who were lynched from 1890 to 1909 testifies to the fact that the threats of deadly violence were real.[122] In 1893 former slave Rev. Peter Randolph wrote regarding the plight of his people in America: "Will extermination satisfy? No, it will add insult to injury. . . . There is but one rule, and one only, that can solve the 'Race Problem,' and all difficult problems. . . . It is called the Golden Rule: 'Do unto others as you would have others do unto you.' On this rests the joy or sorrow of America."[123] But as one white southerner put it, white supremacy remained more important than any ethical obligation to the nation: "Before we submit we will kill every Negro in the south. This is not idle boasting or fire-eating, but the cold hard facts stated."[124] In reminiscing about the African American experience during the Civil War many years later, another formerly enslaved woman reflected that ideas about black extermination remained as salient as ever: "You all ain't seen no hard times, and if another war comes they are going to kill the nits and the old ones. So you all try to be happy. It is nice to live."[125]

During the Civil War and post–Civil War years, African Americans were well aware of what they were up against, for the ideas linking race and freedom with black extermination developed nearly two hundred years earlier did not just disappear. In the case of African American soldiers, it was used unsuccessfully to intimidate black recruits from joining the war effort. A renewed sense of hope between blacks in the North and South due to the federal government's stand against enslavement made it possible for them to endure the terrorism of undeclared warfare. The subsequent murder of large numbers of men, women, and children, however, reveals the brutality and trauma experienced by black Americans not only during the Civil War years but also throughout the nineteenth century. It is because of their unflagging determination to survive that more massacres like those perpetrated upon Native Americans did not occur against blacks before and after the Civil War. Yet the massacre of innocent Native Americans demonstrates how these racialized tactics of war continued in America. If we are ever to reconcile our national memory with our national past, then we must acknowledge what African Americans faced every day, enslaved and free, namely, the supposed inevitability of a war between the races and black extermination, the resurgence of the old philosophy that "nits make lice" and the gendered violence against black women and children that this philosophy gave rise to, and finally, the historical trauma and deadly events that these culturally driven ideas fostered. Whom the nation was willing to sacrifice and whom the nation was willing to save was always informed by race and strategies of war used in the past to conquer, to colonize, to oppress—and African Americans navigated their way through this world they did not make during and after enslavement by ultimately making survival their greatest form of resistance.

The "Place for Which Our Fathers Sighed"

When James Weldon Johnson, principal of the segregated Stanton grammar school in Florida, wrote the poem "Lift Every Voice and Sing" to introduce Booker T. Washington during his visit there in 1900, he eloquently linked the past with the present, our present. Quickly transformed into song by his brother John Rosemond Johnson and adopted by the NAACP in 1919 as the Negro National Anthem, the poem calls out to the black community, "Let us march on till victory is won." But right in the middle of this poem-turned-song, Weldon Johnson acknowledged the recent past events in his own time, and in ours, and condemns America, as he says we are "treading" this pathway to victory "through the blood of the slaughtered." He also asks that America become the place that its creators envisioned, a "place for which our fathers sighed," a place where blacks were truly free, and free from the threat of extermination and mass violence. This elusive yet ever-powerful claim to justice and human rights in America has long sustained African American civil rights activism—even into the twenty-first century. Indeed, the last stanza of these powerful lyrics was used in 2009 to introduce the first African American president, Barack Hussein Obama. Yet racial oppression and fears of a race war and black extermination continue to figure prominently in the minds and lives of black leaders and the black community, which is why this history still matters.

Jamaican-born Marcus Garvey, an advocate of Black Nationalism and organizer of the African Universal Negro Improvement Association, was concerned in 1923 that some whites believed that the race question could be settled by "wholesale butchery, by lynching, by economic starvation, by a return to slavery, and legalized oppression. . . . [I]t is this danger that drives me mad." After the First World War, African American soldiers came back in 1918 with a renewed sense of hope, that since they had served bravely for their country, they would gain the rights to full citizenship. Jim Crow would no longer hold sway over American politics. But this turned out not to be the case, and

many whites in the North and South set about reaffirming white supremacy through violence. To Garvey, this meant that blacks across the diaspora
needed to come together to develop complete autonomy instead of integra-
tion, because "on every side we hear the cry of white supremacy—in America,
Canada, Australia, Europe, and even South America. . . . What must the Negro do in the face of such a universal attitude but to align all his forces in the
direction of protecting himself from the threatened disaster of race domination and ultimate extermination?"[1] For Garvey, the solution was to return to
Africa.

Garvey was right in his assessment that the black community faced a dangerous climate of racial hostility that was rife throughout the twentieth century. In *We Charge Genocide*, the Civil Rights Congress (CRC) indicted the
American government with genocide in 1951 as defined by Article II of the
United Nations Convention on the Prevention and Punishment of the Crime
of Genocide, adopted in 1948. According to Article II, "Killing members of a
group, causing serious bodily or mental harm to members of the group, deliberately inflicting on the group conditions of life calculated to bring about
its physical destruction in whole or in part" were acts of genocide. Article III
states that nations would be punished if they were found to have "conspired to
commit genocide" or even for an unsuccessful "attempt to commit genocide."
Signed by William L. Patterson, Paul Robeson, Mary Church Terrell, and
ninety-one others, the 237-page document claimed, with substantive proof,
that in America "comes this record of mass slayings on the basis of race" and
that "what is obvious . . . is the careless disregard for Negro life, liberty, and
person that is the distinctive trait of genocide."[2]

Racial violence increased significantly in the late 1940s after the Second
World War due to the black community's Double V campaign to win the war
"over our enemies from without" and "our enemies within" America. African
Americans demanded full citizenship rights in exchange for fighting in the
war effort, because "surely," twenty-six-year-old James G. Thompson argued,
"those who perpetrate these ugly prejudices here are seeking to destroy our
democratic form of government just as surely as the Axis forces." Blacks were
no longer willing to remain silent about "these evil forces which threaten us."[3]

The forces that Thompson spoke about and the reason CRC members were
protesting were outlined explicitly in the document they submitted to the
United Nations General Assembly:

We are compelled to speak by the unending slaughter of Negroes. The fact of
our ethnic origin, of which we are proud—our ancestors were building the
world's first civilizations 3,000 years before our oppressors emerged from bar-

barism in the forests of western Europe—is daily made the signal for segrega-
tion and murder. . . . Once the classic method of lynching was the rope. Now
it is the policeman's bullet. . . . We submit that the evidence suggests that the
killing of Negroes has become police policy in the United States. . . . But the
majority of Negro murders are never recorded, never known except to the perpetrators and the bereaved survivors of the victim. Negro men and women
leave their homes and are never seen alive again. Sometimes weeks later their
bodies, or bodies thought to be theirs and often horribly mutilated, are found
in the woods or washed up on the shore of a river or lake. . . . These unre-
corded deaths are the rule rather than the exception.[4]

Thus condemning the United States' history of racial violence, the CRC
members submitted their petition to the UN to "demand that the government
of the United States stop and prevent the crime of genocide . . . to assure the
safety of the Negro People of the United States."[5] Although the UN did not
formally answer the petition, the Senate Foreign Relations Committee was
forced (probably under international pressure) to discuss the meaning of genocide and to determine whether genocide had ever occurred "within the United
States." Certainly, recent studies confirm their analysis, that what African
Americans experienced at the hands of white supremacists in America, "the
phenomenon of wasting somebody else's life on a mass scale," was well within
the bounds of what Raphael Lemkin, the originator of the concept in 1944, intended.[6] But Congress determined that lynching and white-on-black violence
were not acts of genocide; therefore, "genocide, as defined in this convention,
has never occurred in the United States."[7] Congress rejected the CRC's call to
action, because the "outcome of complex processes," official and unofficial,
constructed by individuals and the nation who do "not object" and, under
certain circumstances, sanction by inaction the intentional killing of a select
group of people aligns with the history of slavery, and America still refused to
acknowledge that past.[8] Nevertheless, the CRC's outspoken demands for social
justice on an international stage continued to be part of how black Americans
framed their activism.

Civil rights leaders in the 1950s and 1960s had varying philosophical perspectives about how to combat white violence in the pursuit of their civil
rights and what should be done about it. For Martin Luther King Jr., nonviolence was the only way to combat oppression in 1956, because in his view,
black violence would foster "retaliatory violence," and "the dangers of this
method . . . will lead to terrible bloodshed." King's maternal grandfather, Rev.
A. D. Williams, managed to survive the Atlanta massacre of 1906, and this no
doubt influenced King's opinions about how to fight "the forces of injustice."[9]

But we also know that the humanistic ideals of nonviolence as a strategy for fighting for social justice in America and formulated in large part due to fears of exterminatory violence preceded King *and* Mahatma Gandhi by more than a century.

NAACP president and community leader Robert F. Williams in Monroe, North Carolina, however, believed that times had changed in 1962 such that both strategies, of violence and nonviolence, needed to be employed against the racial terrorism that plagued blacks across the country. Although Williams affirmed that "the tactics of non-violence will continue and should continue . . . we shouldn't take the attitude that one method alone is the way to liberation." He was concerned that it was the black community's practice of nonresistance that encouraged white internecine violence and notions of white supremacy. The civil rights leaders who espoused nonviolence were "pacifists" who were mostly concerned that "we do not 'provoke' or enrage them [whites]." Williams argued that these strategies were based upon old assumptions that he and other black men felt in the 1960s were no longer relevant: "They constantly tell us that if we resort to violent self-defense we will be exterminated. They are not stopping violence—they are only stopping defensive violence against white racists out of fear of extermination." This fear of extermination and the philosophy of nonviolence were harmful, because it was "precisely this unchallenged violence that allows a racist social system to perpetuate itself." Moreover, Williams believed that "this fear of extermination is a myth," because with the world watching and the politics of the Cold War in play, the "United States Government . . . could not succeed in exterminating 20,000,000 people. . . . People everywhere in the world would be ready to support our struggle." Nevertheless, he too called on the United Nations to begin "an immediate international investigation into the denial of human rights in Monroe," North Carolina.[10]

For civil rights leader Malcolm X, however, a race war was inevitable because of the new generation of blacks who came of age after 1945, and he did not envision that black extermination was out of the realm of possibility. In a speech given at the University of California in 1963, Malcolm stated that because young black people were going to defend themselves against white violence, "America is faced with her worst crisis since the Civil War. The worst crisis since the Revolutionary War. For America now faces a race war. The entire country is on the verge of erupting into racial violence and bloodshed simply because 20 million ex-slaves here in America are demanding freedom, justice and equality." At the time, Malcolm was still a member of the Black Muslim community, and in line with the philosophy of the Honorable Elijah

Muhammad, he argued that white Americans would "fight a race war to keep from having to share this country on an equal basis with anyone else but himself. Especially on an equal basis with his 20 million former slaves." African Americans should separate themselves entirely from America either in Africa or in their own country.[11]

By 1964 Malcolm no longer believed in a black state, but he did believe that the struggles of African people across the diaspora, particularly in Africa, should be united under one front. His religious and ideological framework shifted such that he was working to create a world "in which people can live like human beings on the basis of equality." In alignment with this vision, Malcolm spearheaded and became chairman of a new secular organization, the Organization of Afro-American Unity (OAAU). When the Organization of African Unity (OAU), a group of thirty-four African heads of state, held its meeting in Cairo in July 1964, Malcolm was able to disseminate the OAAU's eighty-page document, which outlined the organization's concerns. Similar to the 1951 document, *We Charge Genocide*, this new document argued that "the American government is either unable or unwilling to protect the lives and property of your 22 million African American brothers and sisters. We stand defenseless. . . . We have lived for over 300 years . . . in constant fear of losing life and limb. . . . [I]magine the physical and psychological suffering."[12] Malcolm wanted the OAU to endorse the OAAU's efforts to encourage the United Nations to act because he believed what was needed was to push for international intervention, to push the struggle of black people in America beyond civil rights to one of human rights.[13]

With its headquarters in Harlem, New York, the OAAU was composed of various civil rights leaders and organizationally affiliated people of working- and middle-class backgrounds who understood that the mood within black communities in the South, and in the North, was more confrontational and more desperate. Only the day before the OAU met in Cairo, the Harlem community erupted in six nights of outrage and black aggression because of the shooting and murder of fifteen-year-old James Powell by police officer Thomas Gilligan right in front of his friends and other witnesses with impunity.[14] Indeed, what was at stake was that African American people no longer accepted gradualism: "We no longer endorse patience and turning the other cheek. We assert the right of self-defense by whatever means necessary. . . . [I]f we must die anyway, we will die fighting back and we will not die alone. . . . We are well aware that our future efforts to defend ourselves . . . by meeting violence with violence . . . could create the type of racial conflict in America that could easily escalate into a violent, world-wide, bloody race war." Malcolm asked that in "the interests of world peace and security, we . . . recommend an immediate investigation into our problem by the United Nations Commission on Human Rights."[15]

Malcolm's assassination on February 19, 1965, meant the end of the OAAU and his dream of Pan-African solidarity that would galvanize the world into action in demanding human rights for African Americans in the United States. But the ideas expressed by Robert F. Williams and Malcolm X, along with historian John Hendrik Clarke—self-determination and self-realization through education, economic security and political engagement, the right to self-defense, and the development of a Pan-African consciousness to facilitate a new world order that would "assur[e] full human rights" for all people—influenced the black power movement in the ensuing years.[16]

From the very beginning, conservative civil rights leaders were concerned that the more aggressive agendas of the black power movement would derail what had been accomplished through the courts and encourage white backlash. But King's politics of nonviolence also appear to have been shaped by genuine fears of a race war and black extermination. In his telephone conversation with President Lyndon Johnson, King expressed concerns about the Watts "Riot" in 1965. He told Johnson that because of the potential of "retaliation from the white people" and because "people [white] had bought up guns . . . if something isn't done to give a new sense of hope to the people in that area," he feared that "a full-scale race war can develop." Johnson agreed with King about the gravity of the problem, but he equated violence during the Watts Riot with southern racial violence by stating that "a man's got no more right to destroy property with a Molotov cocktail in Los Angeles than the Ku Klux Klan has to go out and destroy a life."[17] Despite Johnson's diminished capacity for understanding the importance of human life, for King the potential for internecine violence loomed ominously over the black community. According to civil rights leader Bayard Rustin, the overt racism of Police Chief Parker, who called "the Negro rioters . . . monkeys," and Parker's "insistence on dealing with the outbreak in Watts as though it were the random work of a criminal element threatened to lead the black community, as Martin Luther King remarked" privately, "into potential holocaust." Rustin also noted that (as was true for Nat Turner's insurrection, John Brown's insurrection attempt, and the Wilmington and Atlanta massacres) the number of black deaths and injuries was not accounted for in the McCone Report on the Watts Riot and that the report was replete with "white stereotypes and shibboleths about . . . the Negro penchant for violence."[18]

Indeed, much of the controversy over the black power movement was centered upon the idea of a race war leading to mass violence. Roy Wilkins, executive director of the NAACP, claimed that the words *black power* denoted "black racism," which would lead to "black death." King stated that he did not have a problem with black pride and the idea of self-defense, but his concern was that he saw "a pattern of violence emerging" and that "the cry 'black power' . . . falls on the ears as racism in the reverse."[19] Wilkins's and King's fear was that white Americans would construe black power to mean "black mastery," an age-old refrain used to stoke white violence against the black community dating back to the days of enslavement. They feared retaliatory violence in a war between the races that would extend beyond the urban cities in the West and North. They feared the white backlash that would inevitably come from white resistance to what whites would call "Negro rule."

For Stokely Carmichael, however, who popularized the term "Black Power" while still a member and eventually the head of the Student Non-Violent Coordinating Committee (SNCC), black power had nothing to do with violence: "Why do white people in this country associate Black Power with violence, and the [answer] is because of their own inability to deal with blackness."[20] As far as Carmichael and other black power movement members were concerned, it was not their problem that white Americans were fearful of black people asserting their rights to full employment, education, decent housing, protection from police brutality, fair and impartial treatment from the criminal justice system, and the right to self-defense.[21] The affirmation that justice and equality belonged to all of America's citizens and should not have to be legislated through law was obvious to most black Americans. And their collective willingness to push back against those who believed that blacks had to wait for racist whites to give those rights to them became evident in the intensity with which the federal government attempted to shut the movement and its leaders down. Nevertheless, Carmichael affirmed, despite concerns that black power would start a race war in America: "We are not going to wait for white people to sanction Black Power. . . . [W]e are tired of trying to prove things to white people. We are tired of trying to explain to white people that we're not gonna to hurt them. We are concerned with getting the things we want, the things we have to have to be able to function. . . . The question is, will white people overcome their racism and allow for that to happen in this country?"[22]

The National Committee of Negro Churchmen offered similar sentiments over the "controversy about black power" in 1966. For these church leaders, from various denominations across the country, the discourse surrounding the term was "not anything new but the same old problem of power and race which has faced our beloved country since 1619." In their view, the problem with black power lay in the historical fact that it had always been acceptable for whites in America to use power to achieve their goals "in getting what they want," while black people were relegated to achieving their goals of social justice only through moral suasion or through appealing to America's "conscience." These black church leaders were clear that while they "deplore the overt violence of riots . . . their basic causes lie in the silent and covert violence" that surrounded the black community, violence that "pin[s] the backs of the masses of Negroes against the steaming ghetto walls—without jobs in a booming economy; with dilapidated and segregated education systems in the full view of unenforced laws against it; in short: the failure of American leaders to use American power to create equal opportunity in *life* as well as *in law*— this is the real problem and not the anguished cry for 'black power.'" Indeed, they argued that black power did not endanger what had already been achieved, for in reality the gains toward "authentic democracy" had been minimal since the 1950s, and those who benefited were mainly middle-class blacks.[23]

Although the clergy members noted that they were glad that none of the civil rights leaders advocating black power were seeking "domination," the black community had to "be reconciled with the white majority." Their reasoning was not based on the fact that blacks were a minority population surrounded and outnumbered by whites: "We see and feel that power every day in the destructions heaped upon our families and upon the nation's cities. . . . [W]e are men, not children, and we are growing out of our fear of that power, which can hardly hurt us any more in the future than it does in the present or has in the past." No, their reasoning for supporting black power, or "group power," as they renamed it, was because it would lead to that place for which their fathers sighed, one of reconciliation "wielded to make visible our common humanity."[24]

Despite the envisioned positive outcome of the black power movement, black fiction writers had a decidedly different outlook on what would happen if members of the black community applied the black power ethos, indeed, the American ethos of freedom from oppression, self-defense, and self-preservation in large urban cities in the late 1960s and 1970s. In *The Spook Who Sat by the Door: A Novel* by Sam Greenlee published in 1969, the main character, ironically named Freeman, desegregates the CIA, learns its tactics, and then pretends to be a community activist in the inner city of Chicago. Instead of dismantling gang organizations, Freeman works with the most powerful gang, the Cobras, and trains them to fight against the injustices that plagued the black community. The fictional character Freeman states: "They were not convinced, those thickheaded cops, that niggers would tolerate no more head whippings. The cops felt sure that the answer to the riots and the increasing lack of respect for the uniform was more blood, more stitches, more battered kidneys. . . . And don't ever think . . . he won't do anything to keep the scene the way it's always been. . . . He could go all the way: barbed wire, concentration camps, gas ovens; a 'final solution' of the Negro problem."[25] For Greenlee's character Freeman, black extermination was a real possibility.

In his novel *Plan B*, Chester Himes imagines what a race war would look like as a result of blacks fighting back against the white supremacy system, and he imagines it from the perspectives of both blacks and whites in America. At the onset of the race war, it was "whites' guilt and fear that eventually saved blacks from extermination. The whites had the means, but they did not have the will. Their guilt would not allow them to exterminate the black race." Instead, the solution in Himes's imagination became that "whites demanded that many large, modern prisons be erected all over the United States, and that all blacks be locked up in them, except for the few needed to look after their food and sanitation." But as blacks continued to fight back, "there was an immediate outcry demanding the use of armed forces to exterminate the black race." As things begin to disintegrate into chaos in Chicago, the main character Tomsson Black reflects: "He had intended to issue an ultimatum to the white race: grant us equality or kill us as a race. . . . In the end, it would all depend on the white man's image of himself. Could the white man reconcile the destruction of the black race with his own image as a just, civilized, and compassionate human? Was he capable of slaughtering twenty million blacks and then continue to live with himself and enjoy his own society? It had been done before. It was a calculated risk to assume that it could never happen again."[26]

In a 1970 interview with fellow author John A. Williams, Chester Himes explained that his intent was to show whites in America what a race war would look like. Himes envisioned that a black revolution would be violent because "when you have resorted to these means, this is the last resort. . . . All you do then is you kill as many people as you can, the black people kill as many of the people of the white community as they can kill. That means children, women, grown men." Although it is black people who are killed in *Plan B*, Himes wanted white America, who he believed were "going around playing games," to envision "what would happen if the black people would *seriously* uprise." When asked if he believed that America would exterminate its black population in a race war, Himes argued that he did not believe that whites would do it, because it would "destroy America. . . . It's not a question of whether they could destroy the blacks physically; it's the fact that they can't do it morally—and exist in the world." The problem, as Himes saw it, was that most blacks did not know that whites would not exterminate them and thus did not challenge white supremacist violence. Because of this passive behavior, Himes argued, whites did not take black violence or threats by black power leaders to assert their rights through force seriously.[27]

Fortunately, there has not been a race war or black extermination as envisioned by Garvey, Malcolm, King, and Himes, but neither has social justice been achieved, nor an end to racial discrimination and race-based violence. There has not been a race war, but millions of people of African descent have died because of the institution of enslavement and the ideas about race and who was eligible for extermination that supported it across the Atlantic World. The formation of activist groups in 2013 like Black Lives Matter in response to the murder of young black men and women like Trayvon Martin, Michael Brown, Tamir Rice, Eric Garner, Michelle Cusseaux, and Tanisha Anderson effectively galvanized organized protest against this long history of violence that black people continue to contend with. Apocalyptic prophecies about the possibility of a race war and the extermination of black bodies continue to circulate on the Internet. Police brutality, black criminality, and the mass incarceration of large numbers of black and brown people have become popular topics due to Michelle Alexander's 2010 book, *The New Jim Crow*, which has helped to dismantle laws that disproportionately and unfairly target black and brown people to serve unreasonable sentences for nonviolent crimes.[28] Will we be able to look back in fifty years, in one hundred years, and see that the criminal justice system finally serves the American people in an equitable fashion? And what about black-on-black crimes of violence? This is not how Africans in America have treated each other historically. Will we finally get at the heart of the suffering and psychic dislocation caused by unlivable environments that display a callous disregard for the humanity of those forced to live in urban ghettos and rural poverty?

Moreover, the murder of nine innocent members of the historic Mother Emanuel African Methodist Episcopal Church in South Carolina on June 17, 2015, should tell us that these ideas, the deep and troubling history that has tied violence and race together in ways that seem inseparable, are indeed alive and well. Twenty-year-old Dylann Roof told authorities that he hoped to start a "race war." He told a survivor of his night of carnage, a massacre of people young and old, that he was killing black people because "you rape our women and your [*sic*] taking over our country."[29] Did he know that these were the very ideas used to justify enslavement, the dismantling of Reconstruction in the South, and the de facto legalization of Jim Crow? Did he know that this was the first and largest historically black church in the South, a denomination of the Methodist tradition that was started by former slaves and where Denmark Vesey organized with other black members to revolutionize the country by dismantling slavery in one of the richest slave states in the country? Did he realize that his use of the words "race war" had a historic context that meant the annihilation of blacks or whites well into the civil rights era? Did he realize the trauma he would cause not only for the black community but also for the white community, shining daylight on the troubling yet ever-persistent ideas about the alleged racial incompatibility of black, brown, and white people in America?

This country desperately needs something like a Truth and Reconciliation Commission as a solution to dealing with our history of racial violence, with white supremacy, and with the reconciliation of that history because it has been and remains a curse upon this nation. We need to cleanse ourselves of our ugly past, to begin to heal the deep fractures and trauma that 250 years of slavery and 150 years of racial oppression have done to the fabric of America and its people. And then, collectively, we must envision what a country that was not based on the ideas of white supremacy, or race war, or black or white extermination would look like. The question we must ask ourselves is: Have we truly moved beyond where America began? Have we, as Americans, white and black, internalized the ideas of the disposability of black people in America that have held sway for over three centuries? Can we as a country move beyond the depictions of blackness as symbols of savagery and barbarianism that were and are inscribed upon black and brown bodies throughout the African diaspora, made manifest in the history of racial violence in America and the Atlantic World?

ACKNOWLEDGMENTS

This book is the manifestation of a long and serious effort to understand racial violence in America. I want to thank all of the wonderful scholars at Rutgers University who encouraged and supported me: Suzanne Lebsock, Nancy Hewitt, Mia Bay, and my outside reader, Walter Johnson. I also want to thank Carolyn Brown, Ann Fabian, Jan Lewis, Donna Murch, and Steve Lawson, who, knowingly or unknowingly, helped to shape how I approached this work. But I especially want to thank Deborah Gray White for her mentorship and unwavering belief in the value of this project.

I am eternally grateful for the generous support I received from the Virginia State Library; the Andrew W. Mellon Research Fellowship from the Virginia Historical Society; the summer research grant from the University of South Carolina; the staff at the South Carolina Department of Archives and History; the Gilder Lehrman Center for the Study of Slavery, Resistance, and Abolition Postdoctoral Fellowship from Yale University; and the summer research grant from Norfolk State University.

My editor, Walter Biggins, has been a gift from God, and I deeply appreciate his support and guidance in this project. And finally, I want to thank my husband, William Lewis, and my children, Adina, Samantha, Victoria, and Marissa, for their love and unwavering generosity in allowing me to fulfill my dream of becoming a historian.

NOTES

Introduction. The Legacy and Human Cost of Slavery

1. *Atlanta Journal*, May 20, 1918.

2. Walter White, "Memorandum for Governor Dorsey from Walter F. White Submitted in Person July 10, 1918," Papers of the NAACP, group 1, series C, box 353, Library of Congress, Washington, D.C. Hampton Smith, who had a reputation as being particularly violent toward his workers, which included Mary's husband, Hayes Turner, was shot in his home. His wife, who was also pregnant, was probably unintentionally injured, but both baby and mother survived, as her injuries were reportedly not serious. Governor Dorsey, defending the mob's actions, claimed that the "unspeakable outrages . . . committed by members of your race" were responsible for the lynching. Yet he knew that the perpetrator, Sidney Johnson, acknowledged that he had acted alone in the crime of murdering the white farmer Hampton Smith because Smith had physically abused Johnson a few days earlier. Johnson's entire family, his mother, father, and all other relatives, were put in jail for their own protection, "owing to the increased feeling among the people" (*Atlanta Journal*, May 20, 1918).

3. Howard Thurman, *The Luminous Darkness* (Richmond, Ind.: Friends United, 1999), 48.

4. Michel-Rolph Trouillot, *Silencing the Past and the Production of History* (Boston: Beacon Press, 1997), 25–28, 93.

5. Claude A. Clegg, *The Price of Liberty: African Americans and the Making of Liberia* (Chapel Hill: University of North Carolina Press, 2004), 21.

6. See Francis Jennings, *The Invasion of America: Indians, Colonialism, and the Cant of Conquest* (Chapel Hill: University of North Carolina Press, 1975).

7. John Grenier, *The First Way of War: American War Making on the Frontier* (Cambridge: Cambridge University Press, 2005), introduction and chap. 1.

8. Unlimited warfare and wars of extermination or extirpation all signify the same action in the seventeenth through the twentieth century, and I use these terms interchangeably throughout the manuscript. Carl von Clausewitz's classic work *On War*, published in 1832, was the first to discuss the use of unlimited war as a military concept.

9. See Nell Irvin Painter, "Soul Murder and Slavery: Toward a Fully Loaded Cost Accounting," in *Southern History across the Color Line* (Chapel Hill: University of North Carolina Press, 2002), 6.

10. A former slave notes that "we had to stand in fear of them, we had no protection." "Kicked Around Like a Mule," in *Unwritten History of Slavery: Autobiographical Accounts*

of Negro Ex-Slaves, ed. Ophelia Settle Egypt, J. Masuoka, and Charles S. Johnson (Nashville: Fisk University Press, 1968), 49.

11. Thurman, *Luminous Darkness*, 25–26.

12. Howard Thurman, *Jesus and the Disinherited* (Boston: Beacon Press, 1996), 37–39.

13. Michelle Balaev, "Trends in Literary Trauma Theory," *Mosaic* (Winnipeg) 41, no. 2 (June 2008): 2–3.

14. Aaron R. Denham, "Rethinking Historical Trauma: Narratives of Resilience," *Transcultural Psychiatry* 45, no. 3 (2008): 392.

15. Julius Sherrard Scott, "The Common Wind: Currents of Afro-American Communication in the Era of the Haitian Revolution" (PhD diss., Duke University, 1986).

16. George M. Frederickson, *The Black Image in the White Mind: The Debate on Afro-American Character and Destiny, 1817–1914* (Middletown, Conn.: Wesleyan University Press, 1971), 4–24.

17. Robert H. Abzug, "The Influence of Garrisonian Abolitionists' Fears of Slave Violence on the Antislavery Argument, 1829–40," *Journal of Negro History* 55, no. 1 (January 1970): 15–26.

18. Joel Williamson, *The Crucible of Race: Black-White Relations in the American South since Emancipation* (New York: Oxford University Press, 1984), 183, 199, 214, 10.

19. Leon Litwack, *Trouble in Mind: Black Southerners in the Age of Jim Crow* (New York: Vintage, 1998), 202–216, 15, 38, 210–214, 374, 420, 424–425.

20. Gregory J. W. Urwin, "'We *Cannot* Treat Negroes . . . as Prisoners of War': Racial Atrocities and Reprisals in Civil War Arkansas," in *Black Flag over Dixie: Racial Atrocities and Reprisals in the Civil War*, ed. Gregory J. W. Urwin (Carbondale: Southern Illinois University Press, 2004), 140, 146.

21. Chandra Manning, *What This Cruel War Was Over: Soldiers, Slavery, and the Civil War* (New York: Vintage Books, 2007), 38, 174.

22. François Furstenberg, "Beyond Freedom and Slavery: Autonomy, Virtue, and Resistance in Early American Political Discourse," *Journal of American History* 89, no. 4 (March 2003): 2–5, 9–12, 15–19, http://www.historycooperative.org/journals/jah/89.4/furstenberg.html.

23. Robert C. Davis, *Christian Slaves, Muslim Masters: White Slavery in the Mediterranean, the Barbary Coast, and Italy, 1500–1800* (New York: Palgrave Macmillan, 2003), xxvii.

24. Catherine A. Reinhardt, *Claims to Memory: French Caribbean Slavery during the Enlightenment* (New York: Oxford University Press, 2006), 8.

25. Trouillot, *Silencing*, 73.

26. Abbé de Raynal, *Philosophical and Political History of the Settlements and Trade of the Europeans in the East and West Indies* (1770), and Marie Jean Condorcet, *Reflections on Negro Slavery* (1781), both in *The French Revolution and Human Rights: A Brief Documentary History*, ed. and trans. Lynn Hunt (Boston: Bedford / St. Martin's Press, 1996).

27. Raynal, *Philosophical and Political History*, 54–55.

28. Condorcet, *Reflections*, 56–57.

29. John Phillip, *Researches in South Africa: Illustrating the Civil, Moral, and Religious Condition of the Progress of the Christian Missions, Exhibiting the Influence of Christianity in Promoting Civilization*, 2 vols. (London, 1828; repr., New York: Negro University Press, 1969), 1:32–33; Sir Charles Lyell, Esq., *Principles of Geology* (London, 1832; repr., Chicago: University of Chicago Press, 1991), 2:14, 156; James Prichard, *The Natural History of Man: Comprising Inquiries into the Modifying Influences of Physical and Moral Agencies on the Dif-*

ferent Tribes of the Human Family (London: Hippolyte Bailliere, 1848), 5–7; Robert Knox, *The Races of Men: A Fragment* (London: Henry Renshaw, 1850), 466–467, 229.

30. Sir Charles Lyell, *A Second Visit to the United States in the Years 1845–6* (New York: Harper and Brothers, 1849), 2:40.

31. U. B. Phillips, *American Negro Slavery* (New York: D. Appleton and Company, 1918), 230–231; "The Slave Labor Problem in the Charleston District," *Political Science Quarterly* 22, no. 3 (September 1907): 421, 437.

32. Phillips, *American Negro Slavery*, 230–231; Phillips, "Slave Labor Problem," 421, 437.

33. Eugene D. Genovese, *Roll, Jordan, Roll: The World the Slaves Made* (New York: Vintage, 1976).

34. I have received a number of questions about paternalism at conferences where Genovese's ideas about reciprocity have been used to explain why black extermination would never have happened.

35. Lacy K. Ford, *Deliver Us from Evil* (Oxford: Oxford University Press, 2009).

36. See Kenneth M. Stampp, *The Peculiar Institution: Slavery in the Ante-bellum South* (New York: Knopf, 1956); Stanley Elkins, *Slavery: A Problem in American Institutional and Intellectual Life* (Chicago: University of Chicago Press, 1959); Genovese, *Roll, Jordan, Roll*; Gaines Foster, "Guilt over Slavery: A Historiographical Analysis," *Journal of Southern History* 56, no. 4 (November 1990): 665.

Chapter 1. "Nits Make Lice"

1. See Jean Andreau and Raymond Descat, *Slavery in Greece and Rome*, trans. Marion Leopold (Madison: University of Wisconsin Press, 2011).

2. The English philosopher John Locke wrote in his *Two Treatises of Government* that slavery was a particularly contentious state in which the bodies of those enslaved were disposable at will. Locke notes that freedom allows us to protect ourselves from those who would do us harm. Slavery, because of the natural desire for freedom, Locke argued, was "nothing else, but the State of War continued, between lawful Conqueror, and Captive" (1698; repr., Cambridge: Cambridge University Press, 1960), 296–297, 302. It seems that the Romans understood this and incorporated into their system of slavery a safety valve called *peculium*, which allowed those enslaved to work toward manumission. The hope of freedom helped motivate slaves and made slavery tolerable. See Andreau and Descat, *Slavery in Greece and Rome*, 82–84, 87–88, 94.

3. Increase Mather, *A Discourse Concerning the Grace of Courage, where in The Nature, Beneficialness, and Necessities of that Vertue for all Christians, is described. Delivered in a Sermon Preached at Boston in New-England. June 5th. 1710* (Corn Hill: Brick Shop, 1710), 39, http://name.umdl.umich.edu/N01237.0001.001.

4. "Kicked Around Like a Mule," in *Unwritten History of Slavery: Autobiographical Accounts of Negro Ex-Slaves*, ed. Ophelia Settle Egypt, J. Masuoka, and Charles S. Johnson (Nashville: Fisk University Press, 1968), 49.

5. Barbara Donagan, *War in England, 1642–1649* (Oxford: Oxford University Press, 2008). Donagan argues that the atrocities committed across Europe during the Thirty Years' War were prelude to the subsequent Irish massacres, contradicting previously held standards of English warfare that protected civilians. See also Wayne E. Lee, "Early American Ways of War: A New Reconnaissance, 1600–1815," *Historical Journal* 44, no. 1 (March 2001): 269–289; Alden T. Vaughan, "'Expulsion of the Savages': English Policy and the Virginia

Massacre of 1622," *William and Mary Quarterly*, 3rd series, 35, no. 1 (January 1978): 57–84; Gary B. Nash, "The Image of the Indian in the Southern Colonial Mind," *William and Mary Quarterly*, 3rd series, 29, no. 2 (April 1972): 198–230; Francis Jennings, *The Invasion of America: Indians, Colonialism, and the Cant of Conquest* (Chapel Hill: University of North Carolina Press, 1975); Nicholas P. Canny, "The Ideology of English Colonization: From Ireland to America," *William and Mary Quarterly*, 3rd series, 30, no. 4 (October 1973): 575–598.

6. The Desmond Rebellions were fought by the followers of the FitzGeralds of Desmond against the English in Munster, Ireland, from 1569 to 1573 and then again from 1579 to 1583. See Thomas Churchyard, *A General Rehearsal of Warres, called Churchyardes choise* (London, 1579), 72–75, Q1-R1, http://gateway.proquest.com/openurl?ctx_ver=Z39.88 -2003&res_id=xri:eebo&rft_id=xri:eebo:image:8316:72.

7. Paul E. J. Hammer, *Elizabeth's Wars: War, Government and Society in Tudor England, 1544–1604* (New York: Palgrave, 2003), 77, 109; David Quinn, *The Voyages and Colonizing Enterprises of Sir Humphrey Gilbert* (London: Hakluyt Society, 1940), 1:188–194. Others who rationalized and practiced extermination as effective war tactics were Edward Barkley, Walter Devereux, the 1st Earl of Essex, Sir John Norris, and Sir Peter Carew. See Canny, "Ideology of English Colonization," 577–582.

8. *Annals of the Kingdom of Ireland by the Four Masters, from the Earliest Period to the Year 1616. Edited from MSS in the Library of the Royal Irish Academy and of the Trinity College Dublin with a Translation and Copious Notes* (compiled 1632–1636), trans. John O'Donovan, Corpus of Electronic Texts Edition T100005E, M1573.8, p. 1665.

9. Canny, "Ideology of English Colonization," 585–586; Donagan, *War in England*, 196–197, 202–204.

10. Canny, "Ideology of English Colonization," 588–590, 593.

11. *Annals of the Kingdom*, M1574.4, p. 1678.

12. Ibid., M1577.14, p. 1696.

13. Donagan, *War in England*, 206.

14. For example, in retaliation and in order to "wreak his vengeance for the slaughter of his people . . . the Irish captain [Adare] slew one hundred and fifty women and children" (*Annals of the Kingdom*, M1581.15, p. 1759).

15. William Edward Hartpole Lecky, *A History of Ireland in the Eighteenth Century*, vol. 1 (London: Elibron, 2006), 82–83, 86–87.

16. Lecky, *History*, 102–103.

17. John Nalson, *An Impartial Collection of the Great Affairs of State, from the Beginning of the Scotch Rebellion in the Year 1639 to the Murther of King Charles I* (London: His Majesty's Special Command, 1683), 2:vii.

18. Lecky, *History*, 85.

19. Mary Frances Cusack, *An Illustrated History of Ireland from AD 400 to 1800* (1868), 491.

20. Charles II declared that the peace agreement with Ireland was no longer enforceable in 1650 (Cusack, *Illustrated History*, 489). See also Lecky, *History*, 104.

21. Patrick M. Malone, *The Skulking Way of War: Technology and Tactics among the New England Indians* (Lanham, Md.: Madison, 1991), 75.

22. "Sir Humphrey Gilbert's Patent, 11 June, 1578," in *The Principal Navigations, Voiages, Traffiques and Discoveries of the English Nation* (1598), ed. Richard Hakluyt, 7:17–23.

23. See "The Peticion Exhibited to His Majestie by the Lords Spirituall and Temporall and Comons in this present Parliament assembled concerning divers Rights and Liber-

ties of the Subjects: with the Kings majesties Royall Aunswere thereunto in full Parliament" (1627), which was ratified by King Charles I in 1628, esp. secs. 3 and 4, http://www.constitution.org/eng/petright.htm.

24. Jennings, *Invasion of America*, 15, 45; Gary B. Nash, "The Image of the Indian in the Southern Colonial Mind," *William and Mary Quarterly*, 3rd series, 29, no. 2 (April 1972): 198–205; Canny, "Ideology of English Colonization," 586–588.

25. Jennings, *Invasion of America*, 146.

26. Sir Richard Grenville and Sir Walter Raleigh also used the same brutal military tactics that they used in Ireland against Native Americans. See ibid., 5, 163–168; Nash, "Image," 203–204, 206. Nash notes that most of the New World explorers had been involved in the English invasions in Ireland. See also Adam J. Hirsch, "The Collision of Military Cultures in Seventeenth-Century New England," *Journal of American History* 74, no. 4 (March 1988): 1188.

27. William Symmonds, "Virginia: A Sermon Preached at White Church" (1609), *Early English Books On Line*, 2–4, http://gateway.proquest.com/openurl?ctx_ver=Z39.88-2003&res_id=xri:eebo&rft_id=xri:eebo:image:11682.

28. Robert Johnson, "Nova Brittannia offering most excellent fruites by Planting in Virginia: exciting all such as be well affected to further the same" (1609), *Early English Books Online*, 9–10, http://gateway.proquest.com/openurl?ctx_ver=Z39.88-2003&res_id=xri:eebo&rft_id=xri:eebo:image:177020.

29. Robert Gray, "Good Speed to Virginia" (1609), *Early English Books On Line*, 5–6, 9, http://gateway.proquest.com/openurl?ctx_ver=Z39.88-2003&res_id=xri:eebo&rft_id=xri:eebo:image:6158. See also Joshua 6:21.

30. Jennings, *Invasion of America*, 5.

31. John Morgan Dederer, *War in America to 1775 before Yankee Doodle* (New York: New York University Press, 1990), 21–22, 32, 175–176. Old Testament usage is prolific in *Cromwell's Soldier's Bible* (1643; London: Elliot Stock, 1895). It was reprinted and given to Union soldiers during the Civil War. See also Donagan, *War in England*, 20–21.

32. John E. Ferling, *A Wilderness of Miseries: War and Warriors in Early America* (Westport, Conn.: Greenwood Press, 1980), 21–22.

33. Malone, *Skulking Way of War*, 75.

34. Helen C. Roundtree, *Pocahontas's People: The Powhatan Indians of Virginia through Four Centuries* (Norman: University of Oklahoma Press, 1990), 136.

35. Nash, "Image," 208–209, 217.

36. Roundtree, *Pocahontas's People*, 10.

37. Mark Nicholls, "George Percy's 'Trewe Relacyon': A Primary Source for the Jamestown Settlement," *Virginia Magazine of History and Biography* 113, no. 3 (2005): 43–44, http://www.jstor.org/stable/4250269. See also Alden T. Vaughan, "'Expulsion of the Savages': English Policy and the Virginia Massacre of 1622," *William and Mary Quarterly*, 3rd series, 35, no. 1 (January 1978): 65–66.

38. Susan Myra Kingsbury, ed., *The Records of the State of Virginia Company of London* (Washington, D.C.: Government Printing Office, 1933), 551.

39. Nash, "Image," 217–218; John Smith, "Smith's Generall Historie, Book IV," in *Narratives of Early Virginia 1606–1625*, ed. Lyon Gardiner Tyler (New York: Scribner, 1907), 357; Vaughan, "Expulsion," 80.

40. Edward Waterhouse, *A Declaration of the State of the Colony and Affaires in Virginia (1622)*, Sabin Americana, 1500–1926 (Gale, February 22, 2012), 14.

41. Kingsbury, *Records*, 556–557.

42. John Smith, "Smith's History of Virginia," in Tyler, *Narratives of Early Virginia*, 364.

43. "A Letter to the Governor and the Council in Virginia," October 7, 1622, in Kingsbury, *Records*, 683; Vaughan, "Expulsion," 77, 81.

44. "The Story of 'Uncle' Moble Hobson," in *Slave Narratives: A Folk History of Slavery in the United States, from Interviews with Former Slaves. Ohio, Virginia, Tennessee Narratives* (St. Clair Shores: Scholarly Press, 1976), 18:31–33.

45. See Jennings, *Invasion of America*, 168; Hirsch, "Collision," 1210; Malone, *Skulking Way of War*, 80.

46. William Strachey, *The Historie of Travell into Virginia Britannia*, 2nd series, ed. Louis B. Wright and Virginia Freund (1612; repr., Cambridge: Hakluyt Society, 1849), 103:68–69, 44. See also Roundtree, *Pocahontas's People*, 10–12, 25–27; Christina Snyder, *Slavery in Indian Country: The Changing Face of Captivity in Early America* (Cambridge, Mass.: Harvard University Press, 2010), 37–38.

47. Strachey, *The Historie of Travaile into Virginia Britannia*, 101, 107; also quoted in *The Indians of the Southeastern United States*, Smithsonian Institution Bureau of American Ethnology Bulletin 137 (Washington, D.C.: Government Printing Office, 1946), 687–688.

48. Snyder, *Slavery in Indian Country*, 65–67.

49. H. R. McIlwaine, ed., *Minutes of the Council and General Court of Colonial Virginia 1622–1632, 1670–1676*, 2nd ed. (1924; repr., Richmond: Virginia State Library, 1979), 488–489.

50. Roundtree, *Pocahontas's People*, 93, 103, 127, 129.

51. Ibid., 95; Stephen R. Potter, "Early English Effects on Virginia Algonquian Exchange and Tribute in the Tidewater Potomac," in *Powhatan's Mantle: Indians in the Colonial Southeast*, ed. Gregory A. Waselkov, Peter H. Wood, and Tom Hatley (Lincoln: University of Nebraska Press, 2006), 231.

52. Martha W. McCartney, "Cockacoeske, Queen of Pamunkey: Diplomat and Suzeraine," in Waselkov, Wood, and Hatley, *Powhatan's Mantle*, 249.

53. Kathleen M. Brown, *Goodwives, Nasty Wenches, and Anxious Patriarchs: Gender, Race, and Power in Colonial Virginia* (Chapel Hill: University of North Carolina Press, 1996), 159.

54. Ibid., 159–160.

55. John Berry and Francis Moryson, "Narrative of Bacon's Rebellion," *Virginia Magazine of History and Biography* 4, no. 2 (October 1896): 126.

56. Roundtree, *Pocahontas's People*, 96; Berry and Moryson, "Narrative of Bacon's Rebellion," 126.

57. Berry and Moryson, "Narrative of Bacon's Rebellion," 124, 126.

58. Brown, *Goodwives*, 164, 168.

59. Berry and Moryson, "Narrative of Bacon's Rebellion," 126, 136; Brown, *Goodwives*, 161.

60. Berry and Moryson, "Narrative of Bacon's Rebellion," 126, 138.

61. Ibid., 140, 138.

62. Brown, *Goodwives*, 168.

63. Berry and Moryson, "Narrative of Bacon's Rebellion," 136.

64. Ibid., 126.

65. Roundtree, *Pocahontas's People*, 97–100.

66. James H. Merrell, *The Indians' New World: Catawbas and Their Neighbors from European Contact through the Era of Removal* (New York: W. W. Norton, 1991), 36.

67. John Rolfe, "A Letter to Sir Edwin Sandys," January 1619/20, *The Thomas Jefferson Papers*, series 8, *Virginia Records Manuscript, 1606–1737*, Susan Myra Kingsbury, ed., *Records of the Virginia Company, 1606–26*, vol. 3: *Miscellaneous Records*, 243, http://hdl.loc .gov/loc.mss/mtj.mtjbib026605; "List of the Living and Dead in Virginia Feb. 16, 1623," Census Records, *USGenWeb Archives*, http://files.usgenwarchives.net/va/jamestown.htm.

68. Roundtree, *Pocahontas's People*, 141–142; Brown, *Goodwives*, 132–136, 197–198.

69. Jack D. Forbes, *Africans and Native Americans: The Language of Race and the Evolution of Red-Black People* (Urbana: University of Illinois Press, 1993), 195–196.

70. J. Leitch Wright, *The Only Land They Knew: The Tragic Story of the American Indians in the Old South* (New York: Free Press, 1981), 154, 160, 169, 253.

71. Snyder, *Slavery in Indian Country*, 132–133, 64, 83, 61–63; Stephanie Smallwood, *Saltwater Slavery: A Middle Passage from Africa to American Diaspora* (Cambridge, Mass.: Harvard University Press, 2007), chap. 5.

72. Roundtree, *Pocahontas's People*, 167, 179–180, 183.

73. Theda Perdue, *Mixed Blood Indians: Racial Construction in the Early South* (Athens: University of Georgia Press, 2003), 83.

74. A. Leon Higginbotham, *In the Matter of Color: Race and the American Legal Process* (New York: Oxford University Press, 1978), 52–53, 55–57.

75. Thomas Jefferson, *Notes on the State of Virginia*, ed. William Peden (Chapel Hill: University of North Carolina Press, 1982), 138. Col. William Byrd II, son of William Byrd I and one of the largest slave owners in Virginia, wrote to the Earl of Edgemont in 1736 about the "public danger" that so many slaves represented. Even James Madison agreed that blacks who were freedmen "would soon be at war with the whites if too near." See Elizabeth Donnan, *Documents Illustrative of the History of the Slave Trade to America* (Washington, D.C.: Carnegie Institute, 1935), 4:132; Winthrop Jordon, *White over Black: American Attitudes toward the Negro, 1550–1812* (Chapel Hill: University of North Carolina Press, 1968), 552.

76. Jefferson, *Notes*, 61, 96, 138, 143, 163. On the "scale of beings," Jefferson placed Native Americans above Africans, but only those who were not mixed with Africans. When Jefferson wrote *Notes*, he portrayed Native Americans in the romantic terms of the day as the superior "noble savage," although, as historian Rhys Isaac points out, this was easy enough for him to do, as few Native Americans remained near Monticello or in Virginia generally. See Rhys Isaac, "The First Monticello," in *Jefferson's Legacies*, ed. Peter Onuf (Charlottesville: University of Virginia Press, 1993), 98–99.

77. Roundtree, *Pocahontas's People*, 105, 180, 183–184; Brown, *Goodwives*, 180–181. After Nat Turner's rebellion in 1831, white paranoia extended to the Gingaskins, many of whom were forced to sell their tribal homes. Eventually, they merged with a sympathetic black community nearby.

78. Dederer, *War*, 176.

79. Roy Harvey Pearce, *The Savages of America: A Study of the Indian and the Idea of Civilization* (Baltimore, Md.: Johns Hopkins University Press, 1965), 20–21.

80. Jennings, *Invasion of America*, 187–281.

81. Capt. John Mason, *Brief History of the Pequot War: Especially of the memorable Taking of their Fort at Mistick in Connecticut in 1637* (Boston: Kneeland and Green, 1736), in

History of the Pequot War: The Contemporary Accounts of Mason, Underhill, Vincent and Gardener, reprinted from the collections of the Massachusetts Historical Society (Cleveland: Helman-Taylor, 1897), 16, 18; Hirsch, "Collision," 1197.

82. Mason, *Brief History*, 18–19. The idea that the Pequots were bent on destroying the English is questionable when considering the total number of deaths by year: seven in 1643, three in 1635, thirteen in 1636, and nine in 1637.

83. Ibid., 25–26, 29.

84. Capt. John Underhill, *Newes from America; or, A New and Experimentall Discoverie of New England* (London, 1638), 80–81. For more references to King David's methods of war, see 1 Samuel 19:8: "And David went out and fought with the Philistines, and killed them with a great slaughter. And they fled from him"; and 1 Samuel 27:9: "And David struck the land, and did not keep alive man nor woman" (KJV).

85. Jennings, *Invasion of America*, 226; Mason, *Brief History*, 31, 35, 36–40.

86. Mason, *Brief History*, 44.

87. Capt. Leif Lion Gardener, "Leif Lion Gardener His Relation of the Pequot Warres," in *History of the Pequot War*, 119.

88. William Apess, *A Son of the Forest and Other Writings*, ed. Barry O'Connell (Amherst: University of Massachusetts Press, 1997), 91.

89. Underhill, *Newes from America*, 84.

90. Gardener, "Leif Lion Gardener," 132.

91. Charles Orr, introduction to *History of the Pequot War*, x–xiii.

92. Hirsch, "Collision," 1211.

93. Pearce, *Savages*, 49.

94. See Richard Slotkin's seminal work on how European anxiety and subsequent rationale for violence shaped the colonial process, *Regeneration through Violence: The Mythology of the American Frontier, 1600–1860* (Norman: University of Oklahoma Press, 2000).

95. The number of incidents is enormous, but a few good examples of total warfare used against Native Americans are the Great Swamp Massacre of 1675, the Gnadenhuetten Massacre of 1782, the Horseshoe Bend Massacre of the Red Sticks in 1814, the Bad Axe River Massacre in 1833, the Bear River Massacre in 1863, and the Sand Creek Massacre in 1864.

96. Capt. John Underhill was hired in 1643–1644 as an English mercenary by the Dutch to conduct a similar campaign in the New Amsterdam region against the Raritan, Wappinger, and Mohawk nations, during which he and his men used the exact same tactics of fire and entrapment that they employed in the Pequot War. See Ward Churchill, *A Little Matter of Genocide* (San Francisco: City Lights, 1997), 198; Increase Mather, *A Brief History of the War* (Boston, 1676), see December 18; Slotkin, *Regeneration through Violence*, 162.

97. Apess, *Son of the Forest*, 105.

98. Gary Nash, *Red, Black, and White: The Peoples of Early America* (Englewood Cliffs, N.J.: Prentice Hall, 1974), 126; Churchill, *Little Matter*, 177.

99. See Jill Lepore's seminal work for a discussion of the importance of writing, who gets to create the narrative of an event, and how it is remembered: *The Name of War: King Philip's War and the Origins of American Identity* (New York: Vantage Press, 1998).

100. Rev. John Heckewelder, *History, Manners, and Customs of the Indian Nations* (1818; repr., Philadelphia: Historical Society, 1876), 337–338.

101. No. 91, 1843, vol. 8, 3rd series, Body of Liberties Collections of the Massachusetts Historical Society, Boston; Higginbotham, *In the Matter of Color*, 61–62.

102. Kenneth Wiggins Porter, "Negroes on the Southern Frontier, 1670–1763," *Journal of Negro History* 33, no. 1 (January 1948): 54; Nash, *Red, Black, and White*, 114.

103. Alan Gallay, *The Indian Slave Trade: The Rise of the English Empire in the American South, 1670–1717* (New Haven, Conn.: Yale University Press, 2002), 299.

104. Peter Wood, *Black Majority: Negroes in Colonial South Carolina from 1670 through the Stono Rebellion* (New York: W. W. Norton, 1974), 40; Sir Harry H. Johnston, *The Negro in the New World* (Plymouth, Mass.: W. Brendon, 1910), 213n1.

105. Snyder, *Slavery in Indian Country*, 5–7.

106. Wood, *Black Majority*, 39; Wright, *Only Land They Knew*, 126–127, 137–138, 140.

107. Gallay, *Indian Slave Trade*, 299.

108. Wright, *Only Land They Knew*, 147–148; Nash, *Red, Black, and White*, 153.

109. Nash, *Red, Black, and White*, 151; Dr. Francis Le Jau, *The Carolina Chronicle of Dr. Francis Le Jau 1706–1717*, ed. Frank J. Klingberg (Berkeley: University of California Press, 1956), 122–123.

110. Snyder, *Slavery in Indian Country*, 37–38; David E. Stannard, *American Holocaust: The Conquest of the New World* (New York: Oxford University Press, 1992), 118–120; Churchill, *Little Matter*, 200–201.

111. Wood, *Black Majority*, 99n.

112. Interview with Mrs. Susan Hamilton, in *Slave Narratives: A Folk History of Slavery in the United States, from Interviews with Former Slaves. South Carolina Slave Narratives*, pt. 2 (St. Clair Shores: Scholarly Press, 1976), 1:235.

113. Gallay, *Indian Slave Trade*, 257–258, 301–302. Massachusetts, New Hampshire, Connecticut, and Rhode Island all passed laws restricting the importation of Native American slaves from South Carolina after the Yamasee and Tuscarora Wars.

114. Snyder, *Slavery in Indian Country*, 86–87, 37.

115. Paul Lovejoy, "The Children of Slavery—the Transatlantic Phase," *Slavery and Abolition* 27, no. 2 (August 2006): 197, 202, 213.

116. Rev. John Heckewelder, *History, Manners, and Customs of the Indian Nations Who Once Inhabited Pennsylvania and the Neighboring States* (Philadelphia: Historical Society of Pennsylvania, 1876), 339, 337; James E. Seaver, *A Narrative of the Life of Mrs. Mary Jameson*, ed. June Namias (Norman: University of Oklahoma Press, 1992), 117–118; James E. Quinlan, *Tom Quick, the Indian Slayer* (Monticello, N.Y.: De Voe & Quinlan, 1851; repr., Morristown: Digital Antiquaria, 2004), 31, 33; *Diary of David Zeisberger: A Moravian Missionary among the Indians of Ohio* (Cincinnati: Historical and Philosophical Society of Ohio, 1885), March 8, 1782, 80–81, 85, http://www.archive.org/details/diaryofdavid01zeisrich; *True History of the Massacre of Ninety-Six Christian Indians, at Gnadenhuetten, Ohio* (New Philadelphia, Ohio: Gnadenhuetten Monument Society, 1843), 10–11.

117. John H. Hann, *Apalachee: The Land between the Rivers* (Gainesville: University of Florida Press, 1988), chap. 12 and app. 12, 395, quoted in Gallay, *Indian Slave Trade*, 147–148. Gallay estimates that the number of captives was somewhere between two and four thousand, with the larger number probably being more likely. See also Wright, *Only Land They Knew*, 149; William R. Snell, "Indian Slavery in Colonial South Carolina, 1671–1795" (PhD diss., University of Alabama, 1972), 96.

118. In 1663 South Carolina officials instituted laws that only Native Americans captured in a just war could be transported out of the colony. Gallay, *Indian Slave Trade*, 64–65.

119. Ibid., 289.

120. Bartolomé de Las Casas, *A Short Account of the Destruction of the Indies*, trans. and ed. Nigel Griffin (1542; repr., Harmondsworth: Penguin Classics, 1992), 15, 22.

121. Gallay, *Indian Slave Trade*, 261, 267, 270.

122. Wright, *Only Land They Knew*, 117–119, 143–144.

123. Ibid., 112–124, 144; Churchill, *Little Matter*, 200–201; Ian K. Steele, *Warpaths: Invasions of North America* (New York: Oxford University Press), 165–167.

124. Le Jau, *Carolina Chronicle*, 157.

Chapter 2. A "State of War Continued"

1. John Locke, *Two Treatises of Government* (1698; repr., Cambridge: Cambridge University Press, 1960), 297.

2. Ibid., 302–303. Although Locke attempts to qualify the way in which slavery could be lawful, according to Christian standards of war in Europe at the time, prisoners of war could not be made slaves. See also Hugo Grotius's *The Rights of War and Peace: Including the Law of Nature and of Nations* (1625; repr., Washington, D.C.: M. Walter Dunne Press, 1901), specifically bk. 3, chap. 7.

3. See Sylvaine A. Diouf, ed., *Fighting the Slave Trade: West African Strategies* (Athens: Ohio University Press, 2003), x, xi, xvi, 125, 129, and chap. 8, for countless examples of African rejection of their deportation as slaves. This sentiment was also observed by slave ship surgeon Alexander Falconbridge, *Narrative of Two Voyages in the River Sierra Leone during the years 1791, 1792, 1793, with Alexander Falconbridge: An Account of the Slave Trade on the Coast of Africa*, ed. Christopher Fyfe (Liverpool: Liverpool University Press, 2000), 216, 214.

4. See Ismail Rashid, "A Devotion to the Idea of Liberty at Any Price: Rebellion and Antislavery in the Upper Guinea Coast in the Eighteenth and Nineteenth Centuries," chap. 9 in Diouf, *Fighting the Slave Trade*, for compelling evidence that slave resistance actually began in Africa.

5. Paul E. Lovejoy, *Transformations in Slavery: A History of Slavery in Africa*, 2nd ed. (Cambridge: Cambridge University Press, 2000), 70.

6. Michael Gomez, *Exchanging Our Country Mark: The Transformation of African Identities in the Colonial and Antebellum South* (Chapel Hill: University of North Carolina Press, 1998), 64–65, 75–76, 91.

7. Melville J. Herskovits, *Myth of the Negro Past* (Boston: Beacon Press, 1990), 108.

8. Charles Ball, *Slavery in the United States: A Narrative of the Life and Adventures of Charles Ball* (1837; repr., New York: Negro University Press, 1969), 183.

9. See John K. Thornton and Robert S. Smith for a different assessment about the existence of total warfare in Africa: John K. Thornton, *Warfare in Atlantic Africa 1500–1800* (London: UCL Press, 1999), 150, 133, 16; Robert S. Smith, *Warfare and Diplomacy in Pre-Colonial West Africa* (Madison: University of Wisconsin Press, 1989), 35. See also Herskovits, *Myth of the Negro Past*, 108.

10. Joseph Corry, *Observations upon the Windward Coast of Africa* (London: W. Bulmer and Co., 1807; e-book, www.gutenberg.net), 33–34.

11. Martin A. Klein, "Defensive Strategies: Wasula, Masina, and the Slave Trade," in Diouf, *Fighting the Slave Trade*, 62–63.

12. John Barnwell, "The Journal of John Barnwell," *Virginia Magazine of History and Biography* 6, no. 1 (July 1898): 43; see also Le Jau, *Carolina Chronicles*, 103n135.

13. Elizabeth Donnan, *Documents Illustrative of the History of the Slave Trade to America* (Washington, D.C.: Carnegie Institute, 1935), 4:316–317, 351, 319. Henry Laurens, one of the largest slave traders in South Carolina, was particularly adamant about the difficulty that his company had in trying to sell "bite Slaves." Yet when the market demand for slaves was high, even "ordinary Calabar men" sold well. Michael Gomez makes this point as well with respect to levels of various ethnicities in the colonies (*Exchanging Our Country Mark*, 107). Also see Donnan, *Documents*, 4:310, 314, 411–413, 453–454, 504, 521–522, for examples of the number of ships that just listed their cargo of slaves as "Africans"; and see Elizabeth Donnan, "The Slave Trade in South Carolina before the Revolution," *American Historical Review* 33, no. 4 (July 1928): 823n92, for evidence that Igbos were indeed part of the Charleston market. Nevertheless, the largest populations of Igbos were in Virginia, Maryland, and Louisiana, while the Dahomeans and Yorubas from the Bight of Benin were largely sold in Louisiana (Gomez, *Exchanging Our Country Mark*, 149–153).

14. Olaudah Equiano, *The Interesting Life of Olaudah Equiano, or Gustavus Vassa, the African. Written by Himself*, Classic Slave Narratives, ed. Henry Louis Gates Jr. (New York: Mentor, 1987), 18. Olaudah was a powerful antislavery activist in London and one of the founders of the anti–slave trade group the Sons of Africa.

15. Ibid., 18, 25.

16. Ibid., 19.

17. G. I. Jones, *Africa Remembered: Narratives by West Africans from the Era of the Slave Trade*, ed. Philip D. Curtin (Madison: University of Wisconsin Press, 1967), 66.

18. Joseph Wright, "The Narrative of Joseph Wright," in Jones, *Africa Remembered*, 326. Martin R. Delaney observed during his trip to Africa that old people of both genders were put to death when Africans were warring for slaves in southwestern Nigeria among the Yoruba people even in 1859. See "Report of the Niger Valley Exploring Party," in *Martin R. Delany: A Documentary Reader*, ed. Robert S. Levine (Chapel Hill: University of North Carolina Press, 2003), 339–340.

19. Paul Lovejoy, "The Children of Slavery—the Transatlantic Phase," *Slavery and Abolition* 27, no. 2 (August 2006): 205–206.

20. Ball, *Slavery in the United States*, 185.

21. John Ashley Hall, in *House of Commons Sessional Papers*, ed. Sheila Lambert, vol. 72: *Minutes and Correspondence, 1790*, 558; George Francis Dow, "Testimony of James Arnold," in *Slave Ships and Slaving* (Mineola: Dover, 2002), 173.

22. Lovejoy, "Children of Slavery," 197, 200, 213. See Donnan for countless examples of traders requesting that children be around ten years old (*Documents*, 2:159, 244, 250, 289, 292, 327, and 4:57, 360, 451, 456, 586).

23. "Contract between the South Sea Company and the Royal African Company" (1713), in Donnan, *Documents*, 2:159, and 4:323–324, 326, 357, 351.

24. Hugh Thomas, *The Slave Trade: The Story of the Atlantic Slave Trade: 1440–1870* (New York: Simon and Schuster, 1997), 399; Donnan, *Documents*, 4:504, 522; Lovejoy, *Transformations in Slavery*, 76–80.

25. For many nations in Africa, the ritual of circumcision defined warrior status within the community and indicated that the boy (or girl) was initiated into manhood (or womanhood). See Jeff Marck, "Aspects of Male Circumcision in Subequatorial African Culture History," *Health Transition Review*, supplement to vol. 7 (1997): 337, 346–347. Bryan Edwards, a historian, leading member of the colonial assembly in Jamaica, and English politician, wrote on the topic of circumcision. Based on his interviews with his slaves, although

Muslim slaves were circumcised, many slaves from other nations were as well (Edwards, *The History, Civil and Commercial, of the British Colonies in the West Indies* [Dublin: Luke White, 1793], 2:57, 68, 71).

26. John K. Thornton, "African Dimensions of the Stono Rebellion," *American Historical Review* 96 (1991): 1103.

27. Equiano, *Interesting Life*, 18, 25.

28. Edwards, *History*, 2:97.

29. Martin R. Delany, *Frank Rollin's Biography of Martin R. Delany* (1868; repr., New York: Arno Press, 1969), 15–16.

30. Herskovits, *Myth of the Negro Past*, 47–48.

31. "Aunt Ciller," Federal Writers' Project (South Carolina), unpublished ex-slave narratives, 36 MSS Project 1885-1, South Caroliniana Library, University of South Carolina, Columbia.

32. Gomez, *Exchanging Our Country Mark*, 46–52.

33. According to the research of Gwendolyn Midlo Hall, Bambara is inaccurate. "Bambara" is of Muslim African derivation, and it means "barbarian" in Arabic, which is an ethnic slur. See Gwendolyn Midlo Hall, *Slavery and African Ethnicities in the Americas: Restoring the Links* (Chapel Hill: University of North Carolina Press, 2005), 96–98.

34. Gomez, *Exchanging Our Country Mark*, 54. Eric Robert Taylor's work makes clear that African leadership and organizational ability were evident during the numerous insurrections that occurred during the Middle Passage. See *If We Must Die: Shipboard Insurrections in the Era of the Atlantic Slave Trade* (Baton Rouge: Louisiana State University Press, 2006).

35. Samuel Brun, "Samuel Brun's Voyages of 1611–20," in *German Sources for West African History 1599–1699*, trans. Adam Jones (Wiesbaden: Franz Steiner Verlag GmbH, 1983), 93–94. See also clergyman Wilhelm Johann Muller's description in ibid., 198.

36. Stephanie Smallwood, *Saltwater Slavery: A Middle Passage from Africa to American Diaspora* (Cambridge, Mass.: Harvard University Press, 2007), 20–24. See also Thornton, *Warfare in Atlantic Africa*, for a different assessment of early Akan warfare as not "genocide" (132–133).

37. Lovejoy, *Transformations in Slavery*, 84.

38. Gomez, *Exchanging Our Country Mark*, 107.

39. Walter Rodney, *How Europe Underdeveloped Africa* (Washington, D.C.: Howard University Press, 1982), 120–121.

40. Othello, "What the Negro Was Thinking during the Eighteenth Century: Essay on Negro Slavery," *Journal of Negro History* 1, no. 1 (January 1916): 68.

41. Rodney, *How Europe Underdeveloped Africa*, 120; Robin Law, "Dahomey and the Slave Trade: Reflections on the Historiography of the Rise of Dahomey," *Journal of African History* 27, no. 2, Special Issue in Honour of J. D. Fage (1986): 250–251, 266; Edna G. Bay, *Wives of the Leopard: Gender, Politics, and Culture in the Kingdom of Dahomey* (Charlottesville: University of Virginia Press, 1998), 141–142; Robin Law, "Human Sacrifice in Precolonial West Africa," *African Affairs* 84, no. 334 (January 1985): 74.

42. Bay, *Wives of the Leopard*, 58.

43. Thomas Phillips, *A Journal of a Voyage Made in the Hannibal of London, Ann. 1693, 1694, from England to Cape Monseradoe in Africa; And thence along the Coast of Guiney to Whidaw, the Island of St. Thomas, and so forward to Barbadoes*, A Collection of Voyages and Travels, ed. Awnsham and John Churchill (London, 1746), 6:220.

44. Othello, "What the Negro Was Thinking," 67.

45. Rodney, *How Europe Underdeveloped Africa*, 120; Sir Richard Burton, *A Mission to Gelele, King of Dahome* (London, 1853), 57, 155.

46. John Thornton argues that high numbers of Africans captured and sold into slavery were trained soldiers (*Warfare in Atlantic Africa*, 139–147).

47. Warren Alleyne and Henry Fraser, *The Barbados–Carolina Connection* (London: Macmillan, 1988), 1–31; Richard S. Dunn, "The Barbados Census of 1680: Profile of the Richest Colony in English America," *William and Mary Quarterly*, 3rd series, 26, no. 1 (January 1969): 28–29.

48. Donnan, *Documents*, 4:241, 243.

49. Peter Wood, *Black Majority: Negroes in Colonial South Carolina from 1670 through the Stono Rebellion* (New York: W. W. Norton, 1974), 16, 25–26, 45, 49, 100, 105.

50. Donnan, "Slave Trade," 823–827.

51. Daniel C. Littlefield, *Rice and Slaves: Ethnicity and the Slave Trade in Colonial South Carolina* (Champaign: University of Illinois Press, 1991), 31–32, 8–55, 117; Donnan, "Slave Trade"; Margaret Washington Creel, *"A Peculiar People": Slave Religion and Community-Culture among the Gullahs* (New York: New York University Press, 1988), 30–36; Gomez, *Making Our Country Mark*, 40, 106, 241.

52. *South-Carolina Gazette*, June 12, 1749, February 19, 26, 1754, July 30, 1772, July 12, 1804.

53. Donnan, "Slave Trade," 816–817, 811–812.

54. David Richardson, Suzanne Schwarz, and Anthony Tibbles, eds., *Liverpool and Transatlantic Slavery* (Liverpool: Liverpool University Press, 2007), 14–15.

55. Alexander Hewatt, *An Historical Account of the Rise and Progress of the Colonies of South Carolina and Georgia* (London: A. Donaldson, 1779), 2:4–6.

56. Donnan, *Documents*, 4:243, 296–297, 315–449; R. C. Nash, "Trade and Business in Eighteenth Century South Carolina: The Career of John Guerard, Merchant and Planter," *South Carolina Historical Magazine* 95 (1995): 8, 14, 16, 20, 27.

57. See Darold Wax, "Negro Resistance to the Early American Slave Trade," *Journal of Negro History* 51, no. 1 (January 1966): 1–15.

58. Taylor, *If We Must Die*, 2–3, 14, 82, 135. Of the 493 cases that Taylor was able to confirm as insurrections, 120 of them led to the freedom of at least some of those enslaved.

59. Herskovits, *Myth of the Negro Past*, 88–89.

60. Robert Norris, *Memoirs of the Reign of Bossa Ahadee, King of Dahomy, an Inland Country of Guiney. To Which are Added, The Author's Journey to Abomey, The Capital: And Short Account of the African Slave Trade* (London: Lowndes, 1789; electronic ed., Documenting the American South, http://doc.south.unc.edu), 174.

61. David Richardson, "Shipboard Revolts, African Authority, and the Transatlantic Slave Trade," in Diouf, *Fighting the Slave Trade*, 203.

62. For other examples, see "Newport, Rhode Island," *South-Carolina Gazette*, October 4, 1732; "Extract of a Letter from Antigua dated Jan. 11, 1733–4," *South-Carolina Gazette*, August 31–September 7, 1734; "Antigua, Oct. 24," *South-Carolina Gazette*, December 4, 1736; *Great Newes from Barbadoes, or A True and faithful account of the grand conspiracy of the Negroes against the English and happy discovery of the same with the number of those that were burned alive, beheaded, and other wise executed for their horrid crimes* (London: L. Curtis, 1676); U. B. Phillips, *Plantation and Frontier 1649–1863* (New York: Burt Franklin, 1969), 2:100, 117; Donnan, *Documents*, 4:274, and 2:528.

63. Donnan, *Documents*, 4:274.

64. "Newport Octob. 25," *South-Carolina Gazette*, December 2–9, 1732.

65. *South-Carolina Gazette*, October 24, 1743; Donnan, *Documents*, 4:296n6.

66. Donnan, *Documents*, 4:374, 418.

67. Wood, *Black Majority*, 220–225, 222.

68. "An Extract of the Journals of Mr. Commissary Von Reck, who conducted the First Transport of Saltzburgers to Georgia: And of the Reverend Mr. Bolzius, One of their Ministers. Giving an Account of their Voyage to, and happy Settlement in that Province" (1733–1734), *Force's Collection of Historical Tracts* 4, no. 5 (Washington, D.C.: Wm. Q. Force, 1846), 9, 18.

69. *South-Carolina Gazette*, November 1, May 18, 1734, January 18, July 12, September 20, October 11, 1735, July 28, 1739.

70. "Colonel William Byrd to the Earl of Egmont, 1736," in Donnan, *Documents*, 4:132.

71. "Acts Relating to Slaves," Acts of 1712, 1722, and 1735, in *The Statutes at Large of South Carolina*, ed. David J. McCord (Columbia, S.C.: A. S. Johnston, 1840), 7:352, 371, 385; Winthrop Jordan, *White over Black: American Attitudes toward the Negro, 1550–1812* (Chapel Hill: University of North Carolina Press, 1968), 114–115; Wood, *Black Majority*, 236–237.

72. Donnan, *Documents*, 4:257; Thomas Cooper, ed., *Statutes at Large of South Carolina* (Nabu Press, primary source edition, 2013), 2:646–649.

73. Donnan, *Documents*, 4:256.

74. "An Act for Raising and Enlisting Such Slaves as Shall Be Thought Serviceable to This Province in Times of Alarm," no. 237, in McCord, *Statutes at Large*, 7:347–348. This was also true in Virginia, as blacks were free to carry arms and were enlisted in the militia even as late as 1738, although at that point they were required to "appear without arms." See T. H. Breene and Stephen Innes, *"Myne Owne Ground": Race and Freedom on Virginia's Eastern Shore* (New York: Oxford University Press, 1980), 8, 26–27. Blacks in Louisiana enlisted under the French for the first time in 1729. See Roland C. McConnell, *Negro Troops of Antebellum Louisiana: A History of the Battalion of Free Men of Color* (Baton Rouge: Louisiana State University Press, 1968), 2–7.

75. Wood, *Black Majority*, 125–128; Kenneth Wiggins Porter, "Negroes on the Southern Frontier, 1670–1763," *Journal of Negro History* 33, no. 1 (January 1948): 54–56; Herbert Aptheker, *American Negro Slave Revolts* (New York: International Press, 2008), 171–173. Most alarming to slaveholders was the 1712 slave conspiracy in New York during which twenty-five to thirty slaves burned a building and killed nine men before their insurrection was suppressed.

76. Porter, "Negroes on the Southern Frontier," 56.

77. "Richard Ludlam to David Humphreys, St James, Goose Creek, South Carolina. March 22, 1725," in *An Appraisal of the Negro in Colonial South Carolina*, by Frank Klingberg (Washington, D.C.: Associated Publishers, 1941), 47.

78. May 25, 1738, James Glen Papers, South Caroliniana Library, University of South Carolina, Columbia; "An Act for Raising and Enlisting," 7:347–348; Wood, *Black Majority*, 125–128; Porter, "Negroes on the Southern Frontier," 54–56; Alan Gallay, *The Indian Slave Trade: The Rise of the English Empire in the American South, 1670–1717* (New Haven, Conn.: Yale University Press, 2002), 347.

79. Gallay, *Indian Slave Trade*, 348–349.

80. "Lt. Governor Bull to Duke Newcastle" (1739), in Wood, *Black Majority*, 312.

81. Wood, *Black Majority*, 321.

82. Porter, "Negroes on the Southern Frontier," 69; Terry W. Lipscomb, ed., *Journal of the Commons House of Assembly of South Carolina* 33 (October 6, 1757–January 24, 1761): 59; *Charles Town Gazette*, January 17, 1761.

83. Aptheker, *American Negro Slave Revolts*, 198; Donnan, *Documents*, 4:415.

84. Herskovits, *Myth of the Negro Past*, 48.

85. Gomez, *Exchanging Our Country Mark*, 23; W. Roberts Higgins, "Charleston: Terminous and Entrepot of the Colonial Trade," in *The African Diaspora: Interpretive Essays*, ed. Martin L. Kilson and Robert I. Rotberg (Cambridge, Mass.: Harvard University Press, 1976), 118.

86. Donnan, *Documents*, 4:297.

87. Creel, *Peculiar People*, 74; "Missionary John Wikhead to SPG" (1715), Society for the Propagation of the Gospel, reel 6.

88. Wood, *Black Majority*, 220.

89. John Brickell, *The Natural History of North-Carolina with an Account of the Trade, Manners, and Customs of the Christian and Indian Inhabitants* (Dublin: James Carson, 1737), 272–273.

90. John R. Alden, "John Stuart Accuses William Bull," *William and Mary Quarterly* 2, no. 3 (July 1945): 318–319.

91. Donnan, *Documents*, 4:131–132.

92. Brickell, *Natural History*, 274. The term "Guinea" was commonly used to describe all Africans.

93. Dena J. Epstein, "African Music in British and French America," *Music Quarterly* 59, no. 1 (January 1973): 81.

94. Wood, *Black Majority*, 256; *South-Carolina Gazette*, April 26, 1760, July 24, 1769.

95. Thomas Clarkson, *The History of the Rise, Progress, and Accomplishment of the Abolition of the African Slave Trade by the British Parliament* (Whitefish: Kessinger Publishing, 1839), 45, 48. See also Christopher Leslie Brown's *Moral Capital: Foundations of British Abolitionism* (Chapel Hill: University of North Carolina Press, 2006) for a comprehensive overview of the origins of English abolitionism.

96. Donnan, *Documents*, 2:254–255.

97. Law, "Dahomey and the Slave Trade," 250–251; see Rodney, *How Europe Underdeveloped Africa*, 121.

98. Capt. William Snelgrave, *A New Account of Some Parts of Guinea and the Slave-Trade* (1731; repr., London: Frank Cass, 1971), 152, 97, 77.

99. Edwards, *History*, 1:59, 64–65, 80.

100. John Hippisley, "On Populousness of Africa: An Eighteenth-Century Text," *Population and Development Review* 24, no. 3 (September 1998): 605–606.

101. Mungo Park, *Travels in the Interior Districts of Africa* (1799), 283–284, http://www.archive.org/details/travelsininterio1unkngoog.

102. "Account of a Plot formed by the Negroes of Goree, to Destroy All the White People on the Island," *New York Magazine, or Literary Repository*, April 1796 (New York: T. and J. Swords, 1796), 1:108–110, https://books.google.com.

103. English independent traders, merchants, and ship captains, nicknamed the "Ten Percenters," eventually forced the end of the RCA's control of the trade, which allowed the global economy in African slaves to blossom. See Thomas, *Slave Trade*, 205, 209.

104. Clarkson, *History*, 48.

105. H. Shelton Smith, *In His Image, but . . . Racism in Southern Religion, 1780–1910* (Durham, N.C.: Duke University Press, 1972), 12.

106. Anthony Benezet, *A Short Account of That Part of Africa, Inhabited by the Negroes* (Bedford: Applewood Books, 1762), 8–10, 23, 45, 72–73, 79.

107. Alan Gallay, ed., *Voices of the Old South: Eyewitness Accounts, 1528–1861* (Athens: University of Georgia Press, 1994), 149. Whitefield had changed his position about the slave trade as early as 1751 and became a slave owner himself; see Smith, *In His Image*, 13.

108. Clarkson, *History*, 87–88.

109. Alexander Hewatt, *An Historical Account of the Rise and Progress of the Colonies of South Carolina and Georgia* (London: A. Donaldson, 1779), 2:38. Hewatt was pastor from 1763 to 1775; see Smith, *In His Image*, 18.

110. Clarkson, *History*, 224, 265.

111. Ibid., 228–229.

112. Robin Law, "Human Sacrifice in Pre-colonial West Africa," *African Affairs* 84, no. 334 (January 1985): 53–55.

113. Snelgrave, *New Account*, 46–47.

114. Wax, "Negro Resistance," 2–3. See, for example, Randy J. Sparks, *Where Negroes Are Masters: An African Port in the Era of the Slave Trade* (Cambridge, Mass.: Harvard University Press, 2014), for compelling evidence of the power that Ghanaian West Africans wielded in the trade with Europeans.

115. Law, "Human Sacrifice," 66, 69, 73–77.

116. Hewatt, *Historical Account*, 38–39.

117. Locke, *Two Treatises*, 302.

118. "Acts Relating to Slaves," 7:352.

119. Ibid., 7:352, 343, 357, 359–360.

120. "Le Jau to the Secretary," February 20, 1712, in Le Jau, *Carolina Chronicles*, 108; William G. McLoughlin and Winthrop D. Jordon, eds., "Baptist Face the Barbarities of Slavery in 1710," *Journal of Southern History* 29, no. 4 (November 1963): 497, 501.

121. Mia Bay, *The White Image in the Black Mind: African-American Ideas about White People, 1830–1925* (New York: Oxford University Press, 2000).

122. "Acts Relating to Slaves," 7:371.

123. Ibid., 7:382; see also "Act of 1740," in McCord, *Statutes at Large*, 7:413; Wood, *Black Majority*, 273.

124. Wood, *Black Majority*, app. D, 342–343; see also "Stranger," *South-Carolina Gazette*, September 17, 1772.

125. Gregory O'Malley, "Beyond the Middle Passage: Slave Migration from the Caribbean to North America, 1619–1807," *William and Mary Quarterly* 66, no. 1 (2009): 3–5; John Hope Franklin, *From Slavery to Freedom: A History of African Americans* (New York: McGraw-Hill, 1994), 69–70; Lorenzo Greene, *The Negro in Colonial New England 1620–1776* (New York: Columbia University Press, 1942), 35–37; Darold D. Wax, "Preferences for Slaves in Colonial America," *Journal of Negro History* 58, no. 4 (October 1973): 374.

126. "Acts Relating to Slaves," 7:372–373, 417–418, 412.

127. Michael Mullin, "British Caribbean and the North American Slaves in the Era of War and Revolution," in *The Southern Experience in the American Revolution*, ed. Jeffrey J. Crow and Larry E. Tise (Chapel Hill: University of North Carolina Press, 1978), 241; Benjamin Quarles, *Negro in the American Revolution* (Chapel Hill: University of North Carolina Press, 1961), 174.

128. "Acts Relating to Slaves," 7:410.

129. Epstein, "African Music," 78.

130. Wood, *Black Majority*, 276–277.

131. Brickell, *Natural History*, 272.

132. Benjamin Martyn, "An Impartial Inquiry in to the State and Utility of the Province of Georgia," in Gallay, *Voices of the Old South*, 82.

133. Johann Martin Bolzius, "Reliable Answers to Some Submitted Questions Concerning the Land Carolina in Which Answer, However, Regard Is Also Paid at the Same Time to the condition of the Colony of Georgia," in Gallay, *Voices of the Old South*, 234. See Jill Lepore's work for an excellent analysis of the purported 1741 New York slave insurrection: *New York Burning* (New York: Knopf, 2005), 58, xii.

134. Bolzius, "Reliable Answers," 233, 256.

135. Martyn, "Impartial Inquiry," 83.

136. Wood, *Black Majority*, 26, 44, 105; Porter, "Negroes on the Southern Frontier," 72.

137. Wood, *Black Majority*, 152–153, 158. For a discussion of how the increasingly brutal nature of plantation labor correlated to the decline in female fertility and pregnancy and the survival of women, children, and men, see William Dusinberre, *Them Dark Days: Slavery in the American Rice Swamp* (Athens: University of Georgia Press, 2000); Frances Anne Kemble, *Journal of a Residence on a Georgian Plantation* (Charleston: BiblioBazaar, 2006); Jennifer Morgan, *Laboring Women: Reproduction and Gender in New World Slavery* (Philadelphia: University of Pennsylvania Press, 2004); and Sharla Fetts, *Working Cures: Healing, Health, and Power on Southern Slave Plantations* (Chapel Hill: University of North Carolina Press, 2002).

138. "To the Right Honorable the Lord Commissioner for Trade and Plantations," 15–16, May 25, 1738, James Glen Papers, South Caroliniana Library, University of South Carolina, Columbia.

139. Donnan, *Documents*, 4:482–483.

140. Ralph Izard to Mathius Hutchinson, November 20, 1794, Ralph Izard Papers, South Caroliniana Library, University of South Carolina, Columbia.

Chapter 3. "The Past Is Never Dead"

1. William Faulkner, *Requiem for a Nun* (New York: Random House, 1951), 92.

2. John K. Thornton, *Warfare in Atlantic Africa 1500–1800* (London: UCL Press, 1999), 139–147.

3. Vincent Harding, *There Is a River: The Black Struggle for Freedom in America* (New York: Mariner Books, 1993); Manisha Sinha, *The Slave's Cause: A History of Abolition* (New Haven, Conn.: Yale University Press, 2016), chaps. 1 and 2.

4. "Circular fallacy" is a term used by Francis Jennings to describe the thought processes that Europeans used against Native Americans to justify European imperialism and the myths of savagery that I adapt to describe the condition of enslavement. See Francis Jennings, *The Invasion of America: Indians, Colonialism, and the Cant of Conquest* (Chapel Hill: University of North Carolina Press, 1975), 31.

5. Robert Norris, *Memoirs of the Reign of Bossa Ahadee, King of Dahomy, an Inland Country of Guiney. To Which are Added, The Author's Journey to Abomey, The Capital: And Short Account of the African Slave Trade* (London: Lowndes, 1789; electronic ed., Documenting the American South, http://doc.south.unc.edu), 175–176.

6. Richard Ligon, *A True and Exact History of the Island of Barbados* (1657), 45–46. Eric Williams states that enemies to Oliver Cromwell were sent away to the colonies as white laborers, including those who survived the Drogheda massacre, "and thereafter it became his fixed policy to 'barbadoes' his opponents." See *From Columbus to Castro: The History of the Caribbean* (New York: Vintage Press, 1970), 100–101.

7. Noel Sainsbury, ed., *Calendar of State Papers, Colonial Series, America and West Indies 1675–1676* (London: John Menzies, 1893), 291; David Eltis, *The Rise of African Slavery in the Americas* (Cambridge: Cambridge University Press, 2000), 243.

8. *Great Newes from the Barbadoes, or A True and Faithful Account of the Grand Conspiracy of the Negroes against the English . . . with the Number of Those That Were Burned Alive, Beheaded, and Otherwise Executed for Their Horrid Crimes* (London: L. Curtis, 1676), 1.

9. Michael Craton, *Testing the Chains: Resistance to Slavery in the British West Indies* (Ithaca, N.Y.: Cornell University Press, 1982), 109–110.

10. John Poyer, *The History of Barbados, from the First Discovery of the Island in the Year 1605, till the Accession of Lord Seaforth, 1801* (London: Printed for J. Mawman, 1808), 155; *Journal of the Commons House of Assembly of South Carolina* (1692), 15, https://books.google .com/books/content/images/frontcover/6cYBAAAAYAAJ?fife=w300.

11. "Extract of a Letter from a Gentleman in Jamaica, to his Friend in London," Kingston, Jamaica, February 25, 1734, *South-Carolina Gazette*, August 31–September 7, 1734.

12. "Boston, March 15 [1734]," *South-Carolina Gazette*, May 11–18, 1734.

13. "Extract of a Letter," *South-Carolina Gazette*, August 31–September 7, 1734, emphasis added.

14. For full treatment of this topic, see Sylviane Diouf, *Slavery's Exiles: The Story of the American Maroons* (New York: New York University Press, 2014).

15. Martha Warren Beckwith, *Black Roadways: A Study of Jamaican Folk Life* (New York: Negro University Press, 1969), 190–191.

16. *South-Carolina Gazette*, November 1, 1732, May 18, 1734, January 18, July 12, September 20, October 11, 1735, July 28, 1739.

17. Thomas Thistlewood's Journal, 1748–1786, June 7, 1760, pp. 114, 97, series I, box 6, folder 31, Thomas Thistlewood Papers, James Marshall and Marie-Louise Osborn Collection, Beinecke Rare Book and Manuscript Library, Yale University, New Haven, Conn.

18. Ibid., 181, 100.

19. Bryan Edwards, *The History, Civil and Commercial, of the British Colonies in the West Indies* (Dublin: Luke White, 1793), 2:59–61, 87–88.

20. Thistlewood's Journal, 108.

21. Ibid., 221–222, 232, 121.

22. There is evidence that women participated and were made prisoners of war during Tacky's rebellion. A female named Rosanna shaved her head, and a Colonel Spragg made the exception of not destroying rebel women and children in his attempt to regain control of the enslaved population. See ibid., 100, 128, 51.

23. Ibid., 136.

24. Ibid., 134, 200, 116, 109.

25. Edwards, *History*, 2:88.

26. Thistlewood's Journal, 104–105, 154.

27. Edwards, *History*, 2:59–61, 87–88; Edward Long, *History of Jamaica* (London: T. Lowndes Press, 1774), 2:461–462; Craton, *Testing the Chains*, 129, 133, 136–137.

28. Thistlewood's Journal, 114.

29. Craton, *Testing the Chains*, 138.

30. "Report to Governor Mathew of an Enquiry into the Negro Conspiracy," Antigua, December 30, 1736, in "America and West Indies: January 1737," *Calender of State Papers Colonial, America and West Indies: 1737* (1963), 43:20, http://www.british-history.ac.uk/cal-state-papers/colonial/america-west-indies/vol43/pp1-21; for South Carolina, see "Antigua, Oct. 24," *South-Carolina Gazette*, December 4, 1736, and "Charles-town," *South-Carolina Gazette*, January 29–February 5, 1737.

31. "Governor William Mathew to Alured Popple," Saint Christophers, May 11–15, 1737, in "America and the West Indies: May 1737, 11–15," *Calender*, 287.

32. "Report to Governor Mathew."

33. Ibid.

34. Ibid. Michael Craton cites their war dancing as an Akan ritual (*Testing the Chains*, 123).

35. John K. Thornton, "African Dimensions of the Stono Rebellion," *American Historical Review* 96 (1991): 1112.

36. Croton, *Testing the Chains*, 359n18; *Minutes of the Antiguan Council*, January 31, 1737, Colonial Office 9/10.

37. Waldemar Westergaard, ed., "Account of the Negro Rebellion on St. Croix, Danish West Indies, 1759," *Journal of Negro History* 11, no. 1 (January 1926): 57. Further evidence of African rituals of oath taking can be found in Edward Bryan's interviews of his "Koramantyn" slaves in Jamaica (*History*, 67).

38. Westergaard, "Account," 56.

39. Ibid., 58–59.

40. Creel, *Peculiar People*, 117.

41. Michael Gomez argues that it was not until the 1830s that perhaps the large numbers (over 82 percent) of American-born Africans influenced the acculturation process in the everyday lives of those enslaved (*Exchanging Our Country Mark*, 194–195, and see 22–23 for demographic breakdown).

42. Edwin C. Holland, *A Refutation of the Calumnies Circulated against the Southern and Western States, Respecting the Institution and Existence of Slavery among Them* (Charleston: A. E. Miller, 1822), 63–65.

43. J. Leitch Wright, *Only Land They Knew: The Tragic Story of the American Indians in the Old South* (New York: Free Press, 1981), 275; Herbert Aptheker, *American Negro Slave Revolts* (New York: International Press, 2008), 175–176; Kenneth Wiggins Porter, "Negroes on the Southern Frontier, 1670–1763," *Journal of Negro History* 33, no. 1 (January 1948): 63.

44. Wood, *Black Majority*, 299; Creel, *Peculiar People*, 114.

45. "Charleston March 26," *South-Carolina Gazette*, March 26–April 2, 1737.

46. Thornton, "African Dimensions," 1103.

47. Wood, *Black Majority*, 314–316.

48. Thornton, "African Dimensions," 1102. Spain offered freedom to all slaves who could reach Spanish territory.

49. Wood, *Black Majority*, 313–314.

50. George Cato, Federal Writers' Project (South Carolina), unpublished ex-slave narratives at the South Caroliniana Library, 36 MSS Project 1655.

51. *Boston Weekly News-Letter*, November 8, 1739; Wood, *Black Majority*, 318.

52. Wood, *Black Majority*, 318–322.

53. Porter, "Negroes on the Southern Frontier," 67.

54. Aptheker, *American Negro Slave Revolts*, 258–259.

55. C. L. R. James, *The Black Jacobins: Toussaint L'Ouverture and the San Domingo Revolution* (New York: Vintage Press, 1989), 20–21, 241–242; "The Revolution of Saint-Domingue," in *Facing Racial Revolution: Eyewitness Accounts of the Haitian Insurrection*, ed. Jeremy D. Popkin (Chicago: University of Chicago Press, 2007), 6.

56. Yves Benot, "The Insurgents of 1791, Their Leaders and the Concept of Independence," in *The World of the Haitian Revolution*, ed. David Patrick Geggus and Norman Fiering (Bloomington: Indiana University Press, 2009), 102.

57. "The Revolution of Saint-Domingue," 53.

58. "Mon Odyssee," in Popkin, *Facing Racial Revolution*, 76.

59. "Historick Recital of the Different Occurrences in the Camps of Grande-Reviere, Dondon, Sainte-Suzanne, and Others from the 26th of October, 1791, to the 24th of December, of the Same Year," in Popkin, *Facing Racial Revolution*, 144–145.

60. "Mon Odyssee," 77.

61. James, *Black Jacobins*, 242; Laurent Dubois, "Avenging America: The Politics of Violence in the Haitian Revolution," in Geggus and Fiering, *World of the Haitian Revolution*, 112–113.

62. "Mon Odyssee," 78–79, 89.

63. "Historick Recital," 144, 152, 132.

64. "Revolution of Saint-Domingue," 55; Dubois, "Avenging America," 115.

65. "Revolution of Saint-Domingue," 56.

66. "Mon Odyssee," 77.

67. Ibid., 58.

68. "Historick Recital," 134.

69. Ibid., 153. In Saint-Domingue, as it was in America and across the African diaspora, sex between white planters and black females was common. This resulted in a mulatto class that was often privileged with manumission by their fathers. They often owned land, were educated, and acquired personal wealth that situated them in a class above those enslaved. Some even owned slaves.

70. "Historick Recital," 154–155.

71. "A Journalist's Account of the Destruction of Cap Français," in Popkin, *Facing Racial Revolution*, 194–195.

72. "Excerpts from Extrait d'une Lettre," in Popkin, *Facing Racial Revolution*, 220–221.

73. Napoleon Bonaparte, "Proclamation to the Citizens of Santo Domingo," Paris, December 1799, *Letters and Documents of Napoleon*, vol. 1, *The Rise to Power* (New York: Oxford University Press, 1961), 370, http://www.archive.org/details/lettersofdocumen006632mbp.

74. "Charles Victor Emanuel LeClerc Letter" (1802), Digital History, University of Houston, http://www.digitalhistory.uh.edu/era.cfm?eraID=4&smtID=3.

75. "Letter from Leclerc to Napoleon Bonaparte," October 7, 1802, in *Napoleon: Symbol for an Age: A Brief History with Documents*, trans. Rafe Blaufarb (Boston: Bedford / St. Martin's, 2008), 165.

76. "Speech to the Legislature on the Reestablishment of Slavery," May 20, 1802, in Blaufarb, *Napoleon*, 159.

77. "*Boston Centinel*, Dec. 8. French West-Indies," *Courier of New Hampshire*, December 16, 1802.

78. Dubois, "Avenging America," 120, emphasis added.

79. "The Governor-General to General Dessalines, Commander-in-Chief of the Army

of the West," February 8, 1802, *Letters and Documents by Toussaint Louverture,* http://the
louvertureproject.org.

80. *"Boston Centinel,* Dec. 8."

81. Michel-Étienne Descourtilz, "Voyages d'un naturaliste," in Popkins, *Facing Racial
Revolution,* 306.

82. Honoré Lazarus Lecompte, "The Short Account of the Extraordinary Life and
Travels of H.L.L.," in Popkins, *Facing Racial Revolution,* 319, 325.

83. Carlo Célius, "Neoclassicism and the Haitian Revolution," in Geggus and Fiering,
World of the Haitian Revolution, 359; Descourtilz, "Voyages," in Popkins, *Facing Racial
Revolution,* 276, 288–289, 353.

84. James, *Black Jacobins,* 22, 241–242. For full treatment of this topic, see Laurent
Dubois, *A Colony of Citizens: Revolution and Slave Emancipation in the French Caribbean,
1787–1804* (Chapel Hill: University of North Carolina Press, 2004).

85. Célius, "Neoclassicism," 359–360.

86. Ashli White, *Encountering Revolution: Haiti and the Making of the Early Republic*
(Baltimore, Md.: Johns Hopkins University Press, 2010), 177, 179.

87. White, *Encountering Revolution,* 179.

88. Davis P. Geggus, "The Garadeux and Colonial Memory," in *The Impact of the Haitian Revolution in the Atlantic World,* ed. David P. Geggus (Columbia: University of South
Carolina Press, 2001), 232.

89. Ralph Izard to Mathius Hutchinson, November 20, 1794, Ralph Izard Papers 1742–
1804, South Caroliniana Library, University of South Carolina, Columbia.

90. Mary Pinckney to Mrs. Manigault, February 5, 1798, Manigault Family Papers
1750–1900, folder 20, South Caroliniana Library, University of South Carolina, Columbia.

91. Craton, "Proto-Peasant Revolts? The Late Slave Rebellions in the British West Indies 1816–1832," *Past and Present* 85, no. 1 (1979): 100.

92. My analysis does not rely on any of the contested evidence that Michael P. Johnson
interrogates in his article "Denmark Vesey and His Co-conspirators." But because no African American that I know of contested the trial or accusations waged against Vesey in the
antebellum era, I am convinced that people like David Walker, Rev. Morris Brown, Bishop
Richard Allen, T. Hamilton, and Robert Vesey, Denmark Vesey's son, who eventually
rebuilt Charleston's African Methodist Episcopal Church in 1865, would have spoken out
against the murder of dozens of black people for absolutely no reason whatsoever, which
would have been the case if one believes that Vesey's insurrection plot was fabricated. Because these black men lived in South Carolina around or during the time of the incident,
they would have, at some point, spoken out. Indeed, what one observes instead is the black
community's continuous reverence for what Vesey attempted to do throughout the antebellum era. Moreover, the black community writ large would have had nothing to gain
by pretending that an insurrection was planned when one was not, but they would have
gained much antislavery sympathy *against* southern white slaveholders who slaughtered or
sent into exile 131 innocent blacks.

93. Lionel H. Kennedy and Thomas Parker, *An Official Report of the Trials of Sundry
Negroes Charged with an Attempt to Raise an Insurrection in the State of South Carolina*
(Charleston, 1822), reprinted as *The Trial Record of Denmark Vesey,* ed. John Killens (Bos-
ton: Beacon Press, 1970), 4.

94. See Michael Craton's *Testing the Chains* and Edward Pearson's introduction to *Designs against Charleston: The Trial Record of the Denmark Vesey Slave Conspiracy of 1822*

(Chapel Hill: University of North Carolina Press, 1999) for more on the continuity of African cultural mores and the influence of Haiti in Denmark Vesey's insurrection plan. Also see Walter C. Rucker, *The River Flows On: Black Resistance, Culture, and Identity Formation in Early America* (Baton Rouge: Louisiana State University Press, 2006), 152–179.

95. Kennedy and Parker, *Trial Record*, 68, 46, 88, 117.

96. "Confession of Bacchus Hammet, the Slave of Mr. Hammet (ca. 12 July)," in Pearson, *Designs against Charleston*, app. 3, 328. In Kennedy and Parker, *Trial Record*, the authors either observed or thought to add for effect that "old daddy" had marks on his face, signifying him as having been part of the warrior class (110).

97. Kennedy and Parker, *Trial Record*, 117. See also Pearson, *Designs against Charleston*, 238–239.

98. Kennedy and Parker, *Trial Record*, 43, 42, 45.

99. Ibid., 45, 47, 41, 95, 79, 82, 120, 44.

100. Ibid., 53, 66, 78, 83, 76, 84, 76–77, 85.

101. Ibid., 110, 120, 17, 31–32.

102. Melville J. Herkovits, *Myth of the Negro Past* (Boston: Beacon Press, 1990), 82; Creel, *Peculiar People*, 2, 46, 51, 59, 181; Gomez, *Exchanging Our Country Mark*, 94–102, 167. Gomez states that the continuity of the secret societies is found in the attraction of blacks to European Masonry and religious organizations, the latter clearly functioning outside of the structure of secrecy.

103. Kennedy and Parker, *Trial Record*, 71, 52, 45, 85, 96, 46, 58.

104. See Joshua 6:20 (KJV).

105. S[tephen] Elliot to William Elliot (Beaufort), July 22, 1822, in Pearson, *Designs against Charleston*, app. 3, 334. There is a history of African slaves rejecting the Christianity of their masters. See Albert J. Raboteau, *Slave Religion: The "Invisible Institution" in the Antebellum South* (Oxford: Oxford University Press, 2004), chap. 6. Margaret Washington Creel argues that outside of Charleston, slaves in the rural areas learned what they knew about Christianity from other blacks (*Peculiar People*, 147).

106. "Testimony of Smart," in Kennedy and Parker, *Trial Record*, 90.

107. "Confession of John," in Pearson, *Designs against Charleston*, app. 3, 337.

108. H. Shelton Smith, *In His Image . . . Racism in Southern Religion, 1780–1910* (Durham, N.C.: Duke University Press, 1972), 54. This is membership reported in May 1818.

109. Kennedy and Parker, *Trial Record*, 53.

110. Hamilton states that the insurrection was instigated by the enactment of repressive legislation that restricted the rights of free people of color and the criminalization of future manumissions of slaves, closing an important avenue of freedom and black prosperity. T. Hamilton, *The Late Contemplated Insurrection in Charleston, S.C. with the Execution of 36 of the Patriots: Death of William Irving, The Provoked Husband: and Joe Devaul, For Refusing to Be the slave of Mr. Roach: with the Capture of the American Slaver Trading between the Seat of Govt. and New Orleans: Together with an Account of the Capture of the Spanish Schooner Amistad (Jan. 1850)*, 3, 5, 8–9, South Caroliniana Library, University of South Carolina, Columbia. Also see "Acts Relating to Slaves," which states that "no slave shall hereafter be emancipated but by act of Legislature" (7:459).

111. Kennedy and Parker, *Trial Record*, 58.

112. Pearson, *Designs against Charleston*, app. 3, 337; Henry Ravenel Papers, South Carolina Historical Society, Charleston.

113. Kennedy and Parker, *Trial Record*, 54, 50, 86.

114. Thomas Wentworth Higginson, *Black Rebellion: Five Slave Revolts* (New York: Arno Press, 1969), 244.

115. Walter Rodney, *How Europe Underdeveloped Africa* (Washington, D.C.: Howard University Press, 1982), 121; Edna G. Bay, *Wives of the Leopard: Gender, Politics, and Culture in the Kingdom of Dahomey* (Charlottesville: University of Virginia Press, 1998), 121; Olaudah Equiano, *The Interesting Life of Olaudah Equiano, or Gustavus Vassa, the African. Written by Himself*, Classic Slave Narratives, ed. Henry Louis Gates Jr. (New York: Mentor, 1987), 18–19.

116. Deborah Gray White, *Ar'n't I a Woman? Female Slaves in the Plantation South* (New York: W. W. Norton, 1985), 63–64; Eric Robert Taylor, *If We Must Die: Shipboard Insurrections in the Era of the Atlantic Slave Trade* (Baton Rouge: Louisiana State University Press, 2006), 88–93, 111.

117. Kennedy and Parker, *Trial Record*, 65, 56, 80, 95.

118. Aptheker, *American Negro Slave Revolts*, 272.

119. Creel, *Peculiar People*, 163.

120. Pearson, *Designs against Charleston*, 351.

121. Richard Furman, *Rev. Dr. Richard Furman's Exposition of the Views of the Baptists, Relative to the Coloured Population of the United States, in A Communication To the Governor of South-Carolina* (Charleston: A. E. Miller, 1823), 4.

122. Pearson, *Designs against Charleston*, 332.

123. "Mary L. Beach to Elizabeth L. Gilchrist (Germantown, Pennsylvania), 5 July 1822," in Pearson, *Designs against Charleston*, app. 3, 324.

124. "Anna Johnson (Charleston) to Elizabeth Haywood (Charleston) 18 July 1822," in Pearson, *Designs against Charleston*, app. 3, 333.

125. "Martha Proctor Richardson (Savannah) to Dr. James Screven (Liverpool), 6 July 1822," in Pearson, *Designs against Charleston*, app. 3, 325.

126. "Martha Proctor Richardson (Savannah) to Dr. James Screven (Liverpool), 7 August 1822," in Pearson, *Designs against Charleston*, app. 3, 341; Arnold and Screven Family Papers, 1762–1903, Southern Historical Collection, Louis Round Wilson Special Collections Library, University of North Carolina, Chapel Hill, emphasis added.

127. "Thomas Bennett to John Calhoun, 30 July 1822," in Pearson, *Designs against Charleston*, app. 3, 340.

128. Holland, *Refutation*, 76, 86.

129. Ibid., 65–66.

130. Adam Rothman, *Slave Country: American Expansion and the Origins of the Deep South* (Cambridge, Mass.: Harvard University Press, 2005), 135.

131. Whitemarsh B. Seabrook, *A Concise View of the Critical Situation and Future Prospects of the Slave-Holding States* (Charleston: A. E. Miller, 1825), 4.

132. Creel, *Peculiar People*, 165.

133. Aptheker, *American Negro Slave Revolts*, 274–275n31; John Hope Franklin, *The Militant South 1800–1861* (Urbana: University of Illinois Press, 2002), 77.

134. "Acts Relating to Slaves," 7:461, 462, 464.

135. Court members were William Drayton, Nathaniel Heyward, J. R. Pringle, Jas. Legare, Robert J. Turnbull, Henry Deas, and of course Thomas Parker and Lionel H. Kennedy, the authorized authors of the *Report*. See Kennedy and Parker, *Trial Record*, 11, 138.

136. Holland, *Refutation*, 62.

Chapter 4. The Abridgment of Hope

1. John Hope Franklin, *Militant South 1800–1861* (Urbana: University of Illinois Press, 2002), 78. The *American Beacon* announced on August 30, 1831, "The war is over." See Henry Irving Tragle, *The Southampton Slave Revolt of 1831: A Compilation of Source Material* (Amherst: University of Massachusetts Press, 1971), 55.

2. Newspaper editors asserted that Nat Turner was known as a "General" or "Captain." See *Richmond Enquirer*, August 30, 1831.

3. Tragle, *Southampton Slave Revolt*, 189, 196, 204, 214.

4. Thomas Wentworth Higginson, *Travellers and Outlaws: Episodes in American History* (Boston: Lee and Shepard, 1889), 282–288; Herbert Aptheker, *Nat Turner's Rebellion* (New York: Humanities, 1966), 44–50. The number of whites killed varies from fifty-seven to sixty-one; the larger number was used by Governor John Floyd.

5. *Richmond Enquirer*, August 30, 1831, September 30, 1831.

6. Ella Williams, in *Weevils in the Wheat: Interviews with Virginia Ex-Slaves*, ed. Charles L. Perdue Jr., Thomas E. Barden, and Robert K. Phillips (Charlottesville: University of Virginia Press, 1976), 313–314.

7. *Richmond Enquirer*, August 30, 1831; Higginson, *Travellers and Outlaws*, 294–296.

8. *Richmond Enquirer*, August 30, 1831.

9. *Richmond Enquirer*, September 4, 1831. See Herbert Aptheker, *American Negro Slave Revolts* (New York: International Press, 2008), 309–312 for evidence of white paranoia in Georgia, Tennessee, Alabama, and South Carolina after Turner's insurrection.

10. Lucy Mae Turner, "The Family of Nat Turner," in *Harlem's Glory: Black Women Writing 1900–1950*, ed. Lorraine Elena Roses and Ruth Elizabeth Randolph (Cambridge, Mass.: Harvard University Press, 1996), 140; Tragle, "Confessions," in *Southampton Slave Revolt*, 310.

11. J. W. C. Pennington, *A Narrative of Events of the Life of J. H. Banks, an Escaped Slave, from the Cotton State, Alabama, in America* (Liverpool: M. Rourke, 1861; electronic ed., Documenting the American South, http://doc.south.unc.edu), 18.

12. Turner, "Family of Nat Turner," 142.

13. Mary E. C. Drew, *Divine Will Restless Heart: The Life and Works of Dr. John Jefferson Smallwood 1863–1912* (Bloomington: Xlibris, 2010), 18; Turner, "Family of Nat Turner," 144.

14. Turner, "Family of Nat Turner," 142–144.

15. Mrs. Colman Freeman, *A North-Side View of Slavery. The Refugee: Of the Narratives of Fugitive Slaves in Canada. Related by Themselves with an Account of the History and Condition of the Colored Population of Upper Canada*, ed. Benjamin Drew (1856; repr., New York: Negro University Press, 1968), 136.

16. Allen Crawford, in Perdue, Barden, and Phillips, *Weevils in the Wheat*, 75–76. Crawford's account is interesting not only for its reference to slinging babies as a way of killing them but also because the *Confessions* narrative written after Nat Turner's capture is silent on who or how the baby was killed. In fact, it states that Nat Turner forgot that the infant was even there but then sent back Henry and Will, and they "killed it." The story told by Turner even at first glance seems rather implausible, as he stated that they had "gone some distance" before he ordered them to return at the onset of their very dangerous mission to begin an insurrection. William Drewry's account, however, states that after Nat left, he remembered that "nits make lice. Nat sent Henry [Travis] and Will [Reeves] back

to take it by its heels and dash its brains out against the bricks of the fireplace." Whether Nat Turner or Henry Porter and Will Francis did the deed, it seems that all three accounts are consistent that the baby was murdered. It is interesting that even in 1900 the phrase "nits make lice" was still used by Drewry; and in 1937 the idea of swinging a baby's head against the wall is still remembered by ex-slaves as a form of execution. See William Sidney Drewry, *The Southampton Insurrection* (1900; repr., Murfreesboro: Johnson Publishing Company, 1968), 36; Thomas C. Parramore, *Murfreesboro, North Carolina and the Roots of Nat Turner's Revolt 1820–1831* (Zebulon: Murfreesboro Historical Association, 2004), 60.

17. *Richmond Enquirer*, 8 November 1831, repr. in Tragle, *Southampton Slave Revolt*, 137.

18. James L. Smith, *Autobiography of James L. Smith, Including, Also, Reminiscences of Slave Life, Recollections of the War, Education of Freedmen, Causes of the Exodus, etc.* (Norwich: Press of the Bulletin, 1881; electronic ed., http://doc.south.unc.edu), 15.

19. "News from the Insurgents," *American Beacon* (Norfolk, Va.), August 29, 1831; also Tragle, *Southampton Slave Revolt*, 49.

20. Tragle, *Southampton Slave Revolt*, 202; *Southampton County Minutebook*, 1830–35, 72–131, Virginia State Library, Richmond.

21. Tragle, *Southampton Slave Revolt*, 223.

22. "The Southampton Tragedy, Jerusalem, September 21, 1831," *Richmond Enquirer*, September 30, 1831.

23. Higginson, *Travellers and Outlaws*, 297.

24. *Richmond Enquirer*, August 26, 1831.

25. Susan Selden, "Spreading Terror and Devastation Wherever They Have Been: A Norfolk Woman's Account of the Southampton Slave Insurrection," ed. Deborah Shea, *Virginia Magazine of History and Biography* 95, no. 1 (January 1987): 72.

26. Tragle, *Southampton Slave Revolt*, 52–53.

27. "Headquarters, Jerusalem, August 28, 1831," *Richmond Enquirer*, September 6, 1831.

28. Robert S. Parker to Rebecca Manney, August 29, 1831, in John Kimberly Papers, Southern Historical Collection, University of North Carolina, Chapel Hill, quoted in Merton L. Dillon, *Slavery Attacked: Southern Slaves and Their Allies 1619–1865* (Baton Rouge: Louisiana State University Press, 1990), 157.

29. Allen Crawford, in Perdue, Barden, and Phillips, *Weevils in the Wheat*, 76.

30. "Savage Barbarity!," *Liberator*, October 1, 1831, repr. in Tragle, *Southampton Slave Revolt*, 115.

31. *Constitutional Whig*, September 3, 1831, repr. in Tragle, *Southampton Slave Revolt*, 69, 71, emphasis added.

32. Tragle, *Southampton Slave Revolt*, 106–107.

33. I am arguing against and making reference to Eugene Genovese's *Roll, Jordan, Roll* and his notion that white paternalism "implicitly recognized the slaves' humanity" or that paternalism undermined "solidarity among the oppressed by linking them as individuals to their oppressors" (5, 317). The work of Patrick Wolff, who argues that slaves were a valued commodity "carefully—albeit not kindly—preserved," also needs reevaluation ("Land, Labor, and Difference," *American Historical Review* 106, no. 3 [June 2001]: 896). The "pious Methodist" woman is quoted in Tragle, *Southampton Slave Revolt*, 106.

34. Tragle, *Southampton Slave Revolt*, 107.

35. *Liberator* (Boston, Mass.), September 17, 1831; *Worcester (Mass.) Spy*, September 1831, repr. in Tragle, *Southampton Slave Revolt*, 84. In the Battle of Horse Shoe Bend or the Red Sticks Massacre, nine hundred Creek Indians were killed in 1814 by forces led by Andrew

Jackson. See Adam Rothman, *Slave Country: American Expansion and the Origins of the Deep South* (Cambridge, Mass.: Harvard University Press, 2005), 135.

36. *Liberator* (Boston, Mass.), September 17, 1831.

37. "Daring Outrage of Virginia Slavites," repr. in Tragle, *Southampton Slave Revolt*, 114; *New York Sentinel*, repr. in the *Liberator* (Boston, Mass.), October 1, 1831.

38. See Scot French, *The Rebellious Slave: Nat Turner in American Memory* (Boston: Houghton Mifflin, 2004), for an excellent overview of this idea. Also see David Brion Davis, *Inhuman Bondage: The Rise and Fall of Slavery in the New World* (Oxford: Oxford University Press, 2006), for his questioning of whether it is appropriate to defend "indiscriminate killing of people who are 'part of' an oppressive system," as it echoes the rationale/psychology used to justify other acts of crimes against humanity, like "the genocide of Jews, Armenians, Tutsis, or Sudanese blacks" (210).

39. Howard Thurman, *The Luminous Darkness* (Richmond, Ind.: Friends United, 1999), 48.

40. Howard Thurman, *Jesus and the Disinherited* (Boston: Beacon, 1996), 37–39.

41. Thurman, *Luminous Darkness*, 25–26.

42. Charity Bowery, interview by Lydia Maria Childs, January 1, 1839, in *The Liberty Bell: By Friends of Freedom (1839–1858)* (Boston: American Anti-Slavery Society, 1839–1858), 42; also found in John Blassingame, ed., *Slave Testimony: Two Centuries of Letters, Speeches, Interviews, and Autobiographies* (Baton Rouge: Louisiana State University Press, 1977), 267; also in Higginson, *Travellers and Outlaws*, 301–302.

43. Harriet Jacobs, *Incidents in the Life of a Slave Girl* (New York: Oxford University Press, 1988), 97–98.

44. Ibid., 102.

45. Freeman, *North-Side View of Slavery*, 332.

46. F. N. Boney, Richard L. Hume, and Rafia Zafar, eds., *God Made Man, Man Made the Slave: The Autobiography of George Teamoh* (Macon, Ga.: Mercer University Press, 1990), 69, 71.

47. Michelle Balaev, "Trends in Literary Trauma Theory," *Mosaic* (Winnipeg) 41, no. 2 (June 2008): 2; also see Aaron R. Denham, "Rethinking Historical Trauma: Narratives of Resilience," *Transcultural Psychiatry* 45, no. 3 (2008): 395.

48. Mifflin Winstar Gibbs, *Shadow and Light: An Autobiography with Reminiscences of the Last and Present Century* (Washington, D.C., 1902; Project Gutenberg e-book, www.gutenberg.org), 21. Mifflin Gibbs was the first African American elected as a municipal judge in the United States. He was also a successful businessman.

49. Denham, "Rethinking Historical Trauma," 398.

50. Albert Raboteau asserts that the enslaved and free communities were very familiar with the theology of the Old Testament (*Slave Religion: The "Invisible Institution" in the Antebellum South* [Oxford: Oxford University Press, 2004], 289–321).

51. Rev. Noah Davis, "A Narrative of the Life of Rev. Noah Davis, a Colored Man," in *Don't Carry Me Back! Narratives of Former Virginia Slaves*, ed. Maurice Duke (Richmond, Va.: Dietz Press, 1995), 154.

52. Henry Box Brown, *Narrative of Henry Box Brown, Who Escaped from Slavery Enclosed in a Box 3 Feet Long and 2 Wide* (Boston: Brown and Stearns, 1849), 40.

53. Bethany Veney, *The Narrative of Bethany Veney, a Slave Woman* (Worcester, Mass., 1889; electronic ed., Documenting the American South, http://docsouth.unc.edu/fpn/veney/veney.html). Veney was seventy-four years old at the time of the publication of her

narrative, which means that she would have been seventeen at the time of Turner's rebellion.

54. John Floyd, "Diary of John Floyd," June 1918, nos. 1 and 2, in *The John P. Branch Historical Papers of Randolph-Macon College*, ed. Charles H. Ambler (Richmond, Va.: Richmond Press, 1918), 5:156.

55. "The pike" was probably the Columbia turnpike, which ran from east to west across Virginia. See Veney, *Narrative*, 31–32.

56. Perdue, Barden, and Phillips, *Weevils in the Wheat*, 375, app. 6, question no. 281.

57. Frances Andrews, Newberry, South Carolina, in *Born in Slavery: Slave Narratives from the Federal Writers' Project, 1936–1938*, 18, http://memory.loc.gov/cgi-bin/ampage ?co11Id=mesn&fileName=022/mesn022.db7recNu.

58. Liney Chambers, Brinkley, Arkansas; and Frances Andrews, Newberry, South Carolina, both in *Born in Slavery*.

59. One marker of trauma is called the "conspiracy of silence," where, Aaron Denham argues, an "explicit or unstated taboo forbids the asking about or discussion of trauma" ("Rethinking Historical Trauma," 398). See also Maria Sutton Clemments, DeValls Bluff, Arkansas, in *Born in Slavery*.

60. See the introduction to Perdue, Barden, and Phillips, *Weevils in the Wheat*.

61. Lydia Maria Childs to Harriet Jacobs, in *Incidents in the Life of a Slave Girl Written by Herself* by Harriet Jacobs, ed. Jean Fagin Yellin (Cambridge, Mass.: Harvard University Press, 1987), 244.

62. Jacobs, *Incidents*, 102–103, 99.

63. Moses Grandy, *Narrative of the Life of Moses Grandy, Late a Slave in the United States of America* (London: Gilpin, 1844), 15.

64. Ibid., 19.

65. Ibid., 20.

66. Pumla Gododo Madikizela, *A Human Being Died That Night: A South African Woman Confronts the Legacy of Apartheid* (New York: First Mariner Books, 2004), 86.

67. Freeman, *North-Side View of Slavery*, 332.

68. Fields Cook, *Fields Observations: The Slave Narrative of a Nineteenth Century Virginian*, ed. Mary Jo Jackson Bratton, in *Virginia Magazine of History and Biography*, 1980, 93, http://docsouth.unc.edu/neh/fields/menu.html. See also Job 3:1–19, 3:21–24, 27 (AKJV).

69. Cook, *Fields Observations*, 92.

70. Ibid., 93. Allen Crawford stated that when Henry Travis's mother hit Turner in her grief and asked him, "Why did you take my son away," Turner's response was that Travis "was as willing to go as I was." All those who believed in the cause, Turner seemed to suggest, did not regret losing their lives.

71. Ibid., 93.

72. Turner, "Family of Nat Turner," 139–140.

73. "Massa's Slave Son," in *Unwritten History of Slavery: Autobiographical Accounts of Negro Ex-Slaves*, ed. Ophelia Settle Egypt, J. Masuoka, and Charles S. Johnson (Nashville: Fisk University Press, 1968), 38.

74. Autobiography VI, in "Slavery Was Hell without Fires," *God Struck Me Dead: Religious Conversion Experiences and Autobiographies of Ex-Slaves*, ed. Clifton H. Johnson (Philadelphia: Pilgrim, 1969), 161.

75. Freeman, *A North-Side View of Slavery*, 283–284.

76. Mrs. Angie Boyce, in *Indiana Slave Narratives from the Federal Writers' Project of*

the W.P.A., 1936–1938 Indiana Narratives, vol. 5, District 6, Marion County, Library of Congress, Manuscript Division, Washington, D.C.

77. As one former slave put it, "White folks crazy 'bout their nigger babies 'cause that's where they got their profit" ("Nigger Ain't Scared of White Folks Now," in Egypt, Masuoka, and Johnson, *Unwritten History*, 56).

78. Mrs. Parthena Rollins, in *Indiana Slave Narratives*.

79. Mrs. Fannie Berry, in Perdue, Barden, and Phillips, *Weevils in the Wheat*, 33.

80. "L. M. Mill's Story," in Blassingame, *Slave Testimony*, 504.

81. Wilma King, "Mad Enough to Kill: Enslaved Women, Murder, and Southern Courts," *Journal of African American History* 92, no. 1 (Winter 2007): 47, 52.

82. Drew, *Divine Will Restless Heart*, 24, 60–61, 112, 199.

83. Geo. H. Burks, *Future: Containing Great Lecturers on the Future of the Colored Race, Nat Turner's Insur[r]ection, the New Insur[r]ection* (New Albany, Ind.: Will A. Dudley, 1890), 11–12, in *African American Perspectives: Pamphlets from the Daniel A. P. Murray Collection, 1818–1907*, Rare Book and Special Collections Division, Library of Congress, 10–12, http://hdl.loc.gov/loc.rbc/lcrbmrp.t2012.

84. Turner, "Family of Nat Turner," 142–144, 149, 155.

85. Daniel Goddard, Columbia, South Carolina, in *Slave Narratives: A Folk History of Slavery in the United States, from Interviews with Former Slaves. South Carolina Narratives*, pt. 2 (St. Clair Shores: Scholarly Press, 1976), 1:150.

86. Jacobs, *Incidents*, 138–139.

87. Anna Washington, Clarendon, Arkansas; Emma Turner, Pine Bluff, Arkansas; and Rev. Frank T. Boone, Little Rock, Arkansas, all in *Born in Slavery*.

88. Cornelia Carney, in Perdue, Barden, and Phillips, *Weevils in the Wheat*, 67. See Joel Chandler Harris, *The Complete Tales of Uncle Remus* (Boston: Houghton Mifflin, 1955), 679–725.

89. Herbert Aptheker calculated that there were 250 revolts and conspiracies for the entire history of slavery in the United States (*American Negro Slave Revolts*, 162).

90. Aptheker defines slave rebellion and conspiracy as ten or more slaves who have freedom as their main objective. I have counted only those where the plot was detailed or specific, where there were recorded reprisals against the accused, and where the plot was confirmed by court conviction or execution of the said guilty parties in order to weed out those that, in my opinion, might merely have been white hysteria or delusions about servile unrest. See ibid., 328–333, 338, 341–343, 346–347, 351, 353–357.

91. Ibid., 351. In Clarksburg, Virginia, ten slaves were arrested in 1859, but there is no further evidence of what happened to them after being arrested. See *Liberator*, July 29, 1859.

92. Rev. William G. Hawkins, *Lunsford Lane; or, Another Helper from North Carolina* (Boston: Crosby and Nichols, 1864), 83.

93. Johnson, *God Struck Me Dead*, 134.

94. Mom Ryer Emmanuel, Marion, South Carolina, in *Slave Narratives... South Carolina*, pt. 2, 1:25.

95. Brown, *Narrative*, 38–39.

96. The hopelessness of the enslaved trying to acquire freedom forcibly was made even clearer in the Great Slave revolt of December 1831 led by Samuel Sharpe in Jamaica, which demonstrated that even peaceful attempts at obtaining freedom end in the massacre of men, women, and children. Just as in America, many religious Jamaican slaves were im-

plicated in the movement, and "dreadful was the retaliation inflicted upon the misguided negroes." At least 207 slaves were killed in the rebellion, and another 312 were executed after a trial in the Slave Courts at Montego Bay. In all, 519 slaves lost their lives compared to 14 whites. See Henry Bleby, *Death Struggles of Slavery: Being a Narrative of Facts and Incidents, Which Occurred in a British Colony, during the Two Years Immediately Preceding Negro Emancipation* (London: Hamilton, Adams, 1853), 113–114; Mary Reckford, "The Jamaica Slave Rebellion of 1831," *Past and Present* 40 (July 1968): 120.

97. Document 10, "Statement of Amount Paid by Public Treasury," in Tragle, *Southampton Slave Revolt*, 445.

98. Aptheker, *American Negro Slave Revolts*, 301; John W. Cromwell, "The Aftermath of Nat Turner's Insurrection," *Journal of Negro History* 5, no. 2 (April 1920): 212.

99. Darlene Clark Hine, William C. Hine, and Stanley Harrold, *The African-American Odyssey*, 6th ed. (Boston: Pearson, 2014), 1:215.

100. "Insurrection in North Carolina," *Providence Journal*, September 21, 1831; "Another Riot," *Rhode Island American & Gazette*, September 27, 1831.

101. Frederick Douglass, *My Bondage and My Freedom* (1855; New York: Dover Press, 1969), 200, 311–312. In Douglass's first narrative, he says that they said that "they *all* ought to be killed." See Frederick Douglass, *Narrative of the Life of Frederick Douglass, an American Slave, Written by Himself* (1845; repr., New York: Dell, 1997), 92.

102. Julie Winch, *A Gentleman of Color* (Oxford: Oxford University Press, 2002), 284–288. See also "To the Honorable the Senate and House of Representatives of the Commonwealth of Pennsylvania," in *A Documentary History of the Negro People in the United States*, ed. Herbert Aptheker (New York: Citadel, 1951), 126.

Chapter 5. "In the Hands of the Master"

1. Alexis de Tocqueville, *Democracy in America*, trans. Henry Reeve (New York: Bantam Press, 2000), 1:433–434.

2. Philip A. Bolling, *The Speeches of Philip A. Bolling (of Buckingham) in the House of Delegates of Virginia on the Policy of the State in Relation to Her Colored Population: Delivered on the 11th and 25th of January, 1832* (Richmond, Va.: Thomas W. White, 1832), 6.

3. Ibid., 1. See also Joseph C. Robert, *Road to Monticello: A Study of the Virginia Slavery Debate of 1832* (Durham, N.C.: Duke University Press, 1941); Charles H. Ambler, *Sectionalism in Virginia from 1776 to 1861* (New York: Russell and Russell, 1964), 196–198; James Curtis Ballagh, *History of Slavery in Virginia* (Baltimore, Md.: Johns Hopkins University Press, 1902), 127–139; Alison Goodyear Freehling, *Drift toward Dissolution: The Virginia Slavery Debate of 1831–1832* (Baton Rouge: Louisiana State University Press, 1982), xi–xvi, 228; Aptheker, *American Negro Slave Revolts*, 316; and William W. Freehling, *The Road to Disunion: Secessionist at Bay 1776–1854* (New York: Oxford University Press, 1990), 190–195, for discussions about the significance (or not) of the Virginia Debates.

4. John Floyd, "Diary of John Floyd," in *The John P. Branch Historical Papers of Randolph-Macon College*, ed. Charles H. Ambler (Richmond, Va.: Richmond Press, 1918), 5:166, 168.

5. *Journal of the House of Delegates of the Commonwealth of Virginia. Begun and Held at the Capitol. In the City of Richmond, on Monday, the Fifth Day of December, One Thousand Eight Hundred and Thirty-One* (Richmond, Va.: Thomas Ritchie, Printer to the Commonwealth, 1831), 9–10, Virginia Historical Society, Richmond.

6. "John Floyd to J. C Harris," in *The Southampton Slave Revolt of 1831: A Compilation of Source Material*, by Henry Irving Tragle (Amherst: University of Massachusetts Press, 1971), 275–276.

7. Charles F. Irons, *The Origins of Proslavery Christianity: White and Black Evangelicals in Colonial and Antebellum Virginia* (Chapel Hill: University of North Carolina Press, 2008), 41, 49–57, 93. White evangelicals probably had little to do with Turner's actions but rather provided the model for how religion and slavery could coexist. As historian Charles Irons argues, white evangelicals crafted the Old Testament model of slavery into ideas of paternalism in the antebellum South.

8. John Floyd, "Letters Pertaining to the Revolt," in Tragle, *Southampton Slave Revolt*, 276.

9. "Floyd to Harris," 275; *Richmond Enquirer*, August 30, 1831.

10. David Walker, "Letter to Thomas Lewis," Virginia: Governor's Office, House of Delegates Executive Communications, 1830, box 14, folder 61, accession no. 36912, State Records Collection, Library of Virginia, Richmond.

11. Freehling, *Drift toward Dissolution*, 82.

12. Ibid., 83.

13. "Floyd to Harris," 276.

14. David Walker, *Walker's Appeal, in Four Articles, Together with a Preamble, to the Colored Citizens of the World, but in Particular, and Very Expressly to Those of the United States of America* (Boston: For the Author, 1829), 69.

15. There exists a complete copy of the second edition of David Walker's *Appeal* in Floyd's Executive Papers. See Virginia: Governor's Office, House of Delegates Executive Communications, 1830, box 14, folder 61, accession no. 36912.

16. Walker, *Walker's Appeal*, 61, 21.

17. Ibid., 27–28, 21.

18. Floyd, "Diary of John Floyd," 157, 158.

19. John Patton to the Governor, "Convention of Free Negroes in Philadelphia," January 23, 1832, Virginia: Governor's Office, John Floyd Executive Papers, 1830–1834, box 324, accession no. 42665.

20. Ibid.

21. "After Nat Turner: A Letter from the North," *Journal of Negro History* 55, no. 2 (April 1970): 145–146, 147, 148.

22. Ibid., 147–148.

23. Ibid., 147–148, 145.

24. Floyd, "Diary of John Floyd," 156, 166, 168.

25. Tragle, introduction to Floyd, "Diary of John Floyd," 249; and "John Floyd to J. C. Harris," in Tragle, *Southampton Slave Revolt*, 276.

26. The writings of Thomas Jefferson reflect ideas about emancipation that would have influenced Floyd and the other members of the legislature. Jefferson foreshadowed the scientific racial theories that emerged in the last half of the nineteenth century. See Thomas Jefferson, *Notes on the State of Virginia*, ed. William Peden (Chapel Hill: University of North Carolina Press, 1982), 138, 143, 163.

27. "Floyd Diary," in Tragle, *Southampton Slave Revolt*, 261, 262.

28. Freehling, *Drift toward Dissolution*, 127; Virginia Legislative Petitions, Loudon County, 1831, Virginia State Library, Richmond.

29. Bolling, *Speeches*, 3–4.

30. Freehling, *Drift toward Dissolution*, 125.

31. The rest of the committee members were Messrs. Fisher, Cobb, Wood of Abermarle, Roane, Moore, Newton, Campbell of Brooke, Smith of Frederick, Gholson, Brown, Stillman, and Anderson of Nottoway. *Journal of the House of Delegates of the Commonwealth of Virginia*, 9, Virginia Historical Society, Richmond.

32. Bolling, *Speeches*, 3; Charles Jas. Faulkner, *The Speech of Charles Jas. Faulkner, (of Berkeley,) in the House of Delegates of Virginia, on the Policy of the State with Respect to Her Slave Population. Delivered on January 20, 1832* (Richmond, Va.: Thomas W. White, 1832), 21; John A. Chandler, *The Speech of John A. Chandler, (of Norfolk County,) in the House of Delegates of Virginia, on the Policy of the State with Respect to Her Slave Population. Delivered January 17, 1832* (Richmond, Va.: Thomas W. White, 1832), 7.

33. James M'Dowell Jr., *The Speech of James M'Dowell, Jr. (of Rockbridge,) in the House of Delegates of Virginia, on the Policy of the State with Respect to Her Slave Population. Delivered January 21, 1832* (Richmond, Va.: Thomas W. White, 1832), 5, 12.

34. "Postnatus," plural "postnati," means "those born after." Postnati emancipation disallowed slaveholder claims on the children of slaves or any person born after the date of emancipation.

35. Freehling, *Drift toward Dissolution*, 126; "Floyd Diary," 263.

36. "Floyd Diary," 263.

37. *Constitutional Whig*, January 17, 1832.

38. William H. Brodnax, *The Speech of William H. Brodnax, (of Dinwiddie,) in the House of Delegates of Virginia, on the Policy of the State with Respect to Her Slave Population. Delivered January 19, 1832* (Richmond, Va.: Thomas W. White, 1832), 39, 26.

39. Faulkner, *Speech*, 8–9.

40. M'Dowell, *Speech*, 31.

41. *Constitutional Whig*, January 20, 1832.

42. U.S. Department of Commerce, table 6, "Negro Population, Slave and Free at Each Census by Division," Bureau of the Census, *Negro Population*, 1790–1915 (Washington, D.C.: Government Printing Office, 1918), 45, 57. In Virginia, the slave population went from 292,627 to 469,757; the white population went from 442,117 to 694,300; the free black population went from 12,866 to 47,348.

43. *Constitutional Whig*, January 17, 1832.

44. M'Dowell, *Speech*, 4, 29; Bolling, *Speeches*, 4.

45. M'Dowell, *Speech*, 18–20.

46. Daniel Goodloe, *The Southern Platform; or, Manual of Southern Sentiment on the Subject of Slavery* (Boston: John P. Jewett, 1858), 47, 48.

47. *Constitutional Whig*, January 7, 1832.

48. Goodloe, *Southern Platform*, 48.

49. Brodnax, *Speech*, 17.

50. *Constitutional Whig*, January 19, 1832.

51. See Walter Johnson, *Soul by Soul: Life inside the Antebellum Slave Market* (Cambridge, Mass.: Harvard University Press, 1999), for how the internal trade in slaves operated in America.

52. Ambler, *Sectionalism in Virginia*, 186–188; Aptheker, *American Negro Slave Revolts*, 321.

53. John A. Chandler, *The Speech of John A. Chandler, (of Norfolk County,) in the House of Delegates of Virginia, on the Policy of the State with Respect to Her Slave Population. Delivered January 17, 1832* (Richmond: Thomas W. White, 1832), 8.

54. *Richmond Constitutional Whig*, January 11, 1832.

55. *Constitutional Whig*, January 17, 1832.

56. *Richmond Inquirer*, January 19, 1832.

57. "Speech of James H. Gholson," *Constitutional Whig*, January 26, 1832.

58. Thomas Marshall, *Speech of Thomas Marshall, (of Fauquier) in the House of Delegates of Virginia, on the Policy of the State with Respect to Her Slave Population. Delivered January 14, 1832* (Richmond, Va.: Thomas W. White, 1832), 8–9.

59. Freehling, *Drift toward Dissolution*, 142.

60. Brodnax, *Speech*, 23–26.

61. The term "disposability" is from Kevin Bales, *Disposable People: New Slavery in the Global Economy* (Berkeley: University of California Press, 1999). See David Brion Davis, *The Problem of Slavery in the Age of Emancipation* (New York: Vintage Books, 2014), chaps. 3 and 4.

62. See Davis, *Problem of Slavery*, chaps. 3 and 4.

63. Theodore S. Wright, "Address of the Rev. Theodore S. Wright, before the Convention of the New York State Anti-Slavery Society, on the Acceptance of the Annual Report, Held at Utica, Sept. 20," *Colored American*, October 14, 1837.

64. This turn to colonization echoed white responses to an earlier insurrection attempt in Virginia. On December 12, 1800, the Virginia House of Delegates met in secret to discuss the attempted insurrection led by a twenty-four-year-old blacksmith living in Richmond named Gabriel (Prosser). The Virginia legislature drafted a proposal requesting that President Thomas Jefferson begin negotiations with other European countries to send America's free or emancipated blacks to their African colonies. Jefferson began talks with the Sierra Leone Company, but nothing came of it. He reached out to the government of Portugal, with no results, and subsequently gave up. See Helen Tunnicliff Catterall, *Judicial Cases Concerning American Slavery and the Negro* (1926; repr., New York: Negro University Press, 1968), 1:73; Appendix, *Letter* II, in William Lloyd Garrison, *Thoughts on African Colonization* (1832; repr., New York: Arno, 1968), 8–9; *Virginia Argus* (Richmond), October 3, 1800; Scot French, *The Rebellious Slave: Nat Turner in American Memory* (Boston: Houghton Mifflin, 2004), 292; Freehling, *Drifting toward Dissolution*, 111; Joshua Coffin, *An Account of Some of the Principal Slave Insurrections, Others, Which Have Occurred, or Been Attempted, in the United States and Elsewhere, during the Last Two Centuries* (New York: ASS, 1860), in *Slave Insurrections: Selected Documents* (Westport, Conn.: Negro University Press, 1970), 28–29.

65. See Issac V. Brown, "Letter to Mr. John P. Mumford," in *Biography of the Rev. Robert Finley, D.D. of Basking Ridge, N.J. with an Account of His Agency as the Author of the American Colonization Society; also a Sketch of the Slave Trade; a View of Our National Policy and That of Great Britain towards Liberia and Africa* (Philadelphia: John W. Moore, 1857), 81–83, 89–93, 97, 99; *Richmond Recorder*, September 22, 1802; Winthrop Jordan, *White over Black: American Attitudes toward the Negro, 1550–1812* (Chapel Hill: University of North Carolina Press, 1968), 469; Henry Noble Sherwood, "The Formation of the American Colonization Society," *Journal of Negro History* 2, no. 3 (July 1917): 212–213.

66. Sherwood, "Formation," 212–213.

67. Brown, "Letter to Mr. John P. Mumford," 99.

68. Rev. Issac Van Brown, *Memoir of the Rev. Robert Finley, D.D. Late Pastor of the Presbyterian Congregation* (New Brunswick, N.J.: Terhune and Letson, 1819), 81–83, 89, 91, 90.

69. Ibid., 93.

70. Ibid., attributed to Elias Boudinot Caldwell, Esq., 90. The idea that racial amalgamation would lead to a war between the races is evident throughout the antebellum era beginning with the provocative sentiments of political pamphleteer and editor of the *Richmond Recorder* James Callender about Thomas Jefferson and his enslaved mistress, Sally Hemings. See *Richmond Recorder*, September 22, 1802; Jordon, *White over Black*, 469. Fanny Wright would make one exceptional effort to promote interracial sex in her utopian community, Nashoba, in Tennessee.

71. From the African American perspective, members of the ACS stoked white fear to galvanize support for their organization. See "Minutes of the Fourth Annual Convention, for the Improvement of the Free People of Color, in the United States (1834)," in *Minutes of the Proceedings of the National Negro Convention 1830–1864*, by Howard Holman Bell (New York: Arno, 1969), 4–5, 7.

72. Issac Brown and many other colonizationists rationalized that even if it meant death and hardship for blacks in the early years of settlement in Africa, it would be nothing out of the ordinary, as the ancestors of white Americans had also suffered in the beginning (*Memoir of the Rev. Robert Finley*, 97).

73. John Thompson Brown, *The Speech of John Thompson Brown, in the House of Delegates of Virginia, on the Policy of the State with Respect to Her Slave Population. Delivered January 18, 1832* (Richmond, Va.: Thomas W. White, 1832).

74. Brodnax, *Speech*, 7.

75. Jefferson, *Notes*, 138.

76. Brodnax, *Speech*, 30.

77. Ibid., 29, 36, 38, 43. Brodnax's objectives, however, went beyond what the ACS outlined. As a southern businessman looking for new markets, Brodnax envisioned that colonization would facilitate white control over West Africa. This could be achieved by writing into the bill the acquisition of additional territory in Africa.

78. *Constitutional Whig*, January 17, 1832.

79. Faulkner, *Speech*, 13, 14, 16; *Constitutional Whig*, January 24, 1832.

80. Faulkner, *Speech*, 18, 16, 10.

81. Freehling, *Drift toward Dissolution*, 148–149.

82. *Constitutional Whig*, January 23, 1832.

83. Freehling, *Drift toward Dissolution*, 164–165.

84. *Richmond Enquirer*, February 7, 1832.

85. Brodnax, "Appendix," in *Speech*, 42.

86. African Americans contested the ACS's plan for colonization from the very beginning. And they were rightly concerned that compulsion might replace the purported voluntary recruitment of free blacks. See William Loren Katz, introduction to Garrison, *Thoughts on African Colonization*, viii–ix; Philip Bell, "An Address to the Citizens of New-York," in Garrison, *Thoughts on African Colonization*, 16–17; *Richmond Enquirer*, February 7, 1832.

87. Brodnax, "Appendix," in *Speech*, 42; *Richmond Enquirer*, February 7, 1832.

88. Ibid.

89. Moses Grandy, *Narrative of the Life of Moses Grandy, Late a Slave in the United States of America* (London: Gilpin, 1844), 24.

90. Brodnax, "Appendix," in *Speech*, 44, 42.

91. Freehling, *Drift toward Dissolution*, 182, 191–192.

92. Claude A. Clegg, *The Price of Liberty: African Americans and the Making of Liberia* (Chapel Hill: University of North Carolina Press, 2004), 134–136; See U.S. Congress, *Senate Roll of Emigrants That Have Been Sent to the Colony of Liberia*, 28th Cong., 2nd sess., 1844, report 150; and "The Long Awaited Statistics," *African Repository*, June 1844, 161–162.

93. Clegg, *Price of Liberty*, 130–160. Out of 4,454 people sent to settle in Liberia from 1820, only 1,736 remained in 1843; 2,198 of them had died, and 608 managed to leave the colony. Also see Garrison, *Thoughts on African Colonization*, 19, 26–30, 34, for black awareness of mortality in Africa.

94. Clegg, *Price of Liberty*, 134–136. See U.S. Congress, *Senate Roll of Emigrants*; and "Long Awaited Statistics."

95. Clegg, *Price of Liberty*, 139.

96. Brodnax, "Appendix," in *Speech*, 43.

97. Clegg, *Price of Liberty*, 134–135.

98. The 1832 Police Bill altered the rights of free blacks to a trial by jury. Now they would share the same legal rights that slaves had. The governor could now sell free blacks into slavery if convicted of a crime punishable by death.

99. Smith remarked that slaves continued to hold meetings at their quarters in secret. See James L. Smith, *Autobiography of James L. Smith, Including, Also, Reminiscences of Slave Life, Recollections of the War, Education of Freedmen, Causes of the Exodus, etc.* (Norwich: Press of the Bulletin, 1881; electronic edition, http://doc.south.unc.edu), 15.

100. Floyd, "Diary of John Floyd," 92.

101. Thomas R. Dew, *Review of the Debate in the Virginia Legislature of 1831 and 1832* (1832; repr., Westport, Conn.: Negro University Press, 1970), 5, 9.

102. Ibid., 15, 19, 18; Hugo Grotius, *Rights of War and Peace: Including the Law of Nature and of Nations* (1625; repr., Washington, D.C.: M. Walter Dunne Press, 1901), chaps. 1 and 7.

103. Dew, *Review*, 11–12, 33, 29, 113–114, 116.

104. Ibid., 32–33.

105. Ibid., 33.

106. See Bell, "Address," 16–17.

107. Brodnax, "Appendix," in *Speech*, 42.

Chapter 6. Would Have to "See His Blood Flow"

1. For the origins of the "Sambo" thesis, see Stanley Elkins, *Slavery: A Problem in American Institutional and Intellectual Life* (Chicago: University of Chicago Press, 1959).

2. Other than the monographs of W. E. B. Du Bois, *The Suppression of the African Slave Trade to the United States of America 1638–1870* (1896; repr., Baton Rouge: Louisiana State University Press, 1969), and Ronald Takaki, *The Proslavery Crusade: The Agitation to Reopen the African Slave Trade* (New York: Free Press, 1971), there are several articles and book chapters written from various perspectives on the reopening of the foreign slave trade. See Harvey Wish, "The Revival of the African Slave Trade in the United States, 1856–1860," *Mississippi Valley Historical Review* 27, no. 4 (March 1941): 569–588; Robert F. Durden, "J. D. B. De Bow: Convulsions of a Slavery Expansionist," *Journal of Southern History* 17, no. 4 (November 1951): 441–461; Barton J. Berstein, "Southern Politics and Attempts to Reopen the African Slave Trade," *Journal of Negro History* 51, no. 1 (January

1966): 16–35; Gerald Horne, *The Deepest South: The United States, Brazil, and the African Slave Trade* (New York: New York University Press, 2007), esp. 83–170; and Manisha Sinha, *The Counterrevolution of Slavery: Politics and Ideology in Antebellum South Carolina* (Chapel Hill: University of North Carolina Press, 2000), 136, 129, 142, and chap. 5.

3. See William Law Mathieson, *Great Britain and the Slave Trade 1839–1865* (New York: Octagon: 1967), 133, 135, 162, 165–166, 179; Eric Williams, *Capitalism and Slavery* (Chapel Hill: University of North Carolina Press, 1944), 176–177.

4. George Fitzhugh, "The Conservative Principle; or, Social Evils and Their Remedies," *De Bow's Review* 22, no. 5 (May 1857): 450.

5. Trafficking in African slaves continued beyond 1807 because the penalties for participation in the trade were minor at best, while profits reached over 30 percent. The problem was that all of the acts established by Congress were essentially a dead letter. Du Bois notes that there was some decline from 1825 to 1830, but then the trade was revived from 1840 to 1860. Thomas Fowell Buxton, *The African Slave Trade and Its Remedy* (1839; repr., London: Frank Cass, 1967), 221–225; Mathieson, *Great Britain*, 5; see also Walter B. Hill, "Living with the Hydra: The Documentation of Slavery and the Slave Trade in Federal Records," *Prologue* 32, no. 4 (Winter 2000): 4–8, https://www.archives.gov/publications/prologue /2000/winter/hydra-slave-trade-documentation-2.html; Hugh Thomas, *The Slave Trade: The Story of the Atlantic Slave Trade, 1440–1870* (New York: Simon and Schuster, 1997), 614; Du Bois, *Suppression*, 112, 114–123, 182–184.

6. William Lowndes Yancey, "Late Southern Convention at Montgomery," *De Bow's Review* 24, no. 6 (June 1858): 585.

7. Du Bois notes that the fitting out of slave ships was a thriving business in New York City in the 1850s. Even in 1808 New York was considered the premier port for the illicit trade, and the cities of Portland and Boston participated in a major way as well. See Du Bois, *Suppression*, 178–179; Thomas, *Slave Trade*, 461–463.

8. Fitzhugh, "Conservative Principle," 450, 456–457.

9. Leonidas W. Spratt, "Report on the Slave Trade," *De Bow's Review* 24, no. 6 (June 1858): 477–478.

10. Edward Bryan, *Notice of the Rev. John B. Adgers's Article on the Slave Trade Published for the Author* (Charleston, S.C.: Steam Power Press of Walker, Evans, 1858), 24, 26.

11. Fitzhugh, "Conservative Principle," 454, 456.

12. Mathieson, *Great Britain*, 42; Frederick C. Drake and R. W. Schufeldt, "Secret History of the Slave Trade to Cuba Written by an American Naval Officer, Robert Wilson Schufeldt, 1861," *Journal of Negro History* 55, no. 3 (July 1970): 225.

13. W. W. Wright, "The Coolie Trade, or the Excomienda System of the Nineteenth Century," *De Bow's Review* 27, no. 3 (September 1859): 304; Drake and Schufeldt, "Secret History," 225, 226.

14. Mathieson, *Great Britain*, 97–99; see also Paul E. Lovejoy, *Transformations in Slavery: A History of Slavery in Africa*, 2nd ed. (Cambridge: Cambridge University Press, 2000), 143; David Eltis and Stanley L. Engerman, "Fluctuations on Sex and Age Ratios in the Transatlantic Slave Trade, 1663–1864," *Economic History Review* 46, no. 2 (1993): 308–323.

15. Mathieson, *Great Britain*, 40–41, 43.

16. Rev. Pascoe G. Hill noted that of the 447 slaves on board the recaptured Brazilian ship the *Progresso* in 1843, 213 were boys, and none of the 189 men exceeded twenty years of age. See *Fifty Days on Board a Slave Vessel* (Baltimore, Md.: Black Classic Press, 1848), 21–22.

17. *An Exposition of the African Slave Trade, from the Year 1840, to 1850, Inclusive. Prepared from Official Documents, and Published by Direction of the Representatives of the Religious Society of Friends, in Pennsylvania, New Jersey and Delaware* (Philadelphia: J. Rakestraw, 1851), 20, 154.

18. Buxton, *African Slave Trade*, 73, 200; John Leighton Wilson, *The Foreign Slave Trade. Can It Be Revived without Violating the Most Sacred Principles of Honor, Humanity, and Religion?* (pamphlet), *Southern Presbyterian Review*, October 1859, Cornell University Library Digital Collection, 13. Thomas Buxton argued that for every ten slaves who survived to reach Cuba or Brazil, at least fourteen were destroyed. And if the victims of the Islamic slave trade were factored in, the mortality rate escalated to over 200 percent.

19. Mathieson, *Great Britain*, 44; Herman Melville, *Moby-Dick; or The Whale* (1851; repr., New York: Oxford University Press, 1981), 280.

20. Buxton, *African Slave Trade*, 189, 202; Mathieson, *Great Britain*, 41, 121; Thomas C. Hansard, *Hansard's Parliamentary Debates* (London: T. C. Hansard, 1844), 76:930.

21. "Slave Trade—Horrible Massacre," *Niles National Register*, May 1, 1847.

22. Buxton, *African Slave Trade*, 183.

23. Hill, *Fifty Days*, 50. Out of a total of 447 captives, 175 Africans died on board the *Progresso*, and according to Hill, many of them were children.

24. Mathieson, *Great Britain*, 44.

25. Drake and Schufeldt, *Secret History*, 228, 231.

26. Hill, *Fifty Days*, 54, 56.

27. Buxton, *African Slave Trade*, 202; *An Exposition*, 63–64.

28. Dr. Van Evne, "Slavery Extension," *De Bow's Review* 15, no. 1 (July 1853): 3, 9–10, 13.

29. Leonidas W. Spratt, "Speech of Mr. Spratt, of South Carolina," *De Bow's Review* 27, no. 2 (August 1859): 213.

30. *Report of the Special Committee of the House of Representatives, of South Carolina, on So Much of the Message of His Excellency Gov. Jas. H. Adams, as Relates to Slavery and the Slave Trade* (Columbia, S.C.: Steam Power Press, 1857), 7–8, 16.

31. Van Evne, "Slavery Extension," 4, 11.

32. James H. Hammond, "Slavery in the Light of Political Science," in *Cotton Is King, and Pro-slavery Arguments: Comprising the Writings of Hammond, Harper, Christy, Stringfellow, Hodge, Bledsoe, and Cartwright, on This Important Subject*, ed. E. N. Elliot (Augusta, Ga.: Pritchard, Abbott & Loomis, 1860), 667–668.

33. "The Results of African Labor in the New World," *Staunton Vindicator* 16, no. 6 (February 10, 1860).

34. Wright, "Coolie Trade," 318–320.

35. "Southern Population—Its Destiny," *De Bow's Review* 13, no. 1 (July 1852): 13, 18.

36. Spratt, "Report on the Slave Trade," 490.

37. Rev. George B. Wheeler, introduction to *The Southern Confederacy and the African Slave Trade: The Correspondence between Professor Cairnes, A.M. and George M'Henry, Esq.* (Dublin: Mcglashan and Gill, 1863), vi, xvii; Spratt, "Report on the Slave Trade," 474.

38. Henry Hughes, "Reopening of the Slave Trade: A Series by 'St. Henry'" (from the *Southern Reveille*, 1857–58), in *Selected Writings of Henry Hughes: Antebellum Southerner, Slavocrat, Sociologist*, ed. Stanford M. Lyman (Jackson: University Press of Mississippi, 1985), 98–99. Hughes created a third American labor system (the other two being free and slave) called "warranteeism," where labor was owed as the duty of an inferior race in a productive society rather than owned. Ultimately, it was slavery called something else.

39. Ibid., 99.

40. L. J. Gogerty, "Southern Convention at Knoxville," *De Bow's Review* 23, no. 3 (September 1857): 318.

41. Wright, "Coolie Trade," 304, 318–320, 316–317. See also Lovejoy, *Transformations in Slavery*, 151–152. Lovejoy contends that the French and Portuguese were the greatest offenders of all the European nations trying to get around the legal barriers to slave trading by using the label "contract laborers." Because these laborers left Africa as slaves, Lovejoy argues, they must be included in the number of slaves exported from Africa in the nineteenth century.

42. Wright, "Coolie Trade," 298.

43. Mr. Preston, "Late Southern Convention at Montgomery," *De Bow's Review* 24, no. 6 (June 1858): 596.

44. Wright, "Coolie Trade," 310; Fitzhugh, "Conservative Principle," 449, 451.

45. Hill, *Fifty Days*, 51.

46. Roger Pryor, "Late Southern Convention at Montgomery," *De Bow's Review* 24, no. 6 (June 1858): 582.

47. "The Slave Trade," *National Era*, June 23, 1859; "Great Changes Coming Over the South," *National Era*, March 24, 1859.

48. Frederick Douglass, *Frederick Douglass Papers*, ed. John W. Blassingame, series 1, vol. 3, 1855–63 (New Haven, Conn.: Yale University Press, 1985), 434.

49. Henry Washington Hilliard, "Late Southern Convention at Montgomery," *De Bow's Review* 24, no. 6 (June 1858): 592.

50. Ibid., 582.

51. James J. Pettigrew, "Protest against the Slave-Trade Revival," *De Bow's Review* 25, no. 3 (September 1858): 292–295.

52. Ibid., 294.

53. "The Recent Southern Convention at Vicksburg," *De Bow's Review* 27, no. 3 (September 1859): 361.

54. Pettigrew, "Protest," 293–295. This notion of warlike Africans aligns with John Thornton's conclusions that high numbers of Africans captured and sold into slavery were trained soldiers. See John K. Thornton, *Warfare in Atlantic Africa 1500–1800* (London: UCL Press, 1999), 139–147.

55. Pettigrew, "Protest," 298–299.

56. "Becoming Africanized," *Franklin Repository*, September 14, 1859, 4.

57. Edmund Ruffin, *Anticipations of the Future: To Serve as Lessons for the Present Time* (1860; repr., Freeport, N.Y.: Books for Libraries, 1972), 238, 237, 385, 243, 76–77.

58. Thomas Jefferson, *Notes on the State of Virginia*, ed. William Peden (Chapel Hill: University of North Carolina Press, 1982), 142.

59. Pettigrew, "Protest," 305.

60. A Florida Farmer, "Southern Prosperity," *De Bow's Review* 27, no. 1 (July 1859): 38.

61. "Southern Convention at Vicksburg," *De Bow's Review* 27, no. 2 (August 1859): 220.

62. John Hope Franklin, *Militant South 1800–1861* (Urbana: University of Illinois Press, 2002), 7, 10, 12–13, 91–92.

63. Spratt, "Report on the Slave Trade," 488–499.

64. Pettigrew, "Protest," 295.

65. "A Quartette of Objections to African Labor Immigration," *New Orleans Delta*, March 9, 1858.

66. François Furstenberg, "Beyond Freedom and Slavery: Autonomy, Virtue, and Resistance in Early American Political Discourse," *Journal of American History* 89, no. 4 (March 2003): 9–12, 23–24.

67. Eugene D. Genovese, *Roll, Jordan, Roll: The World the Slaves Made* (New York: Vintage, 1976), 89–93.

68. John B. Russwurm to [Edward Jones], March 20, 1830, in *The Black Abolitionist Papers*, ed. C. Peter Ripley (Chapel Hill: University of North Carolina Press, 1992), 3:74.

69. Martin R. Delany, "Annexation of Cuba," *North Star*, April 27, 1849, repr. in *Martin R. Delany: A Documentary Reader*, ed. Robert S. Levine (Chapel Hill: University of North Carolina Press, 2003), 161–162.

70. John Brown, *Slave Life in Georgia: A Narrative of the Life, Sufferings, and Escape of John Brown, a Fugitive Slave*, ed. F. N. Boney (1855; repr., Savannah: Beehive, 1991), 163–164; Du Bois, *Suppression*, 114; Thomas, *Slave Trade*, 614.

71. Charley Barber, Winnaboro, S.C., "Ex-Slave 81 Years Old," in *Slave Narratives: A Folk History of Slavery in the United States, from Interviews with Former Slaves. South Carolina Narratives*, pt. 1 (St. Clair Shores: Scholarly Press, 1976), 1:30.

72. Paul Singleton, Savannah Unit, Georgia Writers' Project, Works Projects Administration, *Drums and Shadows: Survival Studies among the Georgia Coastal Negroes* (Athens: University of Georgia Press, 1940), 17.

73. "Revival of the Slave Trade," *Frederick Douglass' Paper*, August 18, 1854.

74. *Frederick Douglass' Paper*, September 15, 1854.

75. "A New Dodge," *Provincial Freeman* (Chatham, Canada West), August 22, 1857.

76. "Anonymous," *Anglo-African Magazine* 1, no. 9 (September 1, 1859; repr., New York: Arno Press and the New York Times, 1968), 310.

77. James McCune Smith, "The Critic at Chess," in *The Works of James McCune Smith: Black Intellectual and Abolitionist*, ed. John Stauffer (Oxford: Oxford University Press, 2006), 110.

78. Smith, "Critic at Chess," 111; see also *Frederick Douglass' Paper*, January 12, 1855.

79. "South Carolina Becoming Africanized," *National Era,* August 18, 1859.

80. Ethiop, "The Anglo-African and the African Slave Trade," *Anglo-African Magazine*, ed. Thomas Hamilton, 1, no. 9 (September 1859; repr., New York: Arno Press and the New York Times, 1968), 284–286.

81. "Editorial by Thomas Hamilton," in *The Black Abolitionist Papers*, vol. 5: *The United States, 1859–1865*, ed. C. Peter Ripley (Chapel Hill: University of North Carolina Press, 1992), 98–99.

Chapter 7. John Brown's Mistake

1. Douglass, *The Life and Times of Frederick Douglass: In His Own Words* (1881; repr., New York: Kensington Press, 1983), 281. For a thorough, albeit more traditional, treatment of Brown, see David S. Reynolds, *John Brown, Abolitionist: The Man Who Killed Slavery, Sparked the Civil War, and Seeded Civil Rights* (New York: Vintage Books, 2005).

2. "Brown to Higginson, February 12, 1858," in *The Life and Letters of John Brown, Liberator of Kansas and Martyr of Virginia*, ed. Frank B. Sanborn (Boston: Roberts Brothers, 1891), 436.

3. Douglass, *Life and Times*, 280.

4. Howard Holman Bell, *A Survey of the Negro Convention Movement 1830–1861* (New York: Arno Press and the New York Times, 1969), 116–118.

5. Henry Bibb, "Narrative of the Life and Adventures of Henry Bibb: An American Slave," in *Puttin On Old Massa*, ed. Gilbert Osofsky (New York: Harper and Row, 1969), 66.

6. Solomon Northup, "Twelve Years a Slave: Narrative of Solomon Northup," in Osofsky, *Puttin On Old Massa*, 363.

7. Samuel Ringgold Ward, Toronto, March 1, 1852, "To Free Black Men of the United States," *Frederick Douglass' Paper*, March 11, 1852.

8. Herbert Aptheker, "Militant Abolitionism," *Journal of Negro History* 26, no. 4 (October 1941): 466–467.

9. Charles B. Dew, "Black Ironworkers and the Slave Insurrection Panic of 1856," *Journal of Southern History* 41, no. 3 (August 1975): 321–338.

10. "Massa's Slave Son," in *Unwritten History of Slavery: Autobiographical Accounts of Negro Ex-Slaves*, ed. Ophelia Settle Egypt, J. Masuoka, and Charles S. Johnson (Nashville: Fisk University Press, 1968), 38.

11. "I Stole My Learning in the Woods," in Egypt, Masuoka, and Johnson, *Unwritten History*, 148.

12. "One of the First Voters in Montgomery County," in Egypt, Masuoka, and Johnson, *Unwritten History*, 60.

13. Dew, "Black Ironworkers," 327, 329–330, 328.

14. Ward, "To Free Black Men."

15. Benj. S. Bebee, "Letter to Rev. McLain," in *The Mind of the Negro as Reflected in Letters Written during the Crisis 1800–1860*, ed. Carter G. Woodson (New York: Russell and Russell, 1926), 130–131.

16. *Frederick Douglass' Paper*, October 23, 1851. Fugitive slave William Parker led a resistance movement in Christiana, Pennsylvania, in 1851. The slave owner, Edward Gorsuch, was killed.

17. *Frederick Douglass' Paper*, October 23, 1851.

18. Mary Ann Shadd Cary, "In a Strait," *Provincial Freeman* (Chatham, Canada West), March 15, 1856.

19. Mary Ann Shadd Cary, "Insurrections, Underground Railroad, Republican Victory, Fugitive Slave Case," draft, November 1857, Mary Ann Shadd Cary Papers, Ontario Archives, Black Abolitionist Archives, Mercy Libraries, University of Detroit.

20. Ibid.

21. *Liberator*, August 13, 1858; Aptheker, *Documents*, 406–408.

22. Benjamin Quarles, *Allies for Freedom* (New York: Da Capo Press, 2001), 83–84.

23. The research of European ethnologists like John Phillip concluded, however, that there were no biological differences between people in 1828. See Phillip, *Researches in South Africa: Illustrating the Civil, Moral, and Religious Condition of the Progress of the Christian Missions, Exhibiting the Influence of Christianity in Promoting Civilization*, 2 vols. (London, 1828; repr., New York: Negro University Press, 1969), 1:32–33.

24. Reginald Horsman, *Race and Manifest Destiny: The Origins of American Racial Anglo-Saxonism* (Cambridge, Mass.: Harvard University Press, 1981), 116–151; Patrick Brantlinger, *Dark Vanishings: Discourse on the Extinction of Primitive Races, 1800–1930* (Ithaca, N.Y.: Cornell University Press, 2003), 18, 71–74, 90.

25. George M. Frederickson, *Black Image in the White Mind: The Debate on Afro-*

American Character and Destiny, 1817–1914 (Middletown, Conn.: Wesleyan University Press, 1971), 100–102.

26. Jeffery Rossbach, *Ambivalent Conspirators: John Brown and the Secret Six, and a Theory of Slave Violence* (Philadelphia: University of Pennsylvania Press, 1982), 10.

27. See John Stauffer, *The Black Heart of Men: Radical Abolitionists and the Transformation of Race* (Cambridge, Mass.: Harvard University Press, 2004), for a full treatment and perhaps a differing perspective of radical abolitionism.

28. Rossbach, *Ambivalent Conspirators*, 9; François Furstenberg, "Beyond Freedom and Slavery: Autonomy, Virtue, and Resistance in Early American Political Discourse," *Journal of American History* 89, no. 4 (March 2003): 28–31.

29. Rossbach, *Ambivalent Conspirators*, 148.

30. Theodore Parker, *The Present Aspect of Slavery in America: Considered in Two Speeches Delivered before the American Antislavery Society, at New York* (Boston: Benjamin H. Greene, 1856), 4–5.

31. Ibid., 7.

32. James Redpath, *Roving Editor or Talks with Slaves in the Southern States* (University Park: Pennsylvania State University Press, 1996), 284–287.

33. Rossbach, *Ambivalent Conspirators*, 169.

34. James Redpath, *Captain John Brown* (Boston: Thayer and Eldridge, 1860), 204–205; Osborne P. Anderson, *A Voice from Harpers Ferry* (Boston: Printed for the Author, 1861), 31.

35. Sanborn, *Life and Letters*, 122, 130.

36. Redpath, *Roving Editor*, 87.

37. Harriet Beecher Stowe, "An Appeal to the Women of the Free States of America on the Present Crisis in Our Country," *Provincial Freeman*, March 25, 1854.

38. Lucy Stone, "The Fugitive Slave Case," *Cincinnati Daily Gazette*, February 14, 1856.

39. Parker, *Present Aspect*, 5, 91.

40. Frederick Douglass, "Is It Right and Wise to Kill a Kidnapper?," *Frederick Douglass' Paper*, June 2, 1854.

41. Solomon Northup, "Twelve Years a Slave," 363.

42. J. Sella Martin, "Speech of Rev. J. S. Martin," *Liberator*, November 11, 1859.

43. James McCune Smith, *The Works of James McCune Smith: Black Intellectual and Abolitionist*, ed. John Stauffer (Oxford: Oxford University Press, 2006), 154.

44. John S. Jacobs, "A True Tale of Slavery," in *Harriet Jacobs Family Papers*, vol. 1, ed. Jean Fagan Yellin (Chapel Hill: University of North Carolina Press, 2008), 300.

45. Andrew Jackson, *Narrative and Writings of Andrew Jackson, of Kentucky* (Syracuse, N.Y.: Daily and Weekly Star, 1847), 8.

46. James W. C. Pennington, *The Fugitive Blacksmith; or, Events in the History of James W. C. Pennington, Pastor of a Presbyterian Church, New York, Formerly a Slave in the States of Maryland, U.S.* (1850; repr., Westport, Conn.: Negro University Press, 1971), xii, xiii.

47. Ibid., 3.

48. Bibb, "Narrative," 156.

49. Stone, "The Fugitive Slave Case."

50. "A Reminiscence of Slavery. The Slave Mother, Margaret Garner. Her Tragic Sacrifice of a Child in This City. Interview with Her Husband," *Cincinnati Chronicle*, March 11, 1870, in Mark Reinhardt, *Who Speaks for Margaret Garner?* (Minneapolis: University of Minnesota Press, 2010), 238–239.

51. Austin Steward, *Twenty-Two Years a Slave and Forty Years a Freeman* (Rochester, N.Y.: William Alling, 1857), 140.

52. Ethiop, "What Shall We Do with the White People?," *Anglo-African Magazine*, February 1860.

53. Frederick Douglass, "The Black Man's Future in the Southern States: An Address Delivered in Boston, Massachusetts, on 5 February 1862," in *Frederick Douglass Papers*, ed. John W. Blassingame, series 1, vol. 3, 1855–63 (New Haven, Conn.: Yale University Press, 1985), 507.

54. Dr. John S. Rock, in *A Documentary History of the Negro People in the United States*, ed. Herbert Aptheker (New York: Citadel, 1951), 402.

55. Ibid., 403, 404.

56. Douglass, *Life and Times*, 323; see also Quarles, *Allies for Freedom*, 80, for a similar conclusion; as well as W. E. B. Du Bois, *John Brown* (Philadelphia: George W. Jacobs & Co. Publishers, 1909), 344.

57. Edward V. Clark, *National Anti-Slavery Standard*, October 10, 1850.

58. *Liberator*, December 9, 1859.

59. Henry Highland Garnet, *Walker's Appeal and Garnet's Address to the Slaves of the United States of America* (1848; repr., Salem: Ayer, 1994), 94–96.

60. Garnet's address has frequently been interpreted to mean that he advocated violence and was in favor of the slaves insurrecting. What Garnet advocated for slave men and women to do was to "physically resist working" in order to disrupt the institution of slavery to such an extent that it would be impossible for the slaveholding South to recover, forcing southern whites to reconceptualize how black labor would function, a harbinger of how labor relations would unfold after the Civil War. This was ultimately the same goal that Brown hoped to achieve as a result of his plan, only he intended to arm the slaves in running away or to insurrect. See ibid., 96.

61. Ibid., 95–96.

62. Douglass, *Life and Times*, 323–324.

63. *Liberator*, November 11, 1859.

64. Du Bois, *John Brown*, 344.

65. Quarles, *Allies for Freedom*, 75.

66. Jean Libby, *Black Voices from Harpers Ferry* (Palo Alto, Calif.: Published by the Author, 1979), 87.

67. Charles H. Langston, "Editor," *Cleveland Plain Dealer*, November 18, 1859.

68. Quarles, *Allies for Freedom*, 75.

69. Ibid., 66; Rev. J. W. Loguen, *The Rev. J. W. Loguen, as a Slave and as a Freeman: A Narrative of Real Life* (1859; repr., New York: Negro University Press, 1969), 398–430.

70. J. W. Loguen, "Letter from J. W. Logan," *Frederick Douglass' Paper*, August 12, 1853.

71. Loguen, *Rev. J. W. Loguen*, 277; see also J. W. Loguen, "Mr. Loguen's Reply," *Liberator*, April 27, 1860, in Woodson, *The Mind of the Negro*, 218.

72. Loguen, *Rev. J. W. Loguen*, 104–133, 224, 276–278; see also J. W. Loguen, "Irish Ladies Anti-Slavery Society," *Douglass' Monthly*, May 1859; J. W. Loguen, *Frederick Douglass' Paper*, July 20, 1855.

73. *Douglass' Monthly*, March 1859, January 1861.

74. *Liberator*, August 26, 1859.

75. Quarles, *Allies for Freedom*, 65.

76. James Cleveland Hamilton, "John Brown in Canada," *Canadian Magazine* 1, no. 1 (November 1894–April 1895): 132; Dorothy Sterling, ed., *Speak Out in Thunder Tones: Letters and Other Writings by Black Northerners, 1787–1865* (Garden City, N.Y.: Doubleday, 1973), 278–280.

77. *National Anti-Slavery Standard*, April 9, 1870; *Detroit Daily Post*, February 23, 1875; *Detroit Advertiser and Tribune*, February 23, 1875.

78. Anderson, *Voice from Harpers Ferry*, 9–10.

79. Richard J. Hinton, *John Brown and His Men* (New York: Funk and Wagnalls Co., 1894), 170–173.

80. Quarles, *Allies for Freedom*, 41.

81. Hamilton, "John Brown in Canada," 134; Karolyn Smardz Frost, *I've Got a Home in Glory Land: A Lost Tale of the Underground Railroad* (New York: Farrar, Straus and Giroux, 2007), 286–287, 307.

82. Hamilton, "John Brown," 43–44.

83. William Wells Brown, "Narrative of William Wells Brown, a Fugitive Slave," in Osofsky, *Puttin On Old Massa*, 216.

84. J. Sella Martin, *Liberator*, November 11, 1859.

85. Hamilton, "John Brown in Canada," 132–133.

86. Ibid., 46, 133.

87. Frank A. Rollins, *Life and Public Service of Martin R. Delany* (New York: Arno Press, 1969), 88, 90.

88. Ibid., 88; Hinton, *John Brown and His Men*, 635.

89. Quarles, *Allies for Freedom*, 50.

90. Hinton, *John Brown and His Men*, 619.

91. Rollins, *Life and Public*, 92–93.

92. Martin R. Delany, *Blake, or The Huts of America*, in Ronald Takaki, *Violence in the Black Imagination: Essays and Documents* (New York: Oxford University Press, 1993), 103–214, 223.

93. Rollins, *Life and Public*, 89, 93–94.

94. Jean M. Humez, "Conversation with Martha C. Wright," in *Harriet Tubman: The Life and the Life Stories* (Madison: University of Wisconsin Press, 2003), 40.

95. Benjamin Quarles, *Black Leaders of the Nineteenth Century*, ed. Leon Litwack and August Meier (Champaign: University of Illinois Press, 1991), 45.

96. J. H. Hammond, "Hammond's Letters on Slavery," in *The Proslavery Argument; as Maintained by the Most Distinguished Writers of the Southern States* (1852; repr., New York: Negro University Press, 1968), 174; Sanborn, *Life and Letters*, 452.

97. See chapter 1 of Deborah Gray White, *Ar'n't I a Woman? Female Slaves in the Plantation South* (New York: W. W. Norton, 1985). Tubman did value being a woman. After being abused and put out of a railroad car where women sat and put into the smoking car where men sat, Tubman instructed the conductor that "she was proud of being a black woman as he was of being white" (Martha Coffin Wright to Marianne Pelham Mott, November 7, 1865, in Humez, *Harriet Tubman*, 301).

98. Harper also faced gender and racial erasure. Harper recalled "some of the remarks which my lectures call forth[:] 'She is a man,' again 'She is not colored, she is painted'" (William Still, *The Underground Railroad: A Record of Facts, Authentic Narratives, Letters, &c.* [Chicago: Johnson Publishing Company, 1970], 80). While lecturing at an antislavery meeting in Indiana in 1858, some proslavery Democrats requested that Sojourner "submit

her breast for inspection" because "her voice was not the voice of a woman, it was the voice of a man" (Olive Gilbert, *Narrative of Sojourner Truth: A Bondswoman of Olden Time* [New York: Oxford University Press, 1991], 138–139).

99. Humez, *Harriet Tubman*, 35.

100. Ibid., 241, 55, 236. Tubman did not accept the idea of failure lightly, as she was known to threaten to shoot any fugitive slaves who expressed an unwillingness to finish traveling with her to Canada.

101. "Letter of John H. Hill to William Still," Toronto, January 19, 1854, in Woodson, *Mind of the Negro*, 589.

102. Quarles, *Allies for Freedom*, 83; Fred Landon, "Canadian Negroes and the John Brown Raid," *Journal of Negro History* 6, no. 2 (April 1921): 174–182, in *Ontario's African-Canadian Heritage: Collected Writings of Fred Landon 1918–1967*, ed. Karolyn Smardz Frost, Bryan Walls, Hillary Bates Neary, and Frederick H. Armstrong (Toronto: Natural Heritage Books, 2009), 203.

103. Osborn Anderson did not arrive at the farm until September 16, 1859 (*Voice from Harpers Ferry*, 62).

104. Douglass, *Life and Times*, 326.

105. Sanborn, *Life and Letters*, 541.

106. Thomas Wentworth Higginson, *Cheerful Yesterdays* (Boston: Houghton, Mifflin and Co., 1898), 229; Libby, *Black Voices from Harpers Ferry*, 149.

107. Sanborn, *Life and Letters*, 542.

108. "My Man Antony," *Putnam's Magazine* 3 (January–June 1869): 448–449.

109. Brown, "Narrative," 216.

110. Bibb, "Narrative," 89.

111. J. Sella Martin, *Liberator*, November 11, 1859.

112. Humez, *Harriet Tubman*, 243.

113. Harrison Berry, *Slavery and Abolitionism, as Viewed by a Georgia Slave* (Atlanta: M. Lynch & Co., 1861), 15, 21.

114. Ibid., 15–16.

115. Ibid., 33.

116. "The Harper's Ferry Affair as Party Capital: The Danger of Using It," *National Era*, November 3, 1859.

117. Herbert Aptheker, *American Negro Slave Revolts* (New York: International Press, 2008), 337–338, 341–343.

118. Lydia Marie Childs to Mary Stearns, November 3, 1859, John Brown / Boyd B. Stutler Collection, MS 78-1, West Virginia Memory Project, West Virginia Division of Culture and History, Charleston, http://www.wvculture.org/history/jbexhibit/bbsms06-0023.html.

119. Du Bois, *John Brown*, 344.

120. Libby, *Black Voices from Harpers Ferry*, 154.

121. "The Outbreak in Virginia," *Anglo-African Magazine* 1, no. 12 (December 1859): 375, 383; Robert E. McGlone, *John Brown's War against Slavery* (New York: Cambridge University Press, 2009), 300.

122. "John Brown's Final Address to the Court, November 2, 1859," in Jean Libby, *John Brown Mysteries* (Missoula: Pictorial Histories Publishing Co., 1999), 102.

123. Edmund Ruffin, *The Diary of Edmund Ruffin*, vol. 1, ed. William Kauffman Scarborough (Baton Rouge: Louisiana State University Press, 1972), 354.

124. David Hunter Strother, "The Trial of the Conspirators," *Harper's Weekly*, November 12, 1859.

125. "Message of Gov. Henry A. Wise December 1859," West Virginia Archives and History, http://www.wvculture.org/history/jbexhibit/bbspro2-0016.html.

126. "Correspondence Between Lydia Maria Childs and Gov. Wise and Mrs. Mason," published by the American Anti-Slavery Society, Boston, 1860, West Virginia Archives and History, http://www.wvculture.org/history/jbexhibit/bbspro2-0016.html.

127. "Letter of Mrs. M. J. C Mason," Alto, King George's Co., Va., November 11, 1859, published by the American Anti-Slavery Society, Boston, 1860, West Virginia Archives and History, http://www.wvculture.org/history/jbexhibit/bbspro2-0016.html.

128. "Message of Gov. Henry A. Wise December 1859."

129. Anderson, *Voice from Harpers Ferry*, 40.

130. "The Burning of Charleston," *Harper's Weekly*, December 28, 1861.

131. Libby, *Black Voices from Harpers Ferry*, 135.

132. William Lloyd Garrison, "Letter from Petersburg, Va.," in *The New Reign of Terror* (1860; repr., New York: Arno Press, 1967), 116.

133. Robert Dewitt, *The Life and Trial and Conviction of Capt. John Brown: Being a Full Account of the Insurrection at Harpers Ferry, Virginia* (New York: Robert M. Dewitt, Publisher, 1859), 4.

134. "Affairs at the South," *Daily Evening Express*, December 31, 1860.

135. Ann Agnes Coe to George Halstead Coe, January 27, 1860, Col. George Halstead Coe 10 mss, folder 7, Coe Family Papers, South Caroliniana Library, University of South Carolina, Columbia.

136. "The Fear of Slave Insurrections," *New York Times*, December 11, 1860.

137. "William S. Pettigrew to James S. Johnston, October 25 1860," in Aptheker, *American Negro Slave Revolts*, 356.

138. John Townsend, *The Doom of Slavery in the Union: Its Safety out of It* (Charleston, S.C.: Evans & Cogswell, 1860), 24, 37.

139. Hinton, *John Brown and His Men*, 325.

140. "John Brown's Raid at Harper's Ferry: An Eyewitness Account by Charles White," ed. Rayburn S. Moore, *Virginia Magazine of History and Biography* 67 (October 1959): 3–4.

141. Anderson, *Voice from Harpers Ferry*, 42–44, 67.

142. Libby, *Black Voices from Harpers Ferry*, 120.

143. "A False Alarm in Somerset County, Maryland," *National Era*, November 17, 1859.

144. "The Burning of Charleston"; see also oversized folder 1, Christensen Family Papers, South Caroliniana Library, University of South Carolina, Columbia.

145. Ruffin, *Diary of Edmund Ruffin*, 1:456.

146. "Affairs at the South," *Daily Evening Express*, December 31, 1860.

147. "Another Negro Insurrection," *Lancaster Daily Evening Express*, October 18, 1860; "Alabama Negro Insurrection," *New York Herald*, December 19, 1860.

148. "The Alabama Insurrection," *New York Times*, October 20, 1860.

149. "Another Negro Insurrection."

150. Donald E. Reynolds, *Editors Make War: Southern Newspapers in the Secession Crisis* (Carbondale: Southern Illinois University Press, 2006), 101.

151. *Daily Picayune*, September 16, 1860.

152. Townsend, *Doom of Slavery*, 36, 34; see also *Austin State Gazette*, August 4, 1860; "Reminiscences about the Troubles," *Dallas Morning News*, July 10, 1892.

153. "Reminiscences about the Troubles."

154. W.R.D.W., "Further Accounts of the Abolition Raid," *Evening Day Book*, August 12, 1860, in Townsend, *Doom of Slavery*, 37.

155. Laura S. Haviland, *A Woman's Life-Work: Labors and Experiences of Laura S. Haviland* (Cincinnati: Walden and Stowe, 1882), 176–177.

156. Libby, *Black Voices from Harpers Ferry*, 84–85.

157. Hinton, *John Brown and His Men*, 325; Du Bois, *John Brown*, 353–355.

158. Ann Agnes Coe to George Halstead Coe, January 27, 1860.

159. Thomas W. Henry, *From Slavery to Salvation: The Autobiography of Rev. Thomas W. Henry of the A.M.E. Church*, ed. Jean Libby (Jackson: University Press of Mississippi, 1994), 53.

160. Libby, *Black Voices from Harpers Ferry*, 133.

161. Garrison, *New Reign of Terror*, 108.

162. Bethany Veney, *The Narrative of Bethany Veney, a Slave Woman* (Worcester, Mass., 1889; electronic ed., Documenting the American South, http://docsouth.unc.edu/fpn/veney/veney.html), 37.

163. See Mary Ann Shadd Cary, "Underground Railroad Business" and "A Stampede," *Liberator*, November 18, 1859.

164. Libby, *Black Voices from Harpers Ferry*, 171.

165. Anne Brown Adams to Alexander M. Ross, January 15, 1882, GLC 03007.10, Gilder Lehrman Institute of American History, New Haven, Connecticut.

166. Libby, *Black Voices from Harpers Ferry*, 188, 195.

167. Allen A. Lane, "A Warning to Colored Seaman," *Weekly Anglo-African*, December 31, 1859.

168. Douglass, *Life and Times*, 325; Quarles, *Allies for Freedom*, 114.

169. John S. Rock, "The Position of the Colored Man Today Is a Trying One," *Liberator*, March 16, 1860, in *Freedom's Journey: African American Voices of the Civil War*, ed. Donald Yacovone (Chicago: Lawrence Hill Books, 2004), 49.

170. H. Ford Douglass, *Anti-Slavery Bugle*, October 6, 1860, in Yacovone, *Freedom's Journey*, 9.

171. Humez, *Harriet Tubman*, 136, 243.

172. Douglass, *Douglass Papers*, series 1, vol. 3, 413–417.

173. Anderson, *Voice from Harpers Ferry*, 5–6, 7–8.

174. "Speech of John S. Rock, Delivered at the Meionaon, Boston, Mass. 5 March 1860," in *The Black Abolitionist Papers*, vol. 5: *The United States, 1859–1865*, ed. C. Peter Ripley (Chapel Hill: University of North Carolina Press, 1992), 59; *Liberator*, March 16, 1860.

175. Thomas Hamilton, "The Nat Turner Insurrection," *Anglo-African Magazine* 1, no. 12 (December 1859): 386.

176. Henry Clarke Wright, *The Natick Resolution, or Resistance to Slaveholders the Right and Duty of Southern Slaves and Northern Freemen* (Boston: By the Author, 1859), 21.

Chapter 8. Making "Hell for a Country"

1. Roy P. Basler et al., eds., *The Collected Works of Abraham Lincoln* (New Brunswick, N.J.: Rutgers University Press, 1953), 5:370–375.

2. Frederick Douglass, *Frederick Douglass Papers*, ed. John Blassingame, series 1, vol. 3, 1855–63 (New Haven, Conn.: Yale University Press, 1985), 477, 484.

3. Jim Downs, *Sick from Freedom: African American Illness and Suffering during the Civil War and Reconstruction* (New York: Oxford University Press, 2012), 21.

4. Edwin Driskell, interviewer, Henry Wright, ex-slave, Atlanta, Georgia, in *Born in Slavery: Slave Narratives from the Federal Writers' Project, 1936–1938,* https://www.loc.gov /resource/mesn.044/?sp=198&st=text.

5. Liney Chambers, Brinkley, Arkansas, in *Born in Slavery.*

6. Frederick Douglass, "The Present and Future of the Colored Race in America: An Address Delivered in Brooklyn, New York, on 5 May 1863," in Douglass, *Douglass Papers,* series 1, vol. 3, 573.

7. Ibid., 574–575.

8. Ibid., 574.

9. Suzie King Taylor, *Reminiscences of My Life in Camp,* in *Black Writers and the American Civil War,* ed. Richard A. Long (Secaucus: Blue and Gray Press, 1988), 131.

10. Abraham Lincoln, "Proclamation 92—Warning to Rebel Sympathizers," July 25, 1862; Abraham Lincoln, "Second Annual Message," December 1, 1862, both in John T. Woolley and Gerhard Peters, *The American Presidency Project,* http://www.presidency.ucsb .edu/ws/index.php?pid=29503.

11. Ibid. Lincoln was a member of the Illinois Colonization Society even before he became president. See Charles H. Wesley, "Lincoln's Plan for Colonizing the Emancipated Negroes," *Journal of Negro History* 4 (January 1919): 7–21. See Phillip W. Magness and Sebastian N. Page, *Colonization after Emancipation: Lincoln and the Movement for Black Resettlement* (Columbia: University of Missouri Press, 2011), 3–5, 13–80, for evidence that Lincoln supported colonization as early as 1857 to prevent amalgamation and that despite the Emancipation Proclamation, Lincoln continued to work with the British government for the resettlement of blacks in British Honduras (Belize) and British Guiana beginning in 1862. He also gave government assistance to the disastrous settlement of contraband on an uninhabited island, Île-à-Vache, off the coast of Haiti before signing the proclamation freeing those enslaved.

12. Basler et al., *The Collected Works,* 5:370–375; "Editorial by Philip A. Bell," June 14, 1862; "R.H.V. to Robert Hamilton"; "Alfred M. Green to Robert Hamilton," October 1861; all in *The Black Abolitionist Papers,* vol. 5: *The United States, 1859–1865,* ed. C. Peter Ripley (Chapel Hill: University of North Carolina Press, 1992), 143, 117–124. Former slave Maria Sutton Clemments claimed that she had "not taken sides wid neither one" (*Slave Narratives: A Folk History of Slavery in the United States, from Interviews with Former Slaves. Arkansas Narratives,* 2:17, https://www.loc.gov/resource/mesn.022/?sp=19). Former slave William Ward claimed that he didn't know if "Sherman intended to keep him in slavery or free him" ("An Account of Slavery Related by William Ward—Ex Slave," in *Slave Narratives: A Folk History of Slavery in the United States from Interviews with Former Slaves. Georgia Narratives,* pt. 4, 131, https://www.loc.gov/resource/mesn.044/?sp=132).

13. "Alfred M. Green to Robert Hamilton," 123.

14. Bishop Daniel A. Payne, "An Open Letter to the Colored People," *Weekly Anglo-African* (1862), quoted in *Christian Recorder,* September 29, 1862; also in William Wells Brown, *The Black Man, His Antecedents, His Genius, and His Achievements* (Washington, D.C.: Library of Congress, 1865), 208–209.

15. "The Extermination of the Negro," *New York Times,* October 16, 1862.

16. "The War, the Proclamation, and the Slaves," *New York Times,* November 6, 1862. The massacre in Cawnpore, India, was a major event in the Indian rebellion in 1857. See

Rudrangshu Mukherjee, *Spectre of Violence* (New Delhi: Penguin Books, 1998), for a full treatment of this rebellion.

17. Douglass, *Douglass Papers*, series 1, vol. 3, 574.

18. "George E. Stephens to Robert Hamilton," in Ripley, *Black Abolitionist Papers*, 199.

19. Benjamin Butler, *Autobiography and Personal Reminiscences of Major General Benjamin F. Butler* (Boston, 1892), 492–494.

20. Maj. Gen. Thomas H. Holmes to Maj. Gen. Samuel R. Curtis, October 11, 1862, in *War of the Rebellion: A Compilation of the Official Records of the Union and Confederate Armies*, series 1 (Washington, D.C.: Government Printing Office, 1899), 13:726–727.

21. Jefferson Davis, "To the Senate and House of Representatives of the Confederate States," in *Journal of the Congress of the Confederate States of America, 1861–1865*, Wednesday, January 14, 1863 (Washington, D.C.: Government Printing Office, 1904), 3:13, https://memory.loc.gov/ll/llcc/003/0000/00150013.tif; "Rebel View of the Proclamation," *Douglass' Monthly*, March 1863.

22. "Reported Negro Plot in Virginia," *Christian Recorder*, October 25, 1862.

23. Allen Parker, *Recollections of Slavery Times by Allen Parker* (Worcester, Mass.: Chas. W. Burbank and Co., 1895), chap. 8.

24. "The Confederate Black Flag" and "Rebels Shooting Negroes," *Liberator* 33, no. 8 (February 20, 1863).

25. William De Loss Love, *Wisconsin in the War of the Rebellion* (Chicago: Sheldon & Co., 1866), 557; Greg Urwin, *Black Flag over Dixie: Racial Atrocities and Reprisals in the Civil War* (Carbondale: Southern Illinois University Press, 2004), 25.

26. Urwin, *Black Flag over Dixie*, 142–143.

27. "Fort Pillow Massacre," U.S. Congress, House, Joint Committee on the Conduct of the War, vol. 1,206, 38th Cong., 1st sess. (Washington, D.C., May 5, 1864), 7.

28. Andrew Ward, *River Run Red: The Fort Pillow Massacre in the American Civil War* (New York: Penguin, 2005), 156–159.

29. "Fort Pillow Massacre," 4.

30. "Testimony of Major Williams" and "Testimony of Alexander Nayron (colored)," 26–28, in "Fort Pillow Massacre."

31. "Testimony of Jacob Wilson (colored)," in *War of Rebellion*, vol. 32, pt. 1, series 4 (Washington, D.C.: Government Printing Office, 1899), 539–540; "Report of Acting Master William Ferguson, U.S. Navy, of the Capture of Fort Pillow," in ibid., 571–572.

32. "Statement of Daniel Stamps, Company E, Thirteenth Tennessee Cavalry," in *War of Rebellion*, vol. 32, pt. 1, series 4, 531.

33. "Statement of William J. Mays, Company B, Thirteenth Tennessee Cavalry," in *War of Rebellion*, vol. 32, pt. 1, series 4, 525.

34. "Statement of James Lewis, Private of Company C, Sixth U.S. Heavy Artillery (Colored)," in *War of Rebellion*, vol. 32, pt. 1, series 4, 537.

35. "Testimony of Surgeon Horace Wardner," in "Fort Pillow Massacre," 13.

36. "Testimony of Elias Falls (Colored)," in "Fort Pillow Massacre," 15.

37. "Testimony of Thomas Adison (Colored) Private, Company C, 6th United States Heavy Artillery," in "Fort Pillow Massacre," 20–21.

38. "Testimony of Manuel Nichols (Colored) Private, Company B, 6th United States Heavy Artillery," in "Fort Pillow Massacre," 21.

39. "Testimony of George Shaw (Colored) Private, Company B, 6th United States Heavy Artillery," in "Fort Pillow Massacre," 25–26.

40. "Testimony of Ransom Anderson (Colored,) Co. B, 6th United States Heavy Artillery," in "Fort Pillow Massacre," 31–32; "Testimony of Jacob Thompson (Colored)," in ibid., 30; "Report of Acting Master William Ferguson," 571.

41. "Testimony of Jacob Thompson (Colored)," in "Fort Pillow Massacre," 30.

42. "Statement of Frank Hogan, Corporal, Company A, Sixth U.S. Artillery," in *War of Rebellion*, vol. 32, pt. 1, series 4, 536.

43. "Report," in "Fort Pillow Massacre," 6.

44. Ward, *River Run Red*, 250, 464n4.

45. "From L. Polk to Major General Forrest" and "Joint Resolution," in *War of Rebellion*, vol. 32, pt. 1, series 1, 619.

46. R.H.C., "Fort Pillow," *Christian Recorder*, April 30, 1864.

47. Urwin, *Black Flag over Dixie*, 145–146; Dudley Taylor Cornish, *The Sable Arm: Negro Troops in the Union Army, 1861–1865* (New York: W. W. Norton, 1966), 176–177; Alan Axelrod, *The Horrid Pit: The Battle of the Crater, the Civil War's Cruelest Mission* (New York: Carroll & Graf, 2007), 177–178; John Cimprich, *Fort Pillow, a Civil War Massacre and Public Memory* (Baton Rouge: Louisiana State University Press, 2005), 104.

48. H. M. Turner, "A Very Important Letter from Chaplain Turner," *Christian Recorder*, July 9, 1864.

49. Ibid., emphasis added.

50. James M. McPherson, *Anti-Negro Riots in the North, 1863* (New York: Arno Press, 1969), iii.

51. Andrew Dickson White, *CopperHead Minstrel: A Choice Collection of Democratic Poems and Songs, for the Use of Political Clubs and the Social Circle* (New York: Feeks and Bancker, 1863), 31–32.

52. Ibid., 33.

53. *A Thrilling Narrative from the Lips of the Sufferers of the Late Detroit Riot, March 6, 1863, with the Hair Breadth Escapes of Men, Women and Children, and Destruction of Colored Men's Property, Not Less Than $15,000* (Detroit, Mich.: Published by the author, 1863), 9, 20.

54. Ibid., 2–3, 6, 24.

55. Ibid., 13, 18, 8.

56. William Webb, *The History of William Webb, Composed by Himself* (Detroit: Egbert Hoekstra, 1873; electronic ed., http://Docsouth.unc.edu/neh/webb/webb.html), 38–39.

57. *Thrilling Narrative*, 13, 15, 1–2.

58. Ibid., 11–12.

59. The 1863 draft riots were motivated by Democratic leaders who successfully riled up many working-class men, most of whom were Irish, to resist being drafted into the Civil War, as they claimed it only benefited African Americans.

60. *Report of the Committee of Merchants for the Relief of Colored People. Suffering from the Late Riots in the City of New York* (New York: George A. Whitehorne, 1863), 22.

61. Ibid., 27, 22, 26.

62. Ibid., 16–17.

63. Ibid., 17.

64. Ibid., 24–25.

65. James L. Smith, *Autobiography of James L. Smith, Including, Also, Reminiscences of Slave Life, Recollections of the War, Education of Freedmen, Causes of the Exodus, etc.* (Norwich: Press of the Bulletin, 1881; electronic edition, http://doc.south.unc.edu), 43.

66. Douglass, *The Life and Times of Frederick Douglass: In His Own Words* (1881; repr., New York: Kensington Press, 1983), 361.

67. Douglass, *Douglass Papers*, series 1, vol. 3, 581.

68. "Congressional Testimony of John S. Smith, Washington, March 14, 1865," Joint Committee on the Conduct of the War, "Massacre of Cheyenne Indians," 38th Cong., 2nd sess. (Washington, D.C., 1865), 4–12, 56–59, 101–108. See also Joe A. Cramer to Major [Edward Wanshaer Wynkoop], December 19, 1864, "Sand Creek Massacre," United States Congress, Senate, *Report of the Secretary of War, Sand Creek Massacre*, Sen. Exec. Doc. No. 26, 39th Cong., 2nd sess. (Washington, D.C.: Government Printing Office, 1867), 29–33.

69. "Letter from Joe A. Cramer to Major," in Joint Committee, "Massacre of Cheyenne Indians."

70. "The Story of the Sand Creek Massacre Retold by One Who Participated in the Bloody Work of That Eventful Day in Colorado's History," *Denver Evening Post*, April 9, 1899, 13, col. A.

71. "The Chivington Massacre" and "Awful State of Affairs in Alabama," *Liberator* 35, no. 34 (August 25, 1865): 135.

72. Butler, *Autobiography*, 903.

73. Steven Hahn, *A Nation under Our Feet: Black Political Struggles in the Rural South from Slavery to the Great Migration* (Cambridge, Mass.: Belknap, 2003), 147–149; Leslie A. Schwalm, *A Hard Fight for We: Women's Transition from Slavery to Freedom in South Carolina* (Urbana: University of Illinois Press, 1997), 128–132, 173–179.

74. Hahn, *Nation under Our Feet*, 194–195.

75. Eliza Frances Andrews, *The War-Time Journal of a Georgia Girl, 1864–1865* (New York: D. Appleton and Company, 1908; electronic ed., Documenting the American South, http://docsouth.unc.edu/fpn/andrews/menu.html).

76. Entry of Mrs. Mary Jones in her journal (Wednesday, January 11, 1865), in *The Children of Pride: Selected Letters of the Family of the Rev. Dr. Charles Colcock Jones from the Years 1860–1868, with the Addition of Several Previously Unpublished Letters*, ed. Robert Manson Myers (New Haven, Conn.: Yale University Press, 1984), 526.

77. "The Government and the Freedmen," *New York Times*, June 6, 1865, 4.

78. "The Policy of the President, in Its Bearings upon the Black Man," *Independent*, October 19, 1865, 1.

79. "North Carolina. The Scheme to Exterminate the Colored Race. From the *Southern Christian Intelligencer* of Aug. 5," *New York Times*, August 22, 1865.

80. "Extermination of the Negroes," *Milwaukee Daily Sentinel*, March 1, 1866, issue 50, col. B.

81. "The South and the Union," *New York Times*, November 6, 1866, 2. See also "The Future of the Negro," *Round Table* (New York), September 9, 23, 1865, for similar analysis of whether emancipation would lead to the extermination of the colored race in the South.

82. Robert Hamilton, "The Emancipation Proclamation Ignored, and a New Scheme of Southern Despotism Boldly Initiated," *Weekly Anglo-African* (New York), September 3, 1865, in Ripley, *Black Abolitionist Papers*, 360, 362, 364.

83. "Awful State of Affairs in Alabama," *Liberator*, August 25, 1865.

84. "Letter of Chas. F. Jackson to Maj. Genl. O. O. Howard, May 22, 1866," "Affidavit of William Davis, July 8, 1867," and "Reports of Outrages, Riots and Murders, Jan. 15, 1866–Aug. 12, 1868," all in *Records of the Assistant Commissioner for the State of Tennessee: Bureau of Refugees, Freedmen, and Abandoned Lands, 1865–1869*, National Archives Micro-

film Publication M999, roll 34. See also Hannah Rosen, *Terror in the Heart of Freedom: Citizenship, Sexual Violence, and the Meaning of Race in the Postemancipation South* (Chapel Hill: University of North Carolina Press, 2009), for more on the use of terror and rape to subjugate African Americans after the Civil War.

85. "Letter of Chas. F. Jackson to Maj. Genl. O. O. Howard dated May 22, 1866." In the years between 1865 and 1868, more than fifteen hundred people were lynched across the South. Data compiled from *The Lynching Century: African Americans Who Died in Racial Violence in the United States Chronology: Dates of Death 1865–1899*, http://www.oocities.org /colosseum/base/8507/NLists.htm.

86. *Testimony Taken by the Joint Select Committee to Inquire into the Condition of Affairs in the Late Insurrectional States*, North Carolina, vol. 2 (Washington, D.C.: Government Printing Office, 1872), 14, 49, 318.

87. Martin R. Delany, "Letter on President Warner of Liberia," *Christian Recorder*, July 21, 1866, 1.

88. Martin R. Delany, "Trial and Conviction," February 28, 1876, in Tunde Adeleke, *Without Regard to Race: The Other Martin R. Delany* (Jackson: University Press of Mississippi, 2003), 227.

89. "Proceedings of a Session Specially Called. Tuesday, March 4, 1873. By the President of the United States of America. A Proclamation," *Journal of the Senate of the United States of America, 1789–1873*, Library of Congress, U.S. Congressional Documents and Debates, 68:602, http://memory.loc.gov/cgi-bin/ampage?collId=llsj&fileName=068/llsj068.db &recNum=596&itemLink=D?hlaw:2:./temp/~ammem_l2WE::%230680597&linkText=1.

90. "The Camp Grant Massacre: Lieut. Whitman's Report—a Fearful Tale—Women and Children Butchered," *New York Times*, July 20, 1871, 1.

91. Jeffrey Ostler, *The Plain Sioux and U.S. Colonialism from Lewis and Clark to Wounded Knee* (Cambridge: Cambridge University Press, 2004), 13, 15, 62.

92. Jeptha "Doc" Choice, Federal Writers' Project: Slave Narrative Project, vol. 16, Texas, pt. 1, Adams–Duhon, 1936, Manuscript / Mixed Material, Library of Congress, https://www.loc.gov/item/mesn161/; Lewis Favor, ex-slave, Georgia, in *Born in Slavery*, 7.

93. Data compiled from *The Lynching Century*. Also see "History of Lynching in the South Documents Nearly 4,000 Names," *New York Times*, February 10, 2015, http://www .nytimes.com/2015/02/10/us/history-of-lynchings-in-the-south-documents-nearly-4000 -names.html?_r=0.

94. Richard Taylor, *Destruction and Reconstruction: Personal Experiences of the Late War* (1979; repr., New York: Longmans, 1955), 306–307.

95. Essic Harris, *Testimony Taken by the Joint Select Committee to Inquire into the Condition of the Affairs in the Late Insurrectionary States, North Carolina* (Washington, D.C.: Government Printing Office, 1872), 2:99, 94, 95.

96. Eric Foner, *Reconstruction: America's Unfinished Revolution 1863–1877* (New York: Perennial Classics, 2002), 426.

97. William Henry Rooks, Arkansas, in *Born in Slavery*.

98. Eli Coleman, Federal Writers' Project: Slave Narrative Project, vol. 16, Texas, pt. 1.

99. Martin R. Delany, "Delany for Hampton," letter to the editor, *News and Courier*, September 26, 1876, 1.

100. See Civil Rights Cases, 109 U.S. 3 (1883).

101. Dr. Henry McNeal Turner, "The Barbarous Decision of the Supreme Court," *Christian Recorder*, November 8, 1883; letter to the editor, *Christian Recorder*, February 22,

1883; both repr. in *Respect Black: The Writings and Speeches of Henry McNeal Turner*, ed. Edwin S. Redkey (New York: Arno Press, 1971), 62–63, 54.

102. T. Thomas Fortune, "Political Independence of the Negro," in *Black and White: Land, and Labor and Politics in the South* (1884), repr. in *African-American Social and Political Thought 1850–1920*, ed. Howard Brotz (New Brunswick, N.J.: Transaction, 1992), 337–343.

103. Frederick Douglass, "The Future of the Colored Race," May 1886, repr. in Brotz, *African-American Social and Political Thought*, 309. Douglass was probably referring to the massacre of Chinese in Wyoming by white miners in 1885. The white miners in Duquoin, Illinois, imitated these actions and warned African American men that they would be next if they did not abandon their claims and leave. See "The Bitter Fruits of the Chinese Massacre in Wyoming Making Their Appearance with Unpleasant Rapidity," *Congregationalist*, October 8, 1885, issue 41, col. B.

104. *Weekly Age-Herald*, August 28, 1889.

105. W. E. B. Du Bois, *Black Reconstruction in America 1860–1880* (1935; repr., New York: Free Press, 1962), 379.

106. Ida B. Wells-Barnett, *On Lynchings* (New York: Humanity Books, 2002), 121.

107. Mary Church Terrell, "Lynching from a Negro's Point of View," *North American Review* 178 (June 1904): 853–854, 860–861, 863, JSTOR Early Journal Content, https://archive.org/details/jstor-25150991.

108. See Jill Lepore, *The Name of War: King Philip's War and the Origins of American Identity* (New York: Vantage Press, 1998), for more on the importance of naming historical events. See also "1898 Wilmington Race Riot Commission Report," May 2006, LeRae Umfleet, Principal Researcher, Research Branch, Office of Archives and History, North Carolina Department of Cultural Resources, http://www.history.ncdcr.gov/1898-wrrc/report/front-matter.pdf. The commission suggests that what happened in Wilmington was an "ethnic riot" defined as "lethal attacks by . . . one ethnic group upon another, designed to degrade the targeted group, inflict harm or kill them, and thus reduce the ethnic heterogeneity of one's region or state" (357).

109. "1898 Wilmington Race Riot Commission Report," 197.

110. J. Allen Kirk, "A Statement of Facts Concerning the Bloody Riot in Wilmington, N.C. of Interest to Every Citizen of the United States" (Wilmington, N.C., 1898), http://docsouth.unc.edu/nc/kirk/menu.html.

111. Ibid.

112. "Letter to William McKinley: President of the United States of America, Nov. 13, 1898," National Archives Material Relating to the 1898 Wilmington Race Riot, RG 60, General Records of the Department of Justice, box 1117A, "Year Files," 1887–1904, file 17743-1898, McKinley Papers, National Archives, Washington, D.C.

113. "1898 Wilmington Race Riot Commission Report," 195, 197–198, 203; Charles Crowe, "Racial Massacre in Atlanta," *Journal of Negro History* 54, no. 2 (April 1969): 167.

114. "Crisis for Negro Race," *New York Times*, June 4, 1900.

115. George White, "George White Speaks Out on Lynching," in *Trade of Puerto Rico; Personal Explanation: Speeches of Hon. George H. White, of North Carolina, in the House of Representatives, Monday, February 5, and Friday, February 23, 1900*, http://memory.loc.gov/cgi-bin/query/r?ammem/murray:@field(DOCID+@lit(lcrbmrpt2112div1).

116. Kirk, *Statement of Facts*, emphasis added.

117. William Pickens, "Jesse Max Barber," *Voice*, December 3, 1906.

118. J. Max Barber, "The Atlanta Tragedy," *Voice of the Negro*, September 22, 1906, 476, 478.

119. Charles Crowe, "Racial Violence and Social Reform—Origins of the Atlanta Riot of 1906," *Journal of Negro History* 53, no. 3 (July 1968): 168, 170.

120. *Atlanta Constitution*, September 25, 1906.

121. "Letter to the Editor," *Atlanta Georgian*, August 26, 1906.

122. *Lynching Calendar*; *Lynching Century*.

123. Rev. Peter Randolph, *From Slave Cabin to the Pulpit. The Autobiography of Rev. Peter Randolph: The Southern Question Illustrated and Sketched of Slave Life* (Boston: James H. Earle, 1893), 44.

124. "Robert W. Winston, N.C., Oct. 2, 1919, to Moorfield Storey," Robert W. Winston Papers, North Carolina State Archives, as found in Leon Litwack, *Trouble in Mind: Black Southerners in the Age of Jim Crow* (New York: Vintage, 1998), 207.

125. Ophelia Settle Egypt, J. Masuoka, and Charles S. Johnson, eds., *Unwritten History of Slavery: Autobiographical Accounts of Negro Ex-Slaves* (Nashville: Fisk University, 1968), 118.

Epilogue. The "Place for Which Our Fathers Sighed"

1. Marcus Garvey, "An Appeal to the Soul of White America" and "The Negro's Place in World Reorganization," repr. in *African-American Social and Political Thought 1850–1920*, ed. Howard Brotz (New Brunswick, N.J.: Transaction, 1992), 555, 557, 567.

2. Civil Rights Congress, *We Charge Genocide: The Historic Petition to the United Nations for the Relief from a Crime of the United States Government against the Negro People* (New York: Civil Rights Congress, 1951), xii, xvi–xviii, 77, 126, 191–192.

3. James G. Thompson, letter to the editor, *Pittsburgh Courier*, January 31, 1942.

4. Civil Rights Congress, *We Charge Genocide*, 8–9.

5. Ibid., 196–197.

6. A. Dirk Moses, "Empire, Colony: Keywords and the Philosophy of History," in *Empire, Colony, Genocide: Conquest, Occupation, and Subaltern Resistance in World History*, ed. A. Dirk Moses (New York: Berghahn Books, 2010), 7, 17–19. Also see Omer Bartov, "'Fields of Glory': War, Genocide, and the Glorification of Violence," in *Catastrophe and Meaning: The Holocaust and the Twentieth Century*, ed. Moishe Postone and Eric Santner (Chicago: University of Chicago Press, 2003), 118, 131; Omer Bartov, "Defining Enemies, Making Victims: Germans, Jews, and the Holocaust," in *Landscaping the Human Garden: Twentieth-Century Population Management in a Comparative Framework*, ed. Amir Weiner (Stanford, Calif.: Stanford University Press, 2003), 136, 146, 152.

7. U.S. Congress, Senate Hearings before the Subcommittee of the Committee on Foreign Relations, *The Genocide Convention*, 81st Cong., 2nd sess., 13 (Washington, D.C.: Government Printing Office, 1950), 47–48.

8. Moses, "Empire, Colony," 7–8.

9. Martin Luther King, "Non-aggression Procedures to Interracial Harmony," address delivered at the American Baptist Assembly and American Home Mission Agencies Conference, July 23, 1956, in *The Papers of Martin Luther King, Jr., Volume III: Birth of a New Age, December 1955–December 1956*, ed. Clayborne Carson, Stewart Burns, Susan Carson, Pete Holloran, and Dana Powell (Berkeley: University of California Press, 1997), 325; Her-

bert Shapiro, *White Violence, Black Response: From Reconstruction to Montgomery* (Amherst: University of Massachusetts Press, 1988), 429.

10. Robert F. Williams, *Negroes with Guns*, ed. Marc Scheifer (Mansfield Center: Martino Publishing, 2013), 82, 76, 70.

11. Malcolm X, "America's Gravest Crisis since the Civil War," speech at the University of California, October 11, 1963, in *Malcolm X: The Last Speeches*, ed. Bruce Perry (New York: Pathfinder Press, 1989), 62–63, 69.

12. Malcolm X, "An Appeal to African Heads of State," in *Malcolm X Speaks: Selected Speeches and Statements*, ed. George Breitman (New York: Merit Publishers, 1965), 74.

13. Ibid., 75–76.

14. The New York Riot occurred on July 16, 1964. "Negro Boy Killed," *New York Times*, July 17, 1964; "Verdict in Harlem," *New York Times*, September 2, 1964.

15. Malcolm X, "Appeal," 77.

16. Malcolm X et al., "Program of the Organization of Afro-American Unity," http://www.malcolm-x.org/docs/gen_oaau.htm.

17. "Lyndon Johnson and Martin Luther King Jr.," August 20, 1965, *Presidential Recordings Program*, http://whitehousetapes.net.

18. Bayard Rustin, "The Watts," *Watts Commentary Magazine*, March 1966. Governor Edward Brown appointed John A. McCone to head a commission to investigate the causes of the Watts riot; the commission published a report titled *Violence in the City—an End or a Beginning*.

19. "Black Power Is Black Death," *New York Times*, July 7, 1966; "Black Power," *New York Times*, July 10 and July 12, 1966.

20. Stokely Carmichael, speech at University of California, Berkeley, October 29, 1966, http://americanradioworks.publicradio.org.

21. The Black Panthers Party Platform, 1966, http://www2.iath.virginia.edu/sixties/HTML_docs/Resources/Primary/Manifestos/Panther_platform.html.

22. Ibid.

23. "Black Power," a statement by the National Committee of Negro Churchmen, July 31, 1966, in *The Black Power Revolt*, ed. Floyd B. Barbour (Toronto: Collier Books, 1969), 313, 314, 315.

24. Ibid., 319.

25. Sam Greenlee, *The Spook Who Sat by the Door: A Novel* (Chicago: Lushena Books, 2002), 111–112.

26. Chester Himes, *Plan B* (Jackson: University Press of Mississippi, 1993), 143, 146, 183, 200–201.

27. Michel Fabre and Robert E. Skinner, eds., *Conversations with Chester Himes* (Jackson: University Press of Mississippi, 1995), 45, 56, 58.

28. Michelle Alexander, *The New Jim Crow: Mass Incarceration in the Age of Colorblindness* (New York: New Press, 2010), 9.

29. "Shooting Suspect in Custody after Charleston Church Massacre," *CNN.com*, June 18, 2015; "Charleston Church Shooter," *Atlanta Daily World*, June 19, 2015.

INDEX

barbarians: Africans as, 48, 52, 80, 133, 211, 226n33; extermination of, 3; Irish as, 12; Native Americans as, 26. *See also* savages

Barber, Charley, 138

Barber, Max J., 198

Barnwell, John, 32, 36

Baylor, Robert W., 167

Beach, Mary L., 79

Bebee, Benj S., 144–145

Bell, T. P., 189

Ben (Va.), 87

Benezet, Anthony, 50

Benin, 36, 39

Bennett, Ned, 78

Bennett, Thomas, 74, 76, 80

Berkeley, William, 19–20

Berry, Fannie, 96

Berry, Harrison, 163–164

Berry, Henry, 112

Biassou (Saint-Domingue), 69

Bibb, Henry, 143, 152, 163

Bible, 15, 77, 95, 222n84; New Testament, 91; Old Testament, 77–78, 81, 91, 219n31, 240n50, 244n7

Bight of Benin, 35, 36, 40

Bight of Biafra, 35, 36, 76

black abolitionists, 59, 104–107, 178; on black manhood, 150–153; female, 161; fugitive slaves and, 145; on reopening of slave trade, 140; scare tactics, 143, 146–147, 161. *See also* abolition of slavery; emancipation; white abolitionists

black disposability, 141, 190, 211, 246n61

black extermination: Civil War era, 175–190; fear of, 2–3, 134, 142–147, 160, 163–171, 201–211; freedom and, 68, 109, 124, 130–131, 175–191; post–Civil War, 190–199; romantic racism and, 149–150; slavery and, 129–131, 133, 141; threat of, 59, 79, 81, 83, 88–89, 99–100, 107–108, 137, 160. *See also* race war; retaliatory violence

black fears: of extermination, 2–3, 134, 142–147, 160, 163–171, 201–211; of race war, 79, 100, 142, 201–211

black flag policy, 180, 182

black labor, 130–132, 141, 170, 255n60

Black Lives Matter, 210

black manhood, 142–143, 149–153

black power movement, 206–208

black religious leaders, 78–79, 104–105, 207–208, 210, 235n92

black trauma, 2–5, 169, 211; Civil War and post–Civil War era, 176, 199–200; after Turner's rebellion (1831), 4, 82, 83, 89–101

black violence, 203–210. *See also* insurrections; nonviolence; servile war; white extermination

Blake (Delany), 160–161

Bolzius, Johann Martin, 56

Boone, Frank T., 98

Boukman, "Zamba," 68–69

Bowery, Charity, 90–91, 93

Bowley, Harkless, 171

Box Brown, Henry, 91–93, 100

Boyce, Angie and Margaret, 96

Boyer, Jean-Pierre, 74

Boykin, F. M., 87

Brazil, slave trade, 125, 126, 128, 130

Brickell, John, 47, 56

Brodnax, William Henry, 86, 109–110, 115–116, 118–121, 124, 247n77

Brodnax-Bryce compromise, 119

Brookes, Walter, 134

Brown, Annie, 170–171

Brown, John (fugitive slave), 138

Brown, John, Harper's Ferry insurrection, 4, 135, 141–174, 255n60; aftermath of, 142, 165–173; black perspectives on, 142, 153–165, 171–173; Brown's racial assumptions, 147–151; capture and execution, 165; "Declaration of Liberty," 160; leadership style, 147, 154, 162–163; "Provisional Constitution for the Proscribed and Oppressed People of the United States," 160; *Sambo's Mistake*, 149; Secret Six supporters, 147–148, 151; Turner's rebellion and, 97

Brown, John, Jr., 157, 161–162

Brown, Michael, 210

Brown, Morris, 79, 235n92

Brown, William Wells, 159, 163

Creeks, 28, 30, 45, 80, 239n35
Creighton, John C., 193
criminal justice system, 1–2, 210
Crokett, James, 42
Cromwell, Oliver, 13–14, 232n6
Cuba, slave trade, 125, 126, 138
Cusseaux, Michelle, 210
Custer, George Armstrong, 194

Dahomey, 39–41, 49, 51–52, 76, 79, 225n13
Davis, Jefferson, 180
Davis, Noah, 91
Dean (S.C.), 75
death: as better than enslavement, 149,
   164; colonization of free blacks and,
   119, 121; in slave trade, 128, 250n18,
   250n23; threat of, 53, 57, 101–102, 137.
   See also exterminatory warfare; infants
   and children, killing of; lynching
DeBaptiste, George, 158
"Declaration of Liberty" (J. Brown), 160
Delany, Martin R., 38, 138, 158, 225n18;
   Blake, 160–161; "Letter on President
   Warner of Liberia," 193–194
De Loss Love, William, 181
Democratic Party, 184–185, 262n59
Desmond Rebellions, 12, 218n6
Dessalines, Jean-Jacques, 72–73
Detroit race riot, 186–187
Dew, Thomas, 122–124
Doegs, 19–20
Douglass, Frederick: Brown's attack
   at Harper's Ferry and, 155–157,
   162, 171–172; on Civil War, 175; on
   insurrections, 133, 144–145; on massacre
   of Chinese in Wyoming, 265n103; on
   "Negro Problem," 177; on New York
   draft riots, 188–189; on nonviolence,
   150–151; on race war and black
   extermination, 153, 178–179, 196; on
   scare tactics, 133; threats against, 101
Douglass, H. Ford, 171
Douglass, Stephen A., 184
Drayton, Charles, 75
Dred Scott case (1857), 139, 155, 184
Drewry, William, 238n16

Drogheda massacre, 13, 28, 232n6
Du Bois, W. E. B., 7, 156, 196, 249n5,
   249n7

Edwards, Bryan, 49, 225n25
Edwards, Hardy, 86
emancipation: gradual, 103–104, 106,
   108–119, 158; postnati, 109, 112–113,
   245n34; in Saint-Domingue, 70. See
   also freedom
Emmanuel, Mom Ryer, 100
England: apprentice system, 132;
   colonization of America, 11–12, 14–16;
   emancipation, 130; Irish massacres, 12–
   14, 32, 217n5
English Parliament, 13, 44, 48, 50
English Privy Council, 50, 51
Enlightenment philosophy, 8–9, 50
Equiano, Olaudah, 36–38, 225n14
ethnology, 9, 147, 253n23
exterminatory warfare: African methods
   of, 3, 8–10, 33–34, 37–41, 48–52, 59, 78;
   defined, 3; European methods of, 3, 8–
   16, 48, 59, 77, 81; racial extermination,
   2–10; use of terms, 215n8. See also
   black extermination; Native American
   extermination; race war; white
   extermination
extirpation, 215n8. See also exterminatory
   warfare

Falls, Elias, 183
Faulkner, Charles, 112, 118
Faulkner, William (Detroit), 186
fear, 11; as African military strategy, 40;
   used to control African slaves, 53–57.
   See also black fears; white fears
Ferguson, William, 182
Finley, Robert, 116; Thoughts on the
   Colonization of Free Blacks, 117
Fitzhugh, George, 126–127
Floyd, John, 92, 103–109, 116, 122, 238n4,
   244n26
Foote, H. S., 136
Forrest, William Bedford, 182–183
Forten, James, 101

Hippisley, John, 49
Hobson, Moble, 18
Holland, Duke, 27
Holland, Edwin, 80
Holmes, Thomas H., 180
Horse Shoe Bend (Red Sticks Massacre), 80, 89, 239n35
Houston, Louis and Solomon, 186
Howe, Samuel Gridley, 147
Hughes, Henry (Miss.), 131–132, 137
human rights, 205
Hunter, Antony, 162–163
Hunter, Robert, 146
Hunting, S. S., 186
Hurlburt, Stephen A., 181–182
Hutchinson, Mathius, 57

Igbos, 36–37, 76, 79, 225n13
indigenous people. *See* Native Americans
infants and children, killing of: African American, 1–3, 149, 152, 182–183, 196, 250n23; African slaves, 37–38, 96–97; Irish, 14; Native American, 30–31; white slave owners' children, 86
insurrections: black opposition to, 143–147; freedom as goal of, 62–63, 67, 84–86, 102, 112, 227n58; on Goree Island, 50; as incited by abolitionists, 104–106, 131, 135; in New York, 56; punishment for resisting, 53, 58; retribution for (*see* retaliatory violence); secrecy about, 76–77; shipboard, 42–44, 79, 129, 226n34; in South Carolina, 65–81; statistics on, 99, 242nn89–90; in Virginia, 82–102, 242n96; in West Indies, 43–44, 59–65, 67–75, 85, 98, 242n96; white male patrols, 54; whites killed in, 63–66, 68–70, 72–73, 77, 84–85, 148, 228n75
internecine war, 4, 6; in Africa, 41; threat of, 82, 124
interracial marriage, 22
interracial sex, 6, 117–118, 234n69, 247n70
Irish immigrants: antiblack violence, 185, 188–189, 262n59; labor, 28
Irish massacres, 12–14, 217n5, 232n6
Islamic slave trade, 226n25, 250n18

Israelites, 11, 15–16, 77, 81
Izard, Ralph, 57, 73

Jack (Antigua), 63
Jackson, Andrew (formerly enslaved), 152
Jackson, Andrew (president and general), 80, 89, 123
Jack the Feather (Nemattanow), 17
Jacobs, Harriet, 90–91, 93, 98
Jacobs, John S., 152
Jamaica, 42–44, 76; slave rebellions, 61–63, 242n96
James Perkins (ship), 121–122
Jamestown, Va., 15–16
Jean-François (Saint-Domingue), 69–70
Jefferson, Thomas, 5, 23, 79, 118, 135, 221n76, 244n26, 246n64, 247n70
Jemison, Mary, 30
Jesse (S.C.), 79
Joe (S.C.), 76
John (S.C.), 78
Johnson, Anna, 79
Johnson, Billy, 64
Johnson, James Weldon, 201
Johnson, John Rosemond, 201
Johnson, Lyndon, 206
Johnson, Rev. Robert, 15
Johnson, Robert (S.C. governor), 42, 44
Jolliffe, William, 42
Jones, James Monroe, 159
Jones, Mary (wife of Charles Colcock Jones), 191
Jones, Mary and John, 157–158
Jones, William, 186
Julius Pringle (ship), 101
Jupiter (ship), 121
just wars, 11, 24–27, 30, 48, 122, 223n118

Kagi, John Henry, 148, 162
Kennedy, Lionel H., 74
Kentucky (slave ship), 129
Kindle (Harper's Ferry mill worker), 168
King, Martin Luther, Jr., 7, 203–204, 206, 207, 210
King Philip's War, 26–27
Kirk, J. Allen, 196, 198
Knapp, Isaac, 104–105

Moultrie, William, 55
Muhammad, Elijah, 204–205
mulattos: military service, 45; in Saint-
Domingue, 69–70, 72, 74, 234n69
Muslim slaves, 226n25, 250n18

Nalson, John, 14
Nancy of the Nile (Nat Turner's mother),
85–86
Nanzemonds, 19
Napoleon Bonaparte, 71
Narragansetts, 25–26
National Committee of Negro
Churchmen, 207
Native American extermination, 4, 123,
150–153; Civil War era, 189, 193–194,
199; colonial era, 16–32; incidents,
222n95. See also exterminatory warfare
Native Americans: collaborations with
Africans, 45–46, 107; legal status, 21–
23, 29; military culture, 16, 18–19, 27;
as "savage," 11, 14–15, 26, 32–33, 123,
221n76
Native American slaves, 11, 21–23, 27–32,
223n113; military service, 45. See also
slavery; slave trade
Native American trauma, 31
nativism, 185
natural law, 8, 20, 81, 106, 122
natural rights, 50
Ned (S.C.), 76
Nemattanow (Jack the Feather), 17
Nero, 107–108
New England, wars against Native
Americans, 24–27
New Era (gunboat), 182
New York: anti-black riots, 101; draft riots
(1863), 187–188, 262n59; insurrection in
1712, 228n75; slave trade, 249n7
Nichols, Manuel, 183
"nits make lice," 14, 27, 30, 40, 74, 77, 189,
199–200, 238n16
nonviolence, 150–151, 154–155, 172–173,
203–204, 206
"no quarter," 180, 182
Norcom, James, 98
Norris, Robert, 43, 60

North: alliance with South, 155; antiblack sentiment and race riots, 100–
101, 184–189; economy, and slavery,
125–126
North Carolina: rumors of insurrections,
84–85, 101; violence against blacks,
94–95, 101, 167, 196–198
Northup, Solomon, 143, 151
Northwest Freedman's Aid Commission,
192
Nott, Josiah C., 147

oaths: by insurrectionists, 64–65, 76–77;
of secrecy, 76–77
Obama, Barack Hussein, 201
O'Connell, Daniel, 189
"old daddy" (S.C.), 75, 236n96
O'Neill, Brian, 13
Organization of African Unity (OAU), 205
Organization of Afro-American Unity
(OAAU), 205

Pamunkeys, 17–18, 20
Pan-African solidarity, 205–206
Pan-Indian alliance, 31–32
Park, Mungo, 49
Parker, Allen, 181
Parker, Robert S., 88
Parker, Theodore, 147–148, 151
Parker, Thomas, 74
Parson, William Henry, 181
Paspaheghs, 16
Patawomecks, 19
paternalism, 9–10, 125, 129, 135, 137, 217n34,
239n33, 244n7
Patterson, William L., 202
Patton, John, 106
Payne, Daniel A., 178
Pennington, James C., 152
Pequot War, 24–27, 56, 77, 222n82, 222n96
Percy, George, 16–17
Petersburg, Battle of, 184
petite guerre, 3, 5, 196. See also
exterminatory warfare
Pettigrew, James Johnston, 134, 137
Pettigrew, William S., 167
Phillip, John, 9, 253n23

and, 1–6, 9, 101–102, 185, 190–199, 202–211

white violence, 1–10; Civil War era, 175–177, 180–190; Northern race riots, 100–101, 186–189, 262n59; post–Civil War, 1–3, 190–199; used to control African slaves, 52–57, 85–86; vigilante violence, 83, 116, 124. *See also* black extermination; exterminatory warfare; infants and children, killing of; lynching; Native American extermination; race war; retaliatory violence; torture

Whydah, 40, 42

Wikhead, John, 47

Wilkins, Roy, 206–207

William (Paul), 78

Williams, A. D., 203

Williams, Ella, 84

Williams, Nelson, 84

Williams, Robert F., 7, 204, 206

Wilmington, N.C., 101; race riot (1898), 196–198, 265n108

Wilson, John Leighton, 128

Wilson, William J. "Ethiop," 140, 152–153

Windward Coast (Ivory Coast), 35, 42

Wise, Henry, 166–167

women: black women's resistance, 64; killing of, 1–3, 182–183; purported rape of white women, 198, 210; rape of black women, 93; stereotypes about, 161, 256n98; warriors, 36–37, 40, 79

Wright, Henry, 176

Wright, Joseph, 37

Wright, Theodore, 116

Wright, W. W., 131–132

Wyandots, 27

Yamasees, 28, 30

Yamasee War, 31–32, 45, 223n113

Yancey, William, 126

Yorubas, 37, 76, 225n13, 225n18